Literacy's Beginnings

FOURTH EDITION

Literacy's Beginnings

Supporting Young Readers and Writers

Lea M. McGee
University of Alabama

Donald J. Richgels
Northern Illinois University

Boston ■ New York ■ San Francisco
Mexico City ■ Montreal ■ Toronto ■ London ■ Madrid ■ Munich ■ Paris
Hong Kong ■ Singapore ■ Tokyo ■ Cape Town ■ Sydney

Series Editor: *Aurora Martínez Ramos*
Editorial Assistant: *Katie Freddoso*
Senior Marketing Manager: *Elizabeth Fogarty*
Editorial-Production Administrator: *Annette Joseph*
Editorial-Production Coordinator: *Holly Crawford*
Editorial-Production Service: *Colophon*
Composition Buyer: *Linda Cox*
Electronic Composition: *Omegatype Typography, Inc.*
Manufacturing Buyer: *Andrew Turso*
Cover Administrator: *Joel Gendron*
Cover Designer: *Suzanne Harbison*

For related titles and support materials, visit our online catalog at www.ablongman.com

Between the time Website information is gathered and then published, it is not unusual for some sites to have closed. Also, the transcription of URLs can result in typographical errors. The publisher would appreciate notification where these errors occur so that they may be corrected in subsequent editions.

Library of Congress Cataloging-in-Publication Data

McGee, Lea M.
    Literacy's beginnings : supporting young readers and writers / Lea M. McGee, Donald J. Richgels.—4th ed.
      p. cm.
    Includes bibliographical references and index.
    ISBN 0-205-38637-7 (alk. paper)
    1. Reading (Early childhood)—United States.   2. Language arts (Early childhood)—United States.   3. Literacy—United States.   I. Richgels, Donald J.   II. Title.

LB1139.5.R43M33 2004
372.6'0973—dc21

2003043730

Printed in the United States of America

10 9 8 7 6 5 4 3 2   HAM   08 07 06 05 04 03

Photo Credits: Laurie Elish Piper, p. 33; all others, including cover photo, Don Richgels.

*To Richard and Kristen,
and to Mary, Ted, and Carrie*

CONTENTS

PART TWO   Classrooms

6   Literacy-Rich Classrooms   143

PREFACE

Point of View

Literacy's Beginnings: Supporting Young Readers and Writers is intended to help preservice and inservice teachers, and other caregivers of young children, to be aware of and supportive of children's literacy knowledge as it grows and changes in the years from birth through early elementary school. Our purpose is to provide a guide to the long continuum of literacy growth, from the very beginning years, when children's reading and writing efforts are difficult to recognize, through the early elementary school years, when children begin to receive formal literacy instruction.

We believe that children's literacy learning is developmental, but not in the sense of proceeding in an irreversible, step-by-step progression. No child's discoveries about and experiments with literacy exactly match those of another child. Furthermore, an individual child's literacy behaviors vary in sophistication depending on the task and the situation.

Literacy learning is developmental in a very commonsensical way to anyone who has spent time writing and reading with children. Literacy learning is developmental in the sense that what an individual child knows about writing and reading changes dramatically over time. Not only do young children's constructions of literacy differ from those of adults, but children's present constructions also differ from their own former and future constructions.

We believe that teachers have an important role to play in young children's literacy learning. The subtitle of our book emphasizes the supportive nature of that role. We hope that our descriptions of literacy events involving young children and our suggestions for classroom support will help teachers to be aware of the directions in which children's literacy knowledge can move over the period covered by this book. Such awareness can make easier one of the most difficult tasks in teaching: the close observation of many different children. From a basis of careful observation, teachers can respect what children know and support children's continued learning in ways that make sense to the children.

Organization of the Text

Literacy's Beginnings is grouped into two parts. The theme of Part One (Chapters 1 through 5) is that of *learners*. This part describes the children and how they grow as writers and readers. Chapter 1 is an overview of learning and literacy. We describe critical changes in children's concepts about four areas of written language: meanings, forms, meaning-form links, and functions. The next four chapters elaborate on that picture of development.

The word *literacy* has many connotations in everyday life. To us, being *literate* means being able to find meaning in written symbols. This definition includes much territory left out by everyday definitions of literacy; for example, a pretend reading of a favorite storybook qualifies as a literate act by our definition, but does not usually qualify under the everyday definition. Still, our definition does not include everything that very young children do with books and writing materials.

The terms *beginner, novice, experimenter,* and *conventional (early, transitional,* and *self-generating) reader and writer* also demand clarification. We use them as convenient shorthand for the developments described in Chapters 2 through 5, but we do not mean for them to define rigid, irreversible stages. Indeed, we do not call them stages. A child may exhibit many of the knowledges in the cluster of knowledges that we associate with one of those four terms. Furthermore, a child who usually reads or writes like a novice in some situations and with some tasks will also read or write like an experimenter. The important point is that, over time, children will more often resemble conventional readers and writers.

Part Two of *Literacy's Beginnings* concerns *classrooms,* and characteristics of school environments and teacher roles that promote children's development from beginners to conventional readers and writers. Chapter 6 is an overview of the elements included in a literacy-rich classroom. Chapter 7 focuses on preschool, Chapter 8 on kindergarten, Chapter 9 on first grade, and Chapter 10 on second grade and third grade. Chapter 11 describes the literacy needs of diverse learners, and Chapter 12 addresses assessment issues and methods.

This fourth edition of *Literacy's Beginnings* has several **new features:**

- Emphasizes making **instruction more direct and systematic** within a child-centered, developmentally appropriate program. This text balances decoding, comprehension, and teacher-guided instruction with student-initiated activities. By addressing the issues raised in Reading First and Early Reading First legislation, young children's reading comprehension will improve.
- As delineated by the **National Reading Panel,** this text discusses **decoding and phonics instruction,** both essential to maintain literacy instruction standards. In order to provide teachers with evaluation tools for their literacy instruction, this text includes more information on using **assessment to screen and monitor children's progress** in reading.
- Highlights **assessments for key areas of reading—phonemic awareness, phonics, comprehension, vocabulary, and fluency**—providing students with a thorough understanding of the Reading First and Early Reading First legislation. (Chapter 12)
- Offers new and updated **discussions of research-based instruction** in phonemic awareness, phonics, and the high levels of comprehension needed to understand informational books and literature.
- Offers updated **suggestions for computer use** to enhance literacy learning for young children.

- Detailed discussion of the use of **leveled texts,** small group **guided reading** instruction, and activities for **struggling readers** in more applications.
- **Updated case studies** at the end of each chapter allow students to apply the text information in real-life settings.
- More information about **using guided reading instruction in the primary grades.**

Each chapter of *Literacy's Beginnings* again has four sections designed to help readers consolidate and apply what they have learned. First, we list the key concepts used in the chapter. Applying the Information presents a case study on children's interactions with written language similar to the many examples given in the chapter. The reader is asked to apply the chapter's concepts to this example. Going Beyond the Text suggests ways for readers to seek out real-life experiences that will test both the chapter's ideas and the readers' understandings. We ask questions and make suggestions to guide readers' planning and reflecting on those experiences. Finally, References provides a list of all publications cited in the chapter.

The Children and Teachers in This Book

Literacy's Beginnings is based in part on a growing body of research about emerging literacy and in part on our experiences with young children, including our own children. We incorporate many descriptions of those experiences. We wish to add here two important cautions that we will repeat throughout the text. The first is about children's ages. We usually give the age of the children in our examples in order to fully represent the facts. However, we do not intend for those ages to serve as norms against which to compare other children.

Our second caution is about backgrounds. Many, but not all, of the children in our examples have had numerous and varied home experiences with books and writing materials. Their meaningful interactions with written language are often what one would expect of children from such environments. Children with different backgrounds may exhibit different initial orientations toward written language. However, our involvement with teachers whose children come to preschool or elementary school with different backgrounds has shown us that nearly all children can benefit from the informed observation and child-centered, meaning-oriented support described in this book.

The classroom support chapters of this book are based on our own teaching experiences and on our observations of teachers. Just as we have known and observed many literate young children, so also have we known and observed many very sensitive, intelligent, and effective teachers of young children. All the samples of children's reading and writing in this book are authentic cases from our own teaching and research and the research of others cited in the text.

Acknowledgments

We owe a great deal to the many children whose experiences with written language were the basis for much of this book. We thank them and their parents for cooperating so generously with us—for supporting *us* in the extended "literacy event" of writing this book. We thank the teachers who shared their classroom experiences with us: Mary Jane Everett, Candice Jones, Karen Kurr, Roberta McHardy, Nancy Miller, Terry Morel, Kathy Walker, Leigh Courtney, Karen King, Jackie Zickuhr, Carolyn Vaughn, Monette Reyes, Karla Poremba, Diane Roloff, Cindi Chandler, Laurie Coleman, Richard Lomax, Michelle Tran, Michelle Bellamy, and Margaret Medders.

We owe much to the editors and their assistants at Allyn and Bacon, including Aurora Martínez Ramos, Virginia Lanigan, Annette Joseph, and Katie Freddoso. We are also grateful to Denise Botelho at Colophon for her careful handling of the manuscript during editing and production. We thank Gail T. Eichman, Cleveland State University; Frances Mallow, University of Houston; and Mary White-Johnson, Delgado Community College for helpful comments and suggestions.

We acknowledge the contributions of our many students. We learned from our discussions with them about literacy's beginnings and from the examples they shared of their interactions with young readers and writers.

Understanding Children's Literacy Development

KEY CONCEPTS

concepts
schemas
features
related concepts
personal experience
tabula rasa
zone of proximal
   development
scaffolding
meaning-form link
pragmatics

semantics
syntax
phonology
functions
meaning
morpheme
contextualization clues
literary language
forms
graphemes
mock letters

left-to-right organization
top-to-bottom organization
linearity
metalinguistic awareness
concept of word
sound–letter relationships
phonemes
phoneme category
phonological knowledge
phonological awareness
phonemic awareness

1

sound–letter correspondences
phonograms
orthographic readers and
    writers
logographic reading and
    writing
awareness and exploration

beginners
novices
alphabetic reading and
    writing
experimental reading and
    writing
experimenters

conventional reading and
    writing
early reading and writing
transitional reading and
    writing
independent and productive
    reading and writing

Language Development

How do children begin the process of becoming successful lifelong readers and writers? We begin to answer that question by looking at theories of language development. Piaget (1955) and Vygotsky (1978) examined how children acquire language and the relationship of language to thinking. Each of their theories makes unique contributions to what we understand about young children's literacy development. We use their theories first to explain learning in general and then to explore how learning and language acquisition are related.

Schemas and Learning

An important idea from both Piaget's and Vygotsky's theories is that learning occurs as children acquire new **concepts,** or **schemas.** A concept or schema is a mental structure in which we store all the information we know about people, places, objects, or activities.

Schemas.   We will use the concept *football* as an example to explain the nature of schemas. If asked to tell everything that comes to mind when they hear the word *football,* many people in the United States will think of the game that is played with a two-pointed, nonspherical ball by two teams on a 100-yard field, with the object of accumulating points by moving the ball into the other team's end zone or kicking it through the goalposts in that end zone. Because football is a game, its **features** include *who*s, *what*s, *how*s, and *why*s, in this case, who the players are (quarterback, tight end, halfback, tackle, etc.), what equipment they use (ball, goalpost, shoulder pad, helmet, etc.), how they perform actions and plays (pass, tackle, touchdown, field goal, etc.), and why they do so (to score touchdowns, field goals, extra point conversions, and touchbacks and to prevent the other team from scoring). If enough features are listed, the concept is adequately defined; that is, those features characterize that concept or schema and no other.

If the concept is named slightly differently, if someone says "a football" instead of "football," then the features will be features of a certain kind of ball, not of a certain game. Those features, then, may include oblong, two-pointed, made of pigskin, inflated, laced, and of a certain size.

Concepts and their features are related. We have already seen that a football is one of the features of the game called football. Furthermore, we can note that the *certain size* of a football is a function of the way the game of football is played. A football must be large enough so that it can be drop-kicked long distances, thrown and caught—and therefore seen and tracked—over long distances, and cradled for carrying securely in the crook of one's arm; it must be small enough so that it can be grasped and thrown with one adult-sized hand.

Both concepts are also related to other concepts. Whether they hear the word *football* or the phrase *a football,* many people in the United States will think of such **related concepts** as autumn, high school, college, professional, Friday night, Saturday afternoon, Sunday afternoon, Monday night, cheerleaders, mascots, marching bands, Green Bay Packers, Brett Favre, other teams, other famous players, pep rally bonfires, stadium parking lot picnics, Superbowl, Superbowl parties, television advertizing during the Superbowl, and so on.

Any concept or schema, its related concepts or schemas, and their features are the products of experience, usually the experience of growing up in a certain context, including within a certain culture. People in the United States often share the earlier mentioned football concepts because football as played in high school, college, and the National Football League (NFL) is a pervasive part of U.S. culture. Football in other cultures means different things; it may be played with a different-sized field, as in Canadian football; or be a different ball and a different game altogether, as in England and much of the rest of the world where football is known as soccer.

Another influence on concept or schema formation is **personal experience.** For example, individuals will have some football-related concepts not shared by all other football fans because of their personal football experiences. When they hear the word *football,* they might think of or feel pride (having scored the winning touchdown in an important game), loneliness (not liking football when everyone else seems to spend every Friday night through Monday night from September to January devoted to it), a letter jacket (having earned a high school or college letter playing football), frostbite (having attended a football game in below-zero weather in Green Bay in January), or hangover (having celebrated too many football victories).

The reason people make these football-related associations—and many more that we did not take the space to list—is that concepts or schemas are organized. That is, as people have personal football experiences (receiving a football as a gift, playing football, watching football games, following the fortunes of favorite football teams), they make mental associations among the word *football* or the phrase *a football,* the concepts for which that word or phrase stand, and the sights, sounds, tastes, smells, and sensations that contributed to the formations of those concepts. They see and feel the shape of a football and automatically make a mental association between the concept of a football and the qualities nonspherical, oblong, and two-pointed. They score a touchdown playing football—whether in a game of tag football with friends or as part of an organized team before a crowd of spectators—and they automatically make another mental association, this time between the concept *football* and the feeling of excitement or exhilaration. Thus are schemas organized through associations.

We have schemas for many things, including objects such as a *computer* or *fire truck;* people, such as a *teacher* or *rock star;* places such as *home* or *restaurant;* and activities, such as *making a sandwich* or *writing a persuasive essay.* Thinking and learning depend on these many schemas and concepts. Thinking involves calling to mind information from schemas and using that information to make inferences, predictions, conclusions, or generalizations. Suppose, for example, that in early August we see someone at an empty high school football field kicking footballs over and over again from different distances, toward a goalpost, sometimes putting the ball through the uprights, sometimes not. We might make the inference that this person is practicing for tryouts to be that high school team's field goal kicker.

Similarly, learning involves adding to or changing schemas. Suppose we see for the first time, a group playing a game that looks like football. They are divided into two teams, each trying to move a football, by carrying or passing it, across the line defended by the other team. But each player is wearing two strips of cloth, one on each side, attached at the waist. When someone carries the football, members of the opposing team do not stop play by tackling the ball carrier, but instead they steal a cloth strip from his or her waist. We might modify our football schema to include a form of the game called flag football.

Infants and Schemas.   Children begin life with few concepts—or even none. Children's minds may be thought of as vacant structures, or empty schemas. There are only empty slots where features can go. This is the **tabula rasa,** or blank slate, notion of the young child's mind. One of Piaget's greatest insights was a suggestion of how children acquire the knowledge to begin filling those slots with features and making connections among schemas. He suggested that the infant's mind is actually far from a blank slate. It is true that young children have no (or very little) knowledge of content or the things (such as football) that will eventually occupy their minds. However, children do have considerable inborn knowledge of processes. They seem to know how to go about acquiring content knowledge, or knowledge of things.

Piaget's idea was that young humans learn through action. They are born with special schemas for how to act and how to respond to their world. These action schemas bring children in contact with reality (things) in ways that produce knowledge of the world. More action produces more knowledge. As children acquire knowledge and continue to act, changes happen to the things they are in contact with (e.g., milk gets spilled) and changes happen to previous knowledge (e.g., the schema for milk changes to include the idea that milk does not behave like a cracker—it doesn't keep a shape). The action schemas themselves change as active, problem-solving children evolve more effective strategies for making their way in the world.

Two very important conclusions can be drawn from Piaget's theory of how children learn. One is that children create their own knowledge by forming and reforming concepts in their minds. The second conclusion is that children's state of knowledge—or view of the world—can be very different from one time to the next, and especially different from an adult's.

The point we wish to emphasize is that, because children construct their own knowledge, this knowledge does not come fully developed and is often quite different from that of an adult. Thus, there are differences between how an adult understands concepts and how a child understands concepts. Similarly, a young child's concepts about reading and writing are naturally different from, but no less important than, an adult's concepts about reading and writing.

The Relation between Language and Learning

We have already discussed the importance of action to Piaget's idea of learning. Children's actions may physically change objects in the world. While helping to wash the family car, a child may immerse a light, dry, stiff sponge into a bucket of water, changing its appearance and texture as it gets wet. That same action may change the child's concept or schema of a sponge, introducing the features *heavy*, *wet*, and *squishy*, and it may allow the child to see a connection between the schemas *water* and *sponge*.

But can children change their schema for *sponge* to include the notion that it can be heavy, wet, and squishy without hearing or using those words? How important is it for the child to have the words *sponge, water, heavy, wet*, and *squishy* available as labels for what is experienced in such a situation? Vygotsky stressed the importance of having someone with the child who can supply such language. According to Vygotsky, a parent who says to the child, "Boy that's a wet sponge!" or "The water sure made that sponge heavy!" or "Now that sponge is squishy!" plays a vital role in the child's learning about sponges and water. Vygotsky placed a strong emphasis on the social component of cognitive and language development.

Social Basis for Learning.   Vygotsky argued that all learning first takes place in a social context. In order to build a new concept, children interact with others who provide feedback for their hypotheses or who help them accomplish a task they could not do on their own. Children's or adults' language is an important part of the social context of learning. Suppose that a child's concept of the letter *W* does not include its conventional orientation (upright). This child may write $\Lambda\!\Lambda$ and call it *W.* Another child who observes this writing may say, "That's not a *W,* that's an *M."* This feedback provides the child with a label for the new concept, *M,* and prompts the child to reconsider the concept of *W* by adding an orientation (upright).

Vygotsky believed that children need to be able to talk about a new problem or a new concept in order to understand it and use it. Adults supply language that fits children's needs at a particular stage or in response to a particular problem. Language can be part of a routinized situation. It can label the situation or parts of the situation, or it can help pose a problem or structure a problem-solving task. As the child gradually internalizes the language that was first supplied by an adult, the language and a routine task that helps in solving the problem become the child's own.

An example of a child's internalizing the language of a routine is how the child learns to use the words *all gone*. The parents of a child might repeatedly hide a favorite toy and then say, "All gone!" Then they reveal the toy and say, "Here it is!" This becomes a game for the child. Eventually, the child may play the game without the adult, using the same language, "All gone" and "Here it is."

We can draw two important conclusions from the "all gone" example. First, it suggests that language and cognition really emerge at about the same time. Perhaps using the word *gone* helps children to solve the cognitive problem of object permanence, or perhaps *gone* suddenly acquires a fascination for children who have just solved that problem, making it a word they are very likely to use (Gopnick & Meltzoff, 1986; Meltzoff, 1985).

Second, it suggests that learning is a matter of internalizing the language and actions of others. A young child's ability to play the game of "all gone" alone means that he or she has internalized the actions and language of his or her mother or father. For Vygotsky, all learning involves a movement from doing activities in a social situation with the support of a more knowledgeable other to internalizing the language and actions of the more knowledgeable other and being able to use this knowledge alone.

Zone of Proximal Development.   Vygotsky spoke of a **zone of proximal development,** which is an opportune area for growth, but one in which children are dependent on help from others. An adult, or perhaps an older child, must give young children advice if they are to succeed within this zone and if eventually, by internalizing that advice, they are to perform independently.

When children are working in their zone of proximal development, they complete some parts of a task, and adults or older children perform the parts of the task that the younger children cannot yet do alone. In this way, young children can accomplish tasks that are too difficult for them to complete on their own. Adults' or older children's talk is an important part of helping young children—it scaffolds the task. **Scaffolding** talk gives advice, directs children's attention, alerts them to the sequence of activities, and provides information for completing the task successfully. Gradually, children internalize this talk and use it to direct their own attention, plan, and control their activities.

Figure 1.1 presents a letter that five-year-old Kristen and her mother wrote together. After Kristen's second day in kindergarten, she announced, "I'm not going to school tomorrow. I don't like being last in line." Apparently, Kristen rode a different bus from any of the other children in her classroom and the teacher called her last to line up for the buses. When Kristen's mother reminded her of all the things she liked to do in school, Kristen replied, "Okay, I'll go [to school], but you tell Mrs. Peters [the teacher] I don't want to be last all the time." Kristen's mother said, "We'll write her a note. You write it and I'll help." Kristen agreed and wrote Mrs. Peter's name as her mother spelled it. Then Kristen said the message she wanted to write ("I always don't want to be the last person in the line"). Her mother said, "The first word is *I*. You can spell that. What letter do you hear?" Kristen wrote the letter *i*, but when her mother began saying the word *always* slowly for

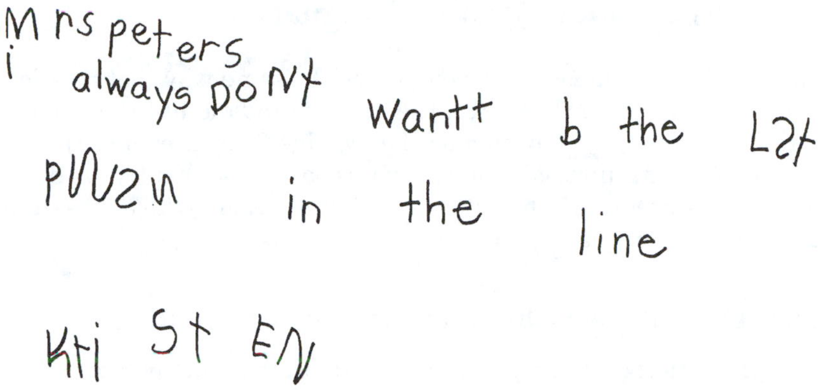

Mrs peters
i always DONt wantt b the Lst
pwsn in the line

Kri St EN

FIGURE 1.1   Kristen's Letter to Her Teacher

Kristen to spell, she refused to spell any more words. So Kristen's mother wrote *always* and then spelled the word *don't* for Kristen to write. She suggested that she write one word and Kristen write one word. As shown in Figure 1.1, the final letter is a combination of Kristen's writing, with invented or incomplete spellings (*t* for *to, b* for *be, Lst* for *last,* and *pwsn* for *person*) as she listened to her mother say each sound in a word, and her mother's writing. Kristen could not have accomplished the task of writing this letter without her mother's scaffolding.

A year and a half later, Kristen ran into the kitchen where her mother was preparing dinner and handed her the note shown in Figure 1.2. This note reads, "I hate when you brought me to Penny's house" (Penny is Kristen's baby-sitter). Kristen had written the note in her room by herself after her mother was late picking her up. This note illustrates the results of scaffolding and working within the zone of proximal development. In kindergarten, Kristen needed her mother's scaffolding to write a letter of protest to her teacher. She needed her mother's support to hear sounds in words, to keep track of what she had written, and to sustain the effort of writing. At the end of first grade, she could write a letter of protest on her own, inventing spellings and reading to keep track of her message as she wrote.

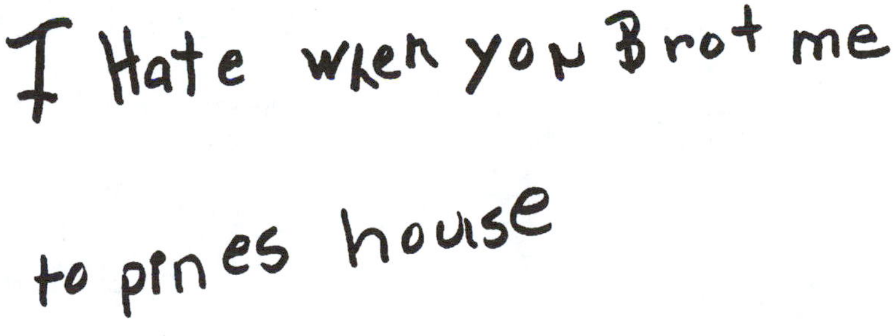

I Hate when you Brot me
to prnes house

FIGURE 1.2   Kristen's Letter to Her Mother

Children's Concepts about Written Language

Children learn written language in much the same way that they learn anything else, including spoken language. They acquire and modify schemas or concepts for various aspects of written language knowledge. They use inborn abilities, and they depend on interactions with others. In this part of the chapter, we describe in detail children's concepts about written language. We begin with a case study of Ted and Carrie as they are playing restaurant.

Ted's Delight: Two Children's Reading and Writing

Ted, who was eight years old, and his sister Carrie, who was three years old, were playing in the corner of the living room. They had set up their card table play-house. Taped on the playhouse was the sign shown in Figure 1.3.

Ted and Carrie had collected Carrie's plastic play food and doll dishes and put them behind the playhouse. When their father entered the room, he looked at the sign and said, "Oh, I think I need some lunch." The children asked him to visit their restaurant. He entered the playhouse, and Carrie presented him with a menu (Figure 1.4).

FIGURE 1.3   "Ted's Delight" Sign

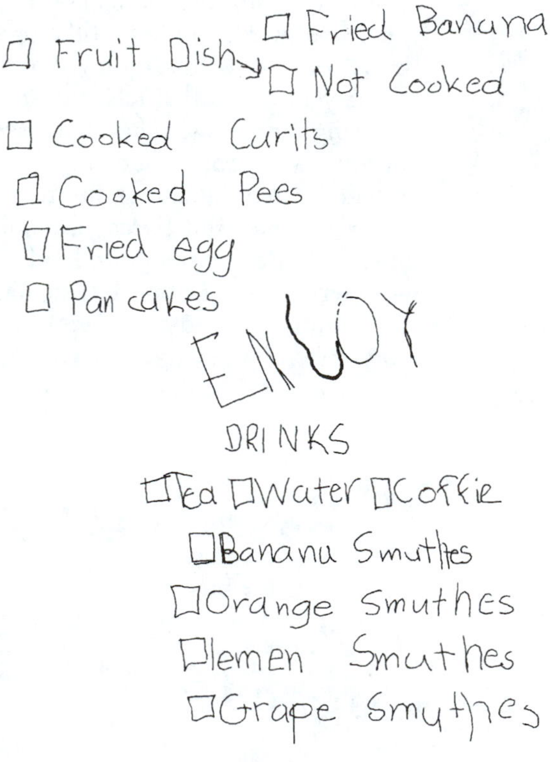

FIGURE 1.4   "Ted's Delight" Menu

FIGURE 1.5   Carrie's Check

Carrie asked, "May I take your order?" Her father read the menu and said, "I'll take pancakes and coffee." Carrie checked off two items on the menu and took it out to Ted, who was behind the playhouse. He pretended to fix pancakes and pour coffee. Ted brought the dishes into the playhouse to his father, who pretended to eat with much relish. When he had finished he asked, "May I have my check, please?" Carrie picked up a pad of paper and a pencil and wrote a check (Figure 1.5). Her father pretended to pay the check and left the playhouse.

Later that evening, the family discussed the restaurant play. Ted said he had made the sign so that the playhouse could be a restaurant. He had asked Carrie if he could use her toy food and dishes. She had wanted to play, too. Ted said that he and Carrie decided to write on the menu the names of the play food they had. In the middle of his writing the menu, Carrie insisted on helping him. "She wrote the letter that looks like a backwards J in the middle of the menu," Ted reported. "I had to turn it into the word *Enjoy* to make sense."

Ted's and Carrie's Concepts about Written Language

What do Ted's and Carrie's reading and writing reveal about their concepts of written language? First, both Ted's and Carrie's behaviors indicate that they understand many ways in which written language is used. Carrie knows that a waitperson writes something when a customer orders and when the customer asks for the check. She seems to be learning, just as Ted is, that writing and reading are functional. Ted and Carrie used written language to get their customer into their restaurant (they made a sign), to let their customer know what was available to eat (they made a menu), and to let their customer know how much the meal cost (they wrote a check).

Second, the sign and menu Ted wrote suggest that he is learning about written language meanings. His sign communicated a message to his father: a restaurant is open for business. Ted also knows that the messages communicated in written language should be meaningful given the written language context. Ted knew that the "backwards J" that Carrie wrote somehow had to be incorporated into a message that could be communicated on a menu. Random letters on menus do not communicate meaningful messages. Ted made the random letter meaningful by incorporating it into the word *Enjoy*. Carrie also showed that she knows that written language communicates meaning. Even though we cannot read her check, her behavior as she gave it to her father (and her father's reactions to the written check) suggests that her writing communicates a message something like "pay some money for your food."

Third, the sign and menu indicate that Ted is learning about written language forms—what written language looks like. These two writing samples certainly look like a sign and a menu. His menu is written in the form of a list. The content of his menu is organized as a menu is usually organized—drinks and food are grouped and listed separately. Carrie is also learning what at least a few written language forms look like. The writing on her check looks something like the letters *E* and *J*. Even though Carrie's letters are not yet conventional, they signal that she is paying attention to what letters look like. Although Carrie's *E*'s sometimes have too many horizontal lines, she has obviously noticed that horizontal lines are included on letters. And, even though Carrie's *J*'s seem to be backwards, she does include the hook expected on this letter. There is one exception. Carrie put a circle on her letter *E*; most letter *E*'s do not include circles. Figure 1.6 (Carrie's name written as her preschool teacher wrote it) suggests why Carrie may have included the circle on her *E*. Her preschool teacher often used what she called "bubble writing," putting small decorative bubbles on each alphabet letter. Carrie noticed that her preschool teacher wrote circles on her letters, so Carrie may have decided to put the same circles on her own letters.

Finally, Ted's and Carrie's writing demonstrates that they are learning a unique system of written language: the manner in which written language conveys meaning. In English, the way written language conveys meaning is that written words map onto spoken words. We call this unique system of written language the **meaning-form link.** In English, the meaning-form link is that written words relate to meaning by being translated into spoken words. Therefore, English is considered an alphabetic language, and learning about sound–letter relationships is an important part of reading and writing. Ted demonstrated his understanding of the alphabetic meaning-form link in his spelling errors. Ted's spelling of *pees* for *peas* shows that he knows that the letters *ee* often take the sound of long *e*.

Carrie's writing demonstrates that she does not yet know sound–letter relationships, the most sophisticated level of the meaning-form link. However, Carrie is using a less sophisticated meaning-form link in her writing. Like many preschoolers, she uses a different concept of meaning-form link. Her concept about how writing can convey meaning is that she writes letters and assumes that a reader, her father, will be able to read her message. We will show that many preschoolers have this concept about the meaning-form link in written language.

FIGURE 1.6   "Carrie" as Written by Her Preschool Teacher

Learning in Social and Cultural Contexts

Ted's and Carrie's reading and writing in the "Ted's Delight" case study provide important insights into *how* children acquire written language concepts. Young children are embedded in social environments constructed, in part, by particular family activities and expectations and, in part, by broader cultural and social group memberships (Gee, 2001). These social and cultural contexts support particular kinds of activities, including activities in which reading and writing are used (Taylor, 1997). They allow children to learn and engage in particular kinds of knowledge as a result of engaging in these activities, including learning concepts about the functions, meanings, forms, and meaning-form links of written language (Purcell-Gates, 1995).

Ted and Carrie were engaging in a play activity that was supported by their father and by the social expectations of their mainstream culture. Ted's and Carrie's father entered the play as a highly experienced playmate, extending their "restaurant" dramatic play by enacting all the events that would be expected to happen in a visit to a real restaurant. He scaffolded their play through his words and actions.

Ted's and Carrie's play was also supported by the *expectations* of their family and mainstream culture. Their father and mother are professionals who expect that their children will become proficient readers and writers. Education is valued in their home, and many opportunities are provided for Ted and Carrie to engage in reading and writing. Ted's and Carrie's play revealed some of the experiences that support their literacy acquisition. They have visited many restaurants and participated in reading menus, selecting entrees and drinks, ordering food, and paying for meals.

Concepts about Written Language: Functions, Meanings, Forms, and Meaning-Form Links

Ted and Carrie have learned a great deal about written language, but their knowledge is not unique. As researchers have studied young children in other literacy events, they have discovered that all children—even those who are not conventionally reading and writing—acquire similar concepts, which we have labeled in our case study, "concepts about written language":

functions	forms
meanings	meaning-form links

We selected these labels for describing children's concepts about written language to reflect that children are developing unique concepts about written language systems. However, these concepts are also related to children's acquisition of four linguistic systems of spoken language:

pragmatics	syntax
semantics	phonology

Pragmatics deals with social and cultural contexts of speaking and conveys the function or purpose of speech. **Semantics** is related to the system of meaning, including the meaning of words and their combinations. **Syntax** is related to the order and organization of words in sentences. **Phonology** is the system of approximately forty-four speech sounds that make up all English words.

Written and Spoken Language Functions

An important part of learning to read and write involves learning about the **functions** or purposes that written language serves. Children have a head start learning about written language's functions because they already use their spoken language to meet a variety of needs. Children, like the adults around them, use their spoken language in functional ways. Halliday (1975) identified seven functions of spoken language. These functions represent different ways in which we use language. Table 1.1 summarizes Halliday's seven functions of language, using examples from children's spoken language as illustrations of each (Halliday, 1975).

Since children are acquainted with using spoken language for several purposes, it is not surprising that they learn how to use written language to accomplish a variety of goals as well. In fact, many of written language's purposes are the same as those of spoken language. Table 1.1 also presents several examples of written language that serve each of Halliday's seven functions.

However, written language also serves unique purposes. We use written language to establish identity or authority. For example, two groups of preschoolers were arguing about the use of a large refrigerator box. One group insisted that the box should be a dollhouse. The other group wanted it to be a fire station. Two boys in the fire station group went to a mother helper and asked her to write the words *fire station*. They copied her writing on a large sheet of paper and taped it to the box. One child pointed to the sign and said, "This is not a house. This is a fire station" (Cochran-Smith, 1984, p. 90).

Written language also has the unique power to make language and thinking permanent and transportable (Stubbs, 1980). We can communicate with others over long distances and share information with people we have never met face-to-face. Because information can be recorded and reread, facts can be accumulated and studied critically. New knowledge is built from a critical analysis of accumulated past knowledge.

Written and Spoken Language Meanings

Meaning is at the heart of both spoken and written language (Halliday, 1975). The human experience demands that we communicate messages to one another, and humans are constantly engaged in meaning-making activities whether through face-to-face conversations or through reading and writing. However, meaning is slippery; we must work hard to get and convey it in everyday conversations and in reading and writing. Messages we construct from conversations are never exact;

TABLE 1.1   Halliday's Language Functions

Language	Function	Spoken Language Examples	Written Language Examples
Instrumental	Satisfies needs and wants	"Gimme that!" "I want pizza!"	Birthday present wish list, sign-up sheet, grant proposal, petition
Regulatory	Controls others	"Stop that!" "Don't spill!"	List of classroom rules, traffic sign, No Smoking sign, policy handbook
Interactional	Creates inter-action with others	"Let's play with the blocks" "Anybody want to paint?"	Party invitation, e-mail to a friend, membership card, "Hello, I'm _____" name tag
Personal	Expresses per-sonal thoughts and opinions	"I like red." "I'm bored."	Letter to the editor, Valentine, journal entry, campaign button
Heuristic	Seeks information	"Are we there yet?" "Why?"	Questionnaire, survey, Internet search entry, insurance claim form, letter of inquiry
Imaginative	Creates imaginary worlds	"This can be our airplane." "You be the robber and I'm the police."	Movie script, short story, novel, poem, label on a play center prop, readers' theater script
Informative	Communicates information	"This is a rectangle." "Today is Wednesday."	Questionnaire results, survey results, Internet site, completed insurance claim form, social studies report, nutrition facts on food package, encyclopedia entry, dictionary entry, class birthday list, school–home newsletter, attendance report, drivers' manual

Adapted from Halliday, 1975.

they always differ in some degree from what was actually spoken. All of us have experienced not being understood; we say, "But, that's not what I meant!" Meaning involves more than just capturing the words others say. It involves interpreting messages.

Semantics in Spoken Language

One aspect of semantics, or the system of meaning, is knowing units of meaning. We usually consider the smallest unit of meaning a word; but units of meaning can actually be smaller than a word. Linguists call the smallest unit of meaning a **morpheme.** The word *start* consists of one morpheme, while the word *restart* has two morphemes: *re* and *start*. *Re* is considered a morpheme because it alters the meaning of the word *start* when it is added to the word. Other morphemes can be added to *start* that will alter meaning by changing the verb tense, such as adding *ed* or *s*. Morphemes can also alter meaning by changing the part of speech, such as when adding *able* to *drink*.

The meaning of words is an important part of the semantic system. We have already discussed how young children begin acquiring word meanings by developing schema or concepts related to words. For example, the meaning of the word *pineapple* may include knowing *spiky, sweet, fruit, yellow, juicy,* and *buy it at the grocery.* We have also stressed that because people have different experiences related to words, they have different meanings associated with them.

Strategies for understanding and conveying meaning in spoken language also apply to written language. Children naturally apply their meaning-making strategies in everyday experiences. When asked what a grocery list might say, a four-year-old will reply, "green beans, bread, coffee." When dictating a letter, five-year-olds say, "I love you." When asked what a traffic sign might say, they reply, "Watch out for children walking." Young children's concepts about meaning are related to their experiences in which different kinds of texts are used. Four-year-olds know the meanings associated with grocery lists because they know the kinds of things found in a grocery store and have shopped with their parents as they read from a grocery list. Young children's concepts about meanings are tied to their awareness of the context in which written language is used and to the variety of written text forms they have observed.

Reading and writing, of course, are only a few of the ways in which we can communicate meanings. We also communicate meanings through facial expression, gesture, dance, art, conversation, and music. For young children, communicating in spoken language and play are very closely related to communicating in written language (Rowe, 1998). Three-year-old Carrie was able to communicate a message through her unconventional writing in the context of restaurant dramatic play. Throughout this book are other examples of children's meaning making as they engage in a variety of playful activities.

Meaning in Written Language

However, strategies that are needed to construct meaning in written language are not always needed for spoken language. One difference, paradoxically, is that written language is not exactly talk written down (Cook-Gumperz, 1986). Meaning in spoken language is often conveyed through gestures, facial expressions, and voice intonation, which provide additional **contextualization clues** to meaning. Much spoken language takes place in a context in which the actual objects discussed can be seen, or between people who know a great deal about each other.

Consider a young child saying, "cookie" to her mother. Without understanding the context—what the mother and child are doing at the time of the utterance—it is difficult to determine the meaning of "cookie." However, suppose we know that it is mid-afternoon, the child has just arisen from a nap, the afternoon routine usually involves a snack, and the child is sitting in her highchair pointing to the cupboard where cookies are kept. Then we know the utterance "cookie" probably means something like, "I'd like my cookie now." In contrast to spoken language, written language does not include contextualization clues such as the context or pointing to objects.

Another difference between spoken and written language is that written language makes more frequent use of unusual words, words that are rarely used in everyday conversation. Words such as *display, exposure, equate, infinite, invariably, literal, luxury, maneuver, participation, provoke,* or *reluctantly* (Cunningham & Stanovich, 1998, p. 10) are found in written stories, newspapers, or textbooks. However, these words are rarely used in daily conversation. Similarly, written language includes **literary language** phrases such as "once upon a time" and "in the previous section," which are not found in everyday spoken language.

Lack of contextualization clues and use of unusual words and literary language are just two examples of the characteristics of written language that require readers and writers to use meaning-making strategies that are not needed by listeners and speakers. As we will show later in the book, reading aloud to young children is a critical pathway to developing the kinds of meaning-making strategies that are necessary for becoming accomplished readers and writers.

Written Language Forms

We use the label written language **forms** to highlight the visual and spatial components of written language. Written language form knowledge includes awareness of visual symbols, spatial directional properties, and spatially organized formats of texts. For example, in the earlier case study, Carrie was learning the visual shapes of alphabet letters. While her letters are not yet totally conventional, she did show attention to many visual features of letters, such as the vertical and horizontal lines found in the letter *E*. Similarly, Ted demonstrated a sophisticated knowledge of the spatial organization of a specific kind of text, a menu. He organized words related to drinks below the words organized as entrees. Ted's menu demonstrated a sophisticated awareness of visual and spatial organization.

Syntax in Spoken Language

Learning the visual shapes and spatial organizational properties of text is unique to learning written language. However, learning about order and organization in written language is similar to learning about order and organization in spoken language. Spoken language relies on order and organization at the levels of words, sentences, and larger discourse units such as stories, jokes, and gossip. One system of spoken language that relies heavily on order and organization is the syntactic system.

Syntax is the set of rules for how to produce and comprehend sentences in language and draws on order and organization. In some languages, including English, the order of words in sentences is crucial (consider, for example, *The boy kicked the goat* versus *The goat kicked the boy*). In other languages, word order is not important. Instead, word endings are critical for understanding who did what to whom (*Lupus agnum portat*, which means, "The wolf carries the lamb," versus *Lupum agnus portat*, which means, "The lamb carries the wolf").

Forms in Written Language

Readers and writers draw upon syntax to construct and convey meaning. However, they also develop a unique set of knowledge about other forms and organizational structures of written language that are not found in spoken language—the form of alphabet letters (which linguists call **graphemes**), words and word spaces, sentences, and text formats.

Alphabet Letters.   One way to find out about children's knowledge of letters and the features which comprise letters is to ask them whether letters are alike or different (Gibson, Gibson, Pick, & Osser, 1962). We might give children the letter *O* and the letter *U* and ask if they are alike or different. (The two letters differ on the feature *closed* versus *open*.) We might show children the letters ⱴ and *A*, which differ on the feature *rotated* versus *upright.* Three-year-olds know that the letters *U* and *O* are different, but they do not know that the letters ⱴ and *A* are different. They know the feature *closed* versus *open,* but they do not know the feature *rotated* versus *upright.* In contrast, seven-year-olds know that both sets of letters are different, because they know both features.

   Children also demonstrate their knowledge of letter features in their writing. Figure 1.7 presents one preschooler's printed letters. This writing does include some conventional or nearly conventional alphabet letter forms (*t, r,* and *M*) as well as many letter-like but unconventional symbols. These symbols look like alphabet letters because they include many letter features, such as vertical, diagonal, and curved lines (Lavine, 1977). Clay (1975) called letters like these **mock letters.**

   Children all over the world construct mock letters, letters that look like the written language children will soon read and write. The features they use in order to write mock letters reveal the unique visual features found in the variety of our world's written languages. In Figure 1.8, a five-year-old Chinese girl has labeled her picture by writing two symbols that resemble Chinese characters, although neither is a real Chinese character.

FIGURE 1.7   A Preschooler's Printed Letters

FIGURE 1.8   A Five-Year-Old's Drawing with Mock Chinese Characters

Words and Sentences.   Children also learn about the features of words. If we wanted to know about children's knowledge of word features, we might ask them to sort cards into two piles, one pile for "words" and one pile for "not words" (Pick, Unze, Brownell, Drozdal, & Hopmann, 1978).

On the cards we would write long and short words and nonwords (such as *keld* or *cafkiton*). Even three-year-olds are willing to perform this task, and they put all the words (and nonwords) with three or more letters in the "word" pile. Thus, their notion of words is that words consist of strings of at least three letters. In contrast, first graders put all the words (including single-letter words, such as *a*, in the word pile, but they reject real words that they cannot read (such as *obese*). Their concept of words is that words may have only one letter but must be readable and meaningful to the reader.

Children also demonstrate their knowledge of word features in their writing (Clay, 1975; Sulzby, 1986). Figure 1.9 presents a letter that five-year-old Zachery wrote to his Aunt Carol. His writing indicates an awareness of words; he separated each word with a dash. Many young children are unsure that a blank space is enough to mark a word boundary. Instead, they make word spaces very obvious, using dots or dashes or circling words to indicate word boundaries to readers. Zachery's writing also demonstrates his strong grasp of the directional principles of written English: he uses **left-to-right** and **top-to-bottom organization.**

This letter also demonstrates Zachery's knowledge of the visual features of two other units of written language: sentences and letter format. Zachery circled each thought unit, which we call a sentence, even though he signaled one sentence boundary with the conventional punctuation mark, a period. His writing also shows a sophisticated awareness of how letters are organized. He begins with a greeting ("Hi Aunt Carol") and ends with a closing ("from Zachery").

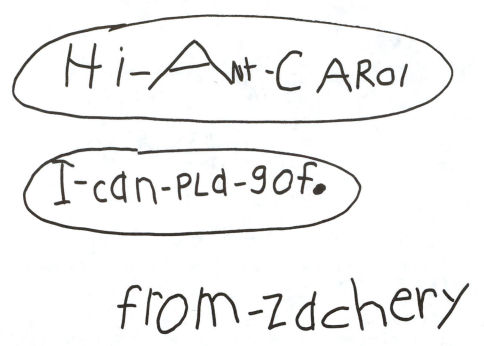

FIGURE 1.9   Zachery's Letter to His Aunt Carol

Text Formats.   There are many kinds of texts, including poems, recipes, maps, newspapers, dictionaries, books, magazine articles, *TV Guides,* and directions. One thing young children learn about these different text forms is how they look.

Figure 1.10 presents a nine-year-old's letter to her principal. The form of the letter reflects Andrea's concepts about letter form, including a greeting, body, and signature. The content is also organized, with a statement of a problem and solution and with arguments for why the principal should consider the solution.

Figures 1.1, 1.2, 1.3, 1.4, 1.9, and 1.10 demonstrate their authors' awareness of **linearity,** that written English appears as horizontal lines of print.

Metalinguistic Awareness of Written Language Units.   We have been using words such as *letter, word, sentence,* and *story,* which make it easy to describe written language. They constitute *language about language.* Children's understanding of and ability to use language about language is a particular kind of knowledge called **metalinguistic awareness** (Yaden & Templeton, 1986). Children acquire several aspects of metalinguistic awareness. One aspect is the ability to examine a written language form apart from the meaning associated with the form (Templeton, 1980). For example, the word *dog* can be examined as a written language form—it is composed of three letters with the graphic shape of ⌐_| . The word *dog* also has meaning—a hairy, four-legged animal. Young children have difficulty examining form apart from meaning. When asked to name a long word, they might reply

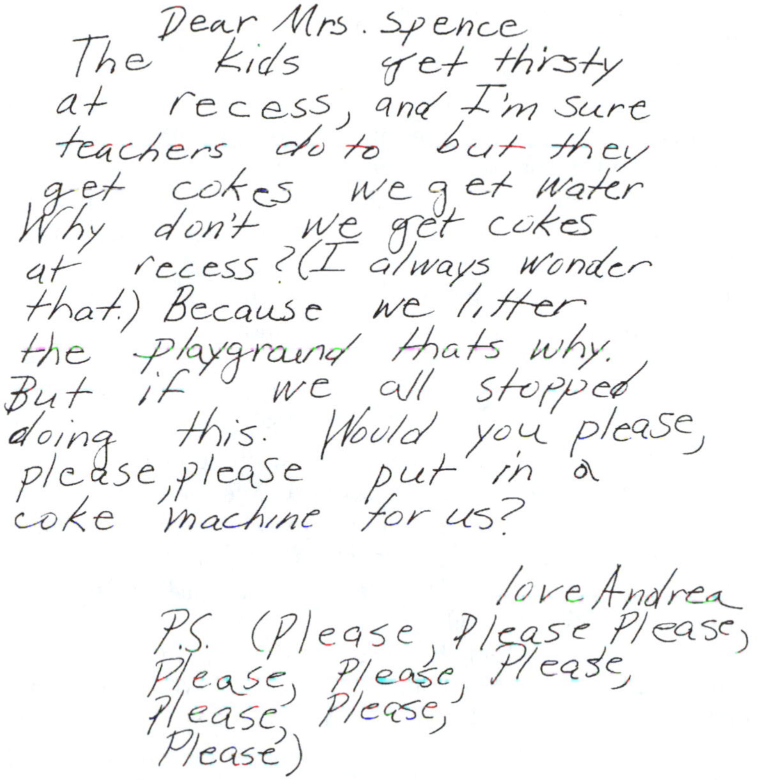

> Dear Mrs. Spence
> The kids get thirsty at recess, and I'm sure teachers do to but they get cokes we get water Why don't we get cokes at recess? (I always wonder that.) Because we litter the playgraund thats why. But if we all stopped doing this. Would you please, please, please put in a coke machine for us?
>
> love Andrea
>
> P.S. (Please, Please Please,) Please, Please, Please, Please, Please, Please)

FIGURE 1.10   A Persuasion Letter

"bus." They are likely to say "paper clip" when asked to name a short word. Young children use the meaning of a word to determine whether a word is long or short. Older children who have metalinguistic awareness would use the form of the written word to identify and name long and short words, such as *encyclopedia* and *I.*

The example of saying that "paper clip" is a short word illustrates another aspect of metalinguistic awareness, **concept of word.** A child who gives this answer does not realize either that the question, "What is a short word?" implies that only one word should be given or that *paper clip* is two words. Concept of word has several components, including the ability to identify a single word in a spoken sentence, the ability to identify a single word in a written sentence, and the ability to answer the question, "What is a word?" (Downing & Oliver, 1973–1974).

Meaning-Form Links

We use the term **meaning-form links** to refer to the way in which meaning is connected to written forms. Ted used the conventional meaning-form link in English—he used letters associated with certain sounds (**sound–letter relationships**) so that his written words corresponded to spoken words and the concepts related to those spoken words. He wrote *pees* using *ee* (as in the word *tree*) to represent the sound of long *e*. Despite Ted's unconventional spelling, we are able to construct the expected meaning (the small, round, green vegetables) because we look for correspondences between expected meanings on a restaurant menu and the letters he chose to represent the sounds in the name of the food item peas.

The link between letters in written words and sounds in spoken words is obvious to experienced readers, but it is not always clear to beginning readers and writers. Despite its not being obvious, young children go about finding a variety of ways to link meaning with printed forms. They draw on their knowledge of written language forms and on their phonological knowledge.

Phonological System in Spoken Language

The phonological system refers to the system of spoken sounds in language. Each language uses some of the few hundreds of possible speech sounds of human languages. English, for example, uses approximately forty-four speech sounds, or **phonemes** (see Table 1.2). Some of English's phonemes are rare: the sound of *i* in *bird* appears in very few other languages. And English does not include some phonemes found in other languages.

Phonemes are the building blocks of words. They are perceivable, manipulable units of sound; they can be combined and contrasted with one another in ways that matter to language users, that is, in ways that make possible the production and perception of words. Consider, for example, the four phonemes /b/, /p/, /i/, and /l/. The last three can be combined to make the word *pill*, and the first two are contrasted when distinguishing the words in the minimal pair *pill* and *bill*. The difference in the pronunciations of the /p/ and the /b/ is slight. It is only that for /p/ we do not use our voices and for /b/ we do; everything else—how we use our tongues and throats, how we shape our lips, how we part our teeth—is identical. Yet speakers and listeners rely on that very small difference, that contrast; it is all that signals two very different English meanings, a dose of medicine versus a duck's mouth.

Phonemes are also abstractions. For example, when we say "the *p* sound," we reference a set of sounds, slightly different in pronunciation from one another, usually depending on the context in which they are pronounced (i.e., what other phonemes precede and follow them). These differences within a **phoneme category** do not matter. Language users can ignore them. The fourth phoneme in *clipped* is /p/; so is the fourth phoneme in *flapping*. But the /p/ in *clipped* is pronounced slightly differently than the /p/ in *flapping*. That difference is real; it has to do with how complete the pronunciations of /p/ are. But it is a difference *within* the /p/ phoneme category, not a difference *between* one phoneme and another. Language users can and do ignore it. To further appreciate the breadth of the category of sounds that constitute /p/ or the *p* sound, notice also the real, but safely ignored difference between /p/ pronunciations in *span* and *pan* (most people do not at first notice this difference, but dangling a piece of paper before their mouths when they say the two words reveals the difference; one word's pronunciation is breathy enough to move the paper, the other's is not).

TABLE 1.2 Common English Phonemes

/a/ cat	/g/ got	/O/ coat	/th/ thing
/A/ Kate	/h/ hot	/oi/ boy	/TH/ this
/ah/ cot	/i/ hit	/oo/ look	/uh/ cut, about
/aw/ caught, fought	/I/ height	/OO/ flute, shoot	/U/ cute
/b/ bought	/j/ Jake	/ow/ shout	/v/ vine
/ch/ chug	/k/ cake	/p/ pat	/w/ wine
/d/ dug	/l/ lake	/r/ rat	/y/ yes
/e/ bed	/m/ make	/s/ sat, city	/z/ zoo
/E/ bead	/n/ win	/sh/ ship	/zh/ treasure
/f/ feed	/ng/ wing	/t/ tip	

Notes:

- Any phoneme list is dialect-sensitive. That is, pronunciations differ from one dialect to another. For example, in some U.S. English dialects, *cot* and *caught* are pronounced the same, both with the middle phoneme /ah/; there is no separate /aw/ phoneme in those dialects.
- There is no "C sound"; C usually spells /k/ (cat) or /s/ (city).
- There is no "Q sound" QU usually spells the two sounds /k/ + /w/ (quick), but sometimes the one sound /k/ (plaque).
- Some phonemes are really combinations of others. The /I/ phoneme is really /ah/ + /E/. The /oi/ phoneme is really /O/ + /E/. The /U/ phoneme is really /y/ + /OO/; notice the difference between the /OO/ in flute and the /y/ + /OO/ in cute. The /ch/ phoneme is really /t/ + /sh/.
- There is no "X sound"; X usually spells the two sounds /k/ + /s/ (box) or the one sound /z/ (xylophone).
- Our list has only thirty-nine phonemes. Many sources give forty-four as the number of English phonemes, so why do we not list forty-four? We could add /hw/ for those whose dialect of English includes an additional /h/-like sound at the beginning of words spelled with WH (those speakers' pronunciation of the beginning of *when* is breathier than their pronunciation of the beginning of *wet*). In addition, some lists of English phonemes include additional sounds for some vowels before /r/. The R sound after a vowel often slightly changes the way the vowel is pronounced, but we do not think the difference is enough for nonlinguists to be concerned with. Finally, some lists of English phonemes include the schwa sound (/ə/) for the vowel sound in many unaccented syllables (about, basket, rapid, cotton), but the schwa sound is the same as the short *U* sound (/uh/); compare about and cut.

Using the phonological system is complex and diverse. **Phonological knowledge** includes abilities to distinguish speech from other kinds of sounds, to distinguish one phoneme from another, to attend to some very slight differences in sounds in some contexts (*zoo* versus *Sue*) but ignore small differences in other contexts (*Sue* pronounced by a child's mother versus *Sue* pronounced by a child's father), to distinguish questions from statements, and so on. For speaking and listening, this kind of phonological knowledge is acquired easily—most preschool and kindergarten children's speech is sufficient for their talking and listening needs, although they will continue to expand their oral language capabilities throughout schooling.

In contrast, **phonological awareness** is necessary for reading and writing. It is a special kind of phonological knowledge that requires the ability to think and talk about these kinds of differences in speech sounds. Children who have phonological awareness notice and identify different sounds units. For example, they can decide if two words rhyme and can clap out syllables in words.

An even more sophisticated level of phonological awareness is called **phonemic awareness.** This is the ability to hear phonemes—for example, to detect if two words begin or end with the same sound. Phonemic awareness is never necessary for speaking or listening. In fact, in everyday speech, phonemes in a word flow together so that it is difficult to say where one phoneme ends and another begins. Nonetheless, because English is an alphabetic language in which alphabet letters correspond to phonemes, acquiring phonemic awareness is important for literacy development (Stahl, Duffy-Hester, & Stahl, 1998; Nation & Hulme, 1997). As we will see later in this book, the ability to segment words into their individual phonemes comes gradually, but is a crucial part of becoming a reader and writer (National Reading Panel, 2000).

Meaning-Form Links in Written Language

The most noticeable meaning-form link in written language is spelling. That is, the way written words look (how they are spelled, what letters are strung together in what order) has a lot to do with what they mean (what words you say for them if you read aloud and what concepts they call to mind whether you read aloud or silently). Thus *slip* and *slap* are two very different words with very different meanings because of the different third letter in those two sequences of letters; similarly, *slip* and *lips* are very different words with very different meanings because of the different ordering of the same four letters.

This noticeable role for letters and sequences of letters—their correspondence with sounds and sequences of sounds—is what makes *sounding out* seem a natural reading and spelling strategy. It is also what makes commercial phonics programs—many directly marketed to parents and grandparents of preschoolers—so beguiling. **Sound–letter correspondences** are the basis for alphabetic writing systems such as English. Each letter in the English alphabet is associated with at least one speech sound. But it is not just that simple. Many letters are associated with additional speech sounds (e.g., the letter *A* with /A/ in *able,* but also with /a/ in *cat,* /ah/ in *car,* and /uh/ in *about*), and some speech sounds are associated with combinations of letters (e.g., the sound /aw/ with *augh* in *caught,* the sound /A/ with *a_e* in *make* and *ai* in *rain,* and the sound /sh/ with *sh* in *shine*).

As noticeable and important as this system of sound–letter correspondences is, it is not the be-all and end-all of reading and writing. Accomplished readers and writers have moved beyond paying attention to individual sound–letter correspondences except as just one of many strategies to use when their reading or spelling falters. Visual processes begin to supplant auditory ones. They recognize and respond to common groupings of letters (**phonograms**), for example, *-ight* in *night, fight, light, sight, slight,* and *tight* and *-an* in *ban, can, fan, tan,* and *plan*. Experience with texts leads them to expect certain combinations of letters; a given letter in a given position produces a greater unconscious expectation for some neighboring letters and not others. The perception of written words and phrases leads more directly to concepts and meanings, with less need for intervening pronunciations.

This more direct linking of spellings to meanings is called **orthographic reading and writing.** Consider a word beginning with the letter *d*. When orthographic readers—who have had much experience with English text—see the *d*, their visual perception mechanisms are primed to expect the second letter to be any vowel, including *y*, or one of only two consonants, *r* and *w*, that commonly follow *d* in English spelling. They are not expecting any of the other consonants. In fact, such expectations feed one another, so that readers come to expect high-frequency sequences of letters. When orthographic spellers make spelling errors, they reveal knowledge of orthographic patterns much like Ted's misspelling of the word *peas* as *pees*.

Sound–letter correspondences are not the first meaning-form links to develop. Well before they learn how letters and sounds work together in written language, most preschoolers attempt in other ways to link meanings and forms. In their letter and scribble strings and in their finger-point reading of familiar texts, they reveal rudimentary knowledge of meaning-form links. They show that they know that the appearance of written language determines what it means.

Meaning-Form Links through Letter and Scribble Strings.   In the case study, Carrie produced a mock letter string (see Figure 1.5). She wrote mock letters without regard for sound–letter relationships. Nonetheless, she expected that her writing would communicate a message. Carrie's father pretended that it indeed was meaningful and paid his bill. Figure 1.11 presents Johanna's picture and story writing. She read her story, pointing to the print from left to right and then down the side and from right to left across the bottom: "Miss Sharon and Mr. K have a new baby, Emily. I hope we will baby-sit Emily. I love Emily Grace." Johanna's text consists of a string of conventional and mock letters wrapped around the edges of the paper framing her illustration. She does not use sound–letter relationships to connect meaning and form. Instead, Johanna's meaning—her story about a beloved new baby and her desire to be with the baby—is told both through the illustration and by spoken language. Johanna knows that print is important—she pointed to her letters as she read the story. The meaning-form link for Johanna was to write and then compose a related story.

Meaning-Form Links by Matching Print with Spoken Units.   An intermediate way that children attempt to link meaning with written language is to match a unit of written language to a unit of spoken language. Sometimes children explore a syllable link between spoken language and written language. For example,

FIGURE 1.11   Johanna's Story

Heather memorized the poem "Twinkle, Twinkle Little Star." Her kindergarten teacher wrote the poem on a chart and asked Heather to read it and "point to each word." Heather performed the task by reading and pointing as follows.

Text:	Twinkle	Twinkle	Little	Star		
Heather:	Twink	le		Twink	le	

Text:	How	I	Wonder	What	You	Are
Heather:	Lit	tle	Star		How	I	Won

Heather hesitated and then pointed back at the beginning of the poem:

Text:	Twinkle	Twinkle	Little	Star	
Heather:	Won	der		What	You

Text:	How	I	Wonder	What	You	Are
Heather:	Are					

Then Heather stopped, pointed to the remainder of the text, and said, "I don't know what the rest says." Heather used a strategy of linking each written word to a spoken syllable.

Table 1.3 summarizes the similarities and differences between the four systems of spoken and written language: pragmatics and function, semantics and meaning, syntax and form, and phonology and meaning-form links. As shown in this table, what children learn as they acquire reading and writing is complex and overlaps with their spoken language development. They acquire these necessary

TABLE 1.3   Systems of Spoken and Written Language

Spoken Language	Written Language
Pragmatics	*Functions*
The contextualized purposes spoken language serves	The purposes written language serves, including establishing identity, recording information, and accumulating knowledge
Semantics	*Meaning*
System of meaning, including word meanings; contextualization clues such as gesture, expression, or intonation; morphology	System of meaning, including word meanings, literary language, unusual words; morphology
Syntax	*Form*
The order and organization of words within sentences and spoken utterances	The order of words within sentences; upper- and lowercase alphabet letters (graphemes); spatial directional principles, including left to right, top to bottom; word spaces; text formats
Phonology	*Meaning-Form Link*
System of approximately forty-four speech sounds (phonemes), which make up spoken English	Phoneme–grapheme relationships: orthographic spelling patterns, including phonograms

concepts for reading and writing gradually, through many experiences and instructional opportunities.

Developmental Changes in Children's Reading and Writing

We have shown how children's concepts change as they have more experiences that include reading and writing. Children have many unconventional concepts about words, alphabet letters, and meaning-form links. Yet all children's concepts become increasingly more conventional. Although the journey to becoming a mature reader and writer is long, what happens during the journey is as valid as the end point. Knowing how children's concepts about written language develop is critical for understanding children's reading and writing.

Since the first edition of this book (McGee & Richgels, 1990) we have described four stages of young readers and writers: beginners, novices, experimenters, and accomplished or conventional readers and writers. In the intervening years, others have documented similar stages in children's literacy development and have used their own labels for them. We will share some of those characterizations, with special attention to a continuum of literacy development given by the International Reading Association (IRA) and the National Association for the Education of Young Children (NAEYC) in their joint position statement about developmentally appropriate literacy education practices (1998). We tell how those characterizations map onto the four stages that we will continue to use in this fourth edition of our book.

Awareness and Exploration

For years before children read and write conventionally, they engage in genuinely literate behavior; they read and write in ways that are not like the reading and writing of adults, but that have many of the characteristics of adults' reading and writing. Reexamine Kristen's letter (Figure 1.2), Carrie's check (Figure 1.5), and Heather's reading (page 24). These children are not operating with conventional knowledge of written language functions, meanings, forms, and meaning-form links, but they do have considerable understanding of many concepts. For example, young children know that the label on their cereal box reads "Rice Krispies." This is an important accomplishment for preschoolers—they realize that print in the environment communicates meaning.

Yet if "Rice Krispies" were printed on a card, preschoolers could not read the words. How, then, can preschoolers read words from familiar environmental print signs? They do so by assigning meaning to logos and illustrations found in familiar print contexts. This is a visual concept of word reading; it depends on seeing print in familiar environments, such as on the front of a cereal box. Their reading depends on context.

Similarly, young children's writing reveals a reliance on context for meaning. When Johanna told her story (see Figure 1.11), she used the context of the illustration in order to construct meaning from her writing. Without being in the context of Johanna's telling of her story, another adult could not read it. Our reading of Johanna's writing is dependent on our being in the context of her story reading. If Johanna were asked to read her story several weeks after writing it, she would likely be unable to reconstruct the story or to retell it in exactly the same way. Researchers have labeled reading and writing that relies on context as **logographic reading and writing** (Ehri, 1991; Juel, 1991).

Logographic reading and writing is just one aspect of a phase of early reading and writing that the IRA and NAEYC (1998) call **Awareness and Exploration.** This phase is characterized by children's special attention to many kinds of print and purposes for print in the world around them. They may notice, for example, that adults in their family consult a *TV guide* in a particular context and for a particular purpose, that is, when deciding what to watch on television. The children may page through the guide themselves and make their own connections between what is in the guide, including some of the print, and their own television experiences. They may, for example, recognize pictures of familiar television actors and actresses in program advertising, and they may even recognize familiar network, station, and program logos.

Other characteristics of the Awareness and Exploration phase include that children are able to

> enjoy listening to and discussing storybooks, understand that print carries a message, engage in reading and writing attempts, . . . participate in rhyming games, identify some letters and make some letter-sound matches, [and] use known letters or approximations of letters to represent written language (especially meaningful words like their name and phrases such as "I love you"). (IRA/NAEYC, 1998, p. 200)

We think that two stages of development are identifiable during this Awareness and Exploration phase. We call these beginning literacy and novice reading and writing.

Beginners are very young children who have meaningful experiences with books and writing materials, experiences that lay necessary foundations for later literacy development. The children we call beginners, however, do not find meaning in printed symbols themselves, and they do not make written marks with the intentions of communicating particular messages.

Novices are aware that printed texts communicate messages, and they write with the intention to communicate meaning, although the ways in which they read and write are unconventional. They learn to name and write some letters of the alphabet, and they make texts that have visual features appropriate to their purposes (e.g., a list that looks like a list rather than a sentence or paragraph, even though it may not contain readable words). They read back and assign meanings to their own writing that match their purposes for writing, and they read other texts in ways that depend on visual clues from the immediate environment (e.g., a picture of an ice cream cone on a sign that says "Ice Cream").

Experimental Reading and Writing

Children eventually come to recognize that meaning is mapped onto print in systematic ways. Heather's matching of words to syllables while reading "Twinkle, Twinkle Little Star" is the beginning of this understanding. Children who attempt to use sound–letter correspondences in their reading and writing do what is called **alphabetic reading and writing** (Ehri, 1991; Juel, 1991).

They know at least some alphabet letters and realize that alphabet letters are associated with certain sounds. When they first acquire this concept, children may perform phonetic cue reading (Ehri, 1991); they read printed words by remembering some sound–letter associations. For example, they may be able to read the word *mom* because they recognize the letter *m* and associate it with the sound /m/.

At this early point in alphabetic reading, knowledge about letters and sounds is not complete. For example, children who can remember *mom* by using the association of the sound /m/ with the letter *m* cannot read the nonsense word *mim*; they cannot yet separate each letter and associate it with a single phoneme. They are not yet able to sound a word phoneme by phoneme (/m/, /i/, and /m/) and then blend the phonemes into the nonsense word *mim*. They might say, "Mom" when reading the word *mim*.

Developing knowledge of and ever more sophisticated use of the alphabetic principle are significant new elements in what IRA and NAEYC (1998) call the **Experimental Reading and Writing** phase. For example, they note that children can "recognize letters and letter–sound matches, show familiarity with rhyming and beginning sounds, . . . [and] begin to write letters of the alphabet and some high-frequency words" (p. 200).

This is just one aspect of experimental reading and writing. In addition to use of the alphabetic principle for decoding and encoding print, IRA and NAEYC (1998) cite other abilities of experimental readers and writers. Experimenters can, for example, "enjoy being read to and themselves retell simple narrative stories or informational texts, use descriptive language to explain and explore, . . . understand left-to-right and top-to-bottom orientation and familiar concepts of print, [and] match spoken words with written ones" (p. 200).

We describe a stage of young children's reading and writing that encompasses much of IRA and NAEYC's Experimental phase. We call it experimenting reading and writing. **Experimenters** use many more conventional tools and strategies than do novices, but most people would not yet mistake them for conventional readers and writers; they are in a process of becoming. They use literary language, they can name and form nearly all the letters of the alphabet, they develop an awareness of words, they become inventive spellers, and they read with the support of familiar, predictable texts.

This stage itself encompasses much development. Experimenters move from the very beginnings of alphabetic reading and writing to showing the first hints that they will soon read and write conventionally. These hints are especially evident in what late-stage experimenters begin to do with sight words, reading more and more words by sight and spelling more and more words without having to work sound-by-sound.

Early, Transitional, and Independent Reading and Writing

The fourth of our stages of literacy development is **conventional reading and writing,** when children read and write in ways that most people in our literate society recognize as *really* reading and writing. For example, they use a variety of reading strategies, know hundreds of sight words, read texts written in a variety of structures, are aware of audience, monitor their own performances as writers and readers, and spell conventionally.

IRA and NAEYC (1998) devote three phases to this increasingly more conventional reading and writing. In the **Early Reading and Writing** phase, children can

> read and retell familiar stories; use strategies (rereading, predicting, questioning, contextualizing) when comprehension breaks down; use reading and writing for various purposes on their own initiative; orally read with reasonable fluency; use letter–sound associations, word parts, and context to identify new words; identify

an increasing number [of] words by sight; sound out and represent all substantial sounds in spelling a word; write about topics that are personally meaningful; [and] attempt to use some punctuation and capitalization. (p. 200)

In IRA and NAEYC's (1998) **Transitional Reading and Writing** phase, children can

read with greater fluency, use strategies more efficiently (rereading, questioning, and so on) when comprehension breaks down, use word identification strategies with greater facility to unlock unknown words, identify an increasing number of words by sight, write about a range of topics to suit different audiences, use common letter patterns and critical features to spell words, punctuate simple sentences correctly and proofread their own work, [and] spend time reading daily and use reading to research topics. (p. 201)

In what IRA and NAEYC (1998) call the **Independent and Productive Reading and Writing** phase, children can

read fluently and enjoy reading, use a range of strategies when drawing meaning from the text, use word identification strategies appropriately and automatically when encountering unknown words, recognize and discuss elements of different text structures, make critical connections between texts, write expressively in many different forms (stories, poems, reports), use a rich variety of vocabulary and sentences appropriate to text forms, revise and edit their own writing during and after composing, [and] spell words correctly in final writing drafts. (p. 201)

One feature that distinguishes conventional readers and writers from experimenters is a greater reliance on visual strategies. Earlier we characterized this as orthographic reading and writing. This is mostly a visual concept of word reading. However, it is far different from the visual concept of logographic reading. With orthographic reading, children are so familiar with the sequences of letters in written words that they automatically see letters in groups, or clusters.

Orthographic writers know the conventional spellings of hundreds of words and spell unfamiliar words with regular spelling patterns. Orthographic reading and writing usually appear toward the end of the primary grades in elementary school. However, highly accomplished readers and writers achieve this level of understanding early. Nonetheless, no single accomplishment establishes a child as a novice, an experimenter, or a conventional reader and writer. The boundaries between these identities are fuzzy; children often waver between them. We use them only to help organize and elaborate the vast amount of information we now have about how children's literacy competence changes from birth to the primary grades.

Chapter Summary

Children's learning is dependent on having experiences that lead to the formation of concepts or schemas. Concepts are mental constructions about objects, people, events or activities, and places. Learning is a matter of acquiring new concepts or adding to and changing old concepts. Language is critical for learning when it provides labels for new concepts and when it is used to scaffold children's attempts at difficult tasks.

Children develop special concepts about written language that they use in reading and writing. They develop concepts about the functions of written language, including using reading and writing to label and record.

Their concepts about written language meanings reflect their experiences with different kinds of texts, such as stories, grocery lists, and traffic signs. They create concepts about written language forms, including learning about letter features, words, sentences, texts, and left-to-right organization. They develop understandings about meaning-form links, including unconventional concepts such using letter strings and matching spoken units with written units.

Children's concepts about written language change and grow with their reading and writing experiences. Children begin with unconventional concepts and gradually acquire conventional concepts. Before reading and writing conventionally, they may proceed through phases of awareness and exploration and experimental reading and writing.

Applying the Information

A case study of a literacy event follows. Read this case study carefully and think about the four domains of written language knowledge. Discuss what each of the children in the case study is learning about written language (1) meanings, (2) forms, (3) meaning-form links, and (4) functions. Figure 1.12 presents a drawing and writing composition jointly produced by Kristen and Carrie.

Kristen, a three-year-old preschooler, and Carrie, a six-year-old kindergartner (not the same Carrie mentioned earlier), were playing school together. Carrie began by demonstrating how to draw. She said, "This is me," as she drew the person (1) in the upper right corner of Figure 1.12. Kristen replied, "I can draw you," and she drew the figure (2) at the middle left of Figure 1.12. Carrie pointed out that the person has no hair, so Kristen drew the figure (3) in the upper left corner. Carrie decided to teach Kristen how to write. She said, "We'll write. Here is a C." She wrote the capital C (4) on the right side of the figure. Kristen wrote the letter (5) in the top middle of the page and said "I can write C, too." Then Carrie wrote the remaining letters in her name, saying the name of each letter as she wrote (6). Kristen wrote similar letters, including an A, several Es, and Rs scattered around the page. The children finished as Carrie drew a tree and Kristen added dots to the picture.

Going Beyond the Text

Observe a literacy event with at least two children. One way to initiate a literacy event is to prepare for some dramatic play with children. Plan a dramatic play activity that could include reading and writing. For example, plan a restaurant

FIGURE 1.12   Kristen's and Carrie's Drawing and Writing

play activity. Bring dramatic props, such as an apron, dishes, and a tablecloth, as well as reading and writing materials, such as large sheets of paper, small pads of paper, crayons or markers, placemats with puzzles, and menus. Suggest to two or three children that they might want to play restaurant and propose that they use the paper and crayons in their play. Observe their actions and talk. Use your observations to find out what the children know about written language meanings, forms, meaning-form links, and functions.

REFERENCES

Clay, M. M. (1975). *What did I write?* Aukland: Heinemann Educational Books.

Cochran-Smith, M. (1984). *The making of a reader.* Norwood, NJ: Ablex.

Cook-Gumperz, J. (Ed.). (1986). *The social construction of literacy.* Cambridge: Cambridge University Press.

Cunningham, A., & Stanovich, K. (1998). What reading does for the mind. *American Educator, 22,* 8–15.

Downing, J., & Oliver, P. (1973–1974). The child's conception of a word. *Reading Research Quarterly, 9,* 568–582.

Ehri, L. (1991). Development of the ability to read words. In R. Barr, M. Kamil, P. Mosenthal, & P. Pearson (Eds.), *Handbook of reading research* (2nd ed., pp. 395–419). New York: Longman.

Gee, J. P. (2001). A sociocultural perspective on early literacy development. In S. B. Neuman & D. K.

Dickinson (Eds.), *Handbook of early literacy research* (pp. 30–42). New York: Guilford.

Gibson, E. J., Gibson, J. J., Pick, A. D., & Osser, H. (1962). A developmental study of discrimination of letter-like forms. *Journal of Comparative Physiological Psychology, 55,* 897–906.

Gopnick, A., & Meltzoff, A. Z. (1986). Relations between semantic and cognitive development in the one-word stage: The specificity hypothesis. *Child Development, 57,* 1040–1053.

Halliday, M. A. K. (1975). *Learning how to mean.* New York: Elsevier.

International Reading Association & National Association for the Education of Young Children. (1998). Learning to read and write: Developmentally appropriate practices for young children. *The Reading Teacher, 52,* 193–216.

Juel, C. (1991). Beginning reading. In R. Barr, M. Kamil, P. Mosenthal, & P. Pearson (Eds.), *Handbook of reading research* (2nd ed., pp. 759–788). New York: Longman.

Lavine, L. O. (1977). Differentiation of letter-like forms in prereading children. *Developmental Psychology, 13,* 89–94.

McGee, L. M., & Richgels, D. J. (1990). *Literacy's beginnings: Supporting young readers and writers.* Boston: Allyn & Bacon.

Meltzoff, A. Z. (1985). In *Baby talk* (NOVA transcript No. 1207). Boston: WGBH Transcripts.

Nation, K., & Hulme, C. (1997). Phonemic segmentation, not onset-rime segmentation, predicts early reading and spelling skills. *Reading Research Quarterly, 32,* 154–167.

National Reading Panel. (2000). *Report of the National Reading Panel.* Washington, DC: National Institutes of Health.

Piaget, J. (1955). *The language and thought of the child.* Cleveland, OH: World.

Pick, A. D., Unze, M. G., Brownell, C. A., Drozdal, J. G., Jr., & Hopmann, M. R. (1978). Young children's knowledge of word structure. *Child Development, 49,* 669–680.

Purcell-Gates, V. (1995). *Other people's words: The cycle of low literacy.* Cambridge, MA: Harvard University Press.

Rowe, D. (1998). The literate potentials of book-related dramatic play. *Reading Research Quarterly, 33,* 10–35.

Stahl, S., Duffy-Hester, A., & Stahl, A. (1998). Theory and research into practice: Everything you wanted to know about phonics (but were afraid to ask). *Reading Research Quarterly, 33,* 338–355.

Stubbs, M. (1980). *The sociolinguistics of reading and writing: Language and literacy.* London: Routledge & Kegan Paul.

Sulzby, E. (1986). Children's elicitation and use of metalinguistic knowledge about word during literacy interactions. In D. B. Yaden, Jr., & S. Templeton (Eds.), *Metalinguistic awareness and beginning literacy* (pp. 219–233). Portsmouth, NH: Heinemann.

Taylor, D. (Ed.). (1997). *Many families, many literacies: An international declaration of principles.* Portsmouth, NH: Heinemann.

Templeton, S. (1980). Young children invent words: Developing concepts of "wordness." *The Reading Teacher, 33,* 454–459.

Vygotsky, L. S. (1978). *Mind in society. The development of higher psychological processes* (Michael Cole, Trans.). Cambridge: Harvard University Press.

Yaden, D. B., Jr., & Templeton, S. (1986). Introduction: Metalinguistic awareness—an etymology. In D. B. Yaden, Jr., & S. Templeton (Eds.), *Metalinguistic awareness and beginning literacy* (pp. 3–10). Portsmouth, NH: Heinemann.

From Birth to Three Years

The Foundations of Literacy Development

KEY CONCEPTS

bbooksharing routines
naming game
bookhandling skills
motor schemes
symbols
scribbling

representational drawing
tadpole
romance representations
ascribing intentionality
interactive bookreading
attention getting strategies

low levels of cognitive
demand
high levels of cognitive
demand
story grammar
concept of story

environmental print
caregiver interactive
   responsiveness
speech density
follow a gaze

immediate events
contextualized language
nonimmediate events
decontextualized
   language

developmentally appropriate
   practices
board books
language play books
first storybooks

The Beginnings of Literacy

Many children, but not all, have literacy experiences with their families as infants and toddlers, and by two years of age, most children have participated in many literacy experiences. They share books with parents and other caregivers, they are invited to use markers and crayons, and they notice the print found in their environment. These early experiences with books and print allow children to acquire concepts that form the foundation for later reading and writing.

Kristen's Early Literacy Experiences

As an example of the rich literacy experiences available to children, we present a case study of Kristen from her birth until she turned three years old. During this time, she demonstrated many literacy behaviors. She could hold books, turn the pages, and eventually identify objects in the illustrations. She made marks with crayons and markers and eventually could draw people. She noticed print in her surroundings, especially McDonald's and Burger King signs. Eventually she recognized the K-Mart sign as "her" sign.

Literacy Experiences from Birth to One.   Early in the first few months of her life, Kristen's mother and father would actively engage her in language activities especially during daily routines. For example, her father would talk with Kristen when he changed her diaper. As Kristen lay on the changing table, her father would say, "I am going to put on a nice dry diaper." Kristen would coo and gurgle, and her father would reply, "I know you like that don't you?" Kristen would wiggle, and her father would continue, "I agree. Dry diapers are the best."

Kristen received her first books when she was just a few months old. Many of these were sturdy cardboard books such as *A Goodnight Hug* (Roth, 1986). They were kept in her toy basket along with her rattles. Her mother and father read to her while she sat in their laps. When just a few months old, Kristen began grabbing her books, picking them up, and holding them. Kristen did not look at the pictures in her books; instead, she made insistent attempts to turn the pages.

When Kristen could sit up by herself (a little before she was six months old), her books were some of her favorite toys. She would pull books out of a basket and dump them on her blanket, grab for books, turn pages, and try to chew on the pages. Her mother and father engaged her in active games with books. When they read a book with nursery rhymes, they would hold Kristen and use actions to engage her attention. As they recited a nursery rhyme, they would hold her close and rock her back and forth. They would hold her arms and hands and help her clap or take her body and gently pretend to fall.

Some months before her first birthday, Kristen could recognize books by their names. Her father would say, "Let's read the Humpty Dumpty book." Kristen would crawl to the book basket and select her "Humpty Dumpty book" (*The Real Mother Goose*, Wright, 1916). She would turn to the page that had the Humpty Dumpty rhyme and sway her body as her father recited the rhyme.

Literacy Experiences from One to Two. By her first birthday, Kristen would hold a book right-side-up and turn the pages from front to back. Sometimes she smiled and patted the pictures or turned pages over from one side to the next, intently checking the pictures on each side of the page.

A few months after her first birthday, Kristen began to point to things around her, saying "dat?" with a rising intonation. She would also point to and ask "dat?" about animals and people pictured in her books. Her mother or father would obligingly name the animals and people. Kristen's mother often requested that she locate animals or people in her books. She would ask, "Where's the kitten?" and Kristen would point to it.

Kristen received crayons as a Christmas present when she was fifteen months old. Her first attempts at drawing were rapid back-and-forth swipes at paper (see Figure 2.1). She would quickly make a few marks and push the paper on the floor, indicating that she wanted another sheet of paper.

When Kristen was about sixteen months old, she began interrupting bookreading by jumping off her father's lap to seek a toy or object in the house. She did this only when she saw certain pictures in her books. Each time Kristen saw a picture of crayons, for example, she would get up and find *her* crayons.

At this age, Kristen would sit by herself and look at her books, saying the names of some of the objects in the pictures while pointing at them. Kristen had

FIGURE 2.1 Back-and-Forth Lines

several ABC books in which she was particularly interested at this time. She noticed the alphabet letters on the endpapers of *Dr. Seuss's ABC Book* (Seuss, 1963a). One day, while she was looking at the letters, her mother sang the ABC song to her and pointed to each letter as she sang. Whenever Kristen read this book, she would turn to the endpapers and repeatedly point at the letters, saying "A-A-A" in her singing voice.

When she was twenty-one months old, Kristen began making round-and-round lines and dots. Her mother and father began drawing to entertain her. They drew people, houses, flowers, cats, dogs, and other familiar objects.

Literacy Experiences from Two to Three.   As Kristen turned two years old, she could recite some of the text in her books. In *Hop on Pop* (Seuss, 1963b), Kristen said, "No. No. No sit" after her mother read, "No, Pat, No. Don't sit on that." As her father read the text of *Goodnight Moon* (Brown, 1947), he would pause for Kristen to fill in part of the rhyme. Kristen began recognizing McDonald's and Burger King signs. She would say "DeDonald's" or "Bugar King" each time she saw the signs. Kristen also pointed to her favorite cereals and cookies in the grocery store, saying "Aisin Ban" and "Oeos."

Drawing continued to be a favorite activity. She began to control her drawing and could make jagged lines, straight lines, and dots. When asked to tell about her drawing, she often replied, "dots." She frequently initiated drawing activities with her parents. She would take paper and crayons to her mother and command, "Draw. Draw little girl." or "Draw little boy." After drawing a little girl, her mother would say, "That's Kristen. Now I'll write Kristen" and she would write her name next to the picture. After drawing a little boy, her mother would say, "That's daddy. I'll write daddy, too."

At twenty-seven months of age, Kristen made concentrated efforts to control her marks. She would slowly draw a continuous line all around the edges of her paper. It seemed as if she were pushing the crayon around the paper and watching its progress. She began making circular shapes of just a single line or a few lines (see Figure 2.2).

Although Kristen continued to thoroughly enjoy drawing, she resisted her mother's attempts to invite her to label her drawings. When asked to tell about her drawings, she would often shrug. However, just before Kristen turned three years old, her mother noticed a change in Kristen's drawings. Now Kristen seemed more intentional about her drawings. She made round shapes and carefully added some straight lines and dots. While her drawings still looked like scribbles, her mother could tell she was trying to draw something, rather than just make marks. One day her mother drew a round shape and asked Kristen to point to where the eyes, nose, mouth, and hair should go. Kristen pointed to where each feature belonged. Her mother coaxed her to draw some eyes. Kristen tried to put eyes on the face, but became frustrated. She announced, "I can't draw that." Another day, Kristen's mother convinced her to draw by saying, "Just do some lines and dots and circles." Kristen selected a blue marker and made several quick line strokes down her page. After making several of these marks, she cried, "Look at the rain." She made sev-

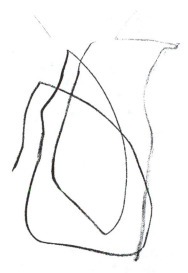

FIGURE 2.2   Circular Shapes

eral more marks, saying, "More rain. Look at the rain, Mommy." Then she began making dots, saying, "Look at all these raindrops (see Figure 2.3).

By the time Kristen was three years old, she was drawing people (see Figure 2.4). She would draw a circle, add two lines for arms, two lines for legs, and some dots for eyes. After drawing the person in Figure 2.4, Kristen said, "This is a picture of Daddy."

At three years of age, Kristen participated in book and familiar print reading in many ways. She made comments about characters and actions depicted in her

FIGURE 2.3   "Rain" and "Raindrops"

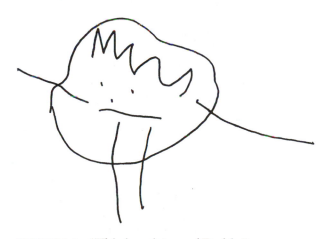

FIGURE 2.4   "This is a picture of Daddy"

books. Pointing to the picture of the wolf in *Walt Disney's Peter and the Wolf* (Disney Productions, 1974), she said, "He needs to be good." She commented about the predicament of Wully-Wully in *Babar and the Wully-Wully* (de Brunhoff, 1975), saying "He's in the cage" and "He got out" as she pointed to the pictures of Wully-Wully captured and rescued.

Concepts about Literacy Acquired from Early Book and Drawing Experiences

As part of these experiences interacting with her parents as they read books with her and using crayons and markers, Kristen acquired six foundational concepts about literacy.

1. *Literacy Activities Are Pleasurable*

Perhaps one of the most important concepts that children can learn at the beginning of their literacy experiences is that reading is a pleasurable activity. When children are read to beginning early in their lives, they play with books as a preferred and frequent activity (Bus, 2001). Bookreading is one of the closest activities parents and children share. Children nestle in Dad's lap or lean over Mom's arm while they take part in this activity. The special feelings generated from this closeness of parents and children are associated with books. It is no wonder that some children will sit alone and look at books far longer than they will sit with their other toys.

Children also enjoy drawing and writing. Adult observers sense children's intense concentration as they hold tightly to both markers and paper and watch intently the shapes they create (Taylor & Dorsey-Gaines, 1988). Kristen often chose drawing and writing over other activities. For her, getting a new box of crayons or a set of markers was an important occasion, followed by hours of pleasurable drawing and writing.

2. *Literacy Activities Occur in Predictable Routines*

Toddlers and their parents learn ways of interacting with each other while reading books. They develop **booksharing routines,** that is, familiar, expected actions and language that accompanied their book reading. Kristen learned how to initiate and participate in bookreading sessions. She frequently selected a book and backed into a lap. She clearly signaled that she wanted to share a book. Once her mother or father began sharing a book, Kristen located characters when asked to do so and solicited comments from her mother or father by pointing to something in the picture or making comments and asking questions. She learned to answer questions. Gradually, she learned to listen to more of the story her mother or father was reading. Kristen discovered that, just like her mother and father, she also had certain roles to play in bookreading (Martin, 1998).

Booksharing routines make it possible for children to show parents what they are learning. Parents respond by giving children opportunities to use their new abilities and expecting children to use them. This results in an increase in children's roles and a decrease in adults' roles. Kristen and her parents demonstrated this in their playing of a routine known as the **naming game** (Ninio & Bruner, 1978). As described earlier, it began with Kristen's mother's pointing to and naming pictured animals, people, and objects; it progressed through Kristen's and her mother's "dat?" and "Where's the kitten?" questions; and it ended with Kristen's pointing to and labeling pictures on her own.

Toddlers and their parents also develop writing and drawing routines. Young children draw both to engage their parents' attention and to engage other children in play. Kristen quickly learned many routines that initiated drawing and writing as social interactions. She would say to her father, "Let's draw. You draw. Draw a little girl." When her father suggested that she draw (because he suspected she needed a new activity), Kristen replied, "No, you draw."

3. *Language Is an Important Part of Reading and Drawing*

Language is an important part of the routine activities of reading books together or drawing. As Kristen's language developed, so did the nature of her reading and drawing. At first, Kristen participated in reading and drawing by actively moving her body. Later, she was expected to use language to participate in these activities. Literacy routines and language development seemed to play mutually supporting roles during Kristen's early years. Repeatedly reading the same books and using the same language provided Kristen with many opportunities to hear and learn the meanings of a few words. As she learned these words, her parents added more words to the routine. As a consequence of learning more words and being able to use words in sentences, Kristen's interactions with books and drawing also became more sophisticated. Interacting with books and drawing supported Kristen's language development. Similarly, language development supported Kristen's growing sophistication in sharing books and drawing.

4. *Literacy Materials Are Handled in Special Ways*

In this beginning period, children also learn **bookhandling skills,** ways of handling and looking at books. Kristen learned how to hold books right-side-up and how to turn pages. She also discovered that books are for viewing and reading and not just for turning pages (Snow & Ninio, 1986).

Children learn motor "schemes" for drawing shapes and lines (Gardner, 1980). **Motor schemes** allow children to control their movements so they can make intentional shapes and lines. In order to be able to put circles and dots on a page where they intend them to go, children must learn how to control their movements. Kristen showed that she was learning to control her movements when she intently watched the progress of her crayons as she drew. As with Kristen, most children first develop motor schemes for making back-and-forth marks, round-and-round lines, dots, and jagged lines. Later, they make circlelike shapes and single lines (Gardner, 1980). Eventually, children learn to make as many as twenty basic scribbles, which become the building blocks of art and writing (Kellogg, 1969).

5. *Literacy Involves the Use of Symbols*

Illustrations in books are **symbols**—they represent or symbolize real objects or people. At first, children treat books as objects. They consider books as interesting objects to manipulate and explore with all their senses. Only gradually do children learn to look at the pictures in books as representations rather than interesting colors, shapes, and lines. Kristen demonstrated her awareness that book illustrations were symbols, or representations, when she sought out her box of crayons after she saw a picture of crayons in a favorite book.

Kristen took longer to understand that her drawings could also be symbols. At first, her drawing consisted of **scribbling**—marks made on a page without any intention of drawing a particular object or person. Then she recognized her mother's and father's drawing as symbols for people. It was not until she was nearly three years old that Kristen created her first **representational drawing**—a symbol for her father. Representational drawings are intentionally constructed and look something like the object or person the child–drawer intends to create. Kristen's drawing of her father is called a **tadpole.** Tadpole "people" have arms and legs emerging from an oversized head. Dots serve as eyes and nose with single lines serving as mouth, arms, and legs. Gradually children add hair, feet, and other details. Bodies do not appear in children's people drawing until much later.

Some children create **romance representations** before they can produce an actual representational drawing. For example, a child might draw round-and-round lines as he imitates the sound of a car motor. After drawing, the child might call his picture "race car." The marks he made (round-and-round scribbles) do not resemble a car; however, after drawing, the child labeled his drawing as if it were a symbol (Gardner, 1980). Kristen's picture of raindrops is probably a romance representation. It was only after drawing that Kristen noticed her lines and dots looked like raindrops. True representational drawings are planned—children intend to draw a person often announcing their intentions as they draw, "I am drawing a picture of my daddy."

Parents' reactions to children's drawings are likely to encourage children to label their pictures. Kristen's mother frequently asked her to "Tell me about your drawing." This request suggested that Kristen was drawing something that could be talked about or labeled rather than merely scribbled. Kristen's mother's request is an example of **ascribing intentionality.** Parents ascribe intentionality when they act as if their child is truly engaging in a communicative activity before they can really do so. For example, Kristen's father acted as if she could engage in a conversation long before she could talk, and her mother acted as if she could make a representational drawing long before Kristen did.

6. *Literacy Involves Communicating Meanings*

A crucial outcome of children's early experiences with books and other kinds of print is that they learn that books and other print materials communicate meaning—they tell a message. Learning to "mean" (Halliday, 2002), to understand what others say and do, is involved in nearly every activity, not only in literacy activities. It is the great undertaking of life—we constantly try to understand the messages that bombard us and to send messages to others. We use many cues to help us understand others and to help others understand us. We use the situation we are in and its clues to meaning (characteristics of the location or people's clothing), as well as spoken language and its clues to meaning (words, stress, and intonation).

Because our society is a literate one, another powerful set of clues to meaning is written language. Written language, too, is used along with situation (getting out a checkbook at the grocery store), with spoken language ("That will be $81.47"), and with written symbols (81.47 printed on the computer display of the cash register).

Home Influences on Literacy Learning

Literacy learning begins in the home. Children's first experiences with literacy are mediated by the ways in which parents and other caregivers use reading and writing in their lives (Purcell-Gates, 1996). One way in which parents invite very young children to participate in literacy activities is to read storybooks aloud. In fact, one predictor of children's reading achievement in school is the number of hours they were read to as preschoolers (Wells, 1986). We also know that preschoolers who interacted more with their parents as they read aloud have larger vocabularies and better story understanding as five-year-olds than do children who contributed less during storybook readings (Leseman & de Jong, 1998). Clearly, reading aloud with young children is an important vehicle through which they acquire literacy concepts.

Parent–Child Interactive Bookreading

We describe the interactions between three children and their parents as they shared books together. These interactions demonstrate the strategies used by parents and other caregivers to support young children's interest in and construction of meaning. They also show how children's abilities to understand books expand as a result of participating in **interactive bookreading.**

The three children play increasingly sophisticated roles in conversations with their parents about books they are reading. The youngest, Kristen, participates in interactive labeling; she labels a picture and anticipates and observes her mother's confirmation. Elizabeth, who is older than Kristen, participates in parent-initiated questioning and answering about picture elements that her mother considers central to plot development. The oldest, Jon-Marc, asks questions about both pictures and text.

Kristen and Her Mother Share **Billy Goats Gruff.**   Figure 2.5 presents a portion of the dialogue between Kristen and her mother as they shared *Billy Goats Gruff* (Hellard, 1986). Kristen was seventeen months old at the time of this interaction. The dialogue demonstrates that Kristen already knew much about how to participate in bookreading. She labeled objects (saying "tee" as she pointed to a picture of a tree) and sought confirmation of her label (she repeated "tee" each time, looking at her mother as if for confirmation of her meaning and label). Kristen also monitored her meaning; she observed her mother's reaction to her label.

Kristen's mother used several strategies to encourage Kristen to participate actively in the booksharing interaction and to expand on what Kristen could currently do. She allowed Kristen to take charge of the reading by turning pages, even

FIGURE 2.5   **Kristen and Her Mother Share** *Billy Goats Gruff* **(Hellard, 1986)**

Bracket indicates portions of the dialogue that occurred simultaneously.

Kristen: (brings *Billy Goats Gruff* to her mother, sits on her mother's lap, holds book, and turns book with cover facing up)

Mother: Three billy goats gruff. (points to each goat on the cover) Look, a little one.
[(points to a small goat) A middle-size—

   K: (opens book and turns two pages, gazes at picture, and points to a picture of a tree) tee (looks up at her mother)

   M: Yes, it's a tree.

   K: (points to another tree) tee (looks up at mother again)

   M: Hm, um.

   K: (points to another tree) tee.

   M: (points to picture of troll, puts her arm around Kristen, and shakes them both) (changes voice to deeper tone) Look at the Trolllllll. I'm going to eat you up.

   K: (laughs, turns page)

when doing so interrupted the reading. She provided feedback to Kristen's labels ("Yes, it's a tree") and helped Kristen focus on the more important narrative elements of the story. She hugged and shook Kristen and used her voice to attract Kristen's attention to a character, the troll.

It is noteworthy that Kristen's mother did not read the text as she shared the book. Instead, she focused on engaging Kristen's active involvement by using gestures and talking about details in the illustrations. Many parents of young children use books as props for interacting with their children rather than as texts for reading aloud (Martin, 1998). Kristen's mother was content to talk about trees in the illustrations and for Kristen to end the book session without ever looking at every page in the text.

***Elizabeth and Her Mother Share* Where's Spot?**   A portion of the interaction between Elizabeth (twenty-six months) and her mother as they shared *Where's Spot?* (Hill, 1980) is presented in Figure 2.6. Elizabeth took charge of the interaction by turning the pages and making comments. She labeled objects in the pictures ("There's a doggy there") and answered her mother's questions.

Elizabeth's mother used many strategies for expanding and supporting Elizabeth's participation in this booksharing event. First, she featured an important narrative element (action and character motivation) by telling Elizabeth that the mother dog was looking for her puppy. She continually used this as a context for helping Elizabeth understand why the dog was looking behind doors and under beds. She matched her reading style to Elizabeth's ability to participate in the bookreading (as did Kristen's mother) by interweaving her talk with reading the text (Martin, 1998). She helped Elizabeth find meaning from the words of the text

FIGURE 2.6   **Elizabeth and Her Mother Share** *Where's Spot?* **(Hill, 1980)**

Paraphrased text is underlined. Brackets indicate portions of the dialogue that occurred simultaneously.

Mother: We are looking for Spot. Let's turn the page. He's a little tiny puppy. Can you see if you can find him <u>behind the door.</u> Is he there?

E: (turns to next page)

M: No?—What's inside the clock? Is he in there?

E: He's in there.

M: That's a snake. That's not a little dog.

E: Let me read it.

M: Okay.

E: It's a snake.

M: Turn the page. Where's Spot? Let's see if we can find the puppy. Is he—

E: (turns back to look at snake again)

M: Let's see what's behind the next page. We need to find Spot. Is he in there? (points to piano)

E: There's a doggy there. (points to Mother Dog, Sally)

M: He's looking for another doggy. Spot's not there.

E: There? (points to Sally on next page)

M: Yes. That's a doggy. He's looking for another doggy, a puppy. Is there a puppy <u>in the piano</u>?

E: No.

---

by using her explanations and expansions on the story as a support for meaning construction. In addition, she asked Elizabeth questions that called for labeling ("What's inside the clock?") and provided feedback to her daughter's answers (correcting Elizabeth when she mistook the mother dog for the puppy).

***Jon-Marc and His Father Share* The Story of Ferdinand.**   Figure 2.7 presents part of a booksharing interaction between Jon-Marc, a three-year-old, and his father. Jon-Marc listened carefully and looked intently at each illustration as his father read *The Story of Ferdinand* (Leaf, 1936). One strategy Jon-Marc used to make meaning was to apply his understanding of events in the real world to make inferences about story events. Jon-Marc asked if Ferdinand would (go home) "And . . . and . . . and love her mother cow?" This question reveals that Jon-Marc used inferences to predict story events (after going home, Ferdinand would love his mother). It also illustrates that he used his own life as a frame of reference for understanding the story. Jon-Marc probably went home to love his mother, so he inferred that Ferdinand would be going home to love his mother.

FIGURE 2.7   Jon-Marc and His Father Share *The Story of Ferdinand* (Leaf, 1936)

Text is presented in all capital letters.

Illustration: Ferdinand in a small cart going over the mountain. A bull ring is the background.

Father: SO THEY HAD TO TAKE FERDINAND HOME.

Jon-Marc: Why?

Father: Because he wouldn't fight. He just wouldn't fight. He didn't like to fight. He just wanted to smell the flowers. (Note, this is a paraphrase of the text that had just been read on the previous pages.)

Jon-Marc: Is that why they wanted to . . . to . . . to fight in the drid?

Father: In Madrid? Yeah, they wanted . . . they wanted him to fight in Madrid. Madrid's the name of a city. They wanted him to fight the matador. But he didn't. He just wanted to go home and smell the flowers.

Jon-Marc: And . . . and . . . and love her mother cow?

Father: Yeah, and . . . and love his mother.

Jon-Marc: Where's her mother cow?

Father: Well, she's back in the book a little bit.

Jon-Marc's father, like Kristen's and Elizabeth's mothers, was skillful at adapting the booksharing event to Jon-Marc's abilities. He expanded on information from the text and related to Jon-Marc's concerns (he explained that Madrid is a city), and he provided more adult models of language ("And love his mother"). He repeated information from the story text to answer Jon-Marc's question and, therefore, made explicit the causal relations among events in the story ("They wanted him to fight the matador. But he didn't. He just wanted to go home and smell the flowers."). All of his talk was contingent on Jon-Marc's talk; that is, it was in response to Jon-Marc's questions and comments.

Participation in Interactive Bookreading

The interactions we presented of Kristen and her mother, Elizabeth and her mother, and Jon-Marc and his father were carefully selected to illustrate how children's participation in and parents' support during interactive read-alouds shift as children gain more language and literacy experience. At first, with older infants and toddlers, parents seem to focus on gaining their children's attention and getting them actively involved. During these interactions parents are not concerned about the story (Martin, 1998); books most parents read at this age are merely a series of interesting pictures (for example, of babies eating, playing, or sleeping) rather than stories. At this age, parents cuddle children closely on their laps, let children hold the book and turn pages, and use motivating and **attention getting strategies** such as pointing and saying, "Look here at this baby." They encourage their children to point and label pictures by asking, "Look, what's that?" as they point to details in an illustration (Bus, 2001). They make comments that connect book ideas to their children by saying, "Look. That blanket is yellow just like yours." Parents follow children's leads by letting them turn the book's pages or close the book, signaling this book is finished.

As children develop a deep sense of enjoyment about books and gain confidence in their role as participants, parents begin taking a more active role in directing children's attention to story characters and events or ideas in an informational book (Martin, 1998). Now parents seem more concerned with helping children understand the basic sequence of events in a story although they still expect their children to be actively involved answering questions, commenting, and labeling pictures. Elizabeth's mother was particularly skillful in both letting Elizabeth turn pages out of order to look at illustrations and redirecting her attention back to the sequence of events in the story. She did this by first letting Elizabeth look at the illustrations that she wanted to, commenting on those illustrations, and then using them as a way to redirect Elizabeth back to searching for the lost puppy. Her mother seems to understand that her role is to help Elizabeth learn to focus on story rather than on interesting illustrations. At this level, these strategies actively engage children and call for them to use thinking at relatively **low levels of cognitive demand.** These strategies are very appropriate for children's literacy learning during this phase of their development.

It takes much experience with interactive bookreading for young children to sit back and quietly enjoy a book that is read aloud as Jon-Marc did. At this stage, parents seem to wait for their children's signals of confusion or misunderstanding. Parents intuitively select books with more complex stories or information perhaps because these books will trigger opportunities for talking about challenging vocabulary and clarifying character traits and motivations. At this level, parents shift from using strategies that focus on lower cognitive demand activities related to understanding the *what* of stories and information books to using strategies that call upon **high levels of cognitive demand** related to understanding the *why* and *how* of stories (Dickinson & Smith, 1994). Figure 2.8 presents a summary of the range of attention getting, low cognitive demand, and high cognitive demand strategies that parents use to elicit their children's participation in interactive bookreading experiences (adapted from Dickinson & Smith, 1994 and Martin, 1999).

Concept of Story

As parents begin reading stories to their children and directing their attention to characters and story events, children develop an awareness of the elements found in typical stories. Most stories have a main character and several supporting characters. The events of the story are set in motion when the main character recognizes a problem or decides to achieve a goal. The plot of the story consists of a series of events in which the main character actively tries to solve the problem or achieve the goal. The story ends as the character solves the problem or achieves the goal (the happily ever after of most fairytales). A **story grammar** describes all the components

FIGURE 2.8   Strategies Parents Use to Support Children's Active Engagement during Interactive Bookreading

Attention Getting and Sustaining Strategies

allowing child to hold book and turn pages

pointing to and labeling or commenting on details in illustrations

helping child imitate or asking child to make gestures or sounds

asking for child to point out details in illustrations

asking for child to label details in illustrations

adjusting language of text for child (may not read text, but talk about illustrations)

answering and responding to child's questions and comments

Low Cognitive Demand Strategies

reading text and pausing for child to supply word

asking child who, what, and where questions calling for recall of information in text

High Cognitive Demand Strategies

asking child why questions calling for inferences (I wonder why . . . ?)

asking child questions calling for making connections between ideas in text and child's personal experience (What does this remind you of . . . ?)

prompting child to predict (What do you think will happen next?)

prompting child to clarify or elaborate

elaborating on child's comments or text

explaining vocabulary word or connections between ideas

commenting on character traits or motivations

that are included in an ideal story (Mandler & Johnson, 1977). Table 2.1 presents the narrative elements of a story grammar and an example of an ideal story (based on Stein & Glenn, 1979). Most adults are at least intuitively aware of the elements included in this story grammar.

Children's awareness of the story elements included in a story grammar is called their **concept of story** (Applebee, 1978). Most toddlers and two-year-olds have undeveloped concepts of stories. When asked to tell stories, they may list the names of their friends or describe the actions of a favorite pet. Some three-year-olds have better developed concepts of stories; they may tell stories with imaginary characters but rely on their knowledge of everyday actions to invent story events. They are not likely to include problems or goals.

Children's concept of story is best observed as they retell favorite stories or engage in dramatic play. At first, children focus on retelling what is happening in each illustration of a story without regard for its significance in the sequence of events in a story. They may label the objects, characters, or actions depicted in the illustrations. For example, when retelling how Goldilocks eats the porridge, breaks the baby bear's chair, and falls asleep in the baby bear's bed in *The Three Bears* story, a child might say, "She eat. Broke chair. Sleeping." Children's dramatic play is also not likely to include sustained actions around a problem until much later. Early on, children act out simple action events such as feeding a doll or pretending to drive a car.

TABLE 2.1   Story Grammar

Narrative Elements	Story Example *A Smart Dog*
Main characters (animals or people)	An old man, his grandson Jim, and their sheepdog Shep
Setting (description of location)	lived on a mountain side
Action or event (introduction of problem)	One dewy morning, while Jim was watching the sheep, Grandpa took Shep and set out to look for wild berries. Grandpa slipped on the wet grass and broke his leg.
Goal (formulation of a goal)	He decided to send Shep for help.
Attempt (actions to solve the problem)	Grandpa tied his scarf around Shep's neck and sent him to find the sheep.
Resolution (outcome of actions)	When Jim saw the scarf around Shep's neck, he knew that Grandpa was in trouble. He left Shep to watch the sheep and followed Shep's tracks in the dewy grass toward where Grandpa lay. Soon he heard Grandpa's calling. Jim helped his grandfather back to their house where they could call a doctor.
Reaction (character's feelings about outcome)	Grandpa and Jim were glad that they had such a smart sheep dog.

Environmental Print

Young children observe and participate in a variety of other literacy activities in addition to sharing books. Children are included in shopping trips for which parents read lists, clip coupons, or write checks. They observe as parents write reminder notes or help older children with homework. The number of literacy events in the home and the willingness and ability of parents to include their children in these activities are related to the amount of knowledge that young children have about literacy. Children whose homes include more frequent literacy events (such as parents' reading magazines and books and writing letters or lists) know more about how reading and writing are used (Burns & Casbergue, 1992; Purcell-Gates, 1996).

Environmental print items play an important part in the beginning literacy experiences of toddlers and two-year-olds. As children eat breakfast, they see a box of Rice Krispies and they hear talk about eating the Rice Krispies. They observe and listen in the grocery store as their parents look for Rice Krispies. As children acquire language, they learn to talk about "Rice Krispies" just as they learn to talk about "ball" or "baby" or "car." Just as children learn that things in pictures have names and can be labeled, they learn that things like cereal boxes and cookie packages can be named as well.

Many toddlers and two-year-olds do not notice or pay much attention to the print on their cereal boxes or cookie packages; nonetheless, the print is there. The print on the packages becomes part of what children know about those objects. Later, children will recognize just the print and stylized picture or logo without the object's being there.

Spoken Language Development and Its Relationship to Literacy Development

As we have seen in the examples of Kristen, Elizabeth, and Jon-Marc, children's spoken language provides the pathway into literacy. Spoken language development supports and provides a foundation for written language development. Children's early language experiences, even in their first few months of life, influence later language and literacy development.

Spoken Language Development

Two factors that are related to children's later language development are **caregiver interactive responsiveness** and **speech density** (Schickedanz, Schickedanz, Forsyth, & Forsyth, 2001). Caregiver interactive responsiveness refers to how effectively a parent or caregiver engages an infant and later toddlers and two-year-olds in a communication interaction. Kristen's father demonstrated a high level of caregiver interactive responsiveness when he talked with Kristen as he changed her diaper. He talked and Kristen wiggled similar to the give-and-take of a real conversation. From interactions such as these, babies learn how to take turns in conversations, how to focus their gaze on a parent, and later how to **follow a gaze** (turn to look at an object or person a parent is looking at). Before acquiring their first words, babies use reaching, gazing, pointing, and giving to take a turn in a conversation; responsive caregivers supply the words and keep the conversation flowing.

Speech density refers to the number of words that infants hear. The more that parents talk to an infant, the higher the speech density. The number of words that children acquire in their spoken language is related to speech density. The more words they hear, the more words they learn. Parents and caregivers who establish interactive responsiveness and produce high levels of speech density are more likely to have children with larger vocabularies and more complex syntax.

Children's vocabularies grow slowly at first, then rapidly increase. Children need responsive conversational partners to accelerate spoken vocabulary development. Adults who talk with children, who honestly try to understand and respond to what children are attempting to communicate, help children become effective language users. Adults naturally seem to repeat and expand on what toddlers say, providing them with a more mature model of their own language. When a toddler comments about a string of lights, "Yights!", a parent may respond "You see those little lights." The toddler may continue the conversation by adding, "Yots." A parent can respond, "There are lots of lights. They are twinkling" (adapted from Post & Hohmann, 2000, p. 78). Effective parents and caregivers encourage conversation by commenting, observing, and acknowledging rather than by asking questions (Post & Hohmann, 2000). They describe what children are seeing and doing: "You see your Mom, Jamal" or "You are sucking your fingers!" Or they describe what they are seeing and doing: "I'm going to put you in this chair for a snack."

Nonimmediate and Decontextualized Spoken Language: Spoken Equivalents to Written Language

While spoken language development includes learning new words and acquiring more complex syntax, it also involves acquiring special spoken language abilities that are related to later language use in reading and writing. Written language used in reading and writing is similar to, but not exactly the same as, spoken language used in conversations. Consider the written language that comprises the text of a favorite novel compared to the spoken language that comprises a good conversation with a long-time friend. Conversations involve turn-taking, thoughts are not completely organized, and ideas are developed jointly through asking questions for clarification, using facial expressions and gestures, and referencing previously shared experiences. On the other hand, readers are constrained by using the words, and only the words, in order to form personal interpretations of a novel. They cannot seek clarification from the author or seek clues by looking around the setting in which they are reading.

Spoken conversations usually center on recent events and familiar people while novels are about imaginary people in settings never before experienced. That is, spoken conversations usually focus on **immediate events** (events that occur in the actual world of here and now) and involve the use of **contextualized language.** Contexualized language draws on sources of meaning outside of words—speakers can communicate meaning by pointing to and looking at people and activities in a shared context or use facial expressions, body language, intonation, and gestures. Written language, in contrast, usually focuses on **nonimmediate events** (events that have occurred in the past or imagination) and draws on the use of **decontextualized language** (language that draws only on words to communicate meaning).

Some children have more opportunities than other children to talk about nonimmediate events and use decontextualized language (Tabors, Roach, & Snow, 2001). Engaging children in conversations at mealtimes in preschool and home seems to be one way that parents and caregivers provide children with opportunities to learn how to talk about nonimmediate events and use decontextualized language strategies. Most children need coaxing to talk about an event from the past and the support of a sensitive caregiver to sustain conversation about that event. Through such language experiences, children learn to recount or retell events of the day, plan for future activities, give explanations, and tell stories. Parents help by asking questions, prompting, and expanding on children's comments (Beals, 2001).

Family and Cultural Influence on Language and Literacy Development

We now consider the question of whether all children learn the same concepts about literacy that Kristen learned and whether her literacy experiences are like those of most young children. We have shown that there are many ways in which literacy is supported in the home long before children go to school—in the ways in which parents and other caregivers interact with children as they share books, draw and write, read environmental print, and engage children in certain oral language routines. Any of these experiences has the potential of helping children become better readers and writers later, when they enter school.

By and large we know that middle class, mainstream families are likely to engage their children in many of these language and literacy activities. But, of course, families differ from one another, and the inclinations of children differ as well. Therefore, even children in the same family do not have exactly the same literacy and language experiences. However, three factors seem to predict language and literacy growth: the number of opportunities children have to engage in sustained dialogue with a parent, the parent's use of unusual or rare words in conversation with the children, and the frequency and quality of interactive book read-alouds and opportunities to write (Tabors, Roach, & Snow, 2001).

Most families vary on their support for a child's language and literacy growth; they may engage the children in lengthy conversations, but fail to introduce rare or unusual words into the conversation. They may read aloud to the children often, but fail to engage the child actively in talking about the book's meaning or vocabulary. Parents who enjoy reading and read frequently themselves tend to share books more often and in more cognitively challenging ways than parents who do not enjoy reading (Bus, 2001); they often encourage their children to pretend to write. Some parents are effective in engaging their children in enjoyable book interactions while other parents are more likely to view reading to children as work or demonstrations of how to behave appropriately (Leseman & de Jong, 1998). Some parents simply do not share books with their children or provide writing experiences for any number of different reasons (Sulzby & Edwards, 1993).

It is especially difficult to make generalizations about early literacy and language experiences across social class lines. Some researchers have found infrequent uses of reading and writing in low-income homes (Purcell-Gates, 1996), although variations within these families also point to difficulties in generalizing across families. Some researchers have shown that the ways in which parents share books with children differ (Heath, 1984), and sometimes parents have difficulty reading with their young children (Edwards, 1994). Other researchers have documented rich and frequent literacy experiences in low-income families (Taylor & Dorsey-Gaines, 1988).

By three years of age, there are remarkable differences between the vocabularies of children from middle-income homes and those of children from low-income homes (Hart & Risely, 1995). Differences in vocabulary development may be linked to differences in experiences with books. That is, home literacy practices seem to outweigh the effects of socioeconomic status (SES) level on vocabulary development (Leseman & de Jong, 1998). Regardless of income level, children whose parents engage them in frequent and sustained conversations as well as frequent and highly interactive bookreading have larger vocabularies and better literacy skills than children with less frequent and less interactive bookreading (Senechal, LeFevre, Hudson, & Lawson, 1996).

However, some researchers have found differences in the ways in which parents from different ethnic backgrounds share books with their children (Bus, Leseman, & Keultjes, 2000). For example, parents in Mexican American and Chinese American families include their children in decontextualized language experiences (Heath, 1986; Pease-Alvarez, 1991). However, Heath (1989) argued that in many cultural groups children are not expected to use language patterns that call upon decontextualized strategies. It is safe to say that not all children come to school with experiences or concepts like Kristen's and that teachers should expect and celebrate the richness these differences bring to the language mix of the classroom. The next section of the chapter describes how teachers can enhance even very young children's literacy learning in child care and nursery school settings.

Implications for Child Care and Nursery School

Soon after they are born, many children spend many of their waking hours in the care of adults at child care centers and nursery schools. We do not believe that infants, toddlers, and two-year-olds ought to have structured literacy activities. However, teachers in these situations can take advantage of what we know about how parents support language and literacy learning to provide appropriate opportunities for young children to expand language and explore literacy.

Developmentally Appropriate Practice

In a joint position statement, adopted in 1998, the International Reading Association (IRA) and the National Association for the Education of Young Children (NAEYC) describe **developmentally appropriate practices** for young children's learning to read and write (IRA and NAEYC, 1998). We support this statement and encourage all teachers of young children to read and follow the recommendations it contains. IRA and NAEYC begin by recognizing the importance of literacy learning to success in school and in later life and by identifying children's first eight years of life as crucial to their literacy learning. This position paper was later extended with recommendations for ways that teachers and caregivers could support children's literacy development (Neuman, Copple, & Bredekamp, 2000). Here we present ideas for caregivers and teachers who are charged with the language and literacy development of infants, toddlers, and two-year-olds.

Make Literacy Experiences Pleasurable

Early language and literacy learning emerges from the tender care of a loving and responsive caregiver or teacher. The power of this early emotional appeal for children is not to be underestimated. "If they do not develop an interest in reading and writing—an eager desire for initiation into print's mysteries and skills—children's progress toward literacy is uncertain. When the going gets tough, they may drop out" (Neuman, Copple, & Bredekamp, 2000, p. 28).

We believe children should be invited to read and draw daily. Exemplary nursery school teachers read aloud to infants, toddlers, and two-year-olds on a daily basis. Two-year-olds sometimes enjoy sharing books in groups of two or three children. This number of children allows teachers to sit close to the children just as parents do in one-on-one booksharing. Teachers can use the same strategies and routines in sharing books with children that parents use. Effective teachers are very willing to share favorite books again and again. They are more likely to talk about the story than to read the text. They invite children to participate by asking questions and making comments. Effective teachers use gestures and intonation to enrich the story meaning, and they tell how pictures and story actions are related to children's real-life experiences.

Arrange the Environment

The environment for infants, toddlers, and young two-year-olds should be thoughtfully arranged to provide frequent opportunities for adult–child language interactions and book read-alouds (Snow, Burns, & Griffin, 1998). Caregivers and teachers need to be at the children's level, sitting on the floor near low shelves or in a chair next to child-sized tables. Classrooms should also include several soft, comfortable adult-sized chairs or sofas where an adult and a few children can sit comfortably together. Unlike preschool classrooms, classrooms for toddlers and young two-year-olds do not need to include printed labels, signs, or a wide variety of printed materials.

Nonmobile infants do not need a special book nook. Instead, books can be placed on blankets or soft pillows with slightly raised edges for babies to explore. Mobile infants and toddlers appreciate a book nook with outward facing shelves. The nook should be out of the traffic of more active play areas and include a small covered mattress and soft pillows, a few stuffed book characters, and a small basket of plastic toys, which might be related to the books included in the nook. However, toddlers are not likely to stay in the book nook to interact with books. They enjoy carrying books around the room and books are later likely to be found in every corner of the room. Caregivers and teachers should establish routines for returning all toys to their storage locations. The best books for infants and toddlers are sturdy, washable cardboard books called **board books.** These books are easier for younger children to manipulate than soft books. Two-year-olds enjoy books with lively language play found in nursery rhymes or books with rhyming words. Many two-year-olds begin to enjoy first storybooks with simple plots (Appendix A presents a list of some board books, **language play books,** and **first storybooks**) appropriate for infants, toddlers, and two-year-olds.

Plan for Language Development

Language development occurs in face-to-face conversations with adult caregivers, parents, or teachers and with other children. Infants and young toddlers need teachers who will "supply words that describe their actions ('Look, Sarah is adding a red block')" (Neuman, Copple, & Bredekamp, 2000, p. 49). They also need teachers who will listen to them, play with them, and talk with them about what they are doing. As children make a remark, teachers reply using many of the child's own words but adding a bit more. Teachers elaborate slightly on children's ideas and provide slightly more sophisticated sentences to stretch children's vocabulary and syntax.

Research has shown that teachers actually talk very little with individual children in preschool (Dickinson & Sprague, 2001). However, teachers engaged children in longer and more sustained conversations when they sat at tables with children during school mealtimes (Cote, 2001). In addition, singing, chanting, and finger-plays provide enjoyable opportunities to stretch children's language. Teachers can expect that toddlers and young two-year-olds learn from using body movements and gestures.

Help Parents Provide Strong Support for Literacy Development at Home

Exemplary caregivers and teachers of very young children form close and supportive relationships with parents or other primary caregivers. Caregivers have daily opportunities for informal conversations with parents as they drop off and pick up their infants and toddlers. They can save toddlers' scribbles and explain to parents the value and importance of providing their children with markers and paper. Most of all, caregivers and teachers are careful to communicate to parents the critical role that they play in their children's language and literacy development even at these early ages. Exemplary caregivers are sensitive to differences in parents' abilities to interact with their children and careful to acknowledge parents' initiatives.

Many early childhood programs provide family literacy programs in which parents are offered educational opportunities as well as invited to special sessions on parenting (Wasik, Dobbins, & Hermann, 2001). Parents are coached in using strategies that help their children accelerate language and cognitive development. They may learn how to sustain longer conversations with their children or how to read aloud interactively with their young children (DeBruin-Parecki, 1999; Edwards, 1994). Many parenting programs actively seek input from parents so that caregivers can build on parents' strengths (Delgado-Gaitan, 1994; Neuman, 1996) and make parenting activities more sensitive to cultural and family differences (Gadsden, 1995). The payoff for parents is clear: Children who have parents who actively seek information about and opportunities to learn more about how to help their children learn do better in school (Purcell-Gates, 2000).

Chapter Summary

Very young children begin their literacy learning when they interact with their parents and other caring adults as they share books or other kinds of print items. Young children who have opportunities to draw and to talk about their drawing are also on their way to knowing about literacy. Infants, toddlers, and two-year-olds are not yet literate (as we describe *literate* in the preface of this book), but they do have many literacy behaviors and they do know something about literacy. They find reading and writing activities pleasurable, and they have bookhandling skills and participate in booksharing routines. Young children gain control over their arms, hands, and fingers as they develop motor schemes for creating shapes they have in mind. They know that the shapes they draw and the pictures they view can be named, are symbols or representations of reality, and communicate meaning.

Young children's home experiences have a powerful influence on their literacy learning. Children acquire literacy concepts through booksharing, through other literacy activities (including interactions with environmental print and drawing), and in decontextualized oral language routines.

As children share books with their parents and other caregivers, they acquire meaning-making strategies and a concept of story. Parents support children's meaning-making through storybook reading that is responsive and interactive. They also support children as they interact with environmental print. They respond to their children's drawings in ways that signal that these drawings are meaningful (ascribe intentionality). Finally, they invite children to participate in decontextualized oral language experiences, including giving explanations and telling stories.

Teachers can also play an important role in young children's literacy learning. They can make literacy materials available, offer literacy experiences, and respond to children's literacy attempts. Figure 2.9 presents a summary of what literacy beginners know about written language meanings, forms, meaning-form links, and functions.

FIGURE 2.9   Summary: What Literacy Beginners Know about Written Language

---

Meaning

know booksharing routines

learn meaning-making strategies

use decontextualized language

develop concepts about stories

Forms

develop motor schemes

recognize the alphabet as a special set of
written signs

Meaning-Form Links

make symbols

Functions

draw and share books as pleasurable activities

use books and drawing to gain the attention
of others

FIGURE 2.10   Steven Retells *Bears in the Night* (Berenstain & Berenstain, 1971)

Story: Bears investigate a sound in the night by creeping out of bed, down a tree, and up a hill.

Steven:	(points to moon)	TEXT: IN BED
	moon	Illustration: Seven bears in bed. Open
	(points to lantern)	window with a crescent moon. A lantern
	i-eet	hangs on the wall.
	(turns page, points to moon)	TEXT: OUT OF BED
	moon	Illustration: One bear out of bed, otherwise
	(points to lantern)	similar to previous page.
	i-eet	
	(turns several pages rapidly, gazes at	TEXT: UP SPOOK HILL
	picture for several seconds)	Illustration: Bear going up hill lantern in
	(turns page)	hand. Moon in sky. Owl at the top of hill.
	shakes head, points at owl bears	Illustration: The word "WHOOOOO," an owl,
	OOOOOOOOOOO	and four frightened jumping up.

Applying the Information

Complete the following case study. Discuss Steven's literacy knowledge and behaviors. Also discuss the role Steven's baby-sitter plays in Steven's learning.

When Steven was nineteen months old, he retold *Bears in the Night* (Berenstain & Berenstain, 1971). He turned the book so that the cover faced him right-side-up. He turned past the first page (title page) quickly. Figure 2.10 presents Steven's retelling.

When Steven was twenty-five months old, he enjoyed drawing with his baby-sitter. She would encourage him to get his crayons, and he would color while she folded clothes or cleaned. He often made nonsense sounds as he colored. His sitter would talk to him as she worked. She would imitate his sounds and he would imitate hers. Sometimes Steven would sing songs he knew as he colored. Figure 2.11 presents one of Steven's pictures. He said, "This is a car."

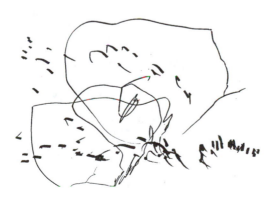

FIGURE 2.11   Steven's Drawing

Going Beyond the Text

Visit a child care center and take note of the literacy materials and activities in the infant, toddler, and two-year-old rooms. What books are available? How often and how do caregivers read with children? How frequently do children draw? Take at least three books to share with a small group of toddlers or two-year-olds. Describe their booksharing strategies. Join the children as they draw. Describe their drawing behaviors and make inferences about their literacy knowledge. Interview at least one caregiver. What does he or she believe about reading and writing for infants, toddlers, and two-year-olds?

REFERENCES

Applebee, A. N. (1978). *The child's concept of story.* Chicago: University of Chicago Press.

Beals, D. (2001). Eating and reading: Links between family conversations with preschoolers and later language and literacy. In D. Dickson & P. Tabors (Eds.), *Beginning literacy with language: Young children learning at home and school* (pp. 75–92). Baltimore, MD: Paul H. Brookes.

Berenstain, S., & Berenstain, J. (1971). *Bears in the night.* New York: Random House.

Brown, M. W. (1947). *Goodnight moon.* New York: Harper and Row.

de Brunhoff, L. (1975). *Babar and the Wully-Wully.* New York: Random House.

Burns, M., & Casbergue, R. (1992). Parent-child interaction in a letter-writing context. *Journal of Reading Behavior, 24,* 289–312.

Bus, A. (2001). Joint caregiver-child storybook reading: A route to literacy development. In S. Neuman & D. Dickinson (Eds), *Handbook of early literacy research* (pp. 179–191).

Bus, A. G., Leseman, P., & Keultjes, P. (2000). Joint book-reading across cultures: A comparison of Surinamese-Dutch, Turkish-Dutch, and Dutch parent-child dyads. *Journal of Literacy Research, 32,* 53–76.

Cote, L. (2001). Language opportunities during mealtimes in preschool classrooms. In D. Dickson & P. Tabors (Eds.), *Beginning literacy with language: Young children learning at home and school* (pp. 205–221). Baltimore, MD: Paul H. Brookes.

DeBruin-Parecki, A. (1999). *Assessing adult/child storybook reading practices.* CIERA Report #2–004. Center for the Improvement of Early Reading Achievement, University of Michigan, Ann Arbor, Michigan.

Delgado-Gaitan, C. (1994). Sociocultural change through literacy: Toward empowerment of families. In B. Ferdman, R. Weber, & A. Ramirez (Eds.), *Literacy across languages and cultures* (pp. 143–170). Albany, NY: State University of New York Press.

Dickinson, D., & Smith, M. (1994). Long-term effects of preschool teachers' book readings on low-income children's vocabulary and story comprehension. *Reading Research Quarterly, 29,* 105–122.

Dickinson, D., & Sprague, K. (2001). The nature and impact of early childhood care environments on the language and early literacy development of children from low-income families. In S. Neuman & D. Dickinson (Eds.), *Handbook of early literacy research* (pp. 263–280). New York: Guilford.

Disney (Walt) Productions. (1974). *Walt Disney's Peter and the wolf.* New York: Random House.

Edwards, P. (1994). Responses of teachers and African-American mothers to a book-reading intervention program. In D. Dickinson (Ed.), *Bridges to literacy: Children, families, and schools* (pp. 175–208). Cambridge, MA: Blackwell.

Gadsden, V. (1995). Representations of literacy: Parents' images in two cultural communities. In L. Morrow (Ed.), *Family literacy: Connections in schools and communities* (pp. 287–303). Newark, DE: International Reading Association.

Halliday, M. A. K. (2002). Relevant models of language. In B. M. Power & R. S. Hubbard (Eds.), *Language development: A reader for teachers, 2nd ed.* (pp. 49–53). Upper Saddle River, NJ: Merrill.

Hart, B., & Risely, T. (1995). *Meaningful differences in the everyday experiences of young American children.* Baltimore, MD: Paul H. Brookes.

Heath, S. B., with Thomas, C. (1984). The achievement of preschool literacy for mother and child. In H. Goelman, A. Oberg, & F. Smith (Eds.), *Awakening to literacy* (pp. 51–72). Exeter, NH: Heinemann.

Heath, S. (1986). Sociocultural contexts of language development. In California State Department of Education (Ed.), *Beyond language: Social and cultural factors in schooling languages* (pp. 143–186). Los Angeles: California State University, Los Angeles.

Heath, S. (1989). The learner as cultural member. In M. Rice & R. Schiefelbusch (Eds.), *The teachability of language* (pp. 333–350). Baltimore, MD: Paul H. Brookes.

Hellard, S. (1986). *Billy goats gruff*. New York: Putnam.

Hill, E. (1980). *Where's Spot?* New York: Putnam.

International Reading Association & National Association for the Education of Young Children (1998). Learning to read and write: Developmentally appropriate practices for young children. *The Reading Teacher, 52,* 193–216.

Kellogg, R. (1969). *Analyzing children's art*. Palo Alto, CA: National Press Books.

Leaf, M. (1936). *The story of Ferdinand*. New York: Viking.

Leseman, P., & de Jong, P. (1998). Home literacy: Opportunity, instruction, cooperation and social-emotional quality predicting early reading achievement. *Reading Research Quarterly, 33,* 3:294–318.

Mandler, L., & Johnson, N. (1977). Remembrance of things parsed: Story structure and recall. *Cognitive Psychology, 9,* 11–51.

Martin, L. (1998). Early book reading: How mothers deviate from printed text for young children. *Reading Research and Instruction, 37,* 137–160.

Neuman, S. (1996). Children engaging in storybook reading: The influence of access to print resources, opportunity, and parental interaction. *Early Childhood Research Quarterly, 11,* 495–513.

Neuman, S. G., Copple, C., & Bredekamp, S. (2000). *Learning to read and write: Developmentally appropriate practices for young children*. Washington, DC: National Association for the Education of Young Children.

Ninio, A., & Bruner, J. (1978). Antecedents of the achievements of labeling. *Journal of Child Language, 5,* 1–15.

Pease-Alvarez, L. (1991). Home and school contexts for language development: The experience of two Mexican-American pre-schoolers. In M. McGroarty & C. Faltis (Eds.), *Language in school and society: Policy and pedagogy* (pp. 487–509). Berlin: Mouton de Gruyter.

Post, J., & Hohmann, M. (2000). *Tender care and early learning: Supporting infants and toddlers in child care settings*. Ypsilanti, MI: High/Scope.

Purcell-Gates, V. (1996). Stories, coupons, and the "TV Guide": Relationships between home literacy experiences and emergent literacy knowledge. *Reading Research Quarterly, 31,* 406–428.

Purcell-Gates, V. (2000). Family literacy. In M. Kamil, P. Mosenthal, P. Perarson, & R. Barr (Eds.), *Handbook of reading research* (vol. 3, pp. 853–870). Mahwah, NJ: Erlbaum.

Roth, H. (1986). *A goodnight hug*. New York: Grosset & Dunlap.

Schickedanz, J. A., Schickedanz, D., Forsyth, P., & Forsyth, G. (2001). *Understanding children and adolescents* (4th ed.). Boston: Allyn and Bacon.

Senechal, M., LeFevre, J., Hudson, E., & Lawson, E. (1996). Knowledge of storybooks as a predictor of young children's vocabulary. *Journal of Educational Psychology, 88,* 520–536.

Seuss, Dr. (Theodore Geisel) (1963a). *Dr. Seuss's ABC Book*. New York: Random House.

Seuss, Dr. (Theodore Geisel) (1963b). *Hop on pop*. New York: Random House.

Snow, C. E., & Ninio, A. (1986). The contracts of literacy: What children learn from learning to read books. In W. H. Teale & E. Sulzby (Eds.), *Emergent literacy: Writing and reading* (pp. 116–138). Exeter, NH: Heinemann.

Snow, C. E., Burns, M. S., & Griffin, P. (Eds.). (1998). *Preventing reading difficulties in young children*. Washington, DC: National Academy Press.

Stein, N., & Glenn, C. (1979). An analysis of story comprehension in elementary children. In R. Freedle (Ed.), *Advances in discourse processes: (Vol 2). New directions in discourse processing* (pp. 53–120). Norwood, NJ: Ablex.

Sulzby, E., & Edwards, P. (1993). The role of parents in supporting literacy development of young children. In B. Spodek & O. Saracho (Eds.), *Language and literacy in early childhood education: Volume 4, Yearbook in early childhood education* (pp. 156–177). New York: Teachers College Press.

Tabors, P., Roach, K., & Snow, C. (2001). Home language and literacy environment: Final results. In D. Dickson & P. Tabors (Eds.), *Beginning literacy with language: Young children learning at home and school* (pp. 111–138). Baltimore, MD: Paul H. Brookes.

Taylor, D., & Dorsey-Gaines, C. (1988). *Growing up literate: Learning from inner-city families.* Portsmouth, NH: Heinemann.

Wasik, B., Dobbins, D., & Hermann, S. (2001). Intergenerational family literacy: Concepts, research, and practice. In S. Neuman & D. Dickinson (Eds.), *Handbook of early literacy research* (pp. 444–458). New York: Guilford.

Wells, G. (1986). *The meaning makers.* Portsmouth, NH: Heinemann.

Wright, B. F. (illustrator) (1916). *The real Mother Goose.* New York: Rand McNally.

3

From Three to Five Years

Novice Readers and Writers in the Phase of Awareness and Exploration

KEY CONCEPTS

novice readers and writers
beginners
intentionality
intention to communicate
awareness of print
repertoire of literacy
    knowledges
literal meaning
inferential meaning
evaluative meaning

reading style
high levels of cognitive
    engagement
analytic talk
story-as-a-whole
sequence
causal relationships
literacy language
organization of informational
    books

pretend readings
timeless present tense
concepts about print
book orientation concepts
directionality concepts
scribble writing
linearity
linear scribble writing
mock cursive
separate units

letter-like forms
symbol salad
features of letters
mock letters
letter orientation
concepts about signatures

text forms
text features
alphabetic principle
contextual dependency
sign concept
rhyming words

phonological awareness
phonemic awareness
beginning phonemes
alliteration

Who Are Novice Readers and Writers?

In this chapter, we examine the literacy learning of many preschoolers, kindergartners, and even a few first graders who are in the phase of Awareness and Exploration (IRA/NAEYC, 1998). Babies, toddlers, and two-year-olds are also in this phase of literacy development. However, we call the children that are discussed in this chapter **novice readers and writers** while we called the children we described in Chapter 2 **beginners.** Our decision to use the word *novice* to describe children's interactions with literacy events in this chapter and the word *beginner* to describe children's interactions with literacy events in Chapter 2 is intentional and we believe important in differentiating what young children discover in the phase of awareness and exploration. At first, when young children are at the very beginning of literacy development, they are included in literacy events and their parents or caregivers help them participate at their level of development. Babies and toddlers learn to point to pictures in books, and as they acquire spoken language, to identify objects or people in book illustrations. As two-year-olds learn to control crayons and markers and engage in simple symbolic play (e.g., by pretending to feed a baby doll), they discover how to use drawing to construct symbols—usually making representational drawings of familiar people. However, novice readers and writers demonstrate several new competencies as literacy users.

Written Language Communicates Messages: Novice Readers' and Writers' New Insights

The first new competency that novice readers and writers demonstrate is what we call **intentionality.** Around the age of three or four, preschoolers sometimes signal they are using print in a new way. They are still far from being able to read and write in a conventional way, but they now intend to read or write rather than to draw. Their behavior, the way they act, and the words they use to explain their actions when they make marks on paper or when they look at books or environmental print, is different. They demonstrate an **intention to communicate** a message with their marks rather than merely to draw. Figure 3.1 presents a scribble-like mark that three-year-old Thomas made. At first glance, we would assume it was a nonrepresentational scribble, and not very remarkable. However, when Thomas handed his paper to his mother, he said, "I have a message for you." His mother asked, "What

FIGURE 3.1 Thomas's Message

does it say?" and Thomas replied, "um, um, I love you." While Thomas' mark looks like a scribble, *he acted and talked as if the scribble was actually a written message*—he even called it a message. Thomas' mother responded to the scribble mark *as if it were actually writing*—she asked him what it said. When asked what his writing said, Thomas was able to construct a plausible message, "I love you." In this literacy event, Thomas acted like a novice writer because he intentionally created a written symbol with the purpose of communicating a message. Thomas did not intend to draw a picture, nor did he treat his written mark as a picture. Instead, he intended to write and treated his writing as if it said something.

A second new competency that novice readers and writers demonstrate is **awareness of print.** Children demonstrate this new awareness as they explore environmental print's role in communicating messages. Novice readers may recognize "Raisin Bran," "McDonald's," and "Coca-Cola" on the familiar cereal box, fast-food restaurant sign, and drink can. However, they go beyond simple recognition of meaning in familiar items or contexts that happen to include printed symbols and words. *Novices react to the meaning communicated in printed signs and labels even when they are not located on the items they represent or in the context in which they are usually found.* They recognize the Raisin Bran and McDonald's logos even when the actual object (the box of cereal) is not present or when the familiar context (the restaurant building) is not available. When they see an unfamiliar environmental print sign, novice readers are likely to ask, "What does that say?" signaling their awareness that print in the environment is intended to communicate messages.

These new insights about literacy allow children sometimes to engage with literacy in new ways. However, it is important to keep in mind that novice readers and writers do not always use their new insights. Children often draw, scribble, and even write whole pages of letter-like forms without intending to do anything other than "draw" or "write." When asked to talk about their writing, many children will describe the colors or lines they use or even say, "It's just writing" rather than attempt to construct a message as Thomas did. Being willing *sometimes* to use scribbles or letter-like forms to construct a message and at other times unwilling to do so is to be expected. Depending on what the task or activity in which they are engaged, children display a **repertoire of literacy knowledge** (Schickedanz, 1999). This means that sometimes—for example, when pretending to be a waitress in a preschool restaurant dramatic play center—children will write with the intention of communicating a message. At other times—for example, when drawing at a preschool art center—children will create marks just for the experience of seeing what they can create.

Examples of Novices

Three literacy events involving Quentin, Kristen, and Courtney are described next. These children have had many experiences sharing books with their parents and nursery school teachers.

Quentin is three and a half years old. He frequently draws with his older sister as she does her homework. Sometimes she draws pictures and writes words or letters at Quentin's request. One day, while his sister was doing her spelling homework, Quentin drew a large circle with one line radiating down from it. He pointed to this primitive *Q* and said "Quentin." Later, when his mother was checking his sister's spelling words, he gave her his paper and said, "I wrote mine."

Kristen is thirty-two months old. One day, while she was riding in the car with her mother, she said, "Pizza man." Her mother looked and finally spotted a Domino's pizza sign. This sign consists of two domino shapes in red, white, and blue and the word *Domino's*. Kristen's family frequently has a Domino's pizza delivered to their home. Kristen had never been to a Domino's pizza place because Domino's only delivers pizzas—it is not a restaurant.

Courtney is twenty-nine months old. When her mother signs birthday cards or makes lists, she gives Courtney paper and pens or crayons and suggests that Courtney write, too. One day, as her mother was writing a letter to accompany a birthday card, Courtney said, "I write 'Happy Birthday to you' " (see Figure 3.2). Courtney's mother suggested that they send her letter, too.

Quentin's, Kristen's, and Courtney's behaviors and talk indicate that they intend for their written symbols to communicate messages and that they recognize that messages can be communicated in written symbols. What is significant about these events is that Quentin, Kristen, and Courtney constructed meaning from *written symbols that they constructed or noticed on their own.*

Kristen constructed the meaning "pizza man" from a printed sign and logo without the clues of an actual pizza, a delivery man, or a familiar location associated with eating pizza. Her behavior indicated a new understanding that printed symbols communicate messages. She knew that written marks in environmental print are significant. Quentin constructed the meaning "Quentin" by printing something like a letter *Q*, and Courtney constructed the meaning "Happy birthday to you" by writing round-and-round and jagged lines. Their behavior, too, indicated their awareness that printed symbols communicate messages. It is significant

FIGURE 3.2   "Happy Birthday to You"

that the messages Quentin and Courtney constructed were part of a larger activity involving writing to communicate. Quentin joined his sister as she practiced her spelling words, and Courtney joined her mother as she wrote a birthday message.

Are they reading and writing? This important question has been the center of controversy for the past few years. Traditionalists define *reading* as the ability to identify words printed in isolation or in simple stories. Similarly, they define *writing* as the ability to write identifiable words in isolation or in simple stories. After careful observation of children such as Quentin, Kristen, and Courtney, some educators have argued that we need a new definition of reading and writing (Baghban, 1984; Goodman, 1980; Harste, Woodward, & Burke, 1984).

Meaning

Novice readers and writers learn to construct meaning from an ever-increasing variety of texts, including menus, *TV Guides,* telephone books, grocery lists, coupons, and, especially, stories. Novice writers make meaning by creating an increasing variety of written symbols.

Constructing the Meaning of Environmental Print

By the age of two-and-a-half or three, many young children find some environmental print symbols meaningful (Hiebert, 1978). Novice readers do not really read the words on environmental print. Unlike beginners, however, they do pay attention to the print on environmental print objects. While beginners respond to such objects as wholes, which include print, novices focus on the print; they point to it. They know that the print is an important part of the object, that somehow it conveys meanings appropriate to the object. They know the kinds of meanings usually associated with the objects and actions signaled by the environmental print item.

For example, a few months after Kristen read the Domino's Pizza sign she said, "Look, Mom, Barbie." Her mother had received an advertisement for ordering magazines. The advertisement included a page of perforated stickers on which the magazine titles were printed. One of the magazines was *The Barbie Magazine,* and the word *Barbie* was printed on the sticker in pink stylized letters just as it appears on the doll box. There was no picture of a Barbie doll on the sticker, and the sticker with *Barbie* written on it was more than halfway down a page of nearly a hundred stickers. Kristen recognized the word *Barbie* without the clues of a toy store, a doll, or even a picture of a doll.

Children expect meaning from many kinds of print items in addition to environmental print. For example, four-year-old Takesha was asked to read a handwritten grocery list. She said, "Green beans, coffee, and bread." She also offered to read a telephone book and said, "Takesha, 75983." Although Takesha did not really read the grocery list or the telephone book, she knew the meanings associated with these kinds of print and used this knowledge to read.

Constructing Meaning While Listening to
Story and Information Book Read-Alouds

In order to construct the meaning of a story being read to them, children must listen to the words of the story. Of course, most books for children include pictures that provide salient contextual cues for understanding the stories. Eventually, however, children must learn to rely only on the text and not on picture context to construct meaning from stories that they read. These strategies are particularly important for later success in reading (Dickinson, 2001).

Most children's early experiences with constructing story meanings take place as they share stories with a parent or other adult. These sessions are highly personalized; they capitalize on children's experiences with particular stories. In Chapter 2 we saw that such personalized booksharing is a context for literacy beginners' learning bookhandling skills and interacting with adults in meaning construction, especially about the pictures in books.

As children approach school age—preschool or kindergarten—their storybook experiences will be in many-to-one situations. Teachers are likely to share books with groups of children rather than with one child at a time. In group story-sharing situations, children are not as close to the pictures as they are in one-to-one story-sharing situations. Thus they have to rely more on the teacher's reading of the words of the text to construct story meaning than on extensive viewing of pictures (Cochran-Smith, 1984).

Children's Meaning-Making Strategies.   Mrs. Jones is a preschool teacher who is skillful in sharing books with her class of four-year-olds. Figure 3.3 presents a portion of the interaction among nine four-year-olds and Mrs. Jones as she shared *There's a Nightmare in My Closet* (Mayer, 1968).

The children's comments and questions demonstrate that they understood much of the **literal meaning** of the story. Obviously, the children understood that there was a nightmare in the closet; they knew that the character needed protection. Their comments and questions demonstrate that they also made many inferences about implied meanings in the story. They made inferences about motivations for the character's actions (he shut the door "Cause he doesn't want the nightmare to come out"); about the character's traits ("He's a scaredy cat"); and about reasons for the character's feelings (he was afraid "cause the wind blow"). The children also made predictions about upcoming story events. Just before Mrs. Jones turned to the last page of the story, which contains an illustration of a second nightmare peeking out of the closet, one child predicted, "There's gonna be another one."

In addition to making inferences and predictions about sequence and causal relations, the children projected themselves into the story ("My momma take the light off, I'm not scared"). They also evaluated the story meaning based on their knowledge of the real world ("I guess he ain't [getting rid of the nightmare] cause that's not a real gun").

In addition, the children paid attention to each other's comments. When one child commented about an action of the character ("Cause he's scared"), another

FIGURE 3.3   A Portion of the Interaction as Mrs. Jones and Her Pre-kindergartners Share *There's a Nightmare in My Closet* **(Mayer, 1968)**

Brackets indicate portions of the dialogue that occurred simultaneously.

Mrs. J: (shows cover of book, invites children to talk about nightmares, reads title and author, and reads first page of text stating the character's belief that a nightmare once lived inside his bedroom closet)

Child 1: He got toys and a gun on his bed.

Mrs. J: Umm, I wonder why?

Child 2: So he can protect him.

Mrs. J: Protect him. Umm. (reads text about closing the door to the closet)

Child 1: Cause he's scared.

⎡ Child 3: He's a scaredy cat.
⎣ Child 1: My momma take the light off, I'm not scared.

Child 4: He might lock it.

Mrs. J: Why would he lock it?

Child 4: Cause he doesn't want the nightmare to come out.

Mrs. J: (reads text about character being afraid to even look in the closet)

Child 1: Cause the wind blow.

Mrs. J: The wind blows?

⎡ Child 3: Yeah, the curtain's out.
⎣ Child 2: It's blowing.

Mrs. J: It must have been a dark, windy night. (continues reading text, making comments, and asking questions)

Children: (continue making comments and asking questions)

Mrs. J: (reads text about character deciding to get rid of the nightmare)

Child 1: I guess he ain't cause that's not a real gun.

Mrs. J: (turns page to illustration of the nightmare coming out of the closet and walking toward the boy in the bed)

⎡ Child 1: There he is.
⎣ Child 5: Why he's awake?

Mrs. J: Well what did it say? He was going to try to get rid of his nightmare, so he stayed awake waiting for his nightmare.

---

one agreed ("He's a scaredy cat"). Similarly, when one child noted that "the wind blow," another child added, "Yeah, the curtain's out."

This short story interaction illustrates that four-year-olds in group story-sharing can construct many kinds of meanings (Martinez, 1983). They understand what the author says—the literal meaning. They understand what the author implies—**inferential meaning.** They make judgments about what the author says—**evaluative meaning.**

Mrs. Jones and her children were reading a narrative or story text together, and the children's comments, questions, and predictions were based on their growing awareness of story elements, more sophisticated language and cognitive development, and experiences listening to books. However, preschoolers and kindergarteners also listen as their teachers read nonfiction or informational books aloud and participate actively in trying to understand the ideas presented in these kinds of texts. Novice readers use many of the same strategies to understand informational texts as they do story texts (Shine & Roser, 1999). For example, they may connect information to personal experiences or imagine themselves engaging with objects and events in the book. They may predict and speculate on behavior of animals or people in the book based on their own experiences. They also ask questions and make inferences (Tower, 2002). For example, as a teacher was reading *Let's Find Out about Ice Cream* (Reid, 1996), a book about the process of making ice cream, a teacher and three children had this discussion about an illustration of a man working in an ice cream freezer:

TEACHER: He has a freezer suit on.

KENNY: Why?

ALTHEA: Cause he won't, cause he can't get cold.

KENNY: Cause he won't catch a cold.

JASON: Yeah, and not get a cough. (Tower, 2002, p. 72)

Young children also use different kinds of strategies for understanding ideas presented in informational text than they do when listening to narrative texts. They rely more heavily on the illustrations in informational text and talk more about what is depicted in those illustrations. They identify, describe, or ask about details or events depicted in the illustrations (Tower, 2002).

Teachers' Roles in Helping Children Understand Interactive Read-Alouds. Figure 3.3 presented only a small portion of the interactive read-aloud of *There's a Nightmare in My Closet,* and from this short excerpt Mrs. Jones' style of reading is not obvious. However, the way in which Mrs. Jones read aloud and talked with her children during the interactive read-aloud influenced the kinds of meanings that her children constructed as they listened to and talked about the story. Mrs. Jones had a very dramatic style. She read with expression and used three different voices: one for the narrator, one for the little boy, and one for the monster. She was so familiar with this story that she frequently turned to look at the children as she read portions of the story so they could see her facial expressions. She pointed to specific places in the pictures as she read, and paused for dramatic effect.

Mrs. Jones' **reading style** (Martinez & Teale, 1993; Smolkin & Donovan, 2002) invites a great deal of participation from the children. She reads the story, but her major concern is for children to enjoy and understand the book. To make sure this happens, she encourages the children to comment and ask questions. She demands **high levels of cognitive engagement.** That is, she helps children make inferences about character traits and their motives. She helps children make connections between events in the story so that they can understand what causes characters to act as they do. She helps children understand the meaning of words and connects events in books to children's experiences. This style of reading helps children engage in **analytic talk** (Dickinson, 2001) in which they are analyzing characters and events rather than merely recalling what happened.

Teachers play many of the same roles as they share informational books with young children. Informational books seem to spontaneously generate more questions than narrative texts and much more description and explanation of information in the illustrations. Effective teachers encourage children's explorations of the illustrations and weave reading of the text of such books into children's comments about the illustrations. Teachers are conscious of connecting children's comments and questions with the technical vocabulary used in the book to describe the actions and objects in the illustrations (Smolkin & Donovan, 2002). For example, while discussing the book about making ice cream, one four-year-old pointed to a picture of sugar cane stalks and asked, "And what are—snakes?" Her teacher clarified, "These are called sugar cane plants" (Tower, 2002, p. 67).

Children's Developing Concept about Story and Informational Text

One of the strategies that children use as they listen to stories in addition to constructing literal, inferential, and evaluative meanings is to pay attention to story elements. We have called children's awareness of elements of story their concept of story, or story schema (see Chapter 2).

Novice readers' and writers' concepts about stories grow as they gain experience with more complex stories. One of the most important ways in which novices' concepts of stories change is that they begin to understand **story-as-a-whole.** Novices learn two important organizational structures that can be used to link events together in stories: **sequence** and **causal relationships.** Novices learn that events in stories occur in sequence and that some events in stories cause other events to occur. They discover that the event of a character's falling down while skating is related to the event of scraping a knee—falling down caused the character's knee to become scraped. Children's concept of story influences many aspects of their literacy behaviors. Children draw on their concept of story as they listen to stories read aloud and construct the stories' meanings. They know to focus on the main characters and their characteristics, including motivations and problems. They know that the events in a story will be related to one another in a specific order. Increasingly, their questions during storybook reading reveal their attention to these elements (see Figure 3.3).

Children's concept of story also influences their creation of text in imaginary play (Wolf & Heath, 1992). They demonstrate their awareness of **literary language** and their ability to enter a story's world. Three-year-old Nat did this when he called his cereal "porridge" and said, "We are the three bears. My chair's broken" (Voss, 1988, p. 275). Three-year-old Kristen was "cooking" on her play stove after she and her mother had shared *Three Little Kittens* (Galdone, 1986). As she slipped on her hot-pad mitten, she said, "Oh, Mother dear, Mother dear. My mitten, my mitten here. Hey, Mommy, you be the mother."

Children draw on their concept of story as they dramatize or compose stories. As we will show later in the chapter, when children write text that they intend as a story, they tend to pretend to read their story using story-like events and language. In contrast, when they write text that they intend to be a grocery list, they pretend to read their list sounding as if it were indeed a list. Similarly, when children read *Crictor* (Ungerer, 1958) and they dramatize narrative events, such as pretending to be a burglar trying to rob from a house, they draw on their understanding of story events and language to support their play.

Constructing Meaning in Pretend Reading and Retelling

Novices also use their concept of story when they attempt to retell stories. A special kind of retelling is when children look at favorite picture books—ones they have shared many times with their parents or teacher—and attempt to reread them on their own. These retellings or rereadings are called **pretend readings** (Pappas, 1993). The pretend readings of novices tell a story. Their retellings and pretend readings may include past tense verbs (as is found in most stories) and an acceptable sequence of story events. At first, retellings are short and leave out much detail. Later, they may include nearly all events and even some of the literary language found in a story.

During the preschool and kindergarten years, children listen to more than just stories. They enjoy poems, songs, and informational books. Just as they gain a growing awareness of the characteristics of storybooks and the organizational patterns in stories, children learn the **organization of informational books** (Duke & Hays, 1998; Pappas & Pettegrew, 1998). From listening to informational books read aloud, children learn that these books tell about classes of things, such as trucks or squirrels or tunnels (Pappas, 1993). Unlike stories, which tell about a particular squirrel (the main character) and his problem, an informational book tells about squirrels in general, what they are like (a description of their characteristics), and what they do (a discussion about their behaviors).

Children's concepts about informational texts also influence their emergent readings, retellings, and compositions of such texts. For example, Jean, a kindergartner, began her retelling of the storybook *The Owl and the Woodpecker* (Wildsmith, 1971), "Once in the forest there was a woodpecker" (Pappas, 1991, p. 455). This sounds like the way a story starts, with a setting and the introduction of a particular woodpecker. The actual text of the book does the same thing. It begins, "Once upon a time in a forest, far away, there lived a Woodpecker." In her retelling of *Squirrels* (Wildsmith, 1974), an information book, however, the same kindergartner used quite different language. She began, "Squirrels are very easy to find cause they have furry bodies and nice furry bodies and some nice furry ears which they stick up" (Pappas, 1991, p. 456). Here Jean is describing squirrels in general. The actual text does that, too. It begins, "It is easy to recognize a squirrel. He is a furry, small animal with a long, bushy tail, two strong back legs, two small front paws, two large tufted ears which stick up, and two big front teeth." The rest of Jean's retellings of these two books show that "she is just as successful in reenacting the information book as she is the story" (Pappas, 1991, p. 450).

Children as young as four differentiate between retelling or pretending to read a story and an informational book (Cox, Fang, & Otto, 1997). They are more likely to identify a specific character and use past tense when pretending to read a storybook. They are more likely to use **timeless present tense** and a generic group of animals or people when pretending to read an informational book. Children's pretend readings begin to sound like the language of books (we will show in Chapter 4 that this transition from pretending to read with book-like language rather than like everyday, conversational language is one indication that children are moving into the next phase of literacy development).

Writing Meaningful Messages

Novices have a new interest in participating in the sending of the message and not just in the activity of writing. Much of novice writers' message making is a part of playful activity. They imitate their parents' or siblings' sending messages in their dramatic play. One day, when Giti and her mother had returned from having a snack at the Big Wheel Restaurant, Giti walked around with a pencil and paper and stood in front of her mother with the pencil held over the pad just as she had seen the waitress at the restaurant do. She said, "You want?" Her mother dictated "Hot dog," and Giti wrote a jagged line. Then her mother said "French fries," and Giti wrote again. After several minutes of this game, Giti said "Ready?" just as her mother had when she was ready to leave the restaurant (Baghban, 1984, pp. 61–62). Giti's behaviors indicated her intention to write something meaningful. She wrote the food orders that her mother dictated. The "words" she wrote ("French fries" and "hot dog") reflected Giti's growing awareness of the content expected in a written food order.

Children's interest in producing written messages can also be initiated through school experiences. Two-year-old Natalie made the zigzag lines in Figure 3.4. She wrote left-to-right zigzags with her right hand and right-to-left zigzags with her left hand. After her first zigzag, she said, "I did it! That's my name. I'll spell your name." Then she made another zigzag and said, "That's your name, Daddy."

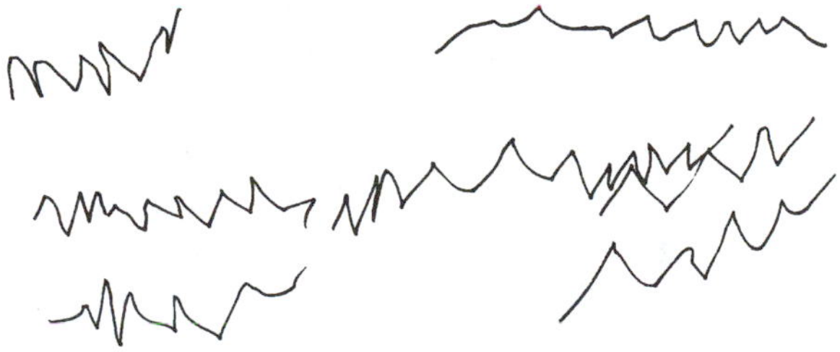

FIGURE 3.4   Natalie's Name Writing

For others she said, "That's Mary's," and "Don's is easy," and, "That's your name, Mommy." We asked Natalie where she learned to write. She said, "I do it at school," referring to her day care center.

Similarly, Vang's kindergarten teacher provides many real-life experiences, such as flying kites, finding caterpillars, and visiting the zoo (Abramson, Seda, & Johnson, 1990). She believes that these experiences are particularly important for the learning of her children, whose first languages include Hmong, Spanish, Laotian, and Cambodian. Several days after visiting the zoo, Vang drew a picture of an elephant and wrote what appears in Figure 3.5, saying "elephant." Then he drew a picture of a second, smaller elephant and discussed it with his teacher (Abramson, Seda, & Johnson, 1990, p. 69)

VANG: Teacher, look it. I made baby. Baby el-fant.

TEACHER: A baby elephant. Oh, that's great. Can you write "baby elephant"?

VANG: Sure!

Vang wrote what appears in Figure 3.5a and 3.5b. Vang knows that writing can be used to label drawings. The meaning he constructed ("elephant" and "baby elephant") is highly dependent both on his picture and on the teacher's suggestion.

Much of children's meaning making in writing depends on their experiences with meaningful uses of reading and writing. Giti would not have used writing to create a food order if she had not observed orders for food being written. Natalie would not have taken up name writing if she had not associated writing at school with classmates' names and then been encouraged by her parents. Vang would not have created a message in his journal if he had not had a highly meaningful trip to the zoo or observed his classmates' daily journal writing and his teacher's responses to those written messages.

Written Language Forms

While they are developing new insights about written language meanings, novices also demonstrate new awarenesses about written language forms. They notice the print on environmental print items and in books, they acquire notions of how print

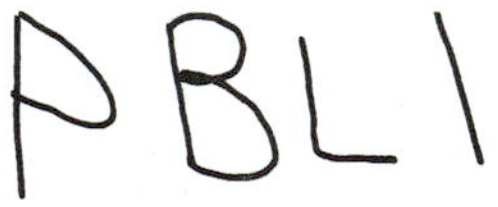

FIGURE 3.5a   "Elephant"    **FIGURE 3.5b   "Baby Elephant"**

From Abramson, S., Seda, I., & Johnson, C. (1990). Literacy development in a multilingual kindergarten classroom. *Childhood Education, 67,* 68–72. Reprinted by permission of the authors and the Association for Childhood Education International, 11501 Georgia Ave., Ste. 315, Wheaton, MD. Copyright © 1991 by the Association.

looks and how it is organized, and they begin to display those notions in their own writing.

Concepts about Print

Children's **concepts about print** are understandings that they have about the visual characteristics, features, and organization of print. As children attend to print, they develop concepts about how print is visually organized and read. They learn that alphabet letters are a special category of visual symbols, that print "says," and that print is read rather than the pictures. In Chapter 2, we described several concepts about print that very young children learn about books; books are held right-side-up (children know which is the top and bottom of a book) and their pages are turned one-by-one from the front of the book to the back. These **book orientation concepts** form the foundation for later discovering **directionality concepts.** Directionality concepts involve children's awareness that print is written and read from left-to-right, line-by-line. Later we will show that novice writers display awareness of directionality in their writing. Novice readers begin this process when they pretend to read a favorite book. They may point to the print as they read, sweeping their hands across the print. Novice readers are not able to point to each word of a book one-by-one (this will come later), but they do display awareness that books are read in a systematic fashion.

From Scribbles to Alphabet Letters

Children's awareness of print and their developing concepts about print influence the kinds of marks they make in their writing. Novice writers attempt to create marks that look like print and are organized on a page like writing. However, children's early writing attempts, called **scribble writing** (Schickedanz, 1999), have virtually none of the features we would expect of writing. They do not include alphabet letters or even forms that somewhat resemble letters. They do not even display awareness of **linearity** (that writing is displayed in a linear fashion across the page). Figure 3.1 (Thomas' "I love you" message) and Figure 3.2 (Courtney's "Happy Birthday to you" message) are examples of scribble writing. Children's **linear scribble writing** (Bloodgood, 1999; Hildreth, 1936) has the feature of linearity and is sometimes called **mock cursive** because of its resemblance to a long line of cursive writing. Figure 3.4 (Natalie's name writing) is an example of a linear scribble.

Eventually, children's writing begins to include **separate units** or symbols although the units may not look very much like alphabet letters. For example, many children's writing attempts consist of a series of circles resembling the letter *O*. Other children may compose symbols using lines and curves along with circle shapes. Figure 3.6 presents an example of writing that consists of separate units presented in a nonlinear arrangement.

As children gain awareness of alphabet letters, their writing includes a mixture of **letter-like forms,** symbols, numbers, and even conventionally formed

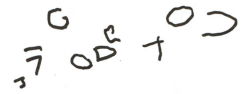

FIGURE 3.6   Writing with Separate Units

alphabet letters. Children seem to enjoy both writing the same form repeatedly in their writing and changing forms to see what new forms they can create (Clay, 1975). Writing with a mixture of letters, numbers, other symbols, and letter-like shapes is sometimes called **symbol salad** (Bear, Invernizzi, Templeton, & Johnston, 2000). Figure 3.7 presents an example of symbol salad writing in which the writer drew on his awareness of both linearity and directionality.

Of course, children frequently draw and write on the same sheet of paper. However, even when they draw and write, children as young as three demonstrate that they differentiate between drawing and writing. Figure 3.8 presents a picture Ryan Patrick drew of himself and his signature. Although his name only consists of a letter-like form that resembles the alphabet letter *P* and a series of scribble-like separate units, his writing is clearly differentiated from his drawing. Notice that his drawing is merely a romance picture of himself rather than a true representational drawing. Ryan Patrick's attention to the letter *P* and its prominence in his writing is also typical of early writers. Often the first conventional letter to appear mixed in with scribble writing or separate units is the first letter in their names (Schickedanz, 1999).

Alphabet Letters

Novices demonstrate in many ways their understanding of the importance of letters of the alphabet, that letters are fundamental units of written language, that they play a basic role in the way written language works. Novices do not yet know what that role is (to represent the fundamental units of spoken language, sounds called phonemes). However, before they learn to name any alphabet letters or to write recognizable letter formations, children discover a great deal about alphabet letters (McGee & Richgels, 1989). One thing they learn is to call this special cate-

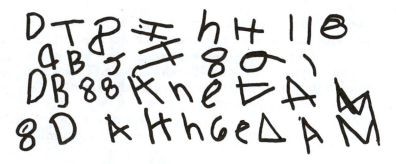

**FIGURE 3.7
Symbol Salad**

FIGURE 3.8 Ryan Patrick's Drawing and Writing

gory of written symbols *the alphabet* or *letters.* They learn that alphabet letters are related to or associated with important people, places, or objects. Kristen (in Chapter 2) thought that *Special K* cereal and *K-Mart* were *her* cereal and *her* store. In one preschool classroom, Jean-Marc always wrote his name with *J* for *Jean-Marc, E* for *Emmanuel, A* for *Andre, N* for *Natalie*—and then he stopped writing because he did not know anyone whose name began with *M* (Ballenger, 1999, p. 45).

Eventually, preschoolers learn the names of the alphabet letters and how to write them. In order to do this, they need a clear visual image of the letter and control over motor schemes to make the lines that they visualize (Schickedanz, 1999). Children build up strong visual images of letters as they experiment with the **features of letters,** the special lines and shapes that make up letters.

The letter *T* is made up of a horizontal and a vertical line; the letter *O* is made up of an enclosed, continuous curved line; and the letter *N* is made up of two vertical lines and a diagonal line. Children must learn to pay attention to letter features in order to distinguish between letters (for example, between the letters *w* and *v* or *l* and *i*).

Children show that they pay attention to letter features in their writing through their mock letters. As we described in Chapter 1, **mock letters** are letter-like shapes with many of the same features of conventional alphabet letters. There are several examples of mock letters found in Figure 3.7. This writer seems to be exploring when the letter *H* can become the letter *I* or *A*. Mock letters are often constructed as children play with **letter orientation.** That is, they rotate letters so they seem to lay sideways or upside down. Letters are frequently written in mirror-image form. It is not surprising that young children are slow to grasp the correct orientation of alphabet letters. For example, a chair is a chair whether it faces left or right. But lower case *b* and *d* are different letters because one faces left and one faces right.

Teachers and parents find that children develop stronger mental images of letters and begin to distinguish between similar letters when adults demonstrate writing letters (Schickedanz, 1999) rather than only providing alphabet letter cards, magnetic letters, or books (although these are useful in learning to name the alphabet letters). For example, when children observe an adult construct the letter *A,* they can observe that it is made up of two long diagonal lines and then a short horizontal line rather than composed of two short diagonal lines, a short horizontal line, and then two connecting diagonal lines.

Many three-year-olds know a few letters and some four-year-olds know nearly all the alphabet letters. Large studies of young children show that on average a four-year-old knows five to nine alphabet letters (Bloodgood, 1999; Smith & Dixon, 1995). Such studies show that children from low income families know fewer alphabet letters, but learn quickly when they are provided alphabet learning activities in preschool (Morgan, 1987).

Signatures

Just as children learn to name and write alphabet letters and acquire concepts about what alphabet letters are, they also learn to write their names and acquire concepts about what written names are. Children's ability to write recognizable signatures develops in an identifiable pattern (Hildreth, 1936). Their ability depends on their growing motor control, awareness of letter features, and knowledge of letters as discrete units. Figure 3.9 presents Robert's name-writing attempts over a nine-month period while he was in a prekindergarten program for four-year-olds. The first example of his signature, produced in early September, was a jagged line. Like Robert's early signatures, many children's initial attempts at writing their names contain no letters at all; they are frequently a single line or shape.

As children gain practice writing their names and begin to notice written language in environmental print or in their parents' writing, they start to produce a number of discrete, letter-like symbols as a part of their signatures. Eventually, children include more conventional formations for all the letters in their signatures. They begin to place the letters in order and to include every letter, although at first the letters are likely to be scattered around the page or in scrambled order.

As children learn to recognize and write their names, their **concepts about signatures** are quite different from those of adults. Ferreiro (1986) described Mariana, who claimed that she could write her name. She wrote five capital letters (*PSQIA*) as she said "Mariana" several times. When asked, "What does it say here?" about the letters *PS,* she replied, "Two Mariana." When asked, "What does it say here?" about the letters *QIA,* she replied, "Three Mariana" (Ferreiro, 1986, p. 37). Her answers reflect that Mariana believed each letter she wrote would say her name.

Mariana's comments about her name illustrate that children do not conceive of signatures as words composed of letters that represent sounds. Their ideas about signatures are interwoven with their concepts of alphabet letters.

FIGURE 3.9   Robert's Signatures

Texts

Novice readers and writers learn a great deal about different kinds of writing, and they use this knowledge to create a variety of texts, especially story texts. Novices come to know a variety of text forms that are used in special contexts and for particular functions. They become aware of and use text features (such as "Dear _____ " at the beginning of a letter). And their concept of story and concept of informational book organization develop (Duke & Hays, 1998).

Novice writers produce many different **text forms.** For example, Courtney wrote a birthday message (Figure 3.2). Later in this chapter we will describe Johanna's birthday list (see Figure 3.12) and Jeremy's "Book of Poems." Much of these texts was included in their talk as they wrote and in the contexts in which the texts were produced. When we look only at Courtney's writing, it does not appear to be a text. It is only apparent that it is a text when we pay attention to her talk, to her actions (she put her writing in an envelope), and to the context (she and her mother were writing birthday cards). It is interesting to note that function plays an important role in novices' creation of texts. Courtney created a birthday message as she participated in the functional activity of sending birthday greetings.

Sometimes the forms found in children's writing signal their growing awareness of the different features of texts. Figure 3.10 presents two pieces of Christopher's

FIGURE 3.10   A Story and a Grocery List

writing. Although Christopher composed both of his pieces using a combination of mock letters and conventional alphabet letters, the two compositions look quite different. One composition was written in the home center when Christopher decided to go grocery shopping with two friends. Christopher said, "I need candy, milk, bread, and cereal." The other composition was written at the writing center. Christopher later read this story to the teacher: "My dad went fishing but he didn't catch any fish. I caught a big fish."

It is easy to distinguish Christopher's grocery list from his story both by the meaning he assigned to his writing and by how each piece of writing looks. The story is composed of three horizontal lines of text with an illustration; the list is composed of a vertical line of text. These features of Christopher's writing indicate his growing awareness of **text features.**

Meaning-Form Links

The conventional way that meaning (the message writers intend) is linked to form (words that writers use) is through the **alphabetic principle.** That is, words are comprised of alphabet letters and alphabet letters are related to phonemes in spoken words. As fluent readers, we are not often consciously aware of the alphabetic principle because we do not draw on it very often. Instead, we immediately recognize most of the words we read without having to look at their letters and "sound out" words letter-by-letter. This is exactly what novice readers and writers do not know. They may recognize letters, and as we will see, may actually be able to isolate and say a phoneme, but they do not understand the relationship between letters and sounds. Instead, they use another method for making their writing meaningful—contextual dependency.

Contextual Dependency

Contextual dependency means that written forms convey meaning through the context of their use or through children's talk about their writing. Thomas's message (Figure 3.1), Courtney's birthday card (Figure 3.2), Vang's journal entry (Figure 3.5), and Christopher's story and grocery list (Figure 3.10) have a common characteristic: the use of contextual dependency to link written form to meaning. If we took the children's writing out of the context in which it was written and did not know what the children said about their writing, we would not be able to determine the messages that the child writers intended to communicate. We can only know the messages that novice writers convey when we know the context in which they wrote and when we listen to what they say about their writing. Clay (1975) called children's dependency on context to link meaning and form the **sign concept.** The sign concept is evident when children use the context of play to construct meaning in their writing and reading.

Matching Print to Spoken Language: More Than Contextual Dependency

Although novice readers and writers depend primarily on the context in which their writing is produced and in which written symbols are found to link meaning and form, some use more than context to link meaning and form. Many researchers have explored children's concepts about the links between meaning and print (Dyson, 1982; Ferreiro & Teberosky, 1982). They have found that not all children have the same concepts about the relations between meaning and form, that their concepts about the relations between meaning and form change as children gain experience using written language, and that children's knowledge of meaning-form links is very complex.

Figure 3.11 presents John's writing and story ("I have a dog. He is big. He is my best friend."). As John read the story, he swept his finger from left to right across each line of text as he said each sentence. He demonstrated contextual dependency in making meaning from his own writing. But, in addition, John noticed that printed text must be matched somehow to the oral message; he matched a line of text with a spoken sentence. Although not yet conventional, this matching of the text with the oral message is a precursor to a later, more-developed kind of meaning-form linking, that is, matching one spoken sound (or phoneme) with one letter (or grapheme).

Figure 3.12 presents Johanna's writing and story. She did not write an actual story, but instead wrote a list of things she wanted for her birthday. Although her list is composed entirely of jagged lines, correlating what Johanna said with her jagged lines reveals that Johanna often matched one continuous jagged line with

I have a dog.

He is big.

FIGURE 3.11 John's Story   He is my best friend.

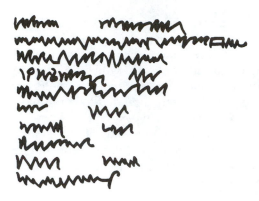

hula hoop
Wishbow kids with a bed
more Mapletown animals
Prince Strongheart
horse for Prince Strongheart
a baby
baby bottles
bonnet
baby clothes
slide

FIGURE 3.12   Johanna's Birthday List

one spoken word. Johanna realized that the written forms she wrote should correspond with the spoken meaning she intended.

Phonological Awareness

As novice readers and writers, young children have many experiences that allow them to develop a special kind of metalinguistic awareness (see Chapter 1). As a result of listening to nursery rhymes, poems, and books with repetitive words and phrases, children begin to play with language.

The rhythm created in nursery rhymes highlights and segments speech sounds in a way that conversation does not. The syllables *PE ter PE ter PUMP kin EAT er* are naturally separated by the stress in the rhyme. This natural play with language sounds invites children to enjoy the music of language. Children who have listened to nursery rhymes and other books with language play soon begin to play with speech sounds themselves. While four-year-old James was playing with a toy typewriter in his preschool room, he muttered "James, Fames, Wames" to himself. James was demonstrating phonological awareness.

Much language play that occurs during preschool and early kindergarten is relatively unconscious. Many children may not realize that they are making up **rhyming words.** They may never have heard the term "rhyming words" or even consciously have attended to the ending sounds in words. Being able to consciously attend to sounds in words apart from words' meanings is a critical component of **phonological awareness.** Some children seem to develop phonological awareness, as indicated by a conscious sense of syllables and rhyming words, without any explicit teaching. Other children need more help hearing and counting syllables in words or identifying rhyming words in order to develop phonological awareness.

A special kind of phonological awareness, known as **phonemic awareness,** requires children consciously to attend to single phonemes in words. Some novice readers and writers, for example, intentionally create rhyming words by isolating **beginning phonemes** and substituting other phonemes for them, especially when their parents, caregivers, or teachers share books that contain many words with **alliteration.** Alliterative words begin with the same beginning sounds such as in the book *Some Smug Slug* (Duncan, 1996).

Using Symbols: The Connections among Dramatic Play, Writing, and Computer Use

Play is a critical component of the preschool years. Children's approach to writing during these years is closely connected to play. Careful observers will notice that preschoolers most often write during play. They will take a phone message when they are pretending to be a mother with a sick baby or take notes on a patient chart when they are pretending to be a doctor. Pretending to write in play involves the use of written symbols (rather than actual written words) to communicate an imaginary message. Children's use of written symbols in pretend writing is very much like their symbolic use of objects in imaginary play. For example, they may create a symbol of a thermometer as they pretend to take a baby's temperature using a spoon as the thermometer. After listening to storybooks or informational books, they often search for objects that can represent characters in the books (Rowe, 1998). Then they can use those objects as characters in their imaginary play about the book. Children's activities on the computer are also playful and involve the use of symbols (Labbo, 1996). They create symbols using drawing and stamping tools and then transform them into pictures. For example, one child created a picture of his sister using a stamp of an ice cream cone to represent or symbolize her nose.

Children's ability to use symbols in highly complex and abstract ways seems to precede their acquisition of more conventional literacy skills. Children can create imaginary symbols in dramatic play by merely gesturing. A four-year-old in the block area can create an imaginary dump truck to drive over his block road by merely pretending to turn the wheel of a truck while make a motor noise. Perhaps such experiences with abstract symbols during play and exploration on the computer and during writing during pretend play provide a foundation for later being able to use the even more abstract symbols of letters and phonemes.

Written Language Functions

During the preschool and kindergarten years, young children acquire an enormous amount of knowledge about literacy. However, what they learn depends on their early experiences with reading and writing. Young children are socialized into their families' ways of using literacy (Gee, 2001; Purcell-Gates, 1996). Many families use literacy in a variety of ways, such as for entertainment (reading novels), for information (surfing the Web for deals on cheap airline tickets), to accomplish family tasks (paying bills and filling out forms to apply for loans). Children observe the ways that family members use literacy and want to be included as they do in all family activities (Taylor & Dorsey-Gaines, 1988).

This willingness, even insistence, on joining in family activities forms a strong foundation for literacy learning. When Dad writes checks to pay bills, his son will want a pen and paper so that he can join in the activity of writing. Later, his son will want to join in the activity of writing checks to pay bills. Children not only observe adults' reading and writing, but also participate in using written language, especially in their play (Gee, 2001).

Many children from literacy-rich homes go beyond using literacy in their play. They use literacy as themes for play. One day Jeremy announced that he was going to make a book (Gundlach, McLane, Scott, & McNamee, 1985, p. 13). His father suggested that he use some index cards and write his book on the typewriter. After Jeremy had finished typing his cards, he and his father stapled the cards together to make the book. When his father asked him what was in his book, Jeremy replied, "A surprise" (p. 13). The next day, Jeremy's father invited him to listen to a radio program of children reading their poetry. After the program, Jeremy asked his mother and father to come into the living room to listen to him read his "Book of Poems." He opened the book he had made the previous day and said, "Page 1." Then he recited a poem that he knew. As he read "Page 2," he could not seem to remember any more poems, so he made up rhyming words and used singsong intonation. His mother and father applauded his reading.

Unlike Jeremy, who uses literacy as a way of playing and gaining the attention of his parents, Tom uses literacy in more functional ways. When Tom was four, he became angry because his mother would not buy him a new toy. His mother said that she would be paid in three weeks and that Tom could have a toy then. Tom asked how many days were in three weeks and went to his room. He made the calendar (a portion of which is presented in Figure 3.13) with a number for each of the twenty-one days remaining until he could get a new toy. Every day as his father read him a story at bedtime, Tom crossed off a day on his calendar, and on the twenty-first day, his mother bought him his new toy.

Written language functions in different ways in different communities (Heath, 1983). In some communities, print serves the practical functions of paying

FIGURE 3.13   Tom's Calendar

bills, providing information about guarantees, and affirming religious beliefs. In other communities, print is used for recreation and entertainment as well; people are likely to read for pleasure. Print serves even wider functions in other communities; it provides a means of critically analyzing political, economic, or social issues. Children growing up in these different communities have different concepts of the functions served by reading and writing (Purcell-Gates, 1996).

A Word of Caution

We add two cautions to our discussion of novice readers and writers. First, we have noted the ages of several of the children we described as novice readers and writers. We believe that many children become novice readers and writers around the ages of two or three. However, children may display knowledge like that of novice readers and writers in one literacy event and knowledge like that of literacy beginners in other events. Many children display novice reading and writing literacy knowledge throughout their preschool years. Many kindergartners and a few first graders seem to operate with novice reading and writing knowledge. We caution that not all three-, four-, or five-year-olds will be novice readers or writers and that novice reading and writing sometimes does not end at age five.

Second, much of the knowledge we have of young preschoolers' literacy derives from research involving middle-class families (Barone, 1999). The ages at which many of these youngsters display novice reading and writing may be deceptive; these children have had early and frequent experiences of the kind that would be expected to support early literacy learning. When preschoolers who have not had many literacy experiences gain access to those experiences, they do acquire literacy concepts (Dickinson & Sprague, 2001; Morgan, 1987).

However, we have been careful in this chapter to include many examples of novice reading and writing from children who do not come from middle-class backgrounds. Vang (Figure 3.5) did not speak any English when he began kindergarten. Gradually, he acquired English, and his writing and talking about writing seemed to be an important vehicle for his learning of English. John's and Christopher's writing was collected from a preschool program for at-risk young children. All these children had parents and teachers who surrounded them with literacy and provided numerous opportunities for children to participate in reading and writing activities (much like those we describe in Chapters 6 and 7).

Chapter Summary

Novice readers and writers approach reading and writing in unconventional but systematic ways. They expect written language to be meaningful, and the meanings they associate with particular kinds of texts (such as environmental print, grocery lists, and stories) reflect their growing awareness of the language associated with these texts. Novice readers and writers find environmental print meaningful. The contextualized nature of this type of print initially supports children's meaning-making efforts, but novice readers respond to environmental print even when it is not in contexts that clue its meaning. Novice readers make strides in understanding the decontextualized print in stories that are read aloud to them. They learn to construct stories-as-wholes. They learn that stories are more than individual pictures, that stories are formed by a causally related series of events. They learn to make inferences and evaluations about characters and events.

Novice writers often intend to communicate a meaning in their writing, and the meaning they communicate reflects how they expect to use their written products (as a birthday card or a story). Novice readers and writers gradually begin to learn names for alphabet letters and to form conventional letters and signatures. Their concepts of letters and signatures differ from those of adults. Their learning to write many kinds of texts reflects knowledge of text features, and their talk about texts reveals an awareness of the content associated with different kinds of texts. In particular, novice readers and writers develop more complex understandings of the content, language, and organization of stories and informational books.

Novices rely on stylized print and pictures to read the logos in environmental print, and they depend on the context of their writing and talk to assign meanings to their writing. They use reading and writing for a variety of purposes, including playing, interacting with others, and conducting the business of daily living in their families and communities. The kinds of reading and writing activities in which children participate may vary, and what children learn about written language functions may differ accordingly.

Figure 3.14 provides a summary of the concepts presented in this chapter. It is important to keep in mind that a concept may appear in more than one section of the figure. For example, children's concept of story is an important part of their knowledge of written language forms. However, concept of story is also an important part of novice readers' and writers' knowledge about written language meanings. They use their concept of story as they construct meanings of the stories read aloud to them and as they compose the content of their own stories. Children's reading and writing ultimately reflect the interdependence of meaning, form, and function.

Applying the Information

Two literacy events follow. The first event concerns Miles' telling a story about a personal experience and then dictating it so his teacher could write his story. The second event concerns Jeffrey's writing a card to his friend Temp. Discuss what each of these events shows about Miles' and Jeffrey's understandings of written language meanings, forms, meaning-form links, and functions.

Miles was in his preschool classroom talking with a visitor. The visitor encouraged him to talk about a recent experience. Miles had this to say presumably about a recent or imaginary shopping trip:

"I buy a Ninja Turtle. I buyed a sweater from the Easter Bunny. I buyed a new bike, a Ninja Turtle one" (Cox, Fang, & Otto, 1997, p. 46).

FIGURE 3.14   Summary: What Novice Readers and Writers Know about Written Language

Meaning Making

intend to communicate meaning in writing

assign meaning to environmental print

assign meaning to a variety of texts by applying knowledge of the content and language used in those texts

apply concept of story in constructing the meaning of stories read aloud, retelling stories, and pretend reading of stories especially using sequence and causality

construct literal meaning

construct inferential meaning

construct evaluative meaning

use some literary language in retelling and pretend reading

Forms

recognize alphabet letters as a special set of graphic symbols

learn alphabet letter names and formations

learn letter features (and may write mock letters)

write own signature

use a variety of text features to construct different kinds of texts

Meaning-Form Links

use contextual dependency

differentiate pictures from print (but sometimes think pictures are read)

pay attention to print (and sometimes know that print is read)

go beyond contextual dependency by matching segments of the printed text with segments of the spoken text (sometimes matching lines to spoken sentences, segments of text to spoken words, or letters to syllables)

develop the beginnings of phonological awareness (by constructing rhyming words and identifying beginning phoneme)

Functions

use reading and writing in play

use reading and writing across time to regulate the behavior of self and others

use reading and writing as part of family and community activities (such as to complete daily-living routines)

Then the visitor praised Miles for telling such an interesting story and asked the child to tell the story so it could be written down as a story for others to read. Miles dictated the following as the visitor wrote his story:

"I got a Ghost Buster man. And I bought a new shoe and bought clothes, too. And I bought me those and I buyed one of those, too. I bought a power car. It's just my size just like my bike. And that's all" (Cox, Fang, & Otto, 1997, p. 46).

Jeffrey was playing with his writing box. He answered his toy telephone and had an imaginary conversation with a friend he had recently visited. "Hi, Temp. This is Jeffrey. Do you want to come play with me? Okay. See you later."

He hung up the phone and looked at his mother. He said, "Temp is sick and needs me to make a card for him." Jeffrey took a sheet of paper from his writing box and cut the paper into two pieces. He cut a rounded shape out of the top center of the larger piece of paper and said, "This is going to be the envelope."

Then he took the smaller paper and wrote four lines of mock cursive. His mother asked, "What does the card say?" Jeffrey ran his finger across each line of

FIGURE 3.15a   Jeffrey's Card   FIGURE 3.15b   Jeffrey's Envelope

text as he read, "I love," "you, Temp," "from," "Jeffrey." Then Jeffrey asked, "How do you spell *Temp?*" He wrote the letters as his mother spelled it for him. Jeffrey's card and envelope are shown in Figure 3.15a and 3.15b.

Going Beyond the Text

Arrange to visit with a family that has a preschooler, or visit a preschool or kinder-garten. Take a book and be prepared to tape-record your interaction as you share the story with the preschooler or kindergartner. Take some paper and markers or crayons and invite the child to draw and write about the story. Record what the child says while drawing and writing. Ask the child to write his or her name and everything else he or she can. Invite the child to read what he or she has written. Describe the child's knowledge of written language meanings, forms, meaning-form links, and functions.

REFERENCES

Abramson, S., Seda, I., & Johnson, C. (1990). Literacy development in a multilingual kindergarten classroom. *Childhood Education, 67,* 68–72.

Baghban, M. (1984). *Our daughter learns to read and write.* Newark, DE: International Reading Association.

Ballenger, C. (1999). *Teaching other people's children: Literacy and learning in a bilingual classroom.* New York: Teachers College Press.

Barone, D. (1999). *Resilient children: Stories of poverty, drug exposure, and literacy development.* Newark, DE: International Reading Association and National Reading Conference.

Bear, D., Invernizzi, M., Templeton, S., & Johnston, F. (2000). *Words their way: Word study for phonics, vocabulary, and spelling instruction* (2nd ed.). Upper Saddle River, NJ: Prentice-Hall.

Bloodgood, J. (1999). What's in a name? Children's name writing and name acquisition. *Reading Research Quarterly, 34,* 342–367.

Carle, E. (1969). *The very hungry caterpillar.* New York: Philomel.

Clay, M. M. (1975). *What did I write?* Auckland: Heinemann.

Cochran-Smith, M. (1984). *The making of a reader.* Norwood, NJ: Ablex.

Cox, B., Fang, Z. & Otto, B. (1997). Preschoolers' developing ownership of the literate register. *Reading Research Quarterly, 32,* 34–53.

Dickinson, D. (2001). Book reading in preschool class-rooms: Is recommended practice common? In

D. Dickinson & P. Tabors (Eds.), *Beginning literacy with language: Young children learning at home and school* (pp. 149–174). Baltimore, MD: Paul H. Brookes.

Dickinson, D., & Sprague, K. (2001). The nature and impact of early childhood care environments on the language and early literacy development of children from low-income families. In S. Neuman & D. Dickinson (Eds), *Handbook of early literacy research* (pp. 263–280). New York: Guilford.

Duke, N. K., & Hays, J. (1998). "Can I say 'Once upon a time'?": Kindergarten children developing knowledge of informational book language. *Early Childhood Research Quarterly, 13,* 295–318.

Duncan, P. (1996). *Some smug slug.* New York: HarperTrophy.

Dyson, A. H. (1982). The emergence of visible language: Interrelationships between drawing and early writing. *Visible Language, 16,* 360–381.

Ferreiro, E. (1986). The interplay between information and assimilation in beginning literacy. In W. H. Teale & E. Sulzby (Eds.), *Emergent literacy: Writing and reading* (pp. 15–49). Norwood, NJ: Ablex.

Ferreiro, E., & Teberosky, A. (1982). *Literacy before schooling.* Exeter, NH: Heinemann.

Galdone, P. (1986). *Three little kittens.* New York: Clarion.

Gee, J. (2001). A sociocultural perspective on early literacy development. In S. Neuman & D. Dickinson (Eds.), *Handbook of early literacy research* (pp. 30–42). New York: Guilford.

Goodman, Y. (1980). The roots of literacy. In M. Douglass (Ed.), *Claremont reading conference, 44th Yearbook* (pp. 1–32). Claremont, CA: Claremont Graduate School.

Gundlach, R., McLane, J. B., Scott, F. M., & McNamee, G. D. (1985). The social foundations of children's early writing development. In M. Farr (Ed.), *Advances in writing research: Vol. 1. Children's early writing development* (pp. 1–58). Norwood, NJ: Ablex.

Harste, J. C., Woodward, V. A., & Burke, C. L. (1984). *Language stories and literacy lessons.* Portsmouth, NH: Heinemann.

Hiebert, E. H. (1978). Preschool children's understanding of written language. *Child Development, 49,* 1231–1234.

Hildreth, G. (1936). Developmental sequences in name writing. *Child Development, 7,* 291–302.

International Reading Association & National Association for the Education of Young Children.

(1998). Learning to read and write: Developmentally appropriate practices for young children. *The Reading Teacher, 53,* 193–216.

Labbo, L. (1996). A semiotic analysis of young children's symbol making in a classroom computer center. *Reading Research Quarterly, 31,* 353–385.

Martinez, M. (1983). Exploring young children's comprehension during story time talk. *Language Arts, 60,* 202–209.

Martinez, M., & Teale, W. (1993). Teacher storybook reading style: A comparison of six teachers. *Research in the Teaching of English, 27,* 175–199.

Mayer, M. (1968). *There's a nightmare in my closet.* New York: Dial.

McGee, L., & Richgels, D. (1989). "K is Kristen's": Learning the alphabet from a child's perspective. *The Reading Teacher, 43,* 216–225.

Morgan, A. L. (1987). The development of written language awareness in Black preschool children. *Journal of Reading Behavior, 19,* 49–67.

Pappas, C. C. (1991). Fostering full access to literacy by including informational books. *Language Arts, 68,* 449–462.

Pappas, C. (1993). Is narrative "primary"? Some insights from kindergartners' pretend readings of stories and information books. *Journal of Reading Behavior, 25,* 97–129.

Pappas, C. C., & Pettegrew, B. S. (1998). The role of genre in the psycholinguistic guessing game of reading. *Language Arts, 75,* 36–44.

Purcell-Gates, V. (1996). Stories, coupons, and the "TV Guide": Relationships between home literacy experiences and emergent literacy knowledge. *Reading Research Quarterly, 31,* 406–428.

Reid, M. (1996). *Let's find out about ice cream.* New York: Scholastic.

Rowe, D. (1998). The literate potentials of book-related dramatic play. *Reading Research Quarterly, 33,* 10–35.

Schickedanz, J. (1999). *Much more than the ABCs: The early stages of reading and writing.* Washington, DC: National Association for the Education of Young Children.

Shine, S., & Roser, N. (1999). The role of genre in preschoolers' response to picture books. *Research in the Teaching of English, 34,* 197–251.

Smith, S., & Dixon, R. (1995). Literacy concepts of low- and middle-class four-year-olds entering preschool. *Journal of Educational Research, 88,* 243–253.

Smolkin, L., & Donovan, C. (2002). "Oh excellent, excellent question!": Developmental differences and comprehension acquisition. In C. Block &

M. Pressley (Eds.), *Comprehension instruction: Research-based best practices* (pp. 140–157). New York: Guilford.

Taylor, D., & Dorsey-Gaines, C. (1988). *Growing up literate: Learning from inner-city families.* Portsmouth, NH: Heinemann.

Tower, C. (2002). "It's a snake, you guys!": The power of text characteristics on children's responses to informational books. *Research in the Teaching of English, 37,* 55–88.

Ungerer, T. (1958). *Crictor.* New York: HarperCollins.

Voss, M. M. (1988). "Make way for applesauce": The literate world of a three year old. *Language Arts, 65,* 272–278.

Wildsmith, B. (1971). *The owl and the woodpecker.* Oxford: Oxford University Press.

Wildsmith, B. (1974). *Squirrels.* Oxford: Oxford University Press.

Wolf, S. A., & Heath, S. B. (1992). *The braid of literature: Children's worlds of reading.* Cambridge, MA: Harvard University Press.

From Five to Seven Years

Experimenting Readers and Writers

KEY CONCEPTS

experimenters
alphabetic writing system
phonics
breaking into print
word-by-word speech-to-
    print matching
literary syntax
metalinguistic awareness
concept of word
invented spelling
concept of word boundaries

mock cursive
stringing letters together
composing by dictation
alliteration
composing by copying
composing by spelling
alphabetic reading
sounding literate
scale of emergent readings
written-language-like talk
dialogue markers

being precise
finger-point reading
voice-to-print match
phoneme
phonemic awareness
relating letters to sounds
manner of articulation
identity of sound
letter name strategy
stages of spelling
    development

non-spelling
emergent spelling
early letter name-alphabetic
    spelling

middle letter name-alphabetic
    spelling
reading and writing to learn
    to read and write

writing to preserve specific
    messages
message concept

Who Are Experimenters?

Learning about written language is a gradual process, and it is not possible to identify absolute milestones. There is no single, great accomplishment that divides beginners and novices from the **experimenters** described in this chapter. A child may act like an experimenter one day and then go back to the ways of a novice for a while. A child may experiment in storyreading, but not yet in spelling. Good observers notice a combination of changes that together suggest that a child is dealing with written language in a new, experimental manner.

Experimenters' New Awareness

One of the most important changes in children as they become experimenters takes place in their *attitude.* Over a period of time, a careful observer can notice a new attitude that might be described as being more aware, thoughtful, tentative, and testing. Experimenters are aware that certain conventions are related to reading and writing. They know that readers and writers attend to print as they read and write, and that print governs what is read and written. But young experimenters know that they cannot do what conventional readers do; they have not yet worked out the puzzle of what exactly readers and writers are doing. However, *experimenters work hard at trying to figure out the conventions that enable conventional reading and writing.* They focus on trying to produce conventional readings of texts and conventionally written texts. In doing so, they work at understanding how the written language system works.

By experimenting with a variety of hypotheses about how written language works, how someone really reads or writes, experimenters eventually (and gradually) come to discover an important insight about conventional reading and writing—that readers read words and that words are composed of letters related to the sounds in spoken words. That is, experimenters eventually discover that the English written language system is an **alphabetic writing system.** They discover the principle of **phonics**—that letters in written words relate to sounds in spoken words.

As we shall see, experimenters' understanding about the relationships between sounds and letters is not the conventional understanding that more accomplished readers and writers hold. Experimenters only gradually become aware of the conventions related to written words and how the letters in words relate to the sounds in spoken words. Yet it is this gradual understanding about words and sound–letter relationships that moves experimenters from emergent reading and writing to the beginnings of conventional reading and writing. Experimenters also acquire new understandings about written language meaning and functions, which are discussed later in the chapter.

What is most important about experimenters, though, is what happens with forms and meaning-form links. Experimenters are **breaking into print;** their reading and writing attempts are influenced by print. Because early experimenters are aware of the shortcomings of such attempts, they are especially prone to frustration and feelings of inadequacy. They are likely to say, "I can't read" or "I don't want to write." Experimenters need understanding, support, and patience.

Experimenters may need adults' encouragement even when they do not finish a task. For example, they may work hard at how to represent the sounds in a single word of a longer message they wish to write, or they may work hard at reading a favorite storybook by concentrating on a single page, its pictures and print, and their memory of what adults have read on that page.

An important distinction between experimenters and more conventional readers and writers is that *experimenters usually concentrate on only one aspect of conventional reading and writing at a time.* Experimenters may want to write a conventional list (for example, when sending a birthday wish list to a grandparent) and refuse to invent spellings. Or, experimenters may look at a storybook page and laboriously try to puzzle out how to read individual words using sound–letter knowledge and ignoring the powerful meaning-making strategies they have been using for years.

The important thing to remember is that experimenters are trying out many pieces of the literacy puzzle and are experimenting with each one. It is an exciting process for both the children and those who support them. In this process, they gain important literacy knowledge that will be used later when they will be better able to put the pieces together.

Examples of Experimenters

Here are two examples of experimenters:

> Three-year-old Sophie listens to her uncle read a storybook. She directs his reading, "Read that. . . . Read that." She always points first to the left-hand page and then to the right-hand page. When they finish the book, Sophie begins pointing to individual words on a page and again says, "Read that. . . . Read that," this time for each word she points to. This pointing proceeds right to left, word by word, until Sophie's uncle has identified every word in a line.

> Five-year-old Ted has been sent to his room for misbehaving. He either does not remember or does not understand why he was sent there. With pencil and paper, he writes the message shown in Figure 4.1. He dashes out of his room, tosses this written query or protest on the floor before his mother, and runs back into his room.

FIGURE 4.1   Ted's Protest: "Mom, why are you punishing me? Ted"

Sophie knows left-to-right directionality for pages. More important, although she does not know left-to-right directionality for word reading, her careful pointing to words shows that she is able to identify word boundaries. She has a concept of written word. She explores the power of written words, the combinations of letters bordered by spaces, to evoke particular spoken words from a reader. Compared with novices, who may point to whole lines of text as representations of anything from a sentence to a word, Sophie has a much more precise **understanding of word-by-word speech-to-print matching.**

Ted's writing is a record not only of his query or protest, but also of his analysis of English words and their component sounds. He knows that he does not know the adult way to spell. At the time he wrote his protest, he often consulted an authority. However, when he was left to his own devices, he knew that he could get his words on paper if he thought about letter names and sounds in words. Compared with novices, who do not know about phonics, Ted has a very mature understanding of how writing works. Although his spelling is not conventional, he systematically pairs letters with sounds. His invented spellings show his knowledge of the alphabetic principle.

Ted's message contains other examples of experimenter traits. He does not always use sound–letter relations to spell. He has learned in school how to read and spell the word *you* conventionally. Unlike novices, experimenters often have school-gained literacy knowledge. They must integrate this with literacy knowledge that they are gaining concurrently from home literacy experiences and that they gained earlier in their lives as preschoolers and literacy novices.

Ted's message shows an intensity that is often characteristic of experimenters. He sometimes worked intensely, especially when a message was as important to him as this one was. Ted's query appears unfinished; he wrote nothing for the word *me.* It is unlikely that he knowingly wrote an incomplete message; perhaps the effort required for this writing task distracted him so much that he did not realize he had omitted a word.

Experimenting with Meaning

The meaning making of experimenters is only slightly more complex than that of novices. Novices and experimenters share a basic orientation toward written language that is one of novices' greatest achievements. Both write in order to communicate a message, and both engage in interactive storybook reading using sophisticated strategies for constructing meaning. Experimenters continue to use the meaning-making strategies they devised as novices.

For example, experimenters are likely to have a fully developed concept of story or story schema (see Chapter 2). They use their concept of story both to make sense of stories that are read aloud to them and as they compose their own stories. Later in this chapter we will describe experimenters' new attention to the literary properties of stories and informational texts. They have learned that written stories and informational books have certain language forms and word orders not found in spoken language. Experimenters are likely to use literary word order, or **literary syntax,** when composing and recalling stories, for example, "Away we went to grandmother's house."

The most striking new achievements of experimenters are related to their greater control over form and meaning-form links. However, in the face of their students' striking achievements with form and meaning-form links, teachers should not lose sight of the important fact that children do not experiment with form in a vacuum. Solving problems of form is not an exercise for its own sake. The meaning making learned as novices is the basis of all that experimenters do.

Experimenting with Forms

Experimenters go beyond novices' exploring of alphabet letter forms. They have considerable knowledge about letters; they can name most letters, write most letters with conventional formations, and recite the alphabet. Experimenters also have **metalinguistic awareness** of letters; they can talk and think about the names and properties of letters. Sarah, a kindergartner, wanted to write the *M* in *snowman.* Her classmate Jason told her, "*M.*" She asked, "Is that the up-down, up-down one?" Experimenters also show their **concept of word** in their reading and writing. They create a variety of texts using a variety of writing strategies.

Concept of Word

A fully developed concept of written words includes knowledge that they are composed of combinations of letters; that they have boundaries, spaces; and that they have particular letters related to the sounds in spoken words (Roberts, 1992). Experimenters acquire bits and pieces of this concept as they move forward in learning to read and write. They may invent words in their writing for others to read or ask about words others have written. As they read, they may work at recognizing combinations of letters and word boundaries, yet not understand that letters in words have a particular relationship to sounds in spoken words. As they write, they may segment words at syllable boundaries or spell words using sound–letter relationships.

One way children show their interest in words is by inventing words when they write. Figure 4.2 shows some writing that Kathy produced one day as she sat by herself in her room. When her mother asked her to read her writing, she replied, "It's just words." Notice that Kathy's writing is much like a novice's—we could not know the meaning Kathy intended to communicate unless we listened to Kathy read her writing (and, in this case, Kathy did not seem to intend to communicate a message).

Three aspects of Kathy's word inventing are typical of experimenters. First, she is experimenting with letter combinations to produce writing that she calls words. Second, she is experimenting with using spaces between letter combinations to signal boundaries between her words (we will discuss more about children's concepts of word boundaries later in this chapter). Third, Kathy seems to be paying attention to only one aspect of written language, words and how they look, and ignoring other aspects of written language, such as meaning.

Another way experimenters signal their interest in words is by asking questions about words. One day, Carrie's father was silently reading a typewritten letter. Carrie climbed onto his lap, pointed to a word in the letter that began with the letter

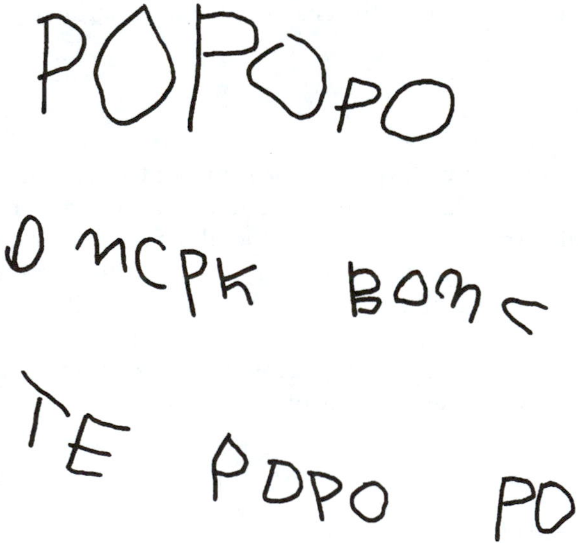

FIGURE 4.2   Kathy's Invented Words

C, and asked what it was. When told that the word was *concern,* she replied, "Oh. It has a *C* like my name." Carrie had noted that the word *concern* was something like her name. Both were composites of letters and both began with a *C.* Carrie then asked, "What's that word?" about several other words in the letter.

Children also signal their attention to words by attempting to write words in which some of the letters in the word capture some of the sounds in spoken words. This process is known as **invented spelling** (Read, 1971) (we will devote considerable attention to this topic later in the chapter). For example, in a story about dinosaurs, Meagan, a kindergartner, wrote Vknl for *volcano.*

Concept of Word Boundaries

As children become aware that words in spoken and written language can be segmented, they develop a **concept of word boundaries.** In conventional writing, we use spaces to show boundaries between individually printed words. Experimenters begin to respond to individual words in environmental print and in books, and they experiment with ways to show the boundaries between words in their own writing. In the example at the beginning of this chapter, Sophie pointed to and asked about individual words in the storybook her uncle read to her. Kathy (see Figure 4.2) used spaces between her invented words, but Paul used dots between words, for example: PAULZ•HOS•PLANF•ELD•VRMAT (Paul's house, Plainfield, Vermont) (Bissex, 1980, p. 22). His dot between PLANF and ELD also shows his awareness of syllables within words; another time he wrote TAL.A.FON for *telephone* (p. 23). A child's writing of the Spanish word *estaba* as *es taba* provides another example of segmenting written words at syllable boundaries (Edelsky, 1982, p. 216).

Other children circle words, put them in vertical arrangements, or even separate them with carefully drawn and blackened squares (Harste, Burke, & Woodward, 1983; Temple, Nathan, Temple, & Burris, 1993).

Figures 4.3 and 4.4 show the ways that two kindergartners separated words in their writing on their sign-in sheets in the middle of November. In addition to writing their own names on their personal sign-in sheets, they followed the current fashion in their classroom: They also wrote their classmates' names, usually by copying from one another's name collars. Eric included Jeff's last name and Tara's last name initial, and he copied Thanksgiving words posted in the room (*turkey, Mayflower, feast*). During the calendar activity at the beginning of the day, he wrote *53* for the 53rd day of school and *15* for November 15. He used vertical lines to separate some, but not all, of his words. Jeff included his own and Freddy's last names and many classmates' last name initials. He also wrote a weather word (*sunny*) during the weather reporting activity at the beginning of the day and *54* for the 54th day of school. He used dashes to separate his entries on his sign-in sheet. Figure 4.5 shows the writing at the same time of year of another kindergartner in this class, Erin. Using a small clipboard, she wrote this list of members of her family while playing in the Housekeeping Center. She circled all but one of her words.

My Sign In Sheet   5.3 15

by: Erica Nokey mary flowera
Jeff
[Last Name] F adst Erin Nicole Taras
Debotoh Alyssa Sdo n Ian

FIGURE 4.3   Eric's Sign-in Writing
with Vertical Lines between Words

My Sign In Sheet   5 4

by: Jeff [Last name and year]

Jason-Eric Nathan H
IANM-Matram
Zack F Elizabeth
Freddy [Last Name]-Tara-steye
Alyssap Gynn
Erri92-4N50
99

FIGURE 4.4   Jeff's Sign-in Writing with Dashes
between Words

FIGURE 4.5   Erin's
Dramatic Play Writing
with Circles around
Words

Texts

Another question of form that young children try to answer during the experimenting stage is, "How do whole written language products look?" They are concerned not only with such components of written language products as words and collections of words, but also with the overall organizational features of different kinds of writing.

Even novices are aware of several text formats when they play with writing in different contexts for various purposes. Chapter 3 included several examples of novices' greeting cards, lists, and stories. Experimenters continue to be interested in a variety of text forms.

The texts that experimenters create usually look more conventional than those produced by novices. Experimenters generate a greater variety of texts as well. There are several reasons for the differences between these two types of writers. Experimenters are more likely to ask for an adult's assistance in constructing their messages because they are aware that they cannot yet produce a readable message on their own. Experimenters also continue to have exposure to a wide variety of texts. Carrie explained that she made the chart shown in Figure 4.6 to keep track of when her parents were nice to her; just at this time, they had made a similar chart to encourage her good table manners (see Figure 4.7).

Like novices, experimenters are interested in writing stories and other kinds of literary texts, such as poems and letters. They write in a variety of ways.

Although it sounds paradoxical (because even novices are willing to write stories), we would expect some experimenters to refuse initially to write a story. Those who refuse are comparing easy writing tasks that they can do well, such as

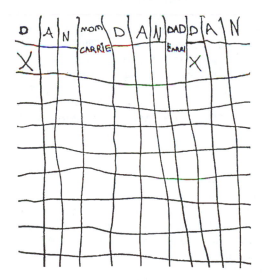

FIGURE 4.6   Carrie's Chart

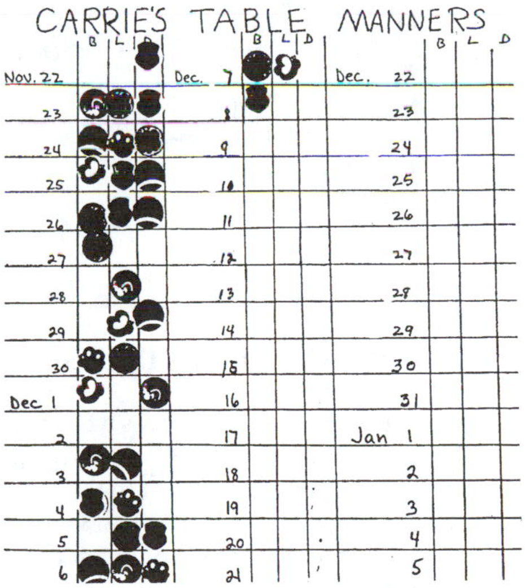

FIGURE 4.7   Good Manners Chart

writing their names, with the more difficult task of writing a story, and they are saying in effect, "I can't do *that!*" This kind of refusal implies some knowledge of what *that* entails. It is not the outright refusal of a beginner. Rather, they know that stories have many more words than they could hope to write on their own.

Eventually, most experimenters can be encouraged to try writing a story, especially if they know that adults will be satisfied with less than a complete story. Then they will take up paper and pencil with the intention of writing a story. This behavior is an example of experimenters' new awareness that we described at the beginning of this chapter.

Experimenters often compose by writing in **mock cursive** or by **stringing letters together** and telling a story as they write. Figure 4.8 presents a story Marianne wrote about seeing a zebra at the zoo.

Figure 4.9 shows another way experimenters **compose—by dictation.** This is a story that Kaitlynn, a kindergartner, dictated to her mother. The story has some

OTOBR

MARIAHhE
ATRREISEErYdoohAsA
AbcdEfGhiUKLMhoPo
ILOVE MMMAIAMAmA

Once upon a time I went to the zoo and saw a zebra. Then I yelled, "Yeah," because I never saw a zebra before. He licked me on the hand. Then I said, "Mom and Dad, look. Sister, look" Then we went home. The end.

FIGURE 4.8   Marianne's Story

FIGURE 4.9   Kaitlynn's Dictated Story

Once upon a time there was a bear who lived in the forest, and his name was Fluffy Bear. His parents went to New York City, so he went out at night to try to catch foxes. He crossed the river to get to the foxes' cave. He met the foxes' family. He was invited to stay for dinner. Mr. Fox showed Fluffy Bear the way home through the forest. When he got home, he drank some milk and played a game. Then he read a story before he went to bed. He woke up when his parents were home.

unity in that it is about events in the day of a main character, Fluffy Bear, but actu-ally, there are two temporally ordered sequences of events. One is the parents' departure, Fluffy Bear's adventures, and the parents' return; the other is Fluffy Bear's dinner, snack and game, bedtime story, and going to sleep.

Kaitlynn shows some sophistication in her story dictation in that she weaves together these two sequences—one exotic with its bears and foxes and caves, the other familiar, with its meals and bedtime activities. Kaitlynn shifts her attitude toward foxes. At first, they are objects of a hunt; Fluffy Bear sets out to catch them. Then they are friendly hosts and guides.

This shift may be because Kaitlynn needs a means of connecting her two sequences. By making the fox family friendly, she can introduce the commonplace event of dinner, and by having Mr. Fox return Fluffy Bear to his home, Fluffy Bear can experience additional commonplace events that usually take place only there, such as bedtime. Another possible explanation for Kaitlynn's shift in attitude about foxes is that Kaitlynn's teacher had recently read two versions of the story of *Goldilocks and the Three Bears* to Kaitlynn's class. In that story, of course, an animal family is shown from two perspectives. At first, the three bears seem to be a typical family, living in a home, owning tables and chairs and beds, preparing a meal, and going for a walk; then, when Goldilocks is wakened by them, she sees them as threatening. Thus, Kaitlynn's storywriting by dictation makes use of both her per-sonal experiences (parents' absences and returns, dinners, bedtimes) and her liter-ary experiences (animal families that can be both friendly and frightening).

Children sometimes dictate literary texts other than stories. Jeffrey dictated a poem to his mother as he ran back and forth across his patio.

> ***The Running Poem***
> *Bubble gun boppers,*
> *Candy heart sneakers,*
> *Sparky love.*
> *Buster slimers,*
> *Booger man,*
> *Barbecue pit.*
> *Blue ribbons win.*
> *The end.*

While the content of Jeffrey's poem relates to what he was doing (running) and seeing (his sneakers, the barbecue pit, and the family dog, Sparky), it also shows Jeffrey's understandings of the conventions of poetry forms. His poem con-sisted of phrases rather than sentences, and he used **alliteration**—five lines of his poem start with words beginning with the sound /b/. It is interesting that Jeffrey ended his poem with "The end," which is the formulaic ending for a story rather than a poem. Still, his poem demonstrates Jeffrey's experimentation with language forms associated with poetry.

Experimenters also **compose by copying.** Figure 4.10 shows a journal entry that Eric (a different Eric from the author of Figure 4.3) composed on the day that chicks hatched in his kindergarten class's incubator. He copied verbatim from *Inside*

Finally the shell
breaks in two
pieces, and the
chick hatches.

FIGURE 4.10   Eric's Copied Journal Entry

an Egg (Johnson, 1982), one of the informational books his teacher had collected for the chick hatching unit. It was an exciting day in Eric's classroom. His careful, time-consuming copying demonstrates the willingness of experimenters to concentrate on literacy tasks and devote considerable energy to their constructions.

As shown in Figure 4.11, children may **compose by spelling.** Ashley drew a picture and then asked her mother to help her spell. Her mother insisted, "If you write it, I'll be able to read it." Ashley said very slowly, "Nora," and wrote the letter *N*; then she said "flies," and wrote the letter *F*; and last she said "kites," and wrote the letter *k*. She wrote ASH and said, "That is my nickname, and here is my real name," (she wrote ASHLEY). Ashley's story was very primitive—she introduced a character and told one thing the character does. However, she listened to

FIGURE 4.11   "Nora Flies Kites"

the spoken words she wanted to write and captured the initial sound of each word in her spelling. Notice that her arrangement of letters was not linear, written in left-to-right order; rather, it seems that Ashley let go of her more sophisticated knowledge about story meanings and the linearity concept in the effort of listening to sounds as she was spelling. This is a good example of experimenters' inability to control all aspects of written language as they experiment with a small part of the written language puzzle.

It is important to keep in mind that experimenters use some of the same conventions as more conventional readers and writers. We tend to think of children at this stage as not yet being very knowledgeable about written language. Even when we are accepting and supportive, what usually catches our attention in children's experimental products are their mistakes. However, there is much that is correct in their products, even by conventional standards.

Experimenting with Meaning-Form Links

Discovering the essentials of how meanings and forms are linked in an alphabetic writing system is the main work of experimenters. It is the achievement that most clearly sets them apart from novices and puts them on the path to conventional reading and writing. In Chapter 3, we saw that novices' ways of linking form and meaning often are limited by their dependence on context, and that novices lack understanding of sound–letter relations. Experimenters' attention to print is much more purposeful than is novices'. Not only do they know that print is important, but they begin to discover how it works—that the alphabetic principle is at the core of the relation between print and meaning.

In their writing, experimenters develop two important kinds of awareness: awareness that their written messages are permanent and stable (they and others can return to them to retrieve their meanings) and awareness of phonemes, the units of sound from which words are built and to which letters are systematically matched. They move from writing by dictating stories, using booklike language, to writing with invented spelling.

Experimenters' writing and reading discoveries interact. For example, phonemic awareness practiced and enhanced during invented spelling is put to use in **alphabetic reading.**

Sounding Literate

One method that children use to link meaning and form might be stated: "Use special words and special combinations of words when you write or read. Everyday conversational talk will not do." Acquiring this special talk is related to experimentation with text forms, such as stories and poems. Examples of special talk include children's use of "Once upon a time" and their use of past tense in stories they tell or write.

Experimenting readers use **sounding literate** when they pretend to read favorite books (Cox, Fang, & Otto, 1997). Recall from Chapter 3 that early emergent reading consists of labeling parts of the illustrations or actions of the characters or telling a story that matches the illustrations. The stories that novices tell in their emergent readings usually do not closely match the words in the text. In contrast, experimenters' emergent readings of favorite storybooks not only closely resemble the words in the text, but even come to be influenced by print. At first, of course, experimenters do not watch print while they read. However, compared to novices, experimenters' emergent readings include much more of the language of the text. Eventually experimenters' emergent readings may be verbatim recreations of the text. Several significant developments fall between these approaches to reading.

Approaches to Pretend Reading.   Sulzby (1985) has documented a developmental **scale of emergent readings** in young children's pretend readings of favorite storybooks. This scale is summarized in Table 4.1, with examples from the descriptions that follow.

Kindergartners were asked to chose a favorite storybook from their classroom collection of storybooks and to read it or pretend to read it to a researcher. Sulzby made several distinctions in the ways children performed this task. A major distinction was that some performances were influenced primarily by the illustrations, others primarily by the text. Sulzby found that when children know they must respond to the text, some simply refuse to read. Others read selectively; they recognize some words and read only those. Still others may read connected text, either making the errors we might expect of a beginner (relying too

---

TABLE 4.1   Types of Storybook Reading

Influenced by Illustrations
- Oral Language-Like (Beginners and Novices)
  - Collections of labels and comments (e.g., "House. Flowers. He's the baby.")
  - Everyday Storytelling (e.g., "There was three bears and . . . and . . . and. . . .")
- Written Language-Like (but not paying attention to the print)
  - Mixed Storyreading and Storytelling (Novices) (e.g., "There was three bears . . . and . . . and . . . tiniest voice of all.")
  - Reading in a Manner Similar to the Original Story (Experimenters) (see Figure 4.12)

- Verbatim Recreation of the Text (Experimenters) (e.g., "Papa bear pounded nails in the roof.")

Influenced by Text (all are written language-like and come from paying attention to the print)

- Refusing (Experimenters) ("I don't know how to read.")
- Selective Reading (Experimenters) ("In. The. The. Baby. Did. On. The.")
- Connected-text Reading (Experimenters and Conventional Readers) ("Papa Bear, put n-n-n-ah-eye-lz, in the rrr-oh-ff, the roaf?" or "Papa bear pounded nails in the roof.")

Adapted from Sulzby (1985).

much on sounding out unknown words, relying too much on predictions based on meanings, omitting too many words, or too often substituting similar words) or reading much like an adult, with fluency and comprehension. The last type, fluent reading, is beyond what experimenters do.

The left column of Figure 4.12 describes the picture and reproduces the text from two facing pages of *The Three Bears* (1952). Suppose this book is familiar to several children who know enough about reading that they pay attention to the print, and suppose we ask them to read. They might just say, "I don't know how." (Note that this refusal is print-related; it comes from children's looking at the words and knowing they can't read them. There are other kinds of refusals, such as a child's unwillingness to take on any kind of storybook reading, even without having looked at the print.) Selective readers might read, "In. The. The. Baby. Did. On. The." Connected-text readers might read, "Papa Bear, put n-n-n-ah-eye-lz, in the rrr-oh-ff, the roaf?" or might even read correctly, "Papa bear pounded nails in the roof."

Sulzby also describes pretend storybook readings when children sound as if they are reading, but they are not paying attention to the print. Although these pretend reading performances now fall into the category of being influenced primarily by the illustrations, they nonetheless resemble print-influenced readings in an important way: The readers' language is similar to the language of books, maybe even to the language of the very books the children have chosen.

Sulzby described three types of these written-language–like readings while not paying attention to the print. First, children's intonation and choice of words may make them sound as if they are telling a story rather than reading it, but they may occasionally insert words that are more typically found in books than in talk;

FIGURE 4.12   Carrie's Emergent Reading

Text	Reading
(From second and third pages. The illustration shows Mama Bear and Baby Bear in the foreground. She is watering tulips. He and a rabbit are doing handstands while a little bird watches. In the background Papa Bear is on the ladder repairing the roof of their house.)	(In an even voice, at a steady pace, until the end, when her voice rises.)
Papa Bear pounded nails in the roof. Mama Bear watered the flowers. Baby Bear did tricks on the lawn.	"And Papa nailed the roof. Mama—Mama watered the flowers. And Baby Bear did tricks on the lawn."
	(Short pause. Laughter. Then in higher pitch, with rising and falling intonation, and faster pace.)
	"The bird's just watching!"

Sulzby called this mixing *storyreading and storytelling*. For *The Three Bears* excerpt in the left column of Figure 4.12, for example, a child might read, "There was three bears living in the woods and there was a mama and a dad and a baby and he had a big voice and she had a medium voice and the baby had the tiniest voice of all." Most of that sentence is the sort of informal recalling a child might provide after watching a movie or television show. It includes run-ons ("and . . . and . . . and . . . "), carelessness about subject-verb agreement ("There was three" instead of "There were three"), and imprecise use of pronouns ("he" coming after "baby" but referring back to "dad"). This pretend storybook reading is not dependent on what is shown in the illustration. At the very end, however, the child slips into written-language-like vocabulary and phrasing ("the tiniest voice of all").

A second type of these written-language–like readings while not paying attention to the print is a pretend reading that is closer to what is on the page than with the first type. It depends more on what is shown in the illustration. It is more patterned; pretend readers may use repetition in ways that the author of the book does. Now pretend readers use reading intonation; their performance as a whole sounds literate. Their pauses, pitches, and stress patterns are those of a reading rather than a casual telling. Sulzby called this *reading in a manner similar to the original story*.

The Three Bears was a favorite book of Carrie's. The right column of Figure 4.12 shows how she read it to her father. Her reading is an example of reading in a manner similar to the original story. It is contextualized; she is bound by what is shown in the picture, which includes elements not usually found in *The Three Bears* story: Papa Bear's repairing the roof, Mama Bear's watering the flowers, and Baby Bear's doing tricks on the lawn. There are three important indications that Carrie's is a written-language-like performance. She uses unique vocabulary, past tense verbs, and reading-like intonation. An example of unique vocabulary is her re-creation of the book's odd description of Papa Bear's behavior. Both the book and Carrie describe him not as repairing the roof or fixing the roof, but as pounding nails in the roof! What convinces a listener of the significance of the verb tense and intonation in Carrie's pretend reading is the contrast between that and what she does when she merely talks with her father. Her shift to conversing with him about a part of the illustration that she finds charming ("The bird's just watching") is marked by present tense and more varied and faster intonation.

The third type of written-language–like reading while not paying attention to the print is a verbatim re-creation of the text. Readers reproduce whole chunks of the text, word-for-word. Adults sometimes dismiss such a performance as "just memorization." This ignores important achievements, including the child's making a fundamental meaning-form link. For the excerpt from *The Three Bears* shown in Figure 4.12, a child may have heard the story read so many times (these are pretend readings of *favorite* storybooks), that seeing the illustration is all that is needed to stimulate the child's memory for the words that are always paired with that illustration. The meaningfulness of those words is demonstrated by the child's pairing them with the illustration and using appropriate intonation. Often a listener can interrupt a verbatim pretend reading to elicit conversation that further demonstrates the reader's understanding of that part of the story.

In addition to all these types of pretend readings, Sulzby describes those that are not like written language at all. These oral-language–like readings may be similar to the mixed storyreading and storytelling described earlier ("There was three bears . . . and . . . and . . . ") but without ever using such written-language-like expressions as "the tiniest voice of all." Or, they may digress even more from the text by being merely collections of discrete labels of or comments about what is shown in the picture, without any re-creation of the story line or use of story structure. For example, reading *The Three Bears* excerpt in Figure 4.12, a child may say, "House. Flowers. He's the baby." These are the storybook performances of beginners and novices as described in Chapters 2 and 3.

Sounding Literate in Writing.   Experimenting writers also use special **written-language-like talk** in their dictated stories and in the stories they write on their own. Recall the story Marianne wrote using letter strings (see Figure 4.8). She read that story as follows:

> Once upon a time I went to the zoo and saw a zebra. Then I yelled, "Yeah," because I never saw a zebra before. He licked me on the hand. Then I said, "Mom and Dad, look. Sister, look." Then we went home. The end.

What is noteworthy about Marianne's story is her use of specialized language found only in written stories and not in spoken language. In everyday speech Marianne would not call her sister "Sister." She likely would not use the **dialogue markers** "I yelled" and "I said" in such a careful, repetitive-yet-varied way. She also would not have included the formulaic literary language used to open and close stories—"Once upon a time" and "The end." Marianne shows that she is experimenting with the special kinds of language forms unique to written stories.

Experimenters know that dictating a story is different from telling a story. They are aware that they are authors. They do not speak in order to communicate with or to entertain their scribe. Instead, they communicate with unknown, non-present future readers. Recall Kaitlynn's dictated story (see Figure 4.9). It shows an experimenter's attention to the literary language and forms found in written stories.

Being Precise

A second way in which children link meaning and form might be stated: "Be precise about which words you (or your scribe) write and about which words you read back from your writing (or from someone else's). Only the words that the author formulated while writing may be read when the author or someone else reads what was written." In other words, reading is different than telling.

Being precise in reading begins as experimenting readers track print in order to capture the story text nearly verbatim. They not only have learned the language of the text (as when they sound literate), but also can match the text language to the exact page of the storybook. Thus, being precise leads to another kind of matching, finger-point reading. **Finger-point reading** is when children say a word from the story while pointing to a word in the printed text (Ehri & Sweet, 1991; Morris, 1993); it is also called **voice-to-print match.** At first, finger-point reading may not be completely accurate. For example, children may match a spoken syllable with a written word (see page 24). Eventually (as their concepts of spoken and written words and their perceptions of word boundaries mature), children begin to match each spoken word with a written word as they pretend read. Children who are accurate finger-point readers are not yet conventionally reading, but they are watching the print and coordinating what they say with the printed text.

Children may also demonstrate precision in writing. They reveal this by the way they attempt to reread their own writing. Figure 4.13 presents a Father's Day card that four-year-old Brooke composed. On the front of her card she drew a bird and some flowers. On the inside she wrote nine letters: *R, A, Y, g, P, G, O, G,* and *I.* Afterward, she read her writing to her mother, pointing to the first five letters one at a time: "I/ love/ you/ dad/ dy." Then she paused for a few moments and pointed at the remaining four letters one at a time, reading, "ver/ y/ much/ too." Brooke is being precise by carefully matching each letter of her writing with a segment of her spoken message (in this case, a syllable).

Using Sound–Letter Relationships

Experimenters also link meaning with written form through the use of sound–letter relationships in their spellings and emergent readings. Preschool experimenters may gain this knowledge from experiences with text and feedback from supportive adults. For example, a child whose parent frequently reads a book of nursery rhymes may notice that both *Jack* and *Jill* start with the letter *J* and that both words and the letter's name start with /j/ (see Table 1.2 for phoneme symbols). When the child comments about this and the parent acknowledges and confirms this, the child is gaining phonics knowledge. School-age experimenters may gain and consolidate such knowledge from both indirect (Dahl, Scharer, Lawson, & Grogan, 1999) and explicit (McIntyre & Freppon, 1994) phonics instruction.

FIGURE 4.13   Brooke's Father's Day Card

We have provided some examples of children who invent spellings—children who look for systematic relationships between sounds and letters. For example, Ted spelled *why* with a *y* and *punishing* as PNShAn (see Figure 4.1), and Ashley spelled *Nora* with an *N* (see Figure 4.11). It may appear that experimenters are using the relationships between sounds and letters just as more conventional readers and writers do, but this is not always the case.

A System Based on Phonemic Awareness

In order to spell, writers need a system: they need a rather precise, analytic understanding of the relationship between spoken and written language; they need the ability to examine words one sound unit at a time; and they need an awareness of some kind of relationship between spoken sounds and letters. What this means is that young writers must first be able to segment their spoken message into its component parts—words. Then spellers must further segment words into smaller parts—eventually, into phonemes. A **phoneme** is a unit of sound (e.g., /t/, /a/, /n/, /i/, /th/, and /ng/) that can contrast with another unit of sound when such units are combined to make words (e.g., *tan* vs. *tin*, *tin* vs. *thin*, *thin* vs. *thing*). In conventional spelling, phonemes are associated with single letters—such as *t, a, n,*—or with letter combinations—such as *th* or *ng*. Hence teachers call /t/ the "T sound" or /th/ the "T-H sound."

Early inventive spellers do not usually pronounce single phonemes one at a time; this is a later-developing ability. Instead, they may pronounce a multisyllable word one syllable at a time. Even in these cases, however, their spelling efforts begin with paying attention to part of that syllable, often the first part, that is, the first phoneme. Then spellers must decide which letter to use to represent that phoneme. This is a long and complicated process that involves a great deal of conscious attention.

The process of attending to phonemes is part of the phonological awareness we described in Chapter 3. Phonological awareness includes attention to all aspects of the sounds of a language. One of those aspects is phonemes. Paying attention to phonemes, **phonemic awareness,** is most developed when a person can segment a word into each and every one of its phonemes, for example, segmenting the word *tan* into /t/, /a/ and /n/. This most developed kind of phonemic awareness only gradually emerges.

Invented spelling is phonemic awareness in action (Richgels, 2001). Kristen's first spellings provide a case in point. She announced that she could spell and looked around the room for things to spell. She said, "I can spell phone," and repeated the word to herself, saying it slowly, stretching out the initial /f/, "Ffffone, phone. I know—it's spelled *V.*" Then she looked around again and said, "I can spell window, too." Again she slowly repeated the word, stretching out the initial /w/, "Wwwwindow. Window is *Y.*"

Kristen's spellings are not conventional, but they have the characteristics of true spelling; they are systematic, and they demonstrate phonemic awareness. Using only one letter to spell each word is consistent with not pronouncing each phoneme of a word one at a time. She pronounced a whole word and paid attention to the first phoneme in that word. She was not doing the complete phoneme-by-phoneme analysis that demonstrates the most developed form of phonemic awareness, but her attention to each word was at the level of the phoneme.

Ways of Relating Sounds and Letters

Once children can segment smaller-than-a-word sound units, they must also have a way to **relate letters to the sounds** they segment. While attending to the phonemes at the beginnings of *phone* and *window,* Kristen used two clues for choosing an appropriate letter for spelling: **manner of articulation** and identity of sound. Manner of articulation is the placement of the mouth, tongue, and teeth when speaking. Kristen noticed that her upper teeth were touching her lower lip both when she started to say the word *phone* and when she started to say the name of the letter *V.*

With *window* and *Y*, there is another possible explanation of Kristen's spelling. She may have used **identity of sound.** Both *window* and the name of the letter *Y* start with /w/ (the letter name *Y* is made up of two phonemes /w/ and /I/). Spellers can use the phonemes in the letter names and associate them with the phonemes in the spoken words they wish to spell. Ashley did this when she linked the phoneme /k/ in the letter name *K* with the phoneme /k/ in the word *kite* (see Figure 4.11).

Ted's spelling of the word *why* with a *Y* shows another way of linking letters and sounds—using the name of the letter to represent a word or a sound segment in a word that sounds like the letter's name. This is called the **letter name strategy.**

Meagan, a kindergartner, used the same strategy when she wrote r for *are* in a journal entry on May 17: chicks r ranein for *Chicks are running.* Likewise, her classmate Nicole, on March 8, wrote a Z for the middle syllable of *museum* in a story about a dinosaur skeleton display: MZM / TyRANNOSAURUS / RX ZR U a Q PPO [with backwards Zs] for *Museum. Tyrannosaurus Rex. There was a lot of people.*

Figure 4.14 shows the storywriting of three of Megan's and Nicole's classmates' on March 23 of their kindergarten year. Like Nicole, they wrote in story folders, which are manila file folders that open to show a picture, and beneath it the words *Once upon a time* and a space for writing a story to go with the picture. The story folders are laminated and kindergartners write with erasable marker pens. The teacher makes photocopies of students' stories for them to keep and then wipes the folders clean so they can be reused by other kindergarten authors. The first story was written to accompany a picture of a girl hugging a woman, the second story to accompany a picture of a rabbit, and the third story to accompany a picture of two girls holding bouquets of daisies. All three stories are within the range of writing products we would expect of kindergartners two-thirds of the way through the school year. All three authors used invented spelling. However, there are noticeable differences in the spelling strategies that these kindergartners employed.

The first story (A G G N G B for *A girl jumped on Grandma's back.*) is composed of one letter per word. The author's spelling choices are systematic. She

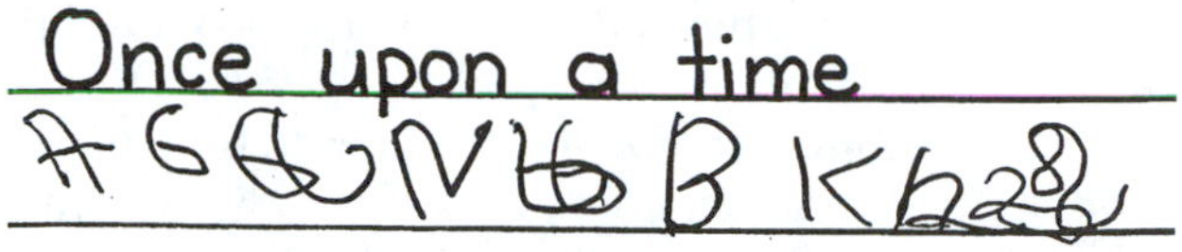

Once upon a time

A G ꝏ N ꝶ B K b2&

A girl jumped on Grandma's back. (Followed by the author's middle and last name initials beginning with K)

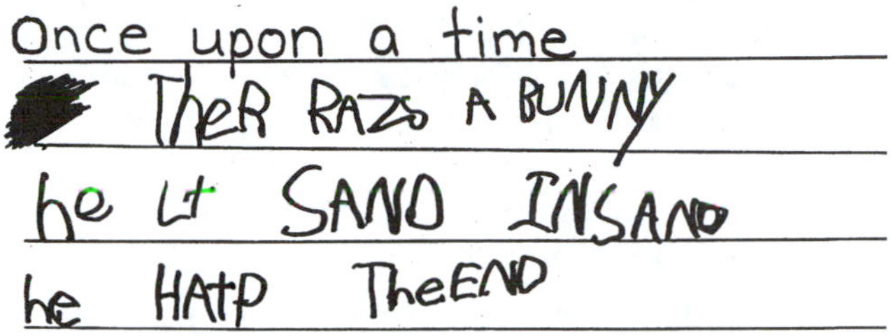

Once upon a time

TheR RAZs A BUNNy

he Lt SAND INSAND

he HAtP TheEND

There was a bunny.
He liked spring. In spring
he hops. The End

Once upon a time

2 GiLS SLNUN.FIiLRS

SeDRA♡ eTh iF TreiAn

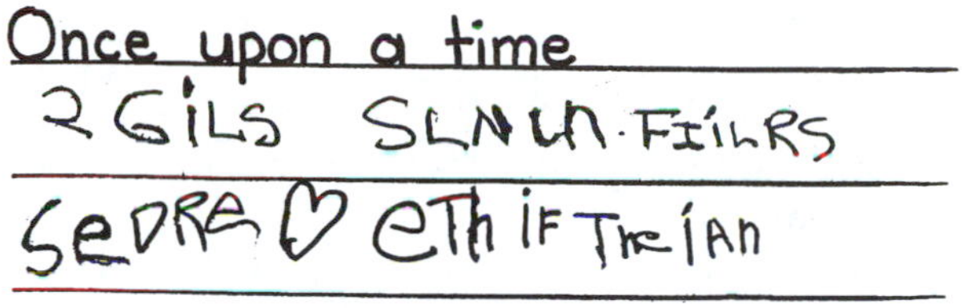

Two girls smelling flowers.
Sister love each of them.

FIGURE 4.14   Story Folder Writing by Three Kindergartners

uses the letter name strategy for the first word, pronounced "aye" like the name of the letter she chooses. Many of her choices are governed by identity of the target sound and a sound in the name of a letter: a letter *G* for the word *jumped* (the name of the letter *G* and the word *jump* both start with /j/), an *N* for the word *in* (the name of the letter *N* and the word *in* both end with /n/), and a *B* for the word *back* (the name of the letter *B* and the word *back* both start with /b/). Twice she uses *G* for /g/ although that sound is not in that letter's name; she knows the conventional /g/-*G* sound–letter correspondence. Although this kindergartner can write her whole first name, she chooses to continue using an initial-letter spelling strategy for writing her name. The *K* for her first name is clear; the remaining two characters are her middle and last name initials as she imagines them to look in cursive.

The second story (TheR RAZS A BUNNy / he Lt SAND INSAND / he HAtP TheEND for *There was a bunny. He liked spring. In spring he hops. The end.*) has discernable spaces between words, except between the two words for *in spring* and the two words for *The end.* The author uses at least two letters per word. He knows that some words require even more letters; the familiar word *and* seems to be a filler for word parts that he can not spell. The spelling for *bunny* was given to him. He routinely uses knowledge of sound–letter correspondences for many other spellings, notably the endings of *there* (TheR), *was* (RAZS), *liked* (Lt), and *hop* (HAtP) (though his spelling omits the final sound of the word as he reads it, "hops"). He uses correct vowel letters for words that are familiar to him: *he, the,* and *end.*

The spelling in the third story (2 GiLS SLNin FliLRS / SeDRE ❤ eTh iF TheiAn for *Two girls smelling flowers. Sister love each of them.*) is even more complete, though still unconventional. The author is willing to use shorthand when possible, a numeral for *two* and a heart for *love,* but most of her spellings are quite ambitious, with an attempt to represent *-ing* (in) in *smelling* and *-er* (RE) in *sister.* Her spellings of *sister* and *of* show attention to manner of articulation; pronunciations of /i/ and the letter name *E,* /uh/ and the letter name *I,* and /v/ and the ending sound in the letter name *F* are very similar. She uses a letter name strategy for the first sound in *each* (eTh). She seems aware of the special nature of the *th* combination of letters; she uses it for two different digraphs, /ch/ in *each* (eTh) and /TH/ in *them* (TheiAn).

Stages of Spelling Development

These examples from Figure 4.14 suggest two hypotheses. First, although none of these kindergarten authors is a conventional speller, all three spell systematically. They know what spelling is supposed to accomplish, that it is an alphabetic code that matches sounds with letters with the goal of enabling readers to retrieve writers' words. Second, invented spelling seems to progress through stages, with the end point being conventional spelling. Each step represented in Figure 4.14 is toward more conventional spelling. Inventive spellers seem to understand not only that they must be systematic, but that they must experiment until they are systematic in the same way that grown-ups are. Then their invented systems will give way to the conventional system.

Research supports these hypotheses, documenting **stages of spelling development,** from invented to conventional (Templeton & Morris, 2000; Templeton, 2003). Table 4.2 describes four stages in that progression. The progression is based on a similar scheme described by Bear, Invernizzi, Templeton, & Johnston (2000), who in turn built on the earlier work of Read (1971) and of Henderson and his students (e.g., Beers & Henderson, 1977; Gentry, 1978; Morris, 1981; Zutell, 1978). The four stages are labeled non-spelling (because it may not even involve letters and is random, not systematic), emergent spelling, early letter name-alphabetic spelling, and middle letter name-alphabetic spelling (for later stages, beginning with late letter name-alphabetic spelling, see Chapter 5).

The first stage, **non-spelling,** is what novices do. They write mock cursive or letter strings to stand for messages (contextually dependent writing). This activity reflects novices' fixation with letters. This stage is primarily characterized by a lack of awareness of sound–letter correspondences. Non-spellers choose letters ran-

TABLE 4.2 Stages of Spelling Development

Non-Spelling (consistent with Bear, Invernizzi, Templeton, & Johnston's, 2000, Early Emergent Spelling and Middle Emergent Spelling) (see Figure 3.8 for an example)

- Uses drawing and writing together, at first interchangeably, later distinguishing between drawing and writing
- Arranges marks horizontally
- Uses letter-like forms

Emergent Spelling (consistent with Bear, Invernizzi, Templeton, & Johnston's, 2000, Late Emergent Spelling)

- Consistently uses left-to-right directionality
- Demonstrates concept of word, but may not always use spaces between words
- Writes some letters of the alphabet
- Occasionally uses sound–letter correspondences or memorized spellings of common words

    Example (from McGee & Richgels, in press):
    MfRETfR - TZRDEfR - KHCDR for *My favorite ride is the roller coaster.*

Early Letter Name-Alphabetic Spelling*

- Writes most letters of the alphabet
- Routinely uses sound–letter correspondences (e.g., MZM for *museum*, FET for *feet*)
- Routinely represents beginning consonants (e.g., T for *telephone*, L for *ladder*)

- Represents some ending consonants (e.g., n for *in*, Tr for *tiger*, SK for *sock*, BD for *bird*, Ht for *hot*)
- Only partially represents consonant blends and digraphs (e.g., BEG for *bridge*, PN for *playing*, pat for *plant*, SID for *slide*, CKS for *chicks*)
- Occasionally represents short vowel sounds using similar articulation of vowel's letter name (e.g., BEG for *bridge*)
- Occasionally represents long vowel sounds using letter whose name is the same as the vowel sound (e.g., FET for *feet*, SID for *slide*, NOZ for *nose*, Her for *here*)

Middle Letter Name-Alphabetic Spelling*

- Routinely represents both beginning and ending consonant sounds (e.g., Hct for *hatched*, WZ for *was*)
- Routinely represents long vowel sounds using the letter whose name is the same as the vowel sound (e.g., PnNO for *piano*, PePL for *people*, ONlE for *only*, AWAK for *awake*)
- Routinely represents short vowel sounds, sometimes using similar articulation of vowel's letter name (e.g., RiCS for *rocks*), sometimes using conventional spellings, especially in high-frequency words (e.g., BAtmAN for *Bat Man*, HOT for *hot*, BIG for *big*)

*Adapted from Bear, Invernizzi, Templeton, & Johnston's (2000) stages with the same names. Examples from research conducted by the authors.

domly. Because they seem to believe in some power of the letters themselves to communicate, non-spellers can also be characterized as lacking a concept of word. Individual letters in their writing are not even representative of beginning sounds in the words of their intended messages.

The second, third, and fourth stages, **emergent spelling, early letter name-alphabetic spelling,** and **middle letter name-alphabetic spelling** represent the kinds of spelling we expect from experimenters. In these three stages experimenters use letters to make words based on analyses of sound units in words and knowledge of sound–letter correspondences. They progress from only partial (initial or initial and final sounds) to nearly complete encoding of word sounds, and from representing only consonant sounds to representing consonants and vowels.

How to Use Spelling Stages.   These stages are intended to clarify the direction of change in children's spelling development. They do not represent a rigid sequence. Children may spell like emergent spellers in a particular context, including particular purposes and assistance, and spell like early or middle letter name-alphabetic spellers in other contexts with other purposes and kinds of assistance.

   Figure 4.15 shows Zack's writing when he was the student helper for the Words for Today routine in his kindergarten classroom (Richgels, 2003). His classmates suggested words for him to write. He wrote *windy* and *rainy* by copying them from the class's weather report chart. His teacher and classmates helped him to hear the sounds, choose the letters, and write the letters for ColD and Krme (*crummy*). For example, his teacher said, "What do you hear in the beginning of *c-c-crummy*?" and Zack answered, "K", and wrote *K* without help. But when she asked, "Crrrrrrr—hear that rrrrr?" she had to prompt Zack with the letter and direct his attention to a model for writing it: "That's an *R*. An *R*. It's

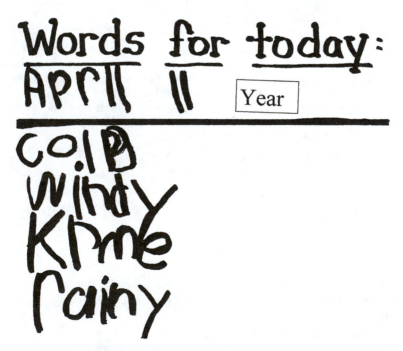

FIGURE 4.15   Zack's Words for Today

the first letter of *rainy.*" She also had to tell Zack that *M* spells the next sound, but he decided on his own that the letter *E* spells the last sound in *crummy.*

On the very same day, Zack's teacher asked him to spell six words without help. Zack's spellings were A for *apple,* D for *ladder,* T for *tiger,* P for *porcupine,* e for *telephone,* and P for *piano.* Just a month earlier, during free play time, Zack was the clerk at a pretend pizza restaurant. With a pencil in hand and a slip of paper on a clipboard, he took a customer's order for "large, thick crust, with pepperoni and black olives." He wrote four wavy lines of mock cursive writing, one for each element of the order: *large, thick crust, pepperoni, black olives* (Richgels, 2003).

At what stage is Zack's spelling? Is he a non-speller, as his wavy-line pizza-store writing might suggest? Is he the early letter name-alphabetic speller that his invented spelling assessment performance indicates? Or is he the middle letter name-alphabetic speller that ColD and Krme suggest? Answers to these questions depend on the context and the level of support that is available. Zack's literacy-related pretend play does not require spelling. Independently, he seems to be an early letter name-alphabetic speller. With help, he can spell like a middle letter name-alphabetic speller. What is important in responding to Zack's invented spellings is not identifying his place in a scheme like the one shown in Table 4.2, but rather, supporting his continued development so that over time, his spellings resemble later stages more often than earlier stages (see Chapter 8 for extensive discussion of such support).

Children's growth in spelling does not stop at the end of the middle letter-name alphabetic stage of spelling development. In Chapter 5 we will describe additional stages of invented spelling that are beyond what experimenters do.

Sound–Letter Relationships in Reading

Children's awareness of systematic (but unconventional) relations between letters and spoken language influences their reading (Richgels, 1995). Children's reading of environmental print, storybooks, and their own writing gradually reflects their awareness of written words and the relationships between letters in words and sounds in spoken language. For example, one day a young child noticed something different about an environmental print sign that she had been reading for quite some time as *Emporium,* . . . "a San Francisco department store whose stylized spelling is dominated by a very large initial *E.* On one of this child's frequent visits to the store, she looked at its name and commented in surprise, 'Mom! That doesn't say Emporium (i.e., *mporium*). That says *E-porium!*' " (Ehri, 1991, p. 411).

Another example of the influence of children's awareness of sound–letter knowledge on their reading occurred when Jeffrey looked at a word book (an alphabet picture book that had several pictures on a page depicting objects and actions associated with a particular letter). He was looking at the *F* page when he called out to his mother, "Do you want to hear me read this page?" Jeffrey's mother knew that he could not really read, but she was willing to be an audience as he pretended to read this favorite book. Jeffrey pointed to the word *fence* and said "fence." He pointed to each of the words or phrases *fruit tree, flag, funny face,* and *four fish* and said the appropriate word or phrase. Then he paused as he scanned the picture of a farmer driving a tractor. The words accompanying this picture were *front wheels* and *fertilizer.* Finally Jeffrey said, "I'm looking for the word *tractor* because this is a tractor. But I can't find it. All of these words have F's. But tractor shouldn't be F. Where is it, Mom? Can you find the word for 'tractor'?"

These examples demonstrate children's attention to letters and their sounds. In the case of *Emporium,* the child was applying a letter name strategy (*m-porium*); and in the case of *tractor,* Jeffrey knew that the word *tractor* did not begin with the phoneme associated with the letter F.

Experimenting with Functions of Written Language

We have presented much information about children's experimentation with the functions of written language. Young experimenters continue what they began as novices. They continue to use written language to communicate for a variety of purposes. Experimenters do, however, cover some new ground in the domain of written language functions. They read and write with the two new **purposes of learning to read and write and of preserving specific messages.**

In this chapter are many examples of experimenters' devoting considerable energy to reading and writing, to *experimenting* with how written language works. Unlike literacy beginners and novices, they are aware of the work involved in becoming literate. Sometimes this means that the experimenter chooses to focus on a small, concentrated part of the whole process of reading and writing. Especially when adults support and encourage such self-assigned work, experimenters come to know that learning to read and write is one of the goals of reading and writing. They learn by doing, even when the doing is at times painstaking. Their appearing to work hard is the result of the careful analysis, the concentrated thinking, and the reasoned trying out that is the essence of experimentation and invention. If it is true that what they are doing at this stage is inventing literacy for themselves (Goodman, 1980), then it is no wonder that such hard work is involved.

We have seen that experimenters, unlike novices, understand that written messages, whether their own or others', are stable and permanent. Ted (see Figure 4.1), Meagan (who wrote chicks r ranein for *Chicks are running*), and three kindergarten story folder authors (see Figure 4.14) knew that by writing a protest, a journal entry, or a story, they rendered their messages retrievable. Ted wanted his parents to notice his protest; Meagan wanted to record the activities of the chicks that had hatched in her classroom; and the story folder authors wanted to take home photocopies of the stories they had created about the folders' pictures. All these children could achieve those goals by writing. All of them had accomplished the most significant function-related conceptual change of the experimental stage, the discovery that written language can preserve a writer's message exactly. This is known as the **message concept** (Clay, 1975).

A Word of Caution

We began this chapter by characterizing experimenters as children who are aware that there is a system to learn, but who do not know what that system is. Throughout the chapter we have described the variety of concepts that children must grasp in order to puzzle out the system, to become what others would judge conventional readers and writers. Children gradually come to have many behaviors and understandings that we call conventional. The understandings that experimenters have about written language are unconventional in many ways (for example, their using manner of articulation to link letters and sounds or their counting syllables or phrases as words). Yet, their reading and writing also have signs of much that is conventional (for example, their using knowledge of literary syntax to compose stories and their using sound–letter knowledge to monitor their reading).

We hope that this chapter does not lead readers to two misconceptions. The first has to do with ages. Ages are not the important part of any description of children as experimenters. The children in our examples have been various ages. We have provided their ages only to accurately present the facts in some of our real-life examples. The ages of these children do not set norms against which to compare other children. Many children come to kindergarten and even to first grade not acting as experimenters. We have no reason to believe that they will fail to learn to read or write, or even that they will fall behind. Of much greater value than age is the behavior that can be observed in a literacy event; what the child knows or learns in the event; and how adults support that behavior, knowledge, and discovery. From this information, teachers can gain insights that will guide instruction.

The second misconception has to do with identification of children as experimenters. Identification is not important for its own sake. It does not really matter whether Carrie or Paul or any other child is called an experimenter. What matters is that teachers know in which literacy behaviors children are willing and able to engage. Then teachers will understand and support children in the provision of resources, in actions, and in talk. We know that some children's literacy behaviors fall in some manner—however imprecisely—within the broad territory described as the experimenter's. We hope that when teachers recognize such children, they will know how to support the children's continued development as writers and readers.

Chapter Summary

Experimenters are aware that there is a system of written language that they only partly understand. Still, they are up to the adventure of exploring the unknown territory. They respond to adults' encouragement with deliberate, focused episodes of reading and writing.

The meaning making that experimenters do is similar to what they did as novices. They continue writing in order to present a message, and they continue using sophisticated strategies for interacting with books.

Some of the most striking new achievements of experimenters are related to their greater control over form and meaning-form links. They make letters of the alphabet that are recognizable according to conventional standards. They acquire a concept of spoken and written words, and they devise means for showing word boundaries in their writing. In addition to knowing what physical arrangements are appropriate for different text forms, they know what special language is appropriate.

Experimenters' reading and writing are increasingly print governed. They achieve phonemic awareness and use it in alphabetic reading and invented spelling. They carefully analyze speech sounds in almost any word they want to write, and match those sounds with letters. Experimenters also show new knowledge of meaning-form links by using special written-language-like talk in literacy events. Often they are aware that written language is more precise than spoken language and that what readers say depends on what writers write.

As with novices, written language serves a variety of functions for experimenters. A new purpose for their reading and writing is simply to experiment. Another is to preserve readable messages.

A summary of what experimenters know about written language meanings, forms, meaning-form links, and functions is presented in Figure 4.16.

Applying the Information

At the beginning of the day that Zack wrote Words for Today (see Figure 4.15), Eric (the same Eric whose journal entry is shown in Figure 4.10) filled his personal sign-in sheet with mostly random letters, frequently letters from his own name (see Figure 4.17). He and his classmates routinely brought their personal sign-in sheets on clipboards with them to opening-of-the-day activities. These activities included number work (which on this day included predicting which numbers on a chart displaying numerals *1* to *110* were masked by a circle, a triangle, a square, and a rectangle), calendar work (which included adding three dates to the calendar, *9, 10,* and *11* for Saturday, Sunday, and Monday, April 9, 10, and 11), a weather report, and the Words for Today routine. Their teacher encouraged them to use their sign-in sheets to record anything they wanted to remember from these activities. With this in mind, and comparing Figures 4.15 and 4.17, what can you say about Eric's writing strategies, especially his spelling?

Later the same day, Eric's teacher asked him to spell six words without help. He wrote A for *apple,* L for *ladder,* T for *tiger,* P for *porcupine,* T for *telephone,* and P for *piano.* Two weeks later, Eric's class viewed the inside of a fertilized chick egg by shining a powerful light through it. Then with the help of an adult, he wrote in a journal about what he saw. His journal entry is shown in Figure 4.18. His message was *A black eye. Veins bring food.* The helper supplied the spelling for the first word, and Eric copied *black* from a black crayon. But Eric decided on the remaining spellings with the same sort of help that his and Zack's teacher had given Zack with *cold* and *crummy* (see p. 110). For example, the adult helper asked, "Do you

FIGURE 4.16 Summary: What Experimenting Readers and Writers Know about Written Language Meanings, Forms, Meaning-Form Links, and Functions

Meaning Making

assign meaning to text by applying knowledge of specialized literary language (such as literary syntax, alliteration, and letter-writing conventions)

Forms

know nearly all alphabet letter names and formations

have metalinguistic awareness of letters

develop concept of spoken words

develop concept of written words

develop concept of word boundaries

use specialized literary knowledge to construct a wide variety of texts

use a variety of strategies to produce conventional texts (including copying, asking for spellings, dictating, and spelling)

Meaning-Form Links

sound literate when assigning meaning to storybooks and compositions

are precise when assigning meaning to storybooks and compositions

develop phonemic awareness

use manner of articulation to associate sounds and letters in spellings

use letter names to associate sounds and letters in spellings

use identity of sounds to associate sounds and letters in spellings

spell at the levels of emergent, early letter name-alphabetic, and middle letter name-alphabetic spelling

use knowledge of sound–letter relationships to monitor emergent reading

use finger-point reading (demonstrating voice-to-print matching)

can use phonetic or alphabetic cues to learn some sight words

Function

read and write to experiment with written language

understand that written language is precise (develop the message concept)

---

have any ideas about how to write *eye?*" and Eric answered, "Just an *I*." The helper asked, "What would *vvvein*—" and before even hearing the end of the word, Eric answered, "*V!*" And when the helper asked, "Do you want to write any other letters for *veinzzzz?*" Eric answered, "Z." With this additional information, what else can you say about Eric's writing and spelling? How are his spelling attempts influenced by context? What sorts of tasks and assistance will be most helpful to Eric's continued spelling development?

Going Beyond the Text

Visit a kindergarten classroom. Join the children who are writing. Notice what their writing activities are. What experimenting behaviors do you observe? What text forms are the children using? How many of them are spellers? Begin your own writing activity (writing a letter, a story, a list of some kind, a reminder to yourself,

My Sign In Sheet
by EriCThoMAS   [Last Name]

● ff ∩ C C   ▲33

■22   ■ AP

Today is ∈ ∩ i C ∩ r E I

∩ C C M C F ∩ C C

∩ r C ∩ C r (∩

E ∩ i ∩ Z   K

COLD UU∈∩ K r ∩ E

APPE A ∩ ∩ R ∩ ((i (

9i0ii r C A C ∩ C i l c c o ∩

FIGURE 4.17   Eric's Sign-in Writing

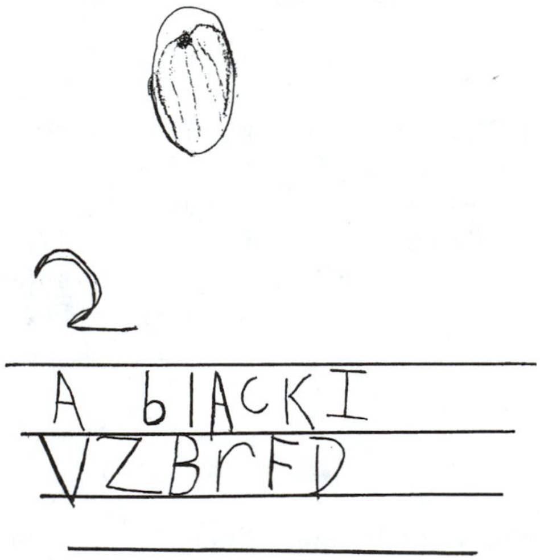

2
A bIACKI
VZBrFD

A black eye
veins bring food

FIGURE 4.18   Eric's Assisted Journal Entry

or a poem). Talk about it with the children. How many of them take up your activity and attempt similar pieces? Does the character of their writing change from what it was for their own activities? Is there more or less invented spelling, more or less word writing, more or less scribbling?

Ask the teacher if children have favorite storybooks. If so, invite children to read their favorites to you. How do they interpret that invitation? If they would rather you read to them, how willing are they to supply parts of the reading? What parts do they know best? What parts do they like best?

REFERENCES

Bear, D. R., Invernizzi, M., Templeton, S., & Johnston, F. (2000). *Words their way: Word study for phonics, vocabulary, and spelling instruction* (2nd ed.). Upper Saddle River, NJ: Merrill.

Beers, J. W., & Henderson, E. H. (1977). A study of developing orthographic concepts among first grade children. *Research in the Teaching of English, 11,* 133–148.

Bissex, G. L. (1980). *GNYS AT WRK. A child learns to write and read.* Cambridge: Harvard University Press.

Clay, M. M. (1975). *What did I write? Beginning writing behavior.* Exeter, NH: Heinemann.

Cox, B., Fang, Z., & Otto, B. (1997). Preschoolers' developing ownership of the literate register. *Reading Research Quarterly, 32,* 34–53.

Dahl, K., Scharer, P., Lawson, L., & Grogan, P. (1999). Phonics instruction and student achievement in whole language first grade classrooms. *Reading Research Quarterly 34,* 312–341.

Edelsky, C. (1982). Writing in a bilingual program: The relation of Ll and L2 texts. *TESOL Quarterly, 16,* 211.

Ehri, L. (1991). Development of the ability to read words. In R. Barr, M. Kamil, P. Mosenthal, & P. Pearson (Eds.), *Handbook of reading research* (2nd ed., pp. 395–419). New York: Longman.

Ehri, L., & Sweet, J. (1991). Finger point reading of memorized text: What enables beginners to process the print? *Reading Research Quarterly, 26,* 442–462.

Gentry, J. R. (1978). Early spelling strategies. *Elementary School Journal, 79,* 88–92.

Goodman, Y. M. (1980). The roots of literacy. In M. P. Douglas (Ed.), *Claremont Reading Conference, 44th Yearbook* (pp. 1–32). Claremont, CA: Claremont Reading Conference.

Harste, J. C., Burke, C. L., & Woodward, V. A. (1983). *Young child as writer-reader, and informant* (Final Report Project NIE-G-80–0121). Bloomington, IN: Language Education Departments, Indiana University.

Johnson, S. A. (1982). *Inside an egg.* Minneapolis: Lerner.

McGee, L. M., & Richgels, D. J. (2003). *Early childhood literacy programs for at-risk three-, four-, and five-year-olds.* New York: Guilford.

McIntyre, E., & Freppon, P. A. (1994). A comparison of children's development of alphabetic knowledge in a skills-based and a whole language classroom. *Research in the Teaching of English, 28,* 391–417.

Morris, D. (1981). Concept of word: A developmental phenomenon in the beginning reading and writing processes. *Language Arts, 58,* 659–668.

Morris, D. (1993). The relationship between children's concept of word in text and phoneme awareness in learning to read: A longitudinal study. *Research in the Teaching of English, 27,* 133–154.

Read, C. (1971). Pre-school children's knowledge of English phonology. *Harvard Educational Review, 41,* 1–34.

Richgels, D. (1995). Invented spelling ability and printed word learning in kindergarten. *Reading Research Quarterly, 30,* 96–109.

Richgels, D. J. (2001). Invented spelling, phonemic awareness, and reading and writing instruction. In S. B. Neuman and D. K. Dickinson (Eds.), *Handbook of early literacy research* (pp. 142–155). New York: Guilford.

Richgels, D. J. (2003). *Going to kindergarten: A year with an outstanding teacher.* Lanham, MD: Scarecrow.

Roberts, B. (1992). The evolution of the young child's concept of word as a unit of spoken and written language. *Reading Research Quarterly, 27,* 124–139.

Sulzby, E. (1985). Children's emergent reading of favorite storybooks: A developmental study. *Reading Research Quarterly, 20,* 458–481.

Temple, C., Nathan, R., Temple, F., & Burris, N. (1993). *The beginnings of writing* (3rd ed.). Boston: Allyn & Bacon.

Templeton, S. (2003). Spelling. In J. Flood, D. Lapp, J. R. Squire, & J. M. Jensen (Eds.), *Handbook of research on teaching the English language arts* (2nd ed., pp. 738–751). Mahwah, NJ: Lawrence Erlbaum Associates.

Templeton, S., & Morris, D. (2000). Spelling. In M. L. Kamil, P. B. Mosenthal, P. D. Pearson, & R. Barr (Eds.), *Handbook of reading research, Vol. 3* (pp. 525–543). Mahwah, NJ: Lawrence Erlbaum Associates.

The Three Bears. (1952). Racine, WI: Western.

Zutell, J. (1978). Some psycholinguistic perspectives on children's spelling. *Language Arts, 55,* 844–850.

5

From Six to Eight Years

Early, Transitional, and Self-Generative Readers and Writers

KEY CONCEPTS

conventional writers and
    readers
early reading and writing
transitional reading and
    writing
self-generative reading and
    writing
high-frequency words
sight words
letter–sound correspondences
personal narratives
recounts
orchestrate
cue systems

writing workshop
first draft
vowel markers
monitor
prior knowledge
predict
confirm
visualize
summarize
metacognitive awareness
fix-up strategies
interpretation
transaction
symbol

referential dimension
morpheme
setting
characters
plot
episodes
conflict
climax
point of view
style
mood
theme
intermediate forms
    of story writing

expositions
topic presentation
description of attributes
characteristic events
category comparison
final summary
consistency
ordered relationships
hierarchical relationships
intermediate forms of
    informational text writing

decoding
early alphabetic decoders
consonant digraphs
long vowels
other vowels
fully phonemic decoding
decoding by analogy
orthographic principles
orthographic decoders
fully phonemic
word families

homophones
later letter name-alphabetic
    spelling
within-a-word spelling
syllable and affix spelling
multisyllabic words
vocabulary
comprehension

Who Are Conventional Readers and Writers?

Learning about reading and writing is a gradual process. It is not possible to identify the exact moment when a child becomes a reader or writer in a conventional sense.

In the beginning of conventional reading, children have only an intuitive understanding of reading strategies. They use a few dozen sight words to read texts that have simple language structures and familiar words from their spoken vocabularies. Young writers rely on invented spellings and a few known spellings to compose text with relatively simple text forms. Eventually, children acquire a variety of reading strategies and thousands of sight words, which they strategically use to read text with complex structures and unfamiliar vocabulary and concepts. They use writing processes and knowledge of many conventional spellings to compose complex texts of different genres for a variety of purposes and audiences. They are **conventional writers and readers.**

Three Phases of Conventional Literacy Development

This chapter covers a broad range of reading and writing development. We provide examples of only a few of the many accomplishments that we can expect children to display during this time of literacy development. In this chapter, we highlight some of the literacy concepts, skills, and strategies children are learning and, where possible, we describe the instructional contexts which allowed children to develop those concepts, skills, and strategies. We discuss children's conventional reading and writing that typically occur during three phases: **early, transitional,** and **self-generative reading and writing** (NAEYC/IRA, 1998).

Early readers are able to read simple texts on their own. These texts have many familiar words that are found in all written texts. These words (such as *the, is, were, she, to, and, of, from,* and *with*) are called **high-frequency words** because they appear frequently in every kind of text. Early readers are able to read many high-frequency words by sight (they can recognize **sight words** immediately when they see them) and **decode** or "sound out" unknown words by using **letter–sound correspondences** (matching a sound or phoneme with a letter and then blending the sounds together to make a word). Although texts that are appropriate for early readers are simple, children learn to direct their attention beyond merely reading the words; they begin to develop early comprehension strategies. Early writers learn to spell words, especially vowels. They compose much longer texts. Most children become early readers during first grade and some children continue in this phase in the early months of second grade.

Transitional readers are able to read more complex text that includes longer sentences and fewer high-frequency words, and they acquire many sight words. They can read more fluently and comprehend more complicated stories and informational texts. They make the transition into reading simple chapter books during this phase, although picture books continue to be an important part of their reading diet. They use more sophisticated decoding strategies that go beyond merely blending individual letters and phonemes, and they develop more complex comprehension strategies. They recognize parts of words, make multiple predictions, monitor their understanding, and draw inferences. Transitional spellers know how to spell many words conventionally, and they learn how to use a variety of strategies for spelling words that they do not yet know how to spell conventionally. They write in several different genres including **personal narratives** (**recounts** about events in their own lives), stories, poems, and science reports (Wollman-Bonilla, 2000). Many children become transitional readers and writers sometime during second grade and continue in this phase of development through third grade.

Some third graders enter an even more sophisticated phase of literacy development. Self-generative readers are becoming highly skilled readers who can control many strategies for reading complex texts, learning from text, and acquiring new vocabulary. Self-generative writers are increasingly able to revise their own writing to communicate for a wide variety of purposes and audiences.

Examples of Early, Transitional, and Self-Generative Readers and Writers

Conventional readers and writers are able to **orchestrate** many different parts of the reading and writing process. Orchestration requires that readers and writers are able to do some reading processes unconsciously so they are freed up to concentrate on other processes. For example, early readers and writers are already fluent at the process of reading from left-to-right and matching one-on-one spoken words with written words. They do not have to think about these processes—they can accomplish them unconsciously. However, these early reading processes must also be orchestrated with other processes such as reading words by sight, decoding words, comprehending, and monitoring the meaning of what they read. Early conventional readers become increasingly planful and strategic as they read and compose. Their attention is focused on understanding what they read and conveying information in their writing so that others will understand.

In order to demonstrate how readers and writers are better able to orchestrate more complex strategies and texts, we present a glimpse into one child's reading and writing as she enters the phases of early and transitional reading and writing and then begins the early steps of self-generative reading and writing. Kristen entered first grade in the experimenting phase of reading and writing. She could not read on her own yet, although she could blend many consonants into word parts such as *at* to create and read new words such as *bat, cat, fat,* and *hat.* She could invent spellings, and Figure 5.1 presents an example of a message that she wrote to her mother at the classroom writing table. Later, when asked to read her message, Kristen said, "I love you" even though her message spelling suggested that she wrote, "I like you."

At this point, Kristen is not yet an early reader. Her reading and writing suggests that she paid attention to only one or two components or **cue systems** of written language. She relied on the graphophonemic cue system (consonant sound–letter correspondences) to spell words and, in part, to read words. She could spell the beginnings and endings of words and pay attention to those parts of words when reading words spelled in a pattern. She ignored word spaces in writing, but in reading showed that she knew what words are. However, she did not yet have sufficient experience with orchestrating the processes required in tracking print word-by-word, recognizing and reading words, and using letter–sound correspondences to decode words.

Kristen entered the phase of early reading and writing mid-year in first grade. Figure 5.2 presents an example of the kinds of text she could read with support at that time. *Go, Dog. Go!* (Eastman, 1961) is considered a pre-primer to primer level text (text that is read during the early-to-mid part of first grade). One year later Kristen became a transitional reader; she was able to read *Frog and Toad Together* (Lobel, 1971), which is considered a second grade text and indicates the beginning of transitional reading. Mid-year in third grade Kristen could read the chapter book titled *The Chocolate Touch* (Catling, 1952), which is considered a third grade text. While she was reading on grade level at this time, Kristen had difficulty comprehending complex stories without instructional support. She would not yet be considered a self-generative reader.

The texts presented in Figure 5.2 highlight the striking differences in idea complexity, number of words, complexity of sentence structure, and level of vocabulary found in texts children read in the first, second, and third grade. As children move through the primary grades, they are expected to make rapid

FIGURE 5.1   Kristen's Message: "I Like You"

FIGURE 5.2   Page 18 from books Kristen read with instructional support at mid-year in the first, second, and third grade.

Grade	Title	Sample Text
1	*Go, Dog. Go!* (Eastman, 1961)	The green dog is up. The yellow dog is down (p. 18).
2	*Frog and Toad Together* (Lobel, 1971)	Frog was in his garden. Toad came walking by. "What a fine garden you have, Frog," he said. "Yes," said Frog. "It is very nice, but it was hard work." "I wish I had a garden," said Toad. "Here are some flower seeds. Plant them in the ground," said Frog (p. 18).
3	*The Chocolate Touch* (Catling, 1952)	A few seconds after the bedroom door had closed behind his mother, John leaped to the floor, got down on his hands and knees, and felt under the bed for the candy box. He soon had it on the pillow and set to work unfastening it. First he took off the thin outer sheet of cellophane. Then he lifted off the lid. Then he removed a sheet of cardboard. Then he pulled off a square of heavy tinfoil. Then he took out a layer of shredded paper. As the wrappings piled up around him, John became rather anxious (paragraph included on p. 18).

growth, as Kristen did, in their ability to read increasingly difficult text with fluency and comprehension.

Kristen made similar strides in writing development during the same time period. Figure 5.3 presents three samples of Kristen's writing collected mid-year in first, second, and third grade. She wrote the first sample ("Do not come in here") on a rainy day when a classmate came to play (see grade 1). Kristen's mother found the note taped to her bedroom door. Earlier she had interrupted the girls' play twice when they were too noisy and engaged in rowdy play. Later, Kristen told her mother she had written the note so that she and her friend could "have some privacy." The writing on the note demonstrates that although Kristen did not use conventional vowels in her spellings (*iw* for *o* in *do, i* for *o* in *come,* and *i* for *e* in *here*), she does have an increasing awareness of the need to use vowels as well as knowledge of some conventional spellings.

FIGURE 5.3   Writing samples composed by Kristen mid-year in the first, second, and third grade.

Grade	Sample	Translation
1	*Diwhoxcimihir*	do not come in here
2	*my room* *I have a room* *Fild with lose of* *toys. Its osem,* *You will not bleve* *Youer eiys,* *I have a bed and a* *dresr. Iv got a* *desch and a sefve* *to put all the* *toys in.*	my room I have a room filled with lots of toys. It's awesome. You will not believe your eyes. I have a bed and a dresser. I've got a desk and a shelf to put all the toys in.
3	*In the winter Caty Cot sleeps on the warm bed Pur* *In the spring Caty Cot sleeps on the window legq Pur* *In the summer Caty Cot sleeps on tile Pur* *In the fall Caty Cot sleeps anywere at all*	

In the winter Catty Cat sleeps on the warm bed, Purr.
In the spring Catty Cat sleeps on the widow ledge, Purr.
In the summer Catty Cat sleeps on the tile, Purr.
In the fall Catty Cat sleeps anywhere at all.

Kristen wrote the second sample presented in Figure 5.3 during **writing workshop** in her second grade classroom, a specific time during the day when children are expected to use the writing process of drafting, revising, and sharing (see more about the writing workshop approach in Chapter 9). This sample was a **first draft** (see grade 2). It demonstrates a dramatic increase in the number of words that Kristen knows how to spell conventionally, control over word spacing and handwriting, and text composition. Her spelling of vowels has shifted from the one-vowel, one-letter strategy she used in first grade to now using **vowel markers.** Vowel markers are the two vowels that are used to spell one long vowel or other vowel phoneme. For example, some long vowels are spelled with a "silent e" at the end of the word to mark the vowel in the word as long (as in the words *cake, bike,* and *stove*) and other long vowels are spelled with the two letters (such as *ai* in the word *wait, eigh* in the word *height,* and *oa* in the word *boat*). Kristen did not yet use vowel markers conventionally in second grade, but she demonstrated awareness of this spelling concept when she spelled *bleve* for the word *believe, eiys* for *eyes,* and *sefve* for *shelf.*

The third writing sample, collected during third grade, was also created as a part of writing workshop; however, it is a second rather than a first draft. Kristen shared her first draft with and got feedback from the other children and her teacher. Based on these comments, she produced the second draft of the poem. This draft was completed in cursive writing although the first draft was written in print. Nearly all words are spelled correctly, with a shift in attention from merely writing a message to writing with attention to literary qualities, such as rhythm and repetition.

Meaning Construction

The children described in this chapter are able to construct meaning from what they read by themselves (What did the author intend?) and in what they write for someone else (How can I convey for others what I intend?). They develop many strategies for understanding the different kinds of texts they read.

Meaning Making in Reading: Using Strategies

One of the first and most important strategies that children use to understand what they read is to **monitor** whether what they are reading makes sense (is meaningful), sounds like language (has acceptable syntax), and looks right (has the sequences of letters that they expect after much experience with texts). Children show that they are monitoring by rereading a portion of the text when what they have read does not make sense or by rereading to correct a word that does not match with the text.

Eventually readers are able to use several different reading strategies to help them understand or comprehend what they read (Paris, Wasik, & Turner, 1991). For example, readers pause to connect what they are reading with what they already know. If they are reading a story about a cat, readers draw on their **prior knowledge** (Pressley, 2002) of cats—what they do, what they eat, where they live, and how they interact with people. Using information from the story and their prior knowledge allows readers to **predict** what will happen, and as they read they look for information to **confirm** or disconfirm their predictions. They **visualize** scenes in stories and **summarize** to themselves what has happened so far. Sometimes readers remember events in their own lives or people they know that are like the events and characters in stories, or they think about characters from other stories.

At first, readers use simple strategies of rereading, sounding out words, and skipping confusing parts of stories. Even these simple strategies may be used deliberately by beginning readers (Freppon, 1991). This conscious use of strategies is called **metacognitive awareness.** Later children develop **fix-up strategies** for fixing up problems they notice while reading (Brown, 1980). Readers may reread a portion of a story when they realize that something does not make sense or that they have missed one of the elements of story form that they know to expect. They may skip a word they do not know if they are aware that they are still able to understand the story. Sophisticated readers may adjust their pace or change their level of engagement, looking for main ideas and a developing gist, or noting finer details. Teachers help children develop these strategies during read-alouds of complex texts, especially informational books (Smolkin & Donovan, 2002). Then, as children gain reading experience, they use comprehension and fix-up strategies automatically (Sinatra, Brown, & Reynolds, 2002).

Meaning Making in Reading: Constructing Interpretations of Literature

An important hallmark of readers is that they go beyond understanding a story—they build interpretations of a story. An **interpretation** is an attempt to understand the story at a more abstract level, using the story to understand one's self or the world (Many, 1991; Sipe, 2000). As they read a story, readers construct their own personal understandings and, sometimes, interpretations of that text, partly based on their unique background experiences. This unique interaction between the text and the reader is called a **transaction** (Rosenblatt, 1978). Transactions also take place for children who listen to stories read aloud.

An important way in which young children build interpretations of literature is to participate in group discussions of books in which children share personal responses to what they read and listen to others' responses. Such experiences lead readers to insightful interpretations of stories, of which they may not have been aware before the group discussion (McGee, 1992; 1998).

Figure 5.4 presents a discussion about *Hey, Al* (Yorinks, 1986) in which children demonstrate their interpretation of two highly abstract literary elements: symbol and theme. A **symbol** is an event, object, person, or activity that represents two meanings—a literal meaning and an abstract meaning. A **theme** is the abstract statement about life or humanity that is reflected in a story or poem (Williams, 2002). The story of *Hey, Al* tells of a janitor who is dissatisfied with his life and is enticed by a strange bird to fly to a paradise. On reaching paradise, Al begins to turn into a bird, but he flies home before he completely loses his identity.

In this discussion Annie made one theme explicit (line 1) when she said, "He (Al) would be better as a janitor instead of up there. *Never talk to strangers.*" "Never talk to strangers" is an abstract statement of theme (more than likely called to mind by the familiar admonition). She also noticed a symbol when she said (line 6),

FIGURE 5.4   First Graders Talk about *Hey, Al* **(Yorinks, 1986)**

1   Annie: I think he (Al) would be better as a janitor instead of up there. Never talk
                to strangers.

2   Ryan: If he stayed up there, he would really be a bird and we don't know if he
                could change back again and his whole body would be a bird.

3   John: He loves his house.

4   T: How do you know?

5   John: Because he was happy to be back and the dog came back and they painted it.

6   Annie: They painted it yellow like the place. He was happy at the end.

7   Chris: Yea, and he got a new shirt like it wasn't the shirt from, like he was a janitor
                again, but he's got a nicer shirt and he looks happy.

8   Alice: Eddy is smiling. Yeah. The story has a happy ending.

Teaching Reading with Literature Case Studies by Tompkins/McGee, © 1993. Reprinted by permission of
Pearson Education, Inc., Upper Saddle River, NJ.

"They painted it yellow *like the place.* He was happy at the end." She noticed that
the yellow color that Al painted his room when he returned from the false paradise
represented both his initial happy experience at the island ("like the place") and his
newfound happiness and contentment with his own life on his return ("He was
happy at the end"). Children's concepts about theme and symbols and their ability
to articulate them develop gradually through the primary grades (Lehr, 1988).

Meaning Making in Writing

Conventional writers draw on many strategies for writing. Rachel wrote the story
presented in Figure 5.5 when she was in second grade. Several elements of this
story are noteworthy. Although Rachel uses knowledge of everyday activities
(such as hide-and-go-seek) and familiar others (such as her friends) in her compositions, she clearly uses these elements to construct a believable and consistent, but
imaginary, story-world. Conventional writers are able to go beyond the personal
and immediate—what is happening or just recently happened—to the abstract—
what has not yet happened or might never really happen. The relation of the writer
with the subject matter (from immediate to abstract) is called the **referential
dimension** of writing (Moffett, 1968).

Written Language Forms

As they become conventional readers and writers, children gain knowledge of the
fine points of form at the word level in English writing. Children's writing begins
to show their achievement of a fully conventional concept of word. They also start
to use narrative form in their writing and their knowledge of a different category
of text form, *exposition*, grows.

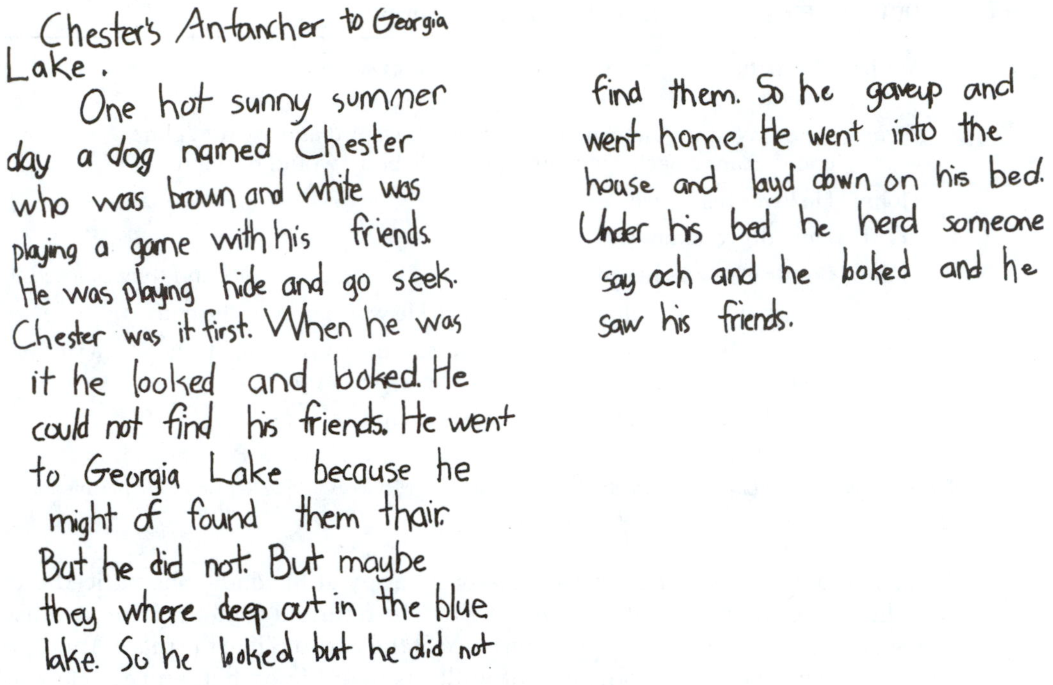

Chester's Antancher to Georgia Lake.

One hot sunny summer day a dog named Chester who was brown and white was playing a game with his friends. He was playing hide and go seek. Chester was it first. When he was

it he looked and boked. He could not find his friends. He went to Georgia Lake because he might of found them thair. But he did not. But maybe they where deep out in the blue lake. So he boked but he did not

find them. So he gaveup and went home. He went into the house and layd down on his bed. Under his bed he herd someone say och and he boked and he saw his friends.

FIGURE 5.5   Chester's Adventure to Georgia Lake

Concept of Word

Conventional readers and writers know how to show word boundaries using word spaces and punctuation. Periods and even commas, question marks, and exclamation marks appear in their writing. In addition, conventional readers and writers learn how morphemes work in written language. A **morpheme** is the smallest unit of meaning in a language. Conventional readers and writers learn that morphemes may be written as individual words, such as the articles *a, an,* and *the,* or they may be written as word parts, such as *-ed, -ing,* and *-s.*

Text Form: Story Compositions

During elementary school, children learn a great deal about how to write many different types of texts including stories, poems, and informational texts (Kamberelis, 1999) including science reports (Wollman-Bonilla, 2000). They learn about the kinds of information or elements that are included in these different text genres and also how to organize that information. In general, the number of elements children include in their compositions increases, the organization of their texts get more complex, and they demonstrate a growing awareness of audience (Wollman-Bonilla, 2001).

Elements Children Include in Story Compositions. One way to examine children's story compositions is to determine whether they include the elements identified in a story grammar (see Table 2.1 in Chapter 2). According to story grammar, characters are sustained throughout the story and introduced in a setting, an initiating event introduces a problem, and the main character (often intuitively) sets a goal to try and solve a problem (this is also called an internal response). The initiating event sets in place a chain of causally related attempts and outcomes in which the main character acts to achieve the goal or solve the problem. Complex stories have a series of attempts and outcomes as the main character must overcome several obstacles before achieving the goal. The story ends as the main character reacts to having achieved the goal. Well-crafted stories also include many literary elements which are similar to the elements in a basic story grammar (Lukens, 1995).

The seven major literary elements include setting, character, plot, point of view, style, mood, and theme. The **setting** introduces the location, time period, and weather in which the story takes place, and reveals mood and character. For example, characters who are put in harsh settings (such as a desert or a lonely island) are often revealed as resourceful, hardworking, and independent. The setting is sometimes used as an antagonist to introduce conflict to the story. For example, a character may have to travel through a snowstorm (an antagonistic setting) in order to get to school.

There are two kinds of **characters** in stories: main characters and supporting characters. The main characters are at the center of the action of the story, and supporting characters serve as helpers to the main characters. Characters are not always people (they can be animals or objects that are animated), but main characters must have human traits—we must come to know them as people. Characters are revealed through their thoughts, actions, words, and appearance. We must be able to see a character in action and hear what a character says and thinks.

The **plot** includes **episodes,** each with a problem and obstacles. The last episode in a story includes the climax and resolution of the story. The main character does not usually solve the problem simply or easily, but encounters difficulties or obstacles along the way that create **conflict.** A critical moment comes when the problem is solved (the **climax**) and the story is resolved (often happily in literature for children). Conflict is an important part of stories, because it produces tension (we do not know how the story will end, although we hope all will go well) and propels the story forward.

Point of view is the perspective from which the story is told. Point of view is particularly important, because it positions the reader inside or outside the story. When point of view allows readers inside the story, they know all the characters' thoughts and feelings.

Style is the way the author uses language, including use of imagery (descriptions that appeal to the senses, such as sight, sound, or touch), word choice, and figurative language (such as the use of simile or metaphor). Each author uses language in unique ways to describe setting and character and to uncover the plot.

Mood is the emotional tone of a story (humorous, somber, lighthearted, mysterious, frightening). **Theme** is the abstract statement about life or humanity revealed by the story as a whole. Through theme, stories achieve a consistency at an abstract level.

Children's Narrative Writing.   What kinds of literary elements might we expect to find in primary schoolchildren's compositions? Return to Rachel's story presented in Figure 5.5. It includes a main character, Chester, the brown and white dog. It also includes Chester's friends (who act as playful antagonists in the game of hide-and-seek and the story). Rachel implied one of Chester's character traits: he is persistent (he looked and looked for his hidden friends). Tension arises naturally from the conflict of searching; the friends are very difficult to find! The story is told consistently from the third-person point of view with a narrator speaking directly to the reader about how clever Chester was for searching for his friends at Georgia Lake. Rachel's literary style includes the use of repetition (looked and looked). The mood is playful, beginning with the title ("Chester's Adventure to Georgia Lake") and continuing through to the climax when "och" reveals Chester's friends hiding under his bed.

Figure 5.6 presents another story written by a primary-grade student. Although the story sometimes loses sequence, it has several characters who act in a consistent manner, as we would expect (a cat chases a chick). The author tells us about the characters by revealing their feelings (the cat is hungry, and the chick is afraid) and by showing us what they say ("Peep, peep" and "Meow"). The story has a problem (the cat is trying to eat the chick) and actions to solve the problem (the mother bites the cat, and the chick hides).

From the stories presented in Figures 5.5 and 5.6, we can conclude that children do use many literary elements of narratives in their stories, but not necessarily all elements, nor are the elements always well developed. We understand that primary schoolchildren's stories may lack plot complexity and descriptive detail. We might expect that young conventional writers' stories would gradually acquire

---

FIGURE 5.6   "Peep Peep" Story

Yo tengo un pollito. El pollito hace—¡pio, pio!—. El pollito se va a jugar y viene. Tiene hambre. El pollito hace—¡pio, pio!—. El gato lo persigue. La madre lo pica y el gato hace—¡miau!— . . . Por eso la gallina y mi pollito dice la gallina y el pollito estaba escondido. Tenía miedo que el gato lo agarrará.

(I have a chick. The chick says, "Peep, peep." The chick goes out to play and comes [back]. He's hungry. The chick says, "Peep, peep." The cat chases him. The mother bites him and the cat goes, "Meow." . . . Therefore the hen and my chick say the hen and the chick was hidden. He was afraid the cat will catch him.)

Writing in a Bilingual Program, Edelsky, C., p. 91. Copyright © 1986. Reprinted with permission of Greenwood Publishing Group, Inc., Westport, CT.

overall story consistency, believability, and detail, but much of this development occurs after the primary grades.

In fact, most first graders do not write stories that include all the elements that would actually qualify their compositions to be called stories (Donovan, 2001). It is not until second and third grade that a majority of children write stories with most of the basic story grammar elements—and, therefore, would qualify to be called stories. Instead, most young children's story compositions are in emergent or intermediate forms. Figure 5.7 presents an explanation of the **intermediate forms of story writing** (adapted from Donovan, 2001). When children are asked to write or dictate a story, these are the kinds of forms their stories take. We present their stories, in order from simple to more complex, without invented spellings to emphasize their form.

FIGURE 5.7   Intermediate Forms of Children's Story Compositions

Label
present tense, word or phrase

This is David. This is Lisa. This is Casey and Wynell and Willima. This is Travis.

Statement
past tense, sentence about an event

Once upon a time there was a witch lived in the forest. (Donovan, 2001, p. 418)

No Structure
story opener, past tense, lacks sequence, and sustained character

Once there was a boy and a dog. The grandmother was dancing. The bunny gave the grandmother a flower.

Action Sequence
past tense, sequence of events, sustained character, no goal

There once was a little boy. He went to the store and bought potato chips. He went to the store and bought milk. He went to the store and bought some junk food. The end.

Reactive Sequence
past tense, causally related sequence of events, no goal

There was an elephant. He climbed up and he fell and bumped his head. The gorilla kissed his head.

Simple Goal Directed
past tense, causally related sequence of events toward resolution of goal

A lady went into a castle. She saw some jewels and she took some. The giant chased her. She put it on and went home. She wore it to bed.

Complex Goal Directed
past tense, causally related sequence of events toward resolution of goal, obstacles and complications

(see Figure 5.6, Chester's Adventure to Georgia Lake)

Adapted from Donovan, 2001.

Text Form: Expositions

Not all texts are stories. Some texts inform or explain, rather than relate a story; these are called **expositions.** Much nonfiction takes this form. We expect conventional writers eventually to compose informative, engaging, and accurate expositions. Of course, readers and writers in the primary grades only begin the process of learning to compose highly structured informational texts and to read and remember ideas from informational books (Kamberelis, 1999). We will first describe the forms of well-structured expository texts and then present what we know about young children's expository writing next.

Elements Children Include in Expository Texts.   One way to examine children's expositions is to determine whether they include the elements expected in informational text (Donovan, 2001). Informational texts include **topic presentation** in which the topic of exposition is introduced (e.g., "Zebras are intelligent animals," p. 426), **description of attributes** in which the topic is described (e.g., "Zebras are very strong," p. 426), **characteristic events** in which typical activities related to the topic are described (e.g., "They eat grass and leaves. They live in packs," p. 426), **category comparison** in which the topic is compared to another similar topic (e.g., "Zebras are smarter than work horses," p. 426), and **final summary** in which all the information presented about the topic is stated in a more general way (e.g., "Zebras are wild animals and shall remain in the wild forever," p. 426). Expositions may not include all of these elements; however, all informational texts must include a topic presentation and at least one or more additional informational text elements.

Another way to examine expositions is to consider three important components found in highly organized informational material: consistency, ordered relationships, and hierarchical relationships (Newkirk, 1987). For a text to have **consistency,** all its ideas must be related to one another. **Ordered relationships** are ideas that are related in some order. For example, two ideas might be related because one idea is an example of or illustrates another idea. Causes and effects, problems and solutions, comparisons, or sequences are all ideas that are ordered— they are related to one another in specific ways.

The last component of expository text structures is **hierarchical relationships.** Most expository texts are complex and can be broken into one or more main topics, which, in turn, can be broken down into subtopics, forming a hierarchy. The relationships among the main topics and between the subtopics and the main topic in expositions are also ordered or related.

Developmental Trends in the Organization of Children's Expositions.   Most young children attempt to write expository texts; however, it is not until second grade that many children include more than one or two elements of informational texts in their expositions (Donovan, 2001). In addition, most children do not include ordered relationships in their informational text writing. Instead, most young children's expositions, like their story compositions, are also in emergent or intermediate forms. Figure 5.8 presents an explanation of the **intermediate forms of informational text writing** (adapted from Donovan, 2001). When children are asked to write or dictate an informational text, these are the kinds of forms their expositions take. They are arranged from simple to more complex form.

FIGURE 5.8 Intermediate Forms of Children's Expositions

Label
present tense, words or phrases

My dog, you, and me

Statement
present tense, sentence, may introduce topic

I know about rabbits

Simple Couplet
present tense, two related statements, second statement describes or extends first statement

The reptiles are snakes and the reptiles are in the zoo

Attribute List
present tense, random list of two or more facts related to topic

Cats get on the couch when it is tired. When it's sleepy, it goes in its bed. When it doesn't want to be by you, it would scratch. And it would hurt you if you hurt it.

Complex Couplet
present tense, attribute list in which two or more statements are related to one another

Dogs
Dogs are very furry. They are also a mammal. Most dogs bark and hear. If dogs can't bark that's because their voice box is not working very well. If dogs can't hear that's because when they were born they were born deaf or they have a real bad ear infection. Dogs can have an ear infection. Dogs are a lot like humans.

Hierarchical Attribute List
present tense, two or more basic attribute lists thus introduces subtopics

Basketball
Basketball is a sport that you play with a ball and someone to play against. Usually it is played on a wooden floor or concrete. You shoot the ball into a basketball net that is held up by a long metal post. The post has a flat piece of wood with a square shape in the middle of the wood. If you take more than three steps it is called traveling and it is the other team's ball. There are four types of shooting the ball. The first one is a set shot. The second is a jump shot. Then a granny shot and lay up shot. I think there are four quarters in a game. In between each quarter is a break that is called halftime. There is an announcer that talks about the game.

Adapted from Donovan, 2001.

Figure 5.8 does not include the most complex forms of expository writing that children are expected to write by the end of elementary school and into the middle school years. Instead, it presents the kinds of expositions we would expect from children through third grade. Even so, most third graders do not yet have control over the most complex structures presented in this figure.

Meaning-Form Links

Early, transitional, and self-generative readers and writers acquire many strategies for decoding and spelling, including using alphabetic and orthographic understandings.

Decoding

Decoding is a term usually applied to what readers do when they try to figure out a word that they do not recognize by sight. In order to decode, readers must use their knowledge of the alphabetic principle—that letters represent the sounds in words and that those sounds can be blended together to pronounce words. So to decode an unknown word, children must know letter–sound correspondences (for example, that the letter l represents the phoneme /l/) and then blend each of the phonemes together (Juel and Minden-Cupp, 2000). Early readers are **early alphabetic decoders** and at first only use initial letters to attempt to decode a word rather than using all of the word's letters. This ability emerges from experimenters' discovery of letter–sound relationships as well as from teachers' instruction.

The trick for early readers is to know where to look beyond the first letter. That is, decoding requires children to look beyond a single letter and attempt to match a phoneme with just that letter. For example, **consonant digraphs** (such as *th, sh, ch,* and *ng*) are comprised of two letters but represent only one phoneme. Similarly most **long vowels** (such as the sound of *a* in the word *way*) and **other vowels** (such as the sound made by *oo* in the word *foot*) are also spelled with two letters (sometimes vowel sounds are spelled by two letters that are not even next to one another such as in the word *tire* where the *e* marks the *i* as long). So, decoding words at the level of early reading often means that children are taught which letter combinations are important to notice and their sound–letter correspondences. Thus, early readers must quickly learn to scan across a word from left-to-right and identify which letters and letter combinations to pay attention to. Then they must match a phoneme with each letter or letter combination and blend those together. The ability to sound out all of a word's letters into phonemes is called alphabetic or **fully phonemic decoding.**

Transitional readers move beyond merely noticing letters or letter combinations. They use familiar word parts to pronounce unknown words. Using word parts to decode an unfamiliar word is called **decoding by analogy** (Ehri & Robbins, 1992). Decoding by analogy is based on an awareness of **orthographic principles,** that certain spelling patterns are always associated with a particular pronunciation (Pressley, 2002). For example, knowing the word *sand* allows readers to use the word part *and* along with its pronunciation to decode many words including *stand, standard,* and *stranded,* among others. As children near the end of transitional reading, they have enough sight words to use dozens and even hundreds of familiar word parts to decode, in turn, hundreds of unfamiliar and fairly rare words seemingly automatically (Share, 1995). Thus, they are on their way to becoming self-generative readers who are able to learn more about decoding merely by reading. Still, self-generative readers do benefit from instruction (especially in spelling) about prefixes, suffixes, and other advanced level word characteristics. They are **orthographic decoders,** and intuitively know how to decide which groups of letters should be pronounced and blended to identify an unknown word.

Spelling

Conventional writers learn new spelling strategies, especially visual ones, that contribute to conventional spelling. As experimenters, they may have spelled the word *weight* as *yt* or *wt*. As early writers they may spell *weight* as *wat*; as transitional writers they may spell it *wayt* or *wate* before finally spelling the word conventionally. We have seen that experimenters' spellings are influenced merely by sound. Early readers and writers are also influenced by sound, especially as their spellings become **fully phonemic** (where an invented spelling includes a letter for nearly every phoneme in a word).

The hallmark of conventional writing is beginning to use new, more visual strategies for spelling. Conventional writers' spellings are influenced by four visual factors: (1) knowledge of the standardized spellings of certain morphemes (*jumped* is spelled with an *ed* even though it sounds like *jumpt*); (2) an expectation of certain letters in certain contexts (for example, the *ight* sequence in *sight, might,* and *fight*)—the similar words that give rise to the expectation described in this second factor are called **word families;** (3) knowledge of spelling patterns for long vowel and other vowel pairs (*meat* is spelled with *ea,* while *meet* is spelled with *ee*), and (4) knowledge of consonant doubling (*stopping* includes the doubled *p*) and adding affixes (*restart* and *placement*).

We now turn to three additional stages of invented spelling: later letter name-alphabetic spelling, within-a-word spelling, and syllables and affix spelling (Bear, Invernizzi, Templeton, & Johnston, 2000). These stages are presented in Table 5.1 (and follow the stages presented in Table 4.2 in Chapter 4). These last three stages of spelling continue considerably beyond the primary years we address in this book; however, we would expect a few second graders and some third graders to exhibit some of the characteristics of the third and final spelling stage.

Later Letter Name-Alphabetic Spelling.   **Later letter name-alphabetic spelling** marks the end of children's sole reliance on listening to sounds in words as a spelling strategy. In this stage, early writers can hear most salient phonemes in a word and assign a letter to spell that sound. Many of the spellings found in Figure 5.3 (grade 1)

TABLE 5.1   Stages of Spelling Development (continued from Table 4.2 on page 109)

Later Letter Name-Alphabetic Spelling*

- Routinely represents one-to-one all salient sounds in a word (also called fully phonemic spelling) (e.g., LadR for ladder)
- Occasionally to routinely spells consonant blends and digraphs conventionally (e.g., KRI for *cry*, BREG for *bridge*, Thr for *there*)
- Routinely uses word spaces
- Occasionally differentiates spellings of **homophones** (words that are pronounced the same but spelled differently) (e.g., *to* and *two, for* and *four*)

Within-a-Word Spelling*

- Routinely spells single syllable short vowel words conventionally
- Occasionally to routinely spells r-controlled vowels conventionally in common single syllable words (e.g., *star, her*)

- Routinely represents long vowel sounds and other vowel sounds using vowel markers (e.g., GRATE for *great*, TEE for *tea*, TOOB for *tube*) sometimes using conventional spellings
- Routinely spells nasals conventionally (e.g., *jump*)
- Routinely spells common morphemes (e.g., *ed, ing, s*) conventionally

Syllables and Affixes Spelling*

- Occasionally to routinely uses consonant doubling at syllable junctures (e.g., *battle, riddle*)
- Occasionally to routinely uses consonant doubling when adding a suffix (e.g., STOPING for *stopping*)
- Occasionally to routinely spells common prefixes and suffixes (e.g., PICHER for *picture*, MOSHUN for *motion*)
- Occasionally to routinely drops e when adding suffixes (e.g., RIDDING for *riding*)

*Adapted from Bear, Invernizzi, Templeton, & Johnston's (2000) stages with the same names

are representative of the middle and later letter name-alphabet spelling stage. The spelling of *come* (*cim*), for example, includes one letter for each of the three phonemes found in the word. All of the spellings include vowels, and two short vowel single-syllable words are spelled conventionally (*not* and *in*) as would also be expected at this stage. However, the spelling of the word *do* as *Diw* heralds the next spelling stage.

Within-a-Word Spelling.   **Within-a-word spelling** is influenced by transitional writers' awareness of visual spelling patterns (how spellings look) as well as by their increasing store of known spellings. By now, nearly all single-syllable short vowel words are spelled conventionally as are consonant blends and digraphs. At this stage, children are aware that most long vowels and some other vowels require more than one vowel letter in their spelling. Thus, Kristen's spelling (in Figure 5.3) of the word *do* as *Diw* demonstrates her growing awareness of possible vowel spelling patterns. Many of Kristen's spellings in Figure 5.3 (grade 2) have characteristics representative of the within-a-word spelling stage. Her spelling of the words *eyes* (as *eiys*) and *shelf* (as *sefve*) reflect a use of a visual spelling strategy. That is, Kristen realizes that the word *eyes* has a *y* in it, so she first spells the long *i* phoneme with the letters *ei* and then adds the *y*. Similarly, Kristen is aware that the word *shelves* includes the letter *v*, so she spells the *f* phoneme with the letter *f* and then adds the *v*. Notice her use of the final *e* visual pattern in the word *believe* (*bleve*) and *shelf* (*sefve*).

Syllable and Affix Spelling.   Children who use **syllable and affix spelling** learn how consonant and vowel patterns work in **multisyllabic words** (words with more than one syllable) and what occurs when syllables join (Bear et al., 2000). At this stage of spelling, children learn how to combine prefixes and suffixes to base words as well as spelling rules associated with adding suffixes to words (for example, when to drop an *e* or double a consonant). During the early parts of this stage, children confuse rules for adding suffixes; however, their spelling errors reveal their awareness of these spelling patterns.

Functions

Conventional readers and writers continue to read and write for their own purposes, but they also learn another set of purposes for reading and writing—school-related purposes. In schools, reading and writing often entail considering the purposes the teacher has set, the special purposes the textbook authors have for writing, and the unique criteria by which classmates will judge one's writing.

In classrooms, students do not always read and write because they need to enter imaginary worlds, to gain information about their own expanding real world, to discover for themselves how written language works, or to create a permanent record of their ideas and wants. They have a new purpose for reading and writing: completing assignments and satisfying their teachers.

Conventional readers and writers have a keen awareness of audience. They have a more constant and pervasive realization that literacy involves creating meaning with someone else in mind, whether it is the author whose book they are reading, the intended reader of their writing, or the listener to whom they are reading. They understand that such meaning making is the single most important element of reading and writing.

The Traditional End Points: Reading and Word Identification, Vocabulary, and Comprehension

We have not used traditional terms to describe what children learn about reading during the early elementary grades. Reading educators traditionally describe the *what* of reading learning in terms of decoding or phonics skills, **vocabulary** knowledge, and **comprehension** ability. Those terms emphasize the view that, in order to become readers, children must do three things. They must learn to identify new words they encounter in print by sounding them out using phonics knowledge, by recognizing known word parts, and by using the context in which the words occur. They must know the meanings of, and know related words for, many of the words that they encounter in their reading. They must be able to understand what they read (for example, by knowing how the complex sentences that they are likely to encounter are constructed and by knowing how main ideas in a passage are supported by details).

Although the descriptions *decoding, vocabulary,* and *comprehension* sound unlike what was used in this chapter, there are similarities. By using the same categories and terms in this chapter that were used in the first four chapters of this book (*meaning making, forms, meaning-form links,* and *functions*), we have tried to call attention to the *origins* of conventional reading and writing, not just what they are. Our terms assume a long period of development in which children truly are readers and writers even though "the person on the street" would not think so. This is a period in which children derive important literacy knowledge, which is the basis for their eventual conventional reading and writing, especially when we acknowledge their accomplishments along the way.

By maintaining the categories and terms we have used throughout this book, we show the importance of respecting children's early developing knowledges and allowing children to use them in their own ways for their own purposes. Invented spelling provides just one example. Letting children experiment early with invented spelling and talking with them about their spellings may eliminate the need for many isolated phonics lessons later, in the primary grades. If so, the same end point is achieved: Children are able to use phonics knowledge efficiently for the word-identification and spelling purposes that make sense to conventional readers and writers.

Chapter Summary

Conventional readers and writers achieve a new independence in their reading and writing, but they are never alone. They are aware of the author who wrote what they read and of the audience that will read what they write. Thus, they show a keen awareness that written language is a communication process. There are three phases of conventional reading and writing: early, transitional, and self-generative.

Conventional readers and writers are able to orchestrate several processes and to control several strategies in extended episodes of writing or reading. They are aware of how well or how poorly their reading is going; they have fix-up strategies for when it goes poorly. Conventional readers' meaning making extends to being able to make interpretations and understand abstract literary elements, including point of view, symbol, and theme. They know the fine points of form at the word level in English; they have a conventional concept of word. They acquire sophisticated awareness of story form that comprises knowledge about setting, characters, plot, point of view, style, mood, and theme.

These children also gain a greater knowledge of text structure than they had as experimenters, especially knowledge of expository text.

Conventional readers and writers have many new spelling strategies. They build on their previous understandings of what spelling is all about by adding mul-

FIGURE 5.9   Summary: What Conventional Readers and Writers Know about Written Language Meanings, Forms, Meaning-Form Links, and Functions

Meaning Making

use metacognitive strategies to focus on meaning while reading, including monitoring that reading makes sense

use strategies for generating ideas during composing, including knowing the expectations of audience

interpret literature and move toward interpretations at the abstract level, including point of view, theme, and symbol

use knowledge of abstract literary elements and style to compose stories and other literary texts

Forms

have fully developed concept of word

understand morphemes

develop an ever-increasing stock of sight words

know conventional spellings of an ever-increasing stock of words

use knowledge of literary elements in narratives to compose stories that include settings, characters, and some plot elements and that signal growing control over point of view, mood, and style

develop knowledge of how exposition is organized, using consistency, ordered relationships, and hierarchical relationships to produce gradually more organized expository text compositions

Meaning-Form Links

develop conventional spelling ability, including learning alternative spelling patterns, phonograms, and morphemes

use orthographic concepts to spell and to decode words in reading (decoding by analogy)

Functions

read and write to meet a variety of personal needs

read and write to join the classroom literate community

---

tiple strategies for representing words in print, some using their earlier knowledge of sound–letter correspondences, and some using visual information in new ways.

Conventional readers and writers have new, school-related purposes for reading and writing. Written language can make them participating members of a literate classroom community and can facilitate a more intense or intimate interaction between authors and audiences than was possible before they reached this stage of reading and writing.

Figure 5.9 summarizes what conventional readers and writers know about written language meanings, forms, meaning-form links, and functions.

Applying the Information

In the following literacy event, a first grader writes a story and shares it with his classmates. Discuss what this event shows about understandings of written language meanings, forms, meaning-form links, and functions.

Figure 5.10 displays Zachary's "whale story." He wrote this as a first draft on six sheets of paper. Later, he read his story aloud to his classmates as part of an author's circle (a gathering of students who listen to others read their compositions,

FIGURE 5.10   Zachary's "Whale Story"

give compliments, and ask questions): "Made and illustrated by Zachary. To my mom and dad. Once upon a time there were two whales. They liked to play. One day when the whales were playing, a hammerhead came along. They fought for a time. Finally it was finished and the whales won. And they lived happily ever after."

After Zachary read his composition, his classmates asked him several questions, including "What kind of whales are they?" "Where do they live—what ocean?" and "How did they win the fight?" After listening to his classmates' questions, Zachary announced, "I am going to change my story by saying they lived in the Atlantic Ocean and they won the fight because they were bigger than the hammerhead and used their tails to defeat him."

Going Beyond the Text

Visit a third grade classroom. Observe the class during a time devoted to reading or writing. Try to identify two children whose behaviors suggest conventional reading or writing. Interview them. How aware are they of their own literacy knowledge and processes? Ask them what they do when they begin a new writing piece. How do they know when a piece is going well? What do they do to make a piece better? Ask how they choose a book to read for enjoyment. What is leisure reading like when it is going well? What makes them see what the author imagined when he or she wrote the book? How do they begin a reading assignment for social studies or science class? What do they do to be sure that they are learning from it what their teacher expects? Ask them if they would be willing to show you something they have written lately. Ask if they would read part of a book or tell about part of a book they are reading.

Do your interview subjects talk easily about reading and writing? Are they aware of what they know about literacy? Are they aware of audience in both reading and writing?

REFERENCES

Bear, D. R., Invernizzi, M., Templeton, S., & Johnston, F. (2000). *Words their way: Word study for phonics, vocabulary, and spelling instruction,* (2nd ed.). Upper Saddle River, NJ: Prentice-Hall.

Calkins, L. M. (1986). *The art of teaching writing.* Portsmouth, NH: Heinemann.

Casbergue, R. M. (1998). How do we foster young children's writing development? In S. B. Neuman & K. A. Roskos (Eds.), *Children achieving: Best practices in early literacy* (pp. 198–222). Newark, DE: International Reading Association.

Catling, P. (1952). *The chocolate touch.* New York: William Morrow.

Donovan, C. (2001). Children's development and control of written story and informational genres: Insights from one elementary school. *Research in the Teaching of English, 35,* 394–447.

Eastman, P. (1961). *Go, dog. Go!* New York: Random House.

Edelsky, C. (1986). *Writing in a bilingual program: Habia una vez.* Norwood, NJ: Ablex.

Ehri, L., & Robbins, C. (1992). Beginners need some decoding skills to read words by analogy. *Reading Research Quarterly, 27,* 12–26.

Freppon, P. (1991). Children's concepts of the nature and purpose of reading in different instructional settings. *Journal of Reading Behavior, 23,* 139–163.

Juel, C., & Minden-Cupp, C. (2000). Learning to read words: Linguistic units and instructional strategies. *Reading Research Quarterly, 35,* 458–492.

Kamberelis, G. (1999). Genre development and learning: Children writing stories, science reports, and poems. *Research in the Teaching of English, 33,* 403–463.

Lehr, S. (1988). The child's developing sense of theme as a response to literature. *Reading Research Quarterly 23,* 337–357.

Lobel, A. (1971). *Frog and Toad together.* New York: HarperCollins.

Lukens, R. (1995). *A critical handbook of children's literature* (5th ed.). Glenview, IL: Scott, Foresman/Little, Brown.

Many, J. (1991). The effects of stance and age level on children's literary responses. *Journal of Reading Behavior, 23,* 61–85.

McGee, L. (1998). How do we teach literature to young children? In S. B. Neuman & K. A. Roskos (Eds.), *Children achieving: Best practices in early literacy* (pp. 172–179). Newark, DE: International Reading Association.

McGee, L. (1992). An exploration of meaning construction in first graders' grand conversations. In C. Kinzer & D. Leu (Eds.), *Literacy research, theory, and practice: Views from many perspectives* (pp. 177–186). Chicago: National Reading Conference.

Moffett, J. (1968). *Teaching the universe of discourse.* Boston: Houghton Mifflin.

Newkirk, T. (1987). The non-narrative writing of young children. *Research in the Teaching of English, 21,* 121–144.

Paris, S., Wasik, B., & Turner, J. (1991). The development of strategic readers. In R. Barr, M. Kamil, P. Mosenthal, & P. Pearson (Eds.), *Handbook of reading research* (2nd ed., pp. 609–640). New York: Longman.

Pressley, M. (2002). Comprehension strategies instruction: A turn-of-the-century status report. In C. Block & M. Pressley (Eds.), *Comprehension instruction: Research-based best practices* (pp. 11–27). New York: Guilford.

Rosenblatt, L. (1978). *The reader, the text, the poem: The transactional theory of the literary work.* Carbondale: Southern Illinois University Press.

Sinatra, G., Brown, K., & Reynolds, R. (2002). Implications of cognitive resource allocation for comprehension strategies instruction. In C. Block & M. Pressley (Eds.), *Comprehension instruction: Research-based best practices* (pp. 62–76). New York: Guilford.

Sipe, L. (2000). The construction of literacy understanding by first and second graders in oral response to picture storybook read-alouds. *Reading Research Quarterly, 35,* 252–275.

Share, D. (1995). Phonological recoding and self-teaching: Sine qua non of reading acquisition. *Cognition, 55,* 151–218.

Smolkin, L., & Donovan, C. (2002). "Oh excellent, excellent question!": Developmental differences in comprehension acquisition. In C. Block & M. Pressley (Eds.), *Comprehension instruction: Research-based best practices* (pp. 126–139). New York: Guilford.

Williams, J. (2002). Using the theme scheme to improve story comprehension. In C. Block & M. Pressley (Eds.), *Comprehension instruction: Research-based best practices* (pp. 126–139). New York: Guilford.

Wollman-Bonilla, J. (2000). Teaching science writing to first graders: Genre learning and recontextualization. *Research in the Teaching of English, 35,* 35–65.

Wollman-Bonilla, J. (2001). Can first-grade writers demonstrate audience awareness? *Reading Research Quarterly, 36,* 184–201.

Yorinks, A. (1986). *Hey, Al.* New York: Farrar, Straus and Giroux.

CHAPTER

6

Literacy-Rich Classrooms

KEY CONCEPTS

developmentally appropriate
literacy-rich classrooms
big books
picture books
chapter books
genres
traditional literature
fables
folktales
myths
legends
fantasy
realistic fiction
historical fiction
biographies

autobiographies
informational books
poetry
wordless picture books
predictable books
alphabet books
reference materials
visual dictionaries
children's magazines
library center
writing center
computer centers
Writing to Read lab
storytelling props
SSR (sustained silent reading)

response-to-literature
   activities
response journal
curriculum
culturally relevant topics
curriculum integration
integrated language arts
multicultural literature
culturally authentic literature
literature theme units
integrated content units
assessment
kid watching
homogeneous reading
   abilities

Developmentally Appropriate Practice

Early childhood professional organizations have taken an active role in defining the kinds of classroom environments, learning activities, and instruction that best support young children's learning. Early childhood professionals argue that the early childhood years, from birth through eight years of age, are crucial for all aspects of children's development: physical, emotional, social, cognitive, and aesthetic. Quality early-childhood education provides opportunities for children to grow in all these areas. Literacy learning is only one part of children's growth and development.

A joint position statement by the International Reading Association (IRA) and the National Association for the Education of Young Children (NAEYC) on developmentally appropriate practices in literacy instruction for young children outlines ambitious goals for young children's literacy development (National Association for the Education of Young Children, 1998). These goals are reflected in later chapters in this book (see Chapters 7 through 10). According to this statement, the goals and expectations for young children's literacy accomplishments should be **developmentally appropriate;** that is, they should be challenging but achievable with adult support. Young children's literacy learning is a result of children's discovery of concepts and understandings and their social interaction with engaging and knowledgeable readers and writers (such as parents, caregivers, and teachers). Developmentally appropriate literacy practices celebrate the current level of children's understandings about literacy but provide strong instructional support for children's taking the next step. Instructional support occurs not just in primary-grade classrooms, where formal reading and writing instruction is expected. It also occurs in day care, preschool, and kindergarten classrooms.

Developmentally appropriate literacy practice is strongly dependent on (1) continuous assessment of children's current levels of understandings and (2) knowledge of the expected continuum of development. Being able to provide instruction that is challenging, but achievable, implies that teachers must constantly assess where children are in the long continuum of literacy learning and plan instruction accordingly. The previous chapters in this book were intended to provide teachers with the kind of knowledge they need in order to assess children's current understandings about literacy and to predict where children might be headed. Later chapters are designed to provide suggestions for instruction that can be tailored to meet the learning needs of children with diverse literacy understandings.

Developmentally appropriate practice is similar to a child-centered early-childhood program. Teachers who use developmentally appropriate practice recognize that children's growth and development can naturally be described in predictable sequences (remember the changes in literacy knowledge discussed in Chapters 2 through 5), but that children also have individual patterns of growth and home experiences that have an impact on what they know and how they learn. Developmentally appropriate practice acknowledges that not all children learn in the same way or need the same experiences at the same time.

A wide range of individual variation in literacy learning is to be expected at all levels from birth through age eight due to differing literacy experiences and expectations. Effective teachers recognize that children will have many different levels of understanding about reading and writing. They will expect that some children may not advance through a sequence of literacy achievements in quite the same way as other children. Therefore, single instructional strategies or sets of materials with lock-step sequences of instruction will not be appropriate to meet the needs of the wide range of children teachers can expect in preschool, kindergarten, or primary-grade classrooms (Snow, Burns, & Griffin, 1998). Instead, teachers will embrace a wide range of literacy instructional practices embedded within literacy-rich classroom environments.

Characteristics of Literacy-Rich Classrooms

Literacy-rich classrooms provide child-centered, developmentally appropriate support for children's literacy learning. All children, whether they have many or few home literacy experiences, whether they speak English or another language at home, and whether they have special learning needs, thrive in such classrooms.

Learners

As a result of being in literacy-rich classrooms, children are reflective, motivated readers and writers who use literacy to learn more about themselves and the world in which they live. This use of literacy begins before the elementary years. For example, four-year-olds who listen to their teacher read about the differences between tortoises and turtles to help identify the animal that one of them brought to school are reflective, motivated readers who use reading to find out more about their world.

Being reflective means that children are thinkers; they construct meanings for themselves and can use the thinking of others to modify those meanings. Reflective readers construct personal understandings from informational books, poems, and stories. Their initial understandings are usually tentative and unfocused. Sharing such undeveloped understandings requires great risk taking. However, reflective readers and writers use their first tentative understandings to build more fully developed and complex knowledge. They often modify their understandings given additional information from books or from talking with their friends or teachers. Similarly, reflective writers compose personally meaningful stories and poems, but also take into account the needs and interests of their audience. Constructing and sharing personal meanings with others both honors the voice of children and creates a "rich broth of meaning" (Oldfather, 1993, p. 676). This concept of literacy emphasizes the social nature of learning.

Being motivated means that children are self-directed and self-motivated (Oldfather, 1993). Many children, especially in the primary grades, are expected to participate in reading and writing activities because the teacher tells them to, but motived learners also participate in many activities because they choose to. Motivating activities have three characteristics: they allow children some choices in materials and experiences, provide challenges but call on strategies previously modeled by the teacher, and require social collaboration (Morrow & Gambrell, 1998).

The Classroom

The goal of all literacy instruction is not merely to produce children who are capable readers and writers (although that is certainly an admirable goal), but also to encourage and support children as they use reading and writing to achieve their own worthwhile personal and social goals. To achieve this aim, teachers must make careful decisions about materials, physical layout of the classroom, classroom routines, curriculum, instruction, grouping, and assessment.

Drawing from research, we argue that literacy-rich classrooms have seven characteristics: (1) an abundance of children's literature and other high-quality literacy materials; (2) physical arrangements that encourage a wide range of reading and writing; (3) daily literacy routines, including read-alouds, independent reading and writing, and sharing; (4) a culturally sensitive curriculum, which integrates the language arts and content study; (5) continuous assessment, which guides instruction; (6) a variety of instructional practices; and (7) a variety of grouping patterns. An overview of the characteristics of a literacy-rich classroom is presented in Figure 6.1.

Literacy Materials

It makes sense that children who have access to quality literature will be highly motivated readers and discerning writers. A good book inspires wonder, curiosity, deep thinking, emotional involvement, and aesthetic pleasure as well as provides models of memorable language.

The Case for Quality Literature

Research confirms that the amount of experience children have with literature correlates with their language development (Chomsky, 1972), reading achievement (Feitelson, Kita, & Goldstein, 1986), and quality of writing (Dressel, 1990). Children who are exposed to quality literature are more likely to learn to love literature and to include reading quality books as an important part of their lives (Hickman, 1979). They are more willing to sustain their involvement with a book through writing, doing projects, and participating in discussions (Eeds & Wells, 1989). Research has also shown that children whose classrooms have a large number of books in a high-quality library center choose to read more often (Morrow & Weinstein, 1982, 1986) and have higher reading achievement (Morrow, 1992).

One of the first decisions that a teacher faces is the selection of literacy materials. Teachers are responsible for using their local resources to locate and evaluate

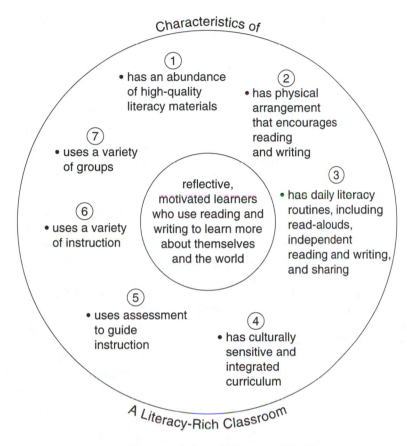

FIGURE 6.1 **Seven Characteristics of Literacy-Rich Classrooms**

materials for their literacy programs. Teachers should gather (1) a large classroom literature collection, (2) a collection of reference materials, (3) children's magazines, and (4) a variety of writing materials.

Classroom Literature Collection

Teachers in literacy-rich classrooms know a great deal about children's literature. They are aware of literary elements, are familiar with many authors and illustrators, and keep up with recent publications (Tomlinson & Lynch-Brown, 2002; Temple, Martinez, Yokota, & Naylor, 1998). They select books on topics of interest to children and that represent a range of difficulty levels.

Teachers choose books in picture book and chapter book format (collections for preschoolers may contain only picture books, but as children get older, they enjoy chapter books as well). Teachers may also include quality **big books** in their classrooms. **Picture books,** such as *Where the Wild Things Are* (Sendak, 1963), *Allison* (Say, 1997), and *The Wall* (Bunting, 1990), present stories or information through both the words of the text and the illustrations. **Chapter books,** such as *Sarah, Plain and Tall* (MacLachlan, 1985), *Ramona Quimby, Age 8* (Cleary, 1981), and *Dominic* (Steig, 1972), present stories or information primarily through text (although some chapter books, especially informational books, may have illustrations).

The process of locating a sufficient number of quality books can be daunting. Experts recommend that the number of books in a high-quality classroom collection should be eight to ten times the number of children (Fractor, Woodruff, Martinez, & Teale, 1993). Teachers can borrow books from local and school libraries, use bonus points from book clubs to obtain free books, and collect inexpensive books from book clubs and bookstores that offer educational discounts. (The Appendix provides lists of suggested literature for a classroom library.)

Genres of Literature.   Literature is generally classified into several broad categories, or **genres,** including traditional literature, fantasy, realistic fiction, historical fiction, biography and autobiography, informational books, and poetry. The classroom literature collection in literacy-rich classrooms includes many books from each of these genres.

Traditional literature has its roots in the oral storytelling tradition of long ago, which still exists today. Familiar stories such as *Goldilocks and the Three Bears* (Cauley, 1981) and *Little Red Riding Hood* (Hyman, 1983) are traditional tales once told by storytellers or family members that have been captured anew by modern illustrators. Traditional stories are found in every culture in the world, and the classroom library collection in a literacy-rich classroom should include many of these multicultural stories. Tales such as *The Brocaded Slipper and Other Vietnamese Tales* (Vuong, 1982) from Vietnam, *The King and the Tortoise* (Mollel, 1993) from Africa, and *Elfwyn's Saga* (Wisniewski, 1990) from Iceland allow children to find out about a wide variety of cultures and literary traditions.

Fables usually have animal characters and an explicitly stated moral. Most children enjoy the familiar fable of *The Town Mouse and the Country Mouse* (Cauley, 1984). Fables can be found in the folk literature of many different countries.

Folktales are usually short, have flat characters (all good, evil, or tricky), and have a happy ending, with good triumphing over evil. Some folktales include animal characters, for instance, *The Three Little Pigs* (Galdone, 1970) and *The Elephant's Wrestling Match* (Sierra, 1992). They may include motifs such as magic or transformations, as in *Frog Prince* (Grimm & Grimm, 1989), or a trickster, as in *Anansi the Spider: A Tale from the Ashanti* (McDermott, 1972).

Myths were created to explain natural occurrences, such as the seasons, constellations, or the creation of life. They include heroes or heroines who have superhuman and magical abilities. **Legends** are similar to myths, but are thought to be based on true stories that grew to exaggerated proportions. Legends contain heroes or heroines who have fantastic powers. Examples of myths and legends include *The Story of Jumping Mouse* (Steptoe, 1984) and *The Fire Children: A West African Creation Tale* (Maddern, 1993).

Fantasy includes elements that could not really happen, such as fantastic characters or fantastic settings. There are many fine examples of fantasies for young children in both picture book and chapter book format. Cassie Louise Light-foot, a young African American girl, takes a fantastic flight above her apartment's roof to marvel at the sparkling beauty of the George Washington Bridge and makes wishes for the good fortune of her family in *Tar Beach* (Ringgold, 1991). *Bunnicula* (Howe & Howe, 1979) is the amusing story of a rabbit who is mistaken for Dracula by the family dog.

Realistic fiction refers to stories about things that could plausibly happen in true life. The characters, setting, and events are realistic and believable. Some realistic fiction presents the humorous side of life, such as Judy Blume's hilarious tale, *The Pain and the Great One* (1974). Other realistic stories help children understand everyday problems, such as dealing with a stepparent, being homesick and lonely, or overcoming prejudice. For example, Alex and his stepfather both learn to respect each other more in *Like Jake and Me* (Jukes, 1984), and a homeless boy manages to keep his hope for a brighter future despite having to live at the airport in *Fly Away Home* (Bunting, 1991).

Historical fiction is set in the past and accurately reflects the time period in which it is set. Often historical fiction is intended to reflect truths about our own society or the universal conflicts that all of us must face, for example, having to overcome fear or learning the value of family relationships. *Dakota Dugout* (Turner, 1985) relates the story of a young woman's first sod house on the prairie, but comments on the values of simple things. *When Jessie Came Across the Sea* (Hest, 1997) tells the story of a young Jewish immigrant girl who earns money sewing lace to pay for her Grandmother's passage to the United States.

Biographies and **autobiographies** are stories about the lives of everyday or famous people. Written accurately and authentically, these texts often include photographs, letters, diaries, newspaper articles, and legal documents to provide supporting evidence. Biographies have been written about sports figures, such as *Teammates* (Golenbock, 1990); bullfighters, such as *El Chino* (Say, 1990); and presidents, such as *The Joke's on George* (Tunnell, 1993).

An autobiography is the life story of its author. Many famous children's authors have written autobiographies, which can be shared with children. Examples include *Bill Peet: An Autobiography* (Peet, 1989) and *The Art Lesson* (de Paola, 1989).

Informational books are books that provide realistic, accurate, and authentic information. Quality informational books avoid stereotyping, present more than one side of issues, have logical organizations, and arouse curiosity. Some examples of quality informational books are *Sugaring Time* (Lasky, 1983), which details the steps of making maple syrup, and *Water* (Canizares & Chanko, 1998), which describes a variety of liquid and solid forms of water; both books are suitable for very young children.

Joanna Cole (1986; 1987; 1989; 1990) has written a series of *Magic School Bus* books, which are very popular with young children. In these stories, set in a classroom, a wacky teacher, Ms. Frizzle, takes the children on fantastic field trips. Howker (1997) uses a similar technique to describe a wolf pack in *Walk with a Wolf*.

Poetry is text that contains condensed language, special lining, and imagery. Poetry often includes elements of rhythm and sound, such as rhyming, alliteration, and repetition. Poetry may capture a single moment in time or allow readers to see everyday events and objects in a new light. It appeals to the senses and calls to mind strong emotions. Some anthologies, or collections, of poems that appeal to young children are *Sing a Song of Popcorn: Every Child's Book of Poems* (de Regniers, Moore, White, & Carr, 1988) and *The Random House Book of Poetry for Children* (Prelutsky, 1983). Other books of poetry include poems written by a single author, such as *Brown Angels* (Myers, 1993), a series of poems inspired by turn-of-the-century photographs of African American children.

Special Picture Book Genres.   In addition to the genres just discussed, there are several additional types of picture books. These books are especially enjoyable for young children, and they have great potential for encouraging children's exploration of literature. Teachers should include several wordless picture books, predictable books, and alphabet books in their classroom libraries.

Wordless picture books portray a story through illustrations only. They appeal to a range of ages, even to adults (Abrahamson, 1981). *Pancakes for Breakfast* (de Paola, 1978) is a favorite of both preschoolers and older children. It illustrates the efforts of a little old woman as she makes pancakes. Young children enjoy the wordless book *Sunshine* (Ormerod, 1981), which illustrates the actions of a young girl who dresses herself while her parents oversleep. Second and third graders enjoy *Deep in the Forest* (Turkle, 1976), especially when they discover its play on the Goldilocks story.

Predictable books contain repeated dialogue or events. For example, the character Gingerbread Boy in the book *The Gingerbread Boy* (Galdone, 1975) repeats actions—he runs past a series of characters who chase him. He also repeats dialogue—each time he runs past a character, he taunts, "I've run away from a little old woman. I've run away from a little old man. And I can run away from you, I can." Predictable books are especially useful for helping children learn to read their first printed words (Bridge, 1986).

Alphabet books use the sequence of the alphabet to organize information or a story. They appeal to both very young and older children. In some alphabet books, a single picture represents the sound associated with an alphabet letter. In *Eating the Alphabet* (Ehlert, 1989), one or two fruits or vegetables are pictured and named for each letter of the alphabet. Other alphabet books tell stories, such as the story of growing, picking, and selling apples in *Applebet* (Watson, 1982). Still other alphabet books present information about a single topic. For example, Jerry Pallotta has written several alphabet books about a variety of topics, including insects, frogs, and reptiles (e.g., *The Yucky Reptile Alphabet Book*, 1986). Still other alphabet books are puzzles for readers to solve. Chris Van Allsburg's *The Z was Zapped* (1987) invites readers to guess what happens to letters by closely examining the illustrations (such as "the *B* was badly bitten," unpaged).

Audiovisual Materials.   Audiovisual materials are an important part of the classroom literacy program. Teachers can borrow copies of audiotapes, films, filmstrips, and videotapes of children's literature from local or school libraries. In addition, children enjoy learning more about favorite authors and illustrators through videotaped and audiotaped interviews. School librarians are especially helpful in locating these materials.

Reference Materials and Magazines.   **Reference materials** include dictionaries, thesauri, atlases, and encyclopedias and are intended to provide information about word meanings, concepts, geography, and other familiar topics. Today, many reference materials are published with detailed photographs and drawings so that even very young children enjoy looking at the illustrations in these materials. Publishers have also made available reference materials at a variety of difficulty levels. For example, very young children find picture dictionaries and encyclopedias intriguing. Two examples appropriate for young children are *My First Dictionary* (Roof, 1993a) and *My First Encyclopedia* (Roof, 1993b). Older children enjoy locating and reading information in *The Random House Children's Encyclopedia* (1992), a single-volume text loaded with diagrams, photographs, and drawings about common topics of study in the primary grades. A specialized dictionary that appeals to primary school-age children is *The Dictionary of Nature* (Burnie, 1994).

A new kind of dictionary, the visual dictionary, seems especially attractive to young children. **Visual dictionaries** rely on illustrations to define words. *The Macmillan Visual Dictionary* (actually intended for adults) defines words by presenting labeled drawings. For example, it includes a drawing of a bird in which more than twenty body parts, such as *pin feather,* are labeled. Other visual dictionaries are written for elementary schoolchildren and focus on single topics. Such dictionaries include *The Visual Dictionary of the Universe, The Visual Dictionary of the Earth,* and *The Visual Dictionary of the Human Body* (all published by Dorling Kindersley, 1993).

Many publishers produce highly useful informational books that children may use as references to locate information about topics of study. Noteworthy are the information series *Eyewitness Books* (published by Knopf) and *Eyewitness Science Books* (published by Dorling Kindersley). These books present detailed photographs, drawings, diagrams, and information about a variety of life science topics. Although the text of these books is often too difficult for many primary schoolchildren to read independently, the illustrations are informative and can heighten children's curiosity about scientific concepts.

Children's magazines are important functional print items in literacy-rich classrooms. They provide stimulating information on a variety of topics in both social studies and science, and they prompt children to experiment with new ideas in art or writing. Many teachers have found that having two or three copies of a magazine encourages children to read together or collaborate on a research project.

Physical Arrangement of Classrooms

Teachers arrange classrooms so that there are spaces for whole-class and small-group gatherings and so that invitations for reading and writing abound. Many early-childhood classrooms, especially those for preschoolers, are center based, and the centers are arranged to encourage the functional use of reading and writing. All literacy-rich classrooms include a library, a writing center, and a computer center. Teachers arrange these spaces so that materials are organized and easily accessible (Isbell & Exelby, 2001).

The Case for Library, Writing, and Computer Centers

Research confirms that the arrangement of space in the classroom library and writing center affects children's reading and writing. Children spend more time reading in classrooms with well-designed library centers (Morrow, 1997; Morrow & Weinstein, 1982, 1986). They generate and test hypotheses about written language and develop self-monitoring strategies in classrooms with well-designed writing centers (Rowe, 1994).

Computers also are an important component of the literacy-rich classroom. Research has shown that introducing computers into the classroom allows children to develop literacy concepts through play (Labbo, 1996). Computers increase social interaction among children as they share ideas and compose jointly (Bruce, Michaels, & Watson-Gregeo, 1985). Computers also encourage expanded explorations and new insights about literacy through multiple kinds of symbol making. For example, children may produce multimedia texts that include icons, drawn scribbles or illustrations, and word-processed text (Labbo, 1996). As a part of this multimedia composition process, children learn that constructing meaning involves manipulation of not just alphabet letters, but also a variety of other symbols. The physical arrangement of a computer center, type of software available, and incorporation of the computer into the overall literacy program affect the amount and quality of interactions that children have with the computer (Labbo & Ash, 1998).

Library Center

All classrooms have a **library center,** which houses a large part of the classroom literature collection. To provide a pleasant space for reading, listening to stories on audiotape, and talking about books, teachers

Place the center label in a prominent location.

Use bookshelves, hanging mobiles, or screens to partition the space from the remainder of the classroom.

Provide space for four to six children.

Arrange pillows, small rugs, or other comfortable seating.

Organize the books (using last name of author or genre).

Display several books with their covers facing outward.

Display props for telling stories, such as three stuffed bears, a doll, and the book for retelling *Goldilocks and the Three Bears.*

Arrange a display of books and objects on a special topic, such as an author, genre, or content topic (Fractor, Woodruff, Martinez, & Teale, 1993; Morrow & Weinstein, 1986).

In addition to spaces for reading books, the classroom library may also have a space for listening to stories on audiotape (or a listening center may be established in a nearby location). A listening center includes several audiotapes of stories that are either commercially available or made by parents or other volunteers. Each tape is accompanied by at least one copy of the story. Tapes and books can be kept in plastic bags and stored in plastic bins or hung on special display racks. Figure 6.2 shows a classroom library and listening center.

FIGURE 6.2   Classroom Library and Listening Center

Writing Center

The **writing center** serves a variety of purposes. For preschoolers it is an important place for groups of children and their teacher to gather, talk, write, and learn. For older primary schoolchildren, the center is used for small groups of children to meet to revise or edit their writing (see the explanation of writing processes presented in Chapter 10). It may also become a publishing center.

To create a writing center, teachers arrange a large table and several chairs of comfortable height for children. The table is large enough to accommodate several children and to include displays of greeting cards, messages, signs, and special words that encourage children to write. Shelves or a rolling cart for storing writing materials are nearby. Writing materials are labeled and easily accessible on the shelves. The materials are changed frequently so that children can explore a variety of writing implements and surfaces. Table 6.1 presents a list of materials that may be included in a writing center.

Computer Center

Computer centers are most effective when they are more centrally placed in the classroom to encourage creative and imaginative interactions rather than relegated to a back corner (Labbo & Ash, 1998). Children often consider their computer center a site for play; and playing on the computer, just like other kinds of dramatic play, can lead to important literacy insights (Labbo, 1996). For example, children may want to bring stuffed animals, informational books, storybooks, and other

---

TABLE 6.1   Materials for a Writing Center

A variety of writing tools, including

  pencils or pens with interesting shapes or fancy toppers such as feathers or objects

  markers such as highlighters, smelly markers, or markers that change colors

  alphabet stamps, tiles, cookie cutters, sponge letters, magnetic letters, felt letters

  crayons, chalk

A variety of writing surfaces, including

  clipboards, small white boards, chalkboards

  lined and unlined paper in a variety of shapes and colors

  a variety of writing pads, including sticky notes, spiral notebooks, to-do lists

  sand tray

A variety of bookbinding materials, including

  a camera to take photos for "all about the author" page

  stapled books of four to eight pages

  computers with word-processing programs and other publishing programs

A variety of reference materials, including

  a photo book of all the children with their first and last names

  special words on index cards (such as seasonal or theme vocabulary)

  pictionaries, dictionaries, visual dictionaries

  handwriting chart

artifacts to the computer center to support their interactions with the computer. Therefore, computers should be placed on large tables that can hold a variety of objects in addition to the computer. For example, when viewing a talking book, children might want to bring a stuffed version of the main character or the print copy of the book with them to the computer.

The computer center should include displays of books, posters, or computer-generated products that will encourage children to engage in creative activities. A "Helpful Hint" poster about basic computer operations also should be displayed. Pictures of icons, examples of illustrations using the "paint brush" and "pencil," or illustrations from children's computer explorations may stimulate further imaginative computer-generated products. Children may also be encouraged to use the computer to enrich dramatic play. For example, when children are playing in a "bank," they can use the computer to generate checks or bank books. Children would enjoy creating imaginative menus for use in a "restaurant" dramatic play center.

Two broad types of software should be available for use in the computer center: expressive and receptive (Labbo & Ash, 1998). Expressive software includes programs that allow children to discover insights about literacy concepts as they create text and graphics (Labbo & Ash, 1998). Programs such as *Kidpix, KidWords 2,* and *Kidwriter Golden Edition* encourage children's active exploration of a variety of symbols, including drawing, painting, assembling images and pictures, and printing text. Receptive software allows children to learn new concepts and share literature through computer automation and graphics, including automated storybook programs. Table 6.2 presents a list of software that might be included in a computer center.

TABLE 6.2 Software for a Computer Center

Alphabet Express by School Zone	*Kidpix* by Broderbund
Arthur's Adventures with DW by The Learning Company	*Mike Mulligan and His Steam Shovel* by Simon and Schuster Interactive
Bailey's Book House by Edmark	*My First Incredible Amazing Dictionary 2.0* by DK Multimedia
Blue's Clues ABC Time by Infogrames Entertainment	*One Duck Stuck* by Tumblebooks
Clifford the Big Red Dog Thinking Adventures by Scholastic	*Reading Blaster* by Knowledge Adventure
Curious George Pre-K ABCs by Pearson Software	*Reading Rabbit* by The Learning Company
Curious George Reads, Writes, and Spells by Pearson Software	*Richard Scarry's Best Reading Ever* by Ingram Micro
Dad, Can I have a T-Rex, Please? by Tumblebooks	*Zoboomafoo Alphabet* by The Learning Company

Many schools already make extensive use of computers in their literacy program through the *Writing to Read* program (Labbo, Murray, & Phillips, 1995–1996). This program is delivered in an IBM computer lab in which children rotate through five "stations": a computer station where children are taught sound–letter relationships; a work journal station where children use paper-and-pencil work sheets to practice saying and writing words, using the sound–letter relationships they were taught at the computer station; a writing–typing station where children may copy words or stories by hand or on an electronic typewriter or computer; a tape library station where children listen to stories that stress the sound–letter relationships being taught; and a make words station where children play games to reinforce their knowledge of sound–letter relationships.

While the **Writing to Read lab** may be successful with some children, with alterations it can be a powerful support for all young children's literacy learning. First, the computer sound–letter learning activities should be embedded in a more meaningful experience provided by a theme that extends over a week or two. For example, if the computer sound–letter lessons focus on the words *cat, dog,* and *fish* for teaching consonants and short vowel sounds, the theme might be "Caring For and Enjoying Pets" (Labbo, Murray, & Phillips, 1995–1996, p. 317). Children can gather together when they first arrive at the lab to listen to their teacher read a story or informational book aloud that is related to the theme. Storytelling, drama, and **storytelling props** (all described later in this chapter) encourage children's active participation. Second, children should be encouraged to experiment with word processors for drawing and writing responses to literature, stories, or other texts rather than copying words. Finally, stories for listening should come from literature and can be selected to focus on the theme.

Literacy Routines

Teachers in literacy-rich classrooms read aloud or tell stories daily and set aside time for children to read and write independently. Children have frequent opportunities to share their writing and engage in activities that extend their responses to literature (Hoffman, Roser, & Battle, 1993). Response-to-literature activities include retelling, drama, writing, talking, and other creative activities.

The Case for Classroom Routines

There is ample evidence that daily reading and writing experiences are crucial for children's literacy development. Children whose teachers read aloud or tell stories to them on a daily basis are highly motivated readers with extensive vocabularies and effective comprehension strategies (Dickinson & Smith, 1994; Dickinson & Sprague, 2001; Feitelson, Kita, & Goldstein, 1986; Morrow & Weinstein, 1982; 1986). Similarly, the more time children spend reading independently, the better their vocabularies, understanding of spelling principles, and comprehension (Adams, 1990; Anderson, Hiebert, Scott, & Wilkinson, 1985).

Research has shown that the amount of independent reading in which children engage has a major impact on their vocabulary knowledge. By fifth grade, the average student reads independently less than five minutes a *day* (Anderson, Wilson, & Fielding, 1988). This yields only 282,000 words read per year. In contrast, a student who reads independently an hour a day, reads over 4,300,000 words per year. Increasing the amount of children's independent reading is a critical component of every reading program.

Sharing experiences about reading and writing is also a critical component of supporting literacy development. Children who talk together about a book, write responses to literature, and share writing with classmates construct interpretations of literature, use higher levels of thinking, and write better quality compositions (Barone, 1990; Eeds & Wells, 1989; Five, 1986; Kelly, 1990; Pressley et al., 2001).

Reading Aloud and Telling Stories

Teachers share literature with children by reading stories, telling stories, or showing films and videos about quality literature. Teachers plan carefully before sharing literature with children. They keep in mind the age and interests of the children as they select books to read aloud. Books selected for reading have illustrations that are large enough for a group of children to see (Glazer, 1981). Teachers preview books carefully to become familiar with story texts and illustrations and to develop purposes for sharing (we will describe more what these purposes might be in later chapters).

Frequently, teachers tell stories using special storytelling props (Cliatt & Shaw, 1988; Ross, 1980). Among the many kinds of literature props that teachers can use to tell a story are objects, clothesline props, flannel board props, puppets, and masks. *Object props* are objects that represent certain characters and actions. Object props for the story *Where the Wild Things Are* (Sendak, 1963) might include a teddy bear (to represent Max sent to bed with no supper), an oar (to represent his travels to the land where the Wild Things Are), and a crown (to represent Max's becoming King of the Wild Things).

Clothesline props include pictures drawn to represent important events in the story. These pictures are clothespinned to a clothesline stretched across the classroom as a story is read or told. *Puppets* make perfect props for storytelling. Finger puppets can be made by drawing characters on paper and carefully cutting them out to include special tabs for fastening around the finger. Stick puppets can be made by coloring characters on stiff paper, cutting them out, and attaching them to soda straws. *Flannel board props* can be made from Velcro, felt, yarn, lace, or other sewing notions.

Children have many creative ideas for constructing their own story-retelling props. First graders used a green pipe cleaner for the hungry caterpillar and punched holes in construction paper food cutouts to retell *The Very Hungry Cater-pillar.* As they retold the story, they slipped each food cutout onto the green pipe-cleaner caterpillar. Third graders worked together to decide the number and content of pictures needed to retell *Nine-in-One. Grr! Grr!* (Xiong, 1989) on a story clothesline. They retold the story collaboratively—each illustrator hung his or her picture on the clothesline and retold that portion of the story.

Independent Reading and Writing

Teachers provide children with plenty of time to browse through and read books of their choice and to write on self-selected topics. Some classrooms and entire schools promote daily reading by using **SSR (sustained silent reading).** During this time, everyone in the classroom (even the teacher) or school (including the principal and other school personnel) reads silently for a specified period of time (usually ten to twenty minutes). However, with so many schools adopting a literature-based read-ing program, time for self-selected reading is usually a part of reading instruction (we discuss more about shared reading and reading workshops—both of which include daily reading of self-selected texts—in later chapters).

One way to establish a daily writing activity is to have children write in a journal (Hipple, 1985; Kintisch, 1986). Each child in the classroom is given his or her own journal. Journals may simply be small books made by stapling paper together, or they may be more elaborate books that children or adults have bound. A special time each day is set aside to write in journals. Children are allowed to write anything they wish.

Sharing Response-to-Literature Activities

Response-to-literature activities encourage children's emotional and intellectual involvement with literature. These activities can serve many purposes, including helping children explore the language of stories, the themes of literature, the media of illustrations, and the connections between literature experiences and life experi-ences. Response activities can support children's imaginative, creative, social, moral, intellectual, and language development (Glazer, 1981). Examples of activities in-clude laughing, writing, drawing, retelling, commenting, questioning, rereading, modeling in clay, pantomiming, dramatizing, dancing, singing, cooking, and paint-ing (Hickman, 1981). Teachers in literacy-rich classrooms plan a variety of these activities from which children can choose and provide time for children to engage in them.

Response-to-literature activities expand and enrich children's understand-ings of literature. One way children respond to literature is by writing in a **response journal.** Primary school-age children's written responses often consist of retellings, evaluations, and related personal experiences (Dekker, 1991). Fig-ure 6.3 presents an entry from a first grader's response journal. Vivian responded to *Hey, Al* (Yorinks, 1986) by describing how Al felt when the bird came into his bathroom.

When he was
in the bath Room
the Bird friten
him

FIGURE 6.3   Vivian's Response to *Hey, Al* (Yorinks, 1986)

Culturally Sensitive and Integrated Curriculum

Curriculum is what children learn related to the disciplines of language arts and literature, social studies, science, mathematics, art, music, health, and physical education. Recent research and theory regarding the literacy curriculum suggest that children learn better when the curriculum is integrated across the language arts and across disciplines and when it is culturally sensitive.

The Case for Culturally Sensitive and Integrated Curriculum

All children belong to cultural groups that in some way shape their attitudes, beliefs, and ways of making meaning with written language (Heath, 1983). When children perceive of a writing task or a text as having content that reaffirms their cultural identities, they are more likely to become engaged in the task and to construct personal meaning (Ferdman, 1990; Meier, 2000). **Culturally relevant topics,** topics that children perceive as culturally affirming, are an important avenue to learning and literacy development (Au, 1993; 1998).

Curriculum integration—teaching broad topics that cover areas in more than one discipline—improves teaching and learning (Dewey, 1933; Vars, 1991). One way of integrating the curriculum is to capitalize on the "interrelationships of the language processes—reading, writing, speaking, and listening" (Routman, 1991, p. 272). **Integrated language arts** activities are those in which children talk, listen, read, and write. For example, writing a poem often includes talking to others about possible topics for writing, listening to others as they talk about topics or read their poems, and reading one's own composition.

Recent recommendations for curriculum development strongly support curriculum integration across content topics (Hughes, 1991). Children learn concepts and ideas related to a topic that cuts across more than one content area, for example, incorporating earth science, geography, and math. This kind of instruction allows children to see connections among facts and theories, provides a focus for selecting instructional activities, provides for coherence of activities, allows children to study topics in depth, and promotes positive attitudes (Lipson, Valencia, Wixson, & Peters, 1993).

Culturally Sensitive Curriculum

The curriculum in literacy-rich classrooms reflects sensitivity for children's cultures in both its content (what is taught and what children are expected to read and write) and its instruction (how concepts are taught). In most classrooms, one or more students have recently arrived in the United States and speak a language other than English at home. Many classrooms include children from a variety of cultural and language backgrounds. Regardless of the mixture of children in a particular classroom, all children need exposure to literature that presents nonstereotyped information about a wide variety of cultural groups.

A culturally sensitive curriculum eliminates the artificial dichotomies created when studying "other" cultures; it includes examples from many cultures as a part of all learning experiences. That is, the content that children study and the material they read naturally present many different cultures. Teachers are careful to include many examples of multicultural literature in all their literature theme units and content units. **Multicultural literature** consists of

> fiction with characters who are from cultural groups that have been underrepresented in children's books: African Americans, Asian Americans, Hispanic Americans, Native Americans, and Americans from religious minorities;
>
> fiction that takes us to other nations and introduces readers to the cultures of people residing outside of the United States; and
>
> information books, including biographies, that focus on African Americans, Asian Americans, Hispanic Americans, Native Americans, Americans from religious minorities, and people living outside the United States. (Zarrillo, 1994, pp. 2–3)

The best in multicultural literature presents culturally authentic information (Bishop, 1992). **Culturally authentic literature** portrays people and the values, customs, and beliefs of a cultural group in ways recognized by members of that group as valid and authentic. Most culturally authentic literature is written or illustrated by members of the cultural group. The Appendix provides a list of multicultural literature including culturally authentic literature.

An important part of a culturally sensitive curriculum is consideration of the language of instruction. Children learn best in their home language. However, many teachers are unable to provide instruction in children's home languages. They may not be qualified speakers of the language, or there may be children with several different home languages in one classroom. Teachers should always be sensitive to children's natural tendency to use home language to communicate complex ideas. Chapter 11 provides more information about teaching children whose home language is not English.

Literature Theme Units

Teachers can integrate activities across the language arts by using literature themes as a focus for curriculum development. **Literature theme units** are units of instruction focused on learning about authors or illustrators, genres, themes, or a single book.

As a part of literature theme units, children engage in activities that include talking, listening, reading, and writing. For example, in a kindergarten literature theme unit comparing versions of "The Gingerbread Boy" story (Tompkins & McGee, 1993), the teacher could read five versions of the story aloud to the class, including

Arno, E. (1985). *The gingerbread man.* New York: Scholastic (this book is also available in big book format).

Brown, M. (1972). *The bun: A tale from Russia.* New York: Harcourt Brace Jovanovich.

Cauley, L. (1988). *The pancake boy.* New York: Putnam.

Galdone, P. (1975). *The gingerbread boy.* New York: Seabury.

Sawyer, R. (1953). *Journey Cake, Ho!* New York: Viking.

Figure 6.4 presents a web of talking, listening, reading, and writing activities that could be included in this literature theme unit.

Integrated Content Units

Integrated content units use themes to plan instruction. Units of instruction are organized around a broad theme that includes learning concepts across more than one content area, active inquiry activities, and activities incorporating all the language arts.

For example, a teacher may use the theme of "growing" as a focus for learning experiences for a group of first graders. This theme explores physical changes that occur as a part of growth in plants, animals, and humans; measurement; and the literary theme "growing up." As a part of the activities included in the theme, the teacher may read aloud folktales in which plants grow to enormous sizes (such as *The Enormous Turnip,* retold by Kathy Parkinson, 1986), stories that contrast children at different ages (such as *Stevie,* by John Steptoe, 1969), poems about childhood

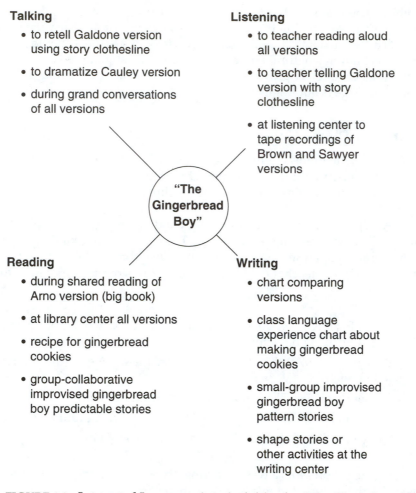

Talking

- to retell Galdone version using story clothesline
- to dramatize Cauley version
- during grand conversations of all versions

Listening

- to teacher reading aloud all versions
- to teacher telling Galdone version with story clothesline
- at listening center to tape recordings of Brown and Sawyer versions

"The Gingerbread Boy"

Reading

- during shared reading of Arno version (big book)
- at library center all versions
- recipe for gingerbread cookies
- group-collaborative improvised gingerbread boy predictable stories

Writing

- chart comparing versions
- class language experience chart about making gingerbread cookies
- small-group improvised gingerbread boy pattern stories
- shape stories or other activities at the writing center

FIGURE 6.4 Integrated Language Arts Activities for "The Gingerbread Boy" Literature Theme

activities at different ages (*I Want to Be*, by Thylias Moss, 1993), and informational books about growing up (such as *Pueblo Boy: Growing Up in Two Worlds*, by Marcia Keegan, 1991). The teacher may guide the children in dramatizing the stories, and children may create storytelling props to use in retelling the folktales.

The teacher may also read informational books about the growth of plants and animals (such as *How a Seed Grows*, by Helen Jordan, 1992, and several books from the *See How They Grow* series published by Dorling Kindersley, 1992, including *See How They Grow: Butterfly, See How They Grow: Frog*, and *See How They Grow: Mouse*).

Assessment, Instruction, and Grouping

We have stressed the social nature of becoming literate: Children expand their understanding of literacy concepts as they interact with others. They learn from each other in a variety of activities in the classroom, such as sitting together at a computer to construct graphics or a story. They also learn from their teacher as she or he talks with them about the story they are composing. Children learn from the multiple models and demonstrations offered in a literacy-rich, talk-filled classroom. However, children also learn from instruction that is thoughtfully planned and based on careful assessment of their current level of literacy accomplishments (see Chapter 12).

Assessment bridges the gap between the specific concepts that an individual child currently uses in reading and writing and instruction that is aimed at enhancing that child's current level of knowledge. In order to know what to teach next, teachers carefully watch what children do as they are reading and writing. **Kid watching** involves direct and informal observation of children as they are using reading and writing in play, reading or writing independently, or working in a cooperative group to accomplish an assigned task (Goodman, 1978).

Good assessment cannot be separated from teaching. While teachers are teaching, they are also assessing. Research confirms that children's literacy learning is enhanced when teachers draw from informed observation during teaching to provide feedback on children's reading and writing (DeFord, Pinnell, Lyons, & Place, 1990) and to plan instruction (McCormick, 1994). A critical component of assessment is determining not just what kind of feedback and instruction individual children need, but how to deliver instruction and provide opportunities for practice.

The Case for a Variety of Instruction

Teachers use a variety of instructional approaches in a literacy-rich classroom in order to meet the needs of their diverse learners. They use instructional talk, modeling, and planned direct instruction.

Talk is an important component in children's literacy learning (Genishi, McCarrier, & Nussbaum, 1988; Linfors, 1988). As children talk together about their compositions, they help each other read, construct ideas, spell, use correct grammar, and clarify information (Kamii & Randazzo, 1985; Rowe, 1994). When children talk with their teachers while they are reading and writing, they learn to use reading strategies (DeFord, Pinnell, Lyons, & Place, 1990). Teachers' talk helps children compose, revise, and edit (Calkins, 1986; Graves, 1983).

Most researchers conclude that talk surrounding literacy activities extends children's literacy understandings because it helps situate them in their zone of proximal development (Vygotsky, 1978; see Chapter 1 for a discussion of the zone of proximal development and its influence on literacy learning). Chapters 7 through 10 provide multiple examples of children learning from a teacher's careful modeling and demonstration of reading and writing strategies.

Research also shows that children learn from direct, planned instruction based on assessment of children's current level of literacy accomplishments. Children's comprehension is enhanced when teachers help students "construct understandings about: (a) the content of the text itself; (b) strategies that aid in interpreting the text; and (c) the nature of the reading process itself" (Dole, Duffy, Roehler, & Pearson, 1991, p. 252). Planned instruction also influences the development of reading skills, especially the ability to decode or "sound out" words. Teachers who provide coaching at the moment of need (such as when a child is struggling to identify or spell a word) and who provide direct, planned instruction in using letter patterns to unlock unknown words have a significant impact on children's reading abilities (Dahl, Scharer, Lawson, & Grogan, 1999; Foorman, Francis, Fletcher, Schatschneider, & Mehta, 1998). Chapters 7 through 10 provide many examples of direct and planned instruction that extends children's reading and writing achievement.

The Case for Multiple Grouping Patterns

Children learn in whole-class groups, small groups, partner or other cooperative tasks, or individual assignments. Children's learning can be fostered through any grouping pattern (Dickinson & Sprague, 2001; Hiebert & Colt, 1989). Whole-class group activities foster a sense of community; small groups provide more natural one-on-one language interactions; and independent activities allow children to pursue personal interests (Berghoff & Egawa, 1991). However, the way in which children are selected for groups is an important factor in their literacy learning. In elementary schools, there is a long history of using reading ability as a criterion for selecting children for reading group membership (Barr & Dreeben, 1991). Traditionally, children grouped for reading had similar, or **homogeneous, reading abilities.** Unfortunately, research has shown that children in low-ability groups receive a different kind of reading instruction from that given to children in high-ability groups (Allington, 1983). Children in lower achieving groups typically get instruction with a stronger focus on reading words, while children in higher achieving groups get instruction with a stronger focus on comprehension. Therefore, some experts have recommended that children not be grouped by ability for reading instruction.

However, when children begin formal reading instruction, it is critical that they spend some time reading challenging, but readable text (Clay, 1991). The text that children read as a part of this kind of instruction should be carefully matched with their level of achievement. Therefore, it is likely that children will spend some time reading with other children of similar reading ability in order to maximize the effectiveness of instruction with appropriate text. Because teachers will be working with small groups of children on a variety of reading levels, it is critical that teachers achieve a balance of instructional focus for all children: instruction that focuses on children's developing a variety of strategies for reading words accurately and fluently and instruction that focuses on helping children acquire a variety of strategies for constructing meaning (McIntyre & Pressley, 1996). It is also critical that children have experiences working in a variety of grouping patterns. Teachers need a framework for instruction that provides children with opportunities to learn in whole-class groups, in small groups with children at a variety of achievement levels, with partners, and alone. They also need a framework that balances teacher-initiated instruction, in which teachers guide, lead, and provide explicit instruction, with child-responsive activities, in which children initiate, guide, and participate in reading and writing experiences (Baumann & Ivey, 1997).

Instructional Framework

A successful instructional framework allows children many opportunities to observe teachers as they model reading and writing. It also makes provisions for children to engage in reading and writing guided by the teacher and independently (Fountas & Pinnell, 1996; Pinnell & Fountas, 1998). Chapters 7 through 10 will include detailed descriptions of many components of such a framework. These include such practices as read-alouds, shared reading, guided reading, reading and writing workshops, cooperative learning groups, partner reading, independent reading, shared writing, interactive writing, and independent writing.

Chapter Summary

Early childhood professional organizations stress the importance of all aspects of children's development. Children's literacy learning should be embedded within child-centered early-childhood programs with developmentally appropriate practices. Exemplary early-childhood programs are found in literacy-rich classrooms where children are reflective, motivated readers and writers who use literacy to learn about their world.

To create literacy-rich classrooms, teachers select quality classroom literature collections that include traditional literature, fantasy, realistic fiction, historical fiction, biography, informational books, poetry, wordless picture books, predictable books, and alphabet books. They select reference materials, audiovisual materials, children's magazines, and writing materials.

Teachers infuse reading and writing materials throughout the room to encourage functional use of literacy. They set up a classroom library center, a writing center, and computer center.

Teachers establish three daily routines using reading and writing. Teachers read or tell stories, poems, or informational books daily; they set aside time for children to read and write on topics of their choice; and they plan activities in which children share their writing and responses to literature.

The curriculum is organized around literature content units that include talking, listening, reading, and writing activities. All units include multicultural literature.

Teachers provide instruction in a variety of settings as they demonstrate reading and writing, guide interactive discussions, and provide direct teaching through modeling. They form a variety of groups, including whole-class gatherings, small groups, and partners, and they set aside time for children to work alone. Groups usually incorporate children with a variety of different ability levels who are encouraged to work cooperatively. Teachers assess children's literacy learning and use information from their assessments, in part, to guide decisions about instruction.

Applying the Information

A description of Mrs. E's kindergarten classroom and literacy activities follows. Use the seven characteristics of a literacy-rich classroom to think about the literacy environment in Mrs. E's classroom. Discuss how Mrs. E's classroom illustrates each of the seven characteristics. What suggestions might you make about room arrangement and instruction?

Mrs. E has twenty-two kindergartners in a relatively small room. Nearly all of the children who attend this school receive free lunch (their families fall below the poverty limit established by the federal government). A map of the classroom is presented in Figure 6.5. This map illustrates that Mrs. E's room is equipped with twenty-four desks and two tables. The entire room is carpeted.

Each morning Mrs. E reads at least one selection of children's literature to the entire class. The children gather around her on the rug in the large-group area. Next, Mrs. E has experience time. During this time, she might demonstrate a science experiment, have a guest speaker, or read nonfiction. Each of these daily experiences is related to a topic of study. For example, one unit of study focused on insects. A man who keeps bees visited the classroom and brought his equipment to the class. The children kept ants in an ant farm. Mrs. E read many books that had insects as characters as well as informational books about insects.

After experience time, the children usually dictate and read accounts of what they learned that day or dictate retellings of favorite stories or charts. Sometimes Mrs. E prepares her own accounts of the previous day's experience for the children to read with her.

Next, Mrs. E holds a five- to ten-minute lesson or discussion designed to motivate the children to write. During the insect unit, children were encouraged to write poems, stories, and predictable stories about insects. One of the lessons Mrs. E taught was to show the children a poster she had made about the letters *b* and *c*. On the poster were several pictures of objects with names beginning with these letters (*boat, bat, beaver, cat, candy, cookie*). Mrs. E reminded the children that as they listened to words they wanted to write, they might hear some sounds like those in the words *boat* or *cat*. They could use the letters *b* and *c*.

After the lesson, the children write at their desks. Mrs. E circulates around the room, asking questions, making comments, and answering children's questions. As the children finish their writing, they read their writing to each other, select books from the library center, or read child-authored poems, stories, and books that are kept on the authors' tables.

Last, Mrs. E holds author's chair. (A special chair is placed in the group area on the rug for a child to sit in as he or she reads his or her writing.) Many children

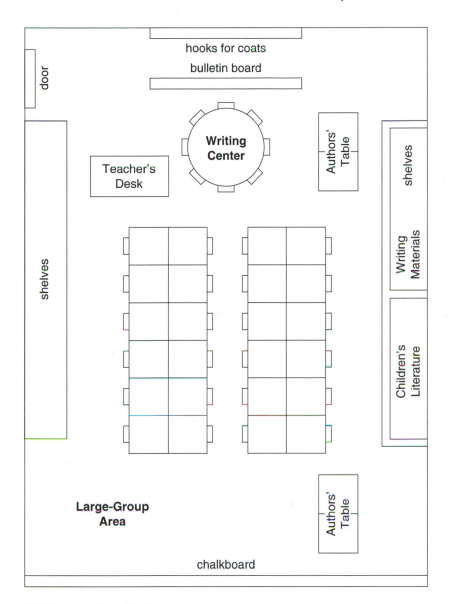

FIGURE 6.5   Mrs. E's Classroom

have opportunities to read their writing. The children know that they may choose to "talk about their writing" or "read what they wrote." They feel very comfortable as the other children make comments and offer praise. Mrs. E always comments on some aspect of the content of the writing, "I didn't know there were ants called carpenters. We will need to read more about them. Will you help me find out about them?"

Going Beyond the Text

Visit a preschool or elementary school classroom and observe literacy instruction and activities. Look carefully at the literacy materials that are available in the room. Note how often children interact with these literacy materials. Observe the children and their teacher as they interact during literacy instruction and as the children work on literacy projects. Use the seven characteristics of literacy-rich classrooms as a guide for discussing your observations.

REFERENCES

Abrahamson, R. F. (1981). An update on wordless picture books with an annotated bibliography. *The Reading Teacher, 34,* 417–421.

Adams, M. (1990). *Beginning to read: Thinking and learning about print.* Cambridge: MIT Press.

Allington, R. (1983). The reading instruction provided readers of differing ability. *Elementary School Journal, 83,* 255–265.

Anderson, R. C., Hiebert, E. H., Scott, J. A., & Wilkinson, I. A. G. (1985). *Becoming a nation of readers: The report of the commission on reading.* Washington, D.C.: The National Institute of Education.

Anderson, R. C., Wilson, P. T., & Fielding, L. G. (1988). Growth in reading and how children spend their time outside of school. *Reading Research Quarterly, 23,* 285–303.

Au, K. (1993). *Literacy instruction in multicultural settings.* New York: Harcourt Brace Jovanovich.

Au, K. (1998). Constructivist approaches, phonics, and the literacy learning of students of diverse backgrounds. In T. Shanahan & F. Rodrigues-Brown (Eds.), *47th Yearbook of the National Reading Conference* (pp. 1–21). Chicago, IL: National Reading Conference.

Barone, D. (1990). The written response of young children: Beyond comprehension. *The New Advocate, 3,* 49–56.

Barr, R., & Dreeben, R. (1991). Grouping students for reading instruction. In R. Barr, M. Kamil, P. Mosenthal, & P. Pearson (Eds.), *Handbook of reading research, vol. 2* (pp. 885–910). White Plains, NY: Longman.

Baumann, J. F., & Ivey, G. (1997). Delicate balances: Striving for curriculum and instructional equilibrium in a second-grade, literature/strategy-based classroom. *Reading Research Quarterly, 32,* 224–275.

Berghoff, B., & Egawa, K. (1991). No more "rocks": Grouping to give students control of their learning. *The Reading Teacher, 44,* 536–541.

Bishop, R. (1992). Multicultural literature for children: Making informed choices. In V. Harris (Ed.), *Teaching multicultural literature in grades K–8* (pp. 37–53). Norwood, MA: Christopher-Gordon.

Blume, J. (1974). *The pain and the great one.* New York: Bradbury.

Bridge, C. (1986). Predictable books for beginning readers and writers. In M. R. Sampson (Ed.), *The pursuit of literacy: Early reading and writing* (pp. 81–96). Dubuque, IA: Kendall/Hunt.

Bruce, B., Michaels, S., & Watson-Gregeo, K. (1985). How computers can change the writing process. *Language Arts, 62,* 143–149.

Bunting, E. (1990). *The wall.* New York: Clarion.

Bunting, E. (1991). *Fly away home.* New York: Clarion.

Burnie, D. (1994). *The dictionary of nature.* London: Dorling Kindersley.

Calkins, L. M. (1986). *The art of teaching writing.* Portsmouth, NH: Heinemann.

Canizares, S., & Chanko, P. (1998). *Water.* New York: Scholastic.

Cauley, L. (1981). *Goldilocks and the three bears.* New York: Putnam.

Cauley, L. (1984). *The town mouse and the country mouse.* New York: Putnam.

Chomsky, C. (1972). Stages in language development and reading exposure. *Harvard Educational Review, 42,* 1–33.

Clay, M. M. (1991). *Becoming literate: The construction of inner control.* Portsmouth, NH: Heinemann.

Cleary, B. (1981). *Ramona Quimby, age 8.* New York: Morrow.

Cliatt, M., & Shaw, J. (1988). The storytime exchange: Ways to enhance it. *Childhood Education, 64,* 293–298.

Cole, J. (1986). *The magic school bus at the waterworks.* New York: Scholastic.

Cole, J. (1987). *The magic school bus inside the earth.* New York: Scholastic.

Cole, J. (1989). *The magic school bus inside the human body.* New York: Scholastic.

Cole, J. (1990). *The magic school bus lost in the solar system.* New York: Scholastic.

Dahl, K. L., Scharer, P. L., Lawson, L. L., & Grogan, P. R. (1999). Phonics instruction and student achievement in whole language first grade classrooms. *Reading Research Quarterly.*

DeFord, D., Pinnell, G., Lyons, C., & Place, Q. (1990). *Report of the follow-up study, Columbus Reading Recovery program 1988–1989* (Report Vol. 11). Columbus: The Ohio State University.

de Paola, T. (1978). *Pancakes for breakfast.* New York: Harcourt Brace Jovanovich.

de Paola, T. (1989). *The art lesson.* New York: Putnam.

Dekker, M. (1991). Books, reading, and response: A teacher-researcher tells a story. *The New Advocate, 4,* 37–46.

de Regniers, B., Moore, E., White, M., & Carr, J. (Compilers). (1988). *Sing a song of popcorn: Every child's book of poems.* New York: Scholastic.

Dewey, J. (1933). *How we think* (rev. ed.). Boston: Heath.

Dickinson, D., & Smith, M. (1994). Long-term effects of preschool teachers' book readings on low-income children's vocabulary and story comprehension. *Reading Research Quarterly, 29,* 104–122.

Dickinson, D. K., & Sprague, K. E. (2001). The nature and impact of early childhood care environments on the language and early literacy development of children from low-income families. In S. B. Neuman & D. K. Dickinson (Eds.), *Handbook of early literacy research* (pp. 263–280). New York: Guilford.

Dole, J., Duffy, G., Roehler, L., & Pearson, D. (1991). Moving from the old to the new: Research on reading comprehension instruction. *Review and Educational Research, 61,* 239–264.

Dressel, J. (1990). The effects of listening to and discussing different qualities of children's literature on the narrative writing of fifth graders. *Research in the Teaching of English, 24,* 397–414.

Eeds, M., & Wells, D. (1989). Grand conversations: An exploration of meaning construction in literature study groups. *Research in the Teaching of English, 23,* 4–29.

Ehlert, L. (1989). *Eating the alphabet.* New York: Harcourt Brace Jovanovich.

Feitelson, D., Kita, B., & Goldstein, Z. (1986). The effects of listening to series stories on first graders' comprehension and use of language. *Research in the Teaching of English, 20,* 336–356.

Ferdman, B. (1990). Literacy and cultural identity. *Harvard Educational Review, 60,* 181–204.

Five, C. (1986). Fifth graders respond to a changed reading program. *Harvard Educational Review, 56,* 395–405.

Foorman, B., Francis, D., Fletcher, J., Schatschneider, C., & Mehta, P. (1998). The role of instruction in learning to read: Preventing reading failure in at-risk children. *Journal of Educational Psychology, 90,* 1–15.

Fountas, I. C., & Pinnell, G. S. (1996). *Guided reading: Good first teaching for all children.* Portsmouth, NH: Heinemann.

Fractor, J., Woodruff, M., Martinez, M., & Teale, W. (1993). Let's not miss opportunities to promote voluntary reading: Classroom libraries in elementary school. *The Reading Teacher, 46,* 476–484.

Galdone, P. (1970). *The three little pigs.* New York: Seabury.

Galdone, P. (1975). *The gingerbread boy.* New York: Clarion.

Genishi, C., McCarrier, A., & Nussbaum, N. R. (1988). Research currents: Classroom interaction as teaching and learning. *Language Arts, 65,* 182–191.

Glazer, J. I. (1981). *Literature for young children.* Columbus, OH: Merrill.

Golenbock, P. (1990). *Teammates.* San Diego: Harcourt Brace Jovanovich.

Goodman, Y. M. (1978). Kid watching: An alternative to testing. *National Elementary Principals Journals, 57,* 41–45.

Graves, D. H. (1983). Teacher intervention in children's writing: A response to Myra Barrs. *Language Arts, 10,* 841–846.

Grimm, J., & Grimm, W. (1989). *Frog prince.* New York: North-South.

Harris, V. J. (1992). *Teaching multicultural literature in grades K–8.* Norwood, MA: Christopher-Gordon.

Heath, S. B. (1983). *Ways with words: Language, life, and work in communities and classrooms.* New York: Cambridge University Press.

Hest, A. (1997). *When Jessie came across the sea.* Cambridge, MA: Candlewick Press.

Hickman, J. (1979). *Response to literature in a school environment. Doctoral dissertation,* The Ohio State University, Columbus, OH.

Hickman, J. (1981). A new perspective on response to literature: Research in an elementary school setting. *Research in the Teaching of English, 15,* 343–354.

Hiebert, E., & Colt, J. (1989). Patterns of literature-based reading instruction. *The Reading Teacher, 43,* 14–20.

Hipple, M. L. (1985). Journal writing in kindergarten. *Language Arts, 62,* 255–261.

Hodges, M. (1984). *Saint George and the dragon.* Boston: Little, Brown.

Hoffman, J., Roser, N., & Battle, J. (1993). Reading aloud in classrooms: From the modal toward a "model." *The Reading Teacher, 46,* 496–503.

Howe, D., & Howe, J. (1979). *Bunnicula: A rabbit tale of mystery.* New York: Atheneum.

Howker, J. (1997). *Walk with a wolf.* Cambridge, MA: Candlewick Press.

Hughes, M. (1991). *Curriculum integration in the primary grades: A framework for excellence.* Alexandria, VA: Association of Supervision and Curriculum Development.

Hyman, T. (1983). *Little red riding hood.* New York: Holiday House.

Isbell, R. T., & Exelby, B. (2001). *Early learning environments that work.* Beltsville, MD: Gryphon House.

Jordan, H. (1992). *How a seed grows.* New York: HarperCollins.

Jukes, M. (1984). *Like Jake and me.* New York: Knopf.

Kamii, C., & Randazzo, M. (1985). Social interaction and invented spelling. *Language Arts, 62,* 124–133.

Keegan, M. (1991). *Pueblo boy: Growing up in two worlds.* New York: Dutton.

Kelly, P. (1990). Guiding young students' response to literature. *The Reading Teacher, 44,* 464–470.

Kintisch, L. S. (1986). Journal writing: Stages of development. *The Reading Teacher, 40,* 168–172.

Labbo, L. D. (1996). A semiotic analysis of young children's symbol making in a classroom computer center. *Reading Research Quarterly, 31,* 356–382.

Labbo, L. D., & Ash, G. E. (1998). What is the role of computer-related technology in early literacy? In S. Neuman & K. Roskos (Eds.), *Children achieving: Best practices in beginning literacy* (pp. 180–197). Newark, DE: International Reading Association.

Labbo, L. D., Murray, B. A., & Phillips, M. (1995–1996). Writing to read: From inheritance to innovation and invitation. *The Reading Teacher, 49,* 314–321.

Lasky, K. (1983). *Sugaring time.* New York: Macmillan.

Linfors, J. W. (1988). From "talking together" to "being together in talk." *Language Arts, 65,* 135–141.

Lipson, M., Valencia, S., Wixson, K., & Peters, C. (1993). Integration and thematic teaching: Integration to improve teaching and learning. *Language Arts, 70,* 252–263.

MacLachlan, P. (1985). *Sarah, plain and tall.* New York: Harper and Row.

The Macmillan visual dictionary. (1992). New York: Macmillan.

Maddern, E. (1993). *The fire children: A West African creation tale.* New York: Dial.

McCormick, S. (1994). A nonreader becomes a reader: A case study of literacy acquisition by a severely disabled reader. *Reading Research Quarterly, 29,* 156–176.

McDermott, G. (1972). *Anansi the spider: A tale from the Ashanti.* New York: Henry Holt.

McGee, L. M. (1998). How do we teach literature to young children? In S. Neuman & K. Roskos (Eds.), *Children achieving: Best practices in beginning literacy* (pp. 162–179). Newark, DE: International Reading Association.

McIntyre, E., & Pressley, M. (1996). *Balanced instruction: Strategies and skills in whole language.* Norwood, MA: Christopher-Gordon.

Mehan, H. (1979). *Learning lessons.* Cambridge: Harvard University Press.

Meier, D. R. (2000). *Scribble scrabble, learning to read and write: Success with diverse teachers, children, and families.* New York: Teachers College Press.

Mollel, T. M. (1993). *The king and the tortoise.* New York: Clarion.

Morrow, L. (1992). The impact of a literature-based program on literacy achievement, use of literature, and attitudes of children from minority backgrounds. *Reading Research Quarterly, 27,* 250–275.

Morrow, L. (1997). *The literacy center: Contexts for reading and writing.* York, ME: Stenhouse.

Morrow, L., & Gambrell, L. B. (1998). How do we motivate children toward independent reading and writing? In S. Neuman & K. Roskos (Eds.), *Children achieving: Best practices in beginning literacy* (pp. 144–161). Newark, DE: International Reading Association.

Morrow, L. M., & Weinstein, C. S. (1982). Increasing children's use of literature through program and physical design changes. *The Elementary School Journal, 83,* 131–137.

Morrow, L. M., & Weinstein, C. S. (1986). Encouraging voluntary reading: The impact of a literature program on children's use of library centers. *Reading Research Quarterly, 21,* 330–346.

Moss, T. (1993). *I want to be.* New York: Dial.

Myers, W. D. (1993). *Brown angels.* New York: Harper Collins.

National Association for the Education of Young Children. (1998). Learning to read and write:

Developmentally appropriate practices for young children. *Young Children, 53,* 30–46.

Oldfather, P. (1993). What students say about motivating experiences in a whole language classroom. *The Reading Teacher, 46,* 672–681.

Ormerod, J. (1981). *Sunshine.* New York: Lothrop.

Pallotta, J. (1986). *The yucky reptile alphabet book.* Watertown, MA: Ivory Tower.

Parkinson, K. (1986). *The enormous turnip.* Niles, IL: Albert Whitman.

Peet, B. (1989). *Bill Peet: An autobiography.* Boston: Houghton Mifflin.

Pinnell, G. S., & Fountas, I. C. (1998). *Word matters: Teaching phonics and spelling in the reading/writing classroom.* Portsmouth, NH: Heinemann.

Prelutsky, J. (1983). *The Random House book of poetry for children.* New York: Random House.

Pressley, M., Allington, R. L., Wharton-McDonald, R., Block, C. C., & Morrow, L. M. (2001). *Learning to read: Lessons from exemplary first-grade classrooms.* New York: Guilford.

The Random House children's encyclopedia (rev. ed.). (1992). New York: Random House.

Ringgold, F. (1991). *Tar beach.* New York: Crown.

Roof, B. (1993a). *My first dictionary.* London: Dorling Kindersley.

Roof, B. (1993b). *My first encyclopedia.* London: Dorling Kindersley.

Ross, R. R. (1980). *Storyteller* (2nd ed.). Columbus, OH: Merrill.

Routman, R. (1991). *Invitations: Changing as teachers and learners K–12.* Portsmouth, NH: Heinemann.

Rowe, D. (1994). *Preschoolers as authors: Literacy learning in the social world.* Cresskill, NJ: Hampton Press.

Say, A. (1990). *El Chino.* Boston: Houghton Mifflin.

Say, A. (1997). *Allison.* Boston: Houghton Mifflin.

Sendak, M. (1963). *Where the wild things are.* New York: Harper and Row.

Sierra, J. (1992). *The elephant's wrestling match.* Toronto: McClelland and Stewart.

Snow, C., Burns, S., & Griffin, P. (Eds.). (1998). *Preventing reading difficulties in young children.* Washington, D.C.: National Academy Press.

Steig, W. (1972). *Dominic.* New York: Farrar, Straus and Giroux.

Steptoe, J. (1969). *Stevie.* New York: Harper and Row.

Steptoe, J. (1984). *The story of jumping mouse.* New York: Mulberry.

Temple, C., Martinez, M., Yokota, J., & Naylor, A. (1998). *Children's books in children's hands: An introduction to their literature.* Boston: Allyn and Bacon.

Tomlinson, C. M., & Lynch-Brown, C. (2002). *Essentials of children's literature* (4th ed.). Boston: Allyn and Bacon.

Tompkins, G., & McGee, L. (1993). *Teaching reading with literature: Case studies to action plans.* New York: Merrill/Macmillan.

Tunnell, M. O. (1993). *The joke's on George.* New York: Tambourine.

Turkle, B. (1976). *Deep in the forest.* New York: Dutton.

Turner, A. (1985). *Dakota dugout.* New York: Aladdin.

Van Allsburg, C. (1987). *The Z was zapped.* Boston: Houghton Mifflin.

Vars, G. (1991). Integrated curriculum in historical perspective. *Educational Leadership, 49,* 14–15.

Vuong, L. (1982). *The brocaded slipper and other Vietnamese tales.* New York: Addison-Wesley.

Vygotsky, L. S. (1978). *Mind in society. The development of higher psychological processes.* Cambridge, MA: Harvard University Press.

Watson, C. (1982). *Applebet.* New York: Farrar, Straus and Giroux.

Wisniewski, D. (1990). *Elfwyn's saga.* New York: Lothrop, Lee and Shepherd.

Xiong, B. (1989). *Nine-in-one. Grr! Grr!* San Francisco: Children's Book Press.

Yorinks, A. (1986). *Hey, Al.* New York: Farrar, Straus and Giroux.

Zarrillo, J. (1994). *Multicultural literature, multicultural teaching: Units for the elementary grades.* New York: Harcourt Brace Jovanovich.

7 Supporting Literacy Learning in Preschools

KEY CONCEPTS

centers	art center	written language talk
block center	book and writing centers	interactive read-alouds
home center	"I can read" bags	clothesline props
sand table	environmental print puzzles	literary prop box
water table	letter game	vocabulary prop box

concept-about-story activities	big books	onset
literary awareness	shared writing	rime
text and toy sets	dictation	"I can hear" talk
dramatic-play-with-print	list making	language play books
centers	pattern innovation	rhyming games
sit and stay	sign-in procedure	
shared reading	write on	

The Preschool Context

In this chapter we describe how to support preschool children's language and literacy growth in a variety of early childhood settings. Children of this age are likely to be attending preschool in Head Start or Even Start programs, in private preschools, or in public pre-kindergarten programs. These programs may last for only a few hours each day, for the entire school day, or for an extended period from early morning to early evening. They will all have a strong parent involvement program, a concern for children's overall health and safety, and a focus on making sure that all areas of children's development are supported. The methods that we describe in this chapter for supporting and accelerating all children's language and literacy development are appropriately embedded in any preschool program.

What Preschoolers Learn about Literacy at Home and in Preschool

As we have described in the earlier chapters in this book, young children who have a strong language and literacy foundation learn a great deal by the end of their preschool years. Before they enter kindergarten, these children have extensive vocabularies and can construct a variety of sentences sometimes with complex syntax. They understand the meaning of environmental print and of stories, poems, and informational books read aloud to them. They begin to recognize alphabet letters, learn to write their names, and develop concepts about print such as book orientation and print directionality. They gradually develop metalinguistic awareness, which allows them to attend to the sound and visual properties of words apart from their meanings. They enjoy playing with the sounds of language—listening to the rhythm created by accented syllables and attending to rhyming and alliterative words. Eventually, they can recognize and create rhyming words or words with the same beginning sounds. Finally (but for most children not yet in preschool), they learn to connect sounds with letters and to recognize a few sight words.

Many preschoolers develop these language and literacy concepts as a result of participating in the everyday routine activities that occur in their families and communities. A great deal of learning occurs as children observe or interact with their parents or caregivers in literacy activities, such as reading a catalog to make decisions about purchasing a gift, writing grocery lists, or signing a birthday card.

As a part of these activities, parents often help their children write their names or dictate a simple message. Through these activities children gain an awareness of how to use language and literacy in particular literacy events, the way that literacy operates, and how literacy use empowers family members (Gee, 2001).

In many preschools, children continue to be involved in literacy activities that are remarkably similar to those they have already experienced in their homes and communities (McGill-Franzen, Lanford, & Adams, 2002). These children have a double dose of highly effective language and literacy learning opportunities. They have supportive parents or caregivers who provide materials, opportunities, and informal teaching about how to interact with books and pretend to read, and how to draw and pretend to write. Further, they have highly skilled preschool teachers who provide additional reading and writing opportunities within a high-quality early-childhood program. As a result, they acquire high levels of literacy development.

However, some children get very few opportunities to engage in sustained language and literacy activities in either home or at preschool (Dickinson, 2001). For a variety of reasons, many parents do not read books aloud to their young children or encourage their children to pretend to write. Children growing up in poverty are more likely to attend a publicly funded preschool that has a low-quality program and an ineffective preschool teacher (McGill-Franzen, Lanford, & Adams, 2002) than middle-class children. Children with low-quality preschool experiences get a double dose of few literacy learning opportunities. It is little wonder that they enter kindergarten with extremely low levels of literacy development.

Therefore, it is crucial that children with few experiences with written language in their homes have especially rich preschool experiences. High-quality preschool experiences do make a difference in young children's lives. Effective preschool teachers can accelerate the learning of children whose parents or caregivers provide low levels of home support for literacy learning (Tabors, Snow, & Dickinson, 2001). Using the activities we describe in this chapter, preschool teachers can create opportunities that will accelerate the language and literacy learning of all children.

The Preschool Classroom

Most preschool programs are founded on several common principles of learning including that young children learn best through active manipulation of materials, through play, and through making choices about activities in which to engage. Thus, most early childhood classrooms are arranged into **centers.** Centers are areas of the classroom in which particular materials are gathered; as children manipulate and play with these materials, they develop certain cognitive abilities. For example, the block center is a typical early childhood center. In this center are housed large wooden blocks along with thematic toys such as cars and trucks, road signs, and small people. Building with blocks and using these thematic toys allows children opportunities to develop spatial relationships and to engage in thematic fantasy play. Over time as children play in the block center, their block constructions and their play in the block center becomes increasingly more complex—demonstrating that children have acquired more complex concepts about balance, size, spatial relationships, and sustaining symbolic play. Teachers support this learning by periodically changing materials in the center and by joining in children's play to pose higher-level problems or engage children in extended conversations. In this way they provide children with ample opportunities to choose and self-direct activities in centers, which is at the heart of most early childhood programs.

Figure 7.1 presents a design for a well-appointed and arranged preschool classroom that includes many traditional centers. The **block center** has bin and shelf storage spaces for large cardboard blocks, large wooden blocks, smaller

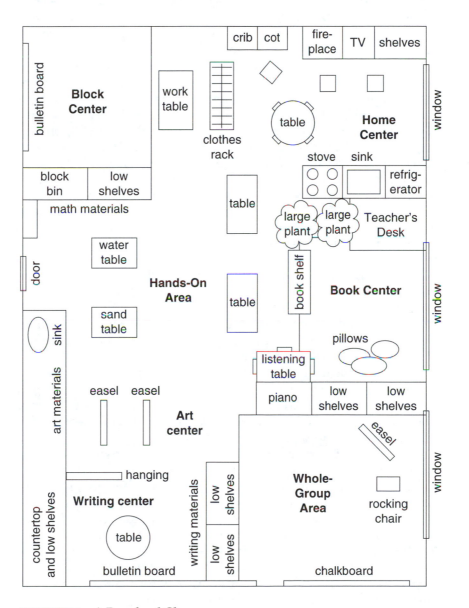

FIGURE 7.1   A Preschool Classroom

wooden blocks, and durable model cars and trucks. It includes a workbench for play with pegs and hammer and wrench. On the bulletin board are posters of city skylines and their distinctive buildings (e.g., the Chicago lakefront with the skyscrapers of The Loop in the background), other distinctive buildings (e.g., Frank Lloyd Wright's Falling Water, a cantilever-constructed house over a waterfall, and the Eiffel Tower), and vehicles (e.g., ocean liners on a travel-agency poster and truck and car posters from a car dealership). These posters contain the print that is part of the poster (e.g., "Chicago," "Cruise the Caribbean") as well as taped-on labels (e.g., "skyscraper," "ship"). On the workbench are hardware-store advertising flyers and a do-it-yourself carpentry book. There are two large, empty pasteboard boxes. There is a large area for playing with blocks.

The **home center** includes a cardboard fireplace with chairs around it, a cardboard television (such as furniture stores use in their entertainment-center displays), shelves, a kitchen set with a small table and four chairs, a small cot, a doll crib, and a doll high chair. The shelves are stocked with magazines, including *TV Guide,* newspapers, a phone book, a few adult books, and a few children's picture books. The kitchen is stocked with plastic food, empty food containers (e.g., cereal boxes, a plastic ketchup bottle, a cottage cheese container), and several illustrated cookbooks, including *My First Cookbook* (Wilkes, 1989). Over the crib is a *Sesame Street* poster picturing Bert and Ernie and displaying their names.

Between the home and block centers is a clothing rack to serve dramatic play in the home and block centers. In both play centers, there are several small, spiral-bound, vertical-flip notebooks, small clipboards with paper, and pencils. In the home center, a waiter or waitress may use these props during restaurant play to take an order, or a mommy or a daddy may use them to take a telephone message or to make a grocery list; in the block center, astronauts may use these items for a countdown checklist.

In the hands-on area are a **sand table,** a **water table,** and the **art center.** There are a sink and storage for supplies, including water toys and plastic aprons, and storage for and places to use children's individual collections of environmental print items, math manipulatives (e.g., Unifix cubes), musical instruments, puzzles, Legos, clay, and science manipulatives (e.g., magnets). There is display space for content centers. All items and storage places are labeled. There is a travel poster of a beach near the sand table and one of Niagara Falls near the water table. The musical instruments are stored near the piano and an easel; sometimes the easel displays the lyrics to a song the children are learning, written on a large piece of posterboard. There are small easels for painting near the art supplies, tables for using many of the manipulatives, and a large, open area for group singing activities and for other large-group activities, such as story performances.

The **book** and **writing centers** are on the opposite side of the room from the play centers. These contain writing materials, a computer, books (including pattern books, movable books, alphabet books, and big books), and space to use them, as described in Chapter 6. A large, round table at the edge of the writing center is the location for children's signing in at the beginning of their day and for checking out and checking in books from the classroom library.

These spaces and materials set the stage for children's learning. As children interact with the materials, each other, and their teacher, they become readers and writers. They are invited to read from familiar big books and pretend to read favorite informational books. They dictate messages that their teacher writes for them and pretend to write messages as they play. In the next section of the chapter, we present case studies of two exemplary preschool teachers who involve their children in daily reading and writing activities.

Reading and Writing in Exemplary Preschool Classrooms

There are three ways that exemplary preschool teachers help children develop language and literacy concepts. The first way is to infuse literacy materials throughout the classroom in nearly every center. The second way is to talk with children and model how to use literacy materials as children are playing in centers. The third way that exemplary preschool teachers help children develop language and literacy concepts is to frequently and routinely include literacy experiences during whole- and small-group activities. In exemplary preschools, literacy activities that occur in small- and whole-groups form a foundation for children's later playful literacy interactions in centers. For example, after a teacher reads aloud a story and helps children dramatize the story using simple props, children enjoy dramatizing the story with a friend in the Book Center. After a teacher writes a thank-you note to a classroom visitor as a shared writing activity, several children pretend to write thank-you notes in the Writing Center.

Literacy in an Exemplary Language- and Print-Rich Environment

We describe one morning in Mrs. Miller's pre-kindergarten classroom for at-risk four-year-olds. She is an exemplary teacher who arranges her classroom so that print is included in every center, and she provides large blocks of time for children to play in the centers. First we describe the children as they play in Mrs. Miller's centers, and then we describe how Mrs. Miller interacts with the children as they play. Finally, we describe some of her whole- and small-group activities that provide a strong foundation for many of the activities in which the children were engaged.

Children at Play. Mrs. Miller's classroom has many centers, including book, McDonald's, writing, games, art, science and math discovery, and home centers. By midmorning, children are working and playing at nearly every center. Two children are on the rug in the book center. They are looking at several books together, commenting about the pictures and talking about the stories. Then they take paper bags labeled with their names and "I can read" from a storage shelf for manipulatives. They look at the coupons, paper bags, and fronts cut from food boxes that they have taken from their **"I can read" bags.** One child gets a doll from the home center, puts it in her lap, and points to each of the items. She reads to her doll by saying a word or two for each item.

Four children are at a McDonald's center. The center is made from a puppet theater to which Mrs. Miller has attached a sign and menu. Inside the theater are empty containers for hamburgers and French fries. Two children are behind the counter in the center. Both have on hats worn by employees at McDonald's. One child is writing on an order pad, and the other is pretending to put a McDLT in a container. Two children are standing in front of the counter. One is dressed in a hat and heels from the home center. She is "Mama." She asks "Baby" what he wants to eat and then orders. The child taking orders announces, "That will be ten dollars." "Mama" looks in her purse for money and pays her bill.

Two children are at the writing center. A number of menus and placemats from local restaurants are displayed at the center. Also displayed are several menus composed by children. Some menus have pictures cut from magazines; some have children's mock letters or mock cursive writing; some have words children have copied from menus or newspapers; and others were written and drawn by parent volunteers. One of the menus on display was composed by Mrs. Miller. It is titled "Miller's Meals" and consists of a drawing of people eating, cutout pictures of food from the food section of the newspaper, and words. One of the children at the center is drawing and writing a menu. She announces, "I'm going to have ice cream," and draws a picture of a double dip cone. The other child comments, "I like ice cream, too. Maybe I'd better write *ice cream*. People might want ice cream on their cake." She writes a scribble on her menu.

Two children are in the games center. They play for several minutes with Legos and other small manipulative toys in the center. Then they remove two **environmental print puzzles** from the game shelf. The puzzles consist of boxes of brownie and cake mixes. Inside each box are pieces cut from the fronts of identical boxes. The children spread the cut-up puzzle pieces on the table. They put the puzzles together by looking at the pieces and then placing them on top of the boxes where they match. They talk together as they complete the puzzles, "I like chocolate. I could eat a whole box of these."

Two other children come to the games center and sit on the floor to play the **letter game.** A large *L* is painted on the front of a pasteboard box and a *K* on another. Attached to one of the boxes is a plastic bag containing several *L*'s and *K*'s that have been cut from construction paper and laminated. The two children play the letter game by sorting the letters and placing them inside the large pasteboard boxes. As they sort the letters, they say, "I'll be the *L* and you be the *K*. I know whose letter *K* is—Kelita's."

One child is in the science and math discovery center. Included in this center is a graph divided into two segments, "No TV Last Night" and "TV Last Night." The first title is accompanied by a picture of a TV with a big *X* over it. The second title is accompanied by a picture of a TV. Under each title some squares of paper have been pasted. Many squares have children's names written on them. Most of the squares are pasted under the "TV Last Night" title. Jermain writes his name on a square of paper and pastes it under the "TV Last Night" title. Displayed on the bulletin board in the center is a graph that the children completed the day before. Under this chart are two sentences: "Two children saw no TV Monday night. Ten children saw TV Monday night."

Three children are in the home center. Two children decide to cook a meal for their babies, using empty food containers and plastic food in the center. One child says, "I think I'll cook some chicken. Let me look up a good recipe." She opens a cookbook on one of the shelves in the center and begins looking through the pages. Another child is sitting in a rocking chair, looking at magazines. Nearby, Mrs. Miller steps into a telephone booth made from a large box. She looks up a number in the telephone book (class telephone book with each child's name and telephone number). She says, "Ring. Ring. Is Melody home?" The child in the rocking chair says, "I'll get that," and answers a toy phone in the center. She says, "Melody is not here. Can I take a message?" She writes on a tablet near the phone and then says, "I'll give her the message. Bye-bye."

The Teacher at Work: Mrs. Miller Teaches about Literacy All Day.   These examples from Mrs. Miller's classroom clearly show that her students can make meanings with and understand the functions of many kinds of print. They are able to do so because she situates the print so as to maintain its original purpose and accepts her children's reading and writing even when it is unconventional. We saw her students making meanings consistent with authentic functions of print when they read coupons to their dolls, used McDonald's wrappers and newspaper food advertising in restaurant play, and consulted a cookbook in their kitchen play.

Most of Mrs. Miller's children's reading and writing is not conventional. Two of the orders written as part of the McDonald's play are presented in Figure 7.2. The children said as they wrote, "Two McDLT's and a Coke" and "Three cheeseburgers and a chocolate shake." The telephone message for Melody that was taken in the home center is presented in Figure 7.3. These examples of children's reading and writing demonstrate that novice readers and writers intend to communicate meaning even when their efforts are unconventional. Mrs. Miller accepts these efforts and treats them as meaningful reading and writing.

FIGURE 7.2   McDonald's Orders   **FIGURE 7.3   Telephone Message**

Mrs. Miller uses the writing of words from environmental print as an opportunity to focus on written language form. As part of their unit on foods, Mrs. Miller's class reads many menus and placemats. These are put in the writing center to stimulate children's writing. Mrs. Miller uses group time to compose environmental and functional print, such as the menu "Miller's Meals." As Mrs. Miller writes, she names letters and points out features of written language, such as specific letters, long or short words, or words that are repeated. She invites children to find letters they know.

Mrs. Miller frequently sits in the writing center so that she can call attention to written language features in the children's writing. In one activity, Mrs. Miller encouraged some children to dictate a "Trash Can Book." The children pasted environmental print items into books made from paper cut in the shape of trash cans. Serita made three pages in her book. She dictated, "I saved Rice Krispies from the trash. I saved Cabbage Patch from the trash. I saved potato chips from the trash." Mrs. Miller drew attention to the words *Rice Krispies, Cabbage Patch,* and *potato chips* written on the environmental print and in the words that she wrote in the book. She asked Serita to talk about the words in the two contexts. She invited Serita to find all the letters that were the same and name the letters she knew. As children focus on form within the meaningful context of the environment, they begin to make connections between written forms (letters and words) and spoken forms (sounds and meaning).

Planned Lessons.   Mrs. Miller uses whole- and small-group activities to present children with more focused opportunities to learn literacy concepts. One activity she planned was to write a letter to Santa Claus. This lesson emerged from her children's interest in the upcoming holiday. During this lesson, she planned to model for children the kinds of language found in a letter, especially a letter to Santa Claus asking for toys for Christmas. She placed a large sheet of paper on an easel near a table so a small group of children could interact with her as she modeled writing the letter. As she wrote her letter to Santa, she used **written language talk** to make explicit many of the concepts she was demonstrating.

She told the children that she would begin the letter by writing "Dear Santa Claus." At the end of her letter, she wrote, "Love, Mrs. Miller." She explained that letters always begin with the word *Dear* and often end with the word *Love.* From this written language talk, the children learned about the text form of a letter.

As Mrs. Miller wrote her Santa letter, her written language talk helped the children learn about meanings. She explained that the letter would start with a sentence about her good behavior in the last year. She reminded the children that Santa would want to know that in order to bring what she wanted for Christmas. Through her talk about meaning, the children learned about the kinds of language found in letters. They also learned the kinds of information appropriate to include in a letter to Santa.

As Mrs. Miller wrote, her written language talk helped the children learn about meaning-form links. She said each word as she wrote it. As she read her letter, she underlined the text with her hands. The children had many opportunities to connect what they heard Mrs. Miller read with the print she was highlighting. Mrs. Miller's talk about letters provided children with information for discovering sound–letter relationships. Some of the children in her class had begun making some of these discoveries. When Mrs. Miller was writing that she wanted a new sewing machine, Serita commented, "I know what letter sewing has, an *S.*" Mrs. Miller knew that Serita only made these sound–letter comments about *S* words. Still, Serita was beginning to display some sound–letter relationship awareness. We will talk more about this knowledge in Chapters 8 and 9.

As Mrs. Miller talked about taking the letter to the post office and mailing it, her written language talk helped the children learn about function. She reminded the children that Santa could keep her letter to remember what she wanted for Christmas. She commented that it was a good thing that Santa would have her letter because he would be getting many, many requests for gifts. She did not want him to forget what she wanted.

Interactive Read-Alouds in Exemplary Preschools

Miss Leslie teaches in a private preschool with an emphasis on academic learning. She is an exemplary teacher who is careful to meet those expectations while maintaining a child-centered approach. One way in which she balances these two needs is through **interactive read-alouds** (see Chapter 6). The interaction comes from children's being expected to answer questions, make comments, and predict outcomes. Miss Leslie plans questions that help children use analytic talk and call for high levels of cognition. She also plans response-to-literature activities to extend the read-aloud experience.

Children Talk about Books and Respond to Literature.   Miss Leslie and six three-year-olds are gathered for storytime on the rug in their classroom. The children are sitting in a square area bordered by tape on the rug. As she announces storytime, Miss Leslie points to a sign entitled "Storytime" that has a picture of a mother reading to two children. On the sign are clothespinned cards with the names of the children who are to come to storytime: Cory, Echo, Leah, Paul, Laura, and Evan. Miss Leslie points to the name on the chart as she calls each child and reminds the child to come to the rug for storytime. As the children approach the rug, she begins to sing one of the children's favorite songs, "Twinkle, Twinkle Little Star."

After she and the children are settled on the rug, Miss Leslie holds up the book *The Little Rabbit Who Wanted Red Wings* (Bailey, 1987). She reads the title, pointing to each word. She reminds the children that she has read this book to them before. The book is about a little rabbit who is not happy with himself and wishes he had what other animals have. The children ask questions and make comments during the booksharing. Miss Leslie reads the text, talks about the illustrations, and asks questions. Figure 7.4 presents a segment of their interactive read-aloud.

Text is presented in all capital letters. Brackets indicate portions of the dialogue that occurred simultaneously.

The illustration depicts a porcupine who is wearing glasses standing under a tree. Little Rabbit is sitting in a large hole in the tree looking at the porcupine.

Miss L: Now who does Little Rabbit see? (points to porcupine)

Child 1: um um its . . .

Child 2: Mr. Beaver.

Child 3: Mr. Porcupine.

Miss L: It does look a little like a beaver. This is Mr. Porcupine.

Child 2: (reaches up and touches the picture of the porcupine) Ouch.

Miss L: Ooh, I wouldn't want to touch that.

Child 1: Me either.

Child 4: Oh, oh.

Miss L: His bristles would stick me. They would stick like a needle.

Child 3: Not me.

Child 2: He sticks you? If you touch him like this? (puts her finger on the picture of the porcupine and pulls it off as if she were stuck)

Miss L: Yes, he might. Those bristles are special. Now I wonder what Little Rabbit likes about Mr. Porcupine?

Child 5: Glasses. (porcupine has on glasses)

Child 1: Needles.

Child 2: I wouldn't want to touch Porcupine.

Miss L: I wouldn't want to touch him either. But what about Little Rabbit? What do you think *he* thinks about those bristles? What do you think Little Rabbit likes?

Child 3: um, um.

Child 4: Glasses.

Child 1: Needles.

Miss L: Do you think *he* wants those bristles? Or maybe those glasses? (laughs, and smiles at Child 1)

Child 1: Yeah.

Miss L: What would *you* like to have like Mr. Porcupine?

Child 2: I want glasses.

Child 5: Bristles.

Child 1: I want needles.

Miss L: Let's see. (looks at book) WHEN MR. PORCUPINE PASSED BY, THE LITTLE RABBIT WOULD SAY TO HIS MOMMY (looks at children as if inviting them to join in), "MOMMY, I WISH I HAD (looks back at print) A BACK FULL OF BRISTLES LIKE MR. PORCUPINE'S."

Child 1: Mommy, I want those needles.

Child 5: I wish I had those bristles.

Child 4: I want some bristles.

Child 2: Mommy, . . .

Then Miss Leslie takes a paper bag from beneath her chair. She tells the children that it contains pictures of each of the animals Little Rabbit met in the story. She asks the children to guess what they are. As the children guess, she pulls out a construction-paper picture of the animal and asks, "What did Little Rabbit like about this animal?" She clothespins each animal picture to a clothesline hung a few feet off the floor behind her chair. She tells the children they might want to use the **clothesline props** to retell the story to a friend during center time. She also suggests that they might want to draw pictures and write about the animals or Little Rabbit in the writing center. All the children are then free to select center activities.

Some children go to the block center. One goes to the home center to join three four-year-olds who have been playing there during storytime. The other three children sit down with the animal props on the clothesline. They take the construction-paper animals and clip each one on the line. As they do this, they talk about the story.

Miss Leslie goes to the writing center and announces that she is going to write. Echo and Cory join her, along with three of the four-year-olds who were not participants in storytime. She says, "I think I'll draw a picture about Little Rabbit. I want to draw his red wings." The children comment on what they might draw, "I'm going to do Mrs. Puddleduck" and "I like trucks." As the children draw and talk, Miss Leslie comments that she is going to write. "I think I'll write that Little Rabbit didn't like the red wings." Cory says, "I'm gonna write, too. I'll write about her feet." Echo says, "I don't want to write." Miss Leslie and the children continue to talk about their pictures and writing. Then Miss Leslie invites the children to read their stories and talk about their pictures.

Miss Leslie's Roles in an Interactive Read-Aloud.   This example from Miss Leslie's preschool interactive read-aloud classroom shows that her children were active participants in the construction of the meaning of the story *The Little Rabbit Who Wanted Red Wings.* One of Miss Leslie's goals is to enhance children's meaning-making strategies, and she uses several techniques for creating such meaning-making opportunities. The first is her skillful interaction with children during reading aloud.

Miss Leslie uses a variety of techniques to help her children understand the story and to encourage their interactions. She encourages children to identify characters (she asks, "Now who does Little Rabbit see?" while pointing to the porcupine in the illustration) and to make predictions ("Now I wonder what Little Rabbit likes about Mr. Porcupine?"). She also encourages children to participate by accepting and extending their comments and questions (when Leah touched the picture of the porcupine and said "Ouch," Miss Leslie commented, "Ooh, I wouldn't want to touch that. His bristles would stick me. They would stick like a needle."). She uses questions that are intended to help children identify with story characters ("What would you like to have like Mr. Porcupine?"). She provides information that will help children understand words used in the story. (Miss Leslie commented that the porcupine's bristles "would stick like a *needle*" to clarify the meaning of the word *bristles* used in the story text.) She also recognizes all of the children's responses—even when they deviate from the story text. Miss Leslie acknowledged the prediction that Little Rabbit wanted Mr. Porcupine's glasses even though that was not a part of the story.

Miss Leslie adjusts to the needs of children. Another reason that her three-year-old listeners were such able meaning makers is that she knows that the best group-reading opportunities for preschoolers are often activities for well-chosen small groups rather than large groups. She has found that the six children she calls together comment more about stories when they are in smaller groups. She included two children in this group whose oral language was more mature than that of the other children. Miss Leslie believes that children learn much from interacting with other children whose abilities are slightly more mature than their own.

Miss Leslie plans response-to-literature activities that extend children's opportunities for meaning making. For example, she encouraged children to use her clothesline props to retell the story during center time, and she provided special rabbit-shaped paper in the writing center to encourage children to write their own stories. Another response-to-literature activity involves special literature props in boxes to stimulate children's dramatic response to literature through play. These **literary prop boxes** include props designed to encourage children's becoming characters from favorite stories. In the *Little Rabbit Who Wanted Red Wings* literary prop box, Miss Leslie gathered several pairs of rabbit ears (made from headbands and construction paper), acorns, glasses, several pairs of rubber boots, a mirror, a pair of red wings (made from construction paper attached to an old vest), several head scarves, a toothbrush, a bowl and spoon, and two fur vests. She placed an extra copy of the book in the prop box along with the other props. Children are encouraged to use the props to act out the story or create their own stories.

What Are the Characteristics of an Exemplary Preschool Literacy Program?

Exemplary literacy programs, such as those we observed in Mrs. Miller's and Miss Leslie's classrooms, include frequent and routine literacy activities that are geared to the developmental levels of children (Neuman, Copple, & Bredekamp, 2000). Much of what preschoolers can do is not conventional—many preschoolers do not yet write alphabet letters conventionally and even their signatures are not fully developed. They ask many questions about books read aloud to them that reveal they often do not understand some vocabulary words or sequences of events. Therefore, exemplary literacy programs for preschoolers are not the same as those found in kindergartens or first grades.

Exemplary preschool literacy programs may have as their desired outcomes that children learn many conventional literacy skills including being able to recognize alphabet letters, write their names, demonstrate phonological awareness (recognize rhyming words and words with the same beginning sounds), demonstrate concepts about print orientation and directionality, and retell stories and informational books read aloud to them with many details and some sophisticated vocabulary and syntax (Whitehurst & Lonigan, 2001). However, in exemplary literacy programs, young children are provided many playful opportunities to achieve these expected conventional literacy outcomes through discovery and experimentation. Mrs. Miller encouraged her children to write orders in the McDonald's center—and most of the children's writing in the activities was unconventional. Yet, Mrs. Miller provided frequent demonstrations of how to write conventional alphabet letters. Miss Leslie encouraged her children to talk about the stories she read aloud and was tolerant of their diverse comments. However, she skillfully guided children to attend to more salient story elements even when their interest focused on personally interesting story details.

Exemplary preschool literacy programs help teachers find a balance between instruction geared toward helping children develop conventional literacy concepts and activities in which children are allowed and encouraged to explore literacy on their own terms. These programs are systematic—they present experiences that are compatible with children's current level of literacy knowledge yet at the same time provide opportunities for children to develop more complex concepts. In the remainder of the chapter we describe instructional activities that strike this balance around three major areas of literacy development in preschool: (1) vocabulary and concept development (meaning and function), (2) concepts about print and alphabet knowledge (form), and (3) phonological awareness (meaning-form links) (Snow, Burns, & Griffin, 1998).

Supporting Vocabulary and Concept Development

Laying the Foundation for Comprehension and Composition

Reading and writing are ultimately about meaning—readers must construct meaning as they read, and writers must convey meaning through their writing. Vocabulary and concept development in preschool play a key role in children's later being able to comprehend highly complex books and write detailed and persuasive compositions (Wells, 1986; Senechal et al., 1996). Therefore, vocabulary and concept development, experience and knowledge of books, and extended conversations form a strong foundation for children's literacy success (Hargrave & Senechal, 2000; Schickedanz et al., 2001). As a natural part of these activities, children also learn more about how print functions.

Interactive Read-Alouds: More than Reading Aloud

Miss Leslie was a master of interactive read-alouds. She prompted discussion before she began to read a book, paused while she read to make comments and ask questions, and continued the discussion after reading. The four purposes of talking about the book before, during, and after interactive reading are to:

- prompt children's active participation in constructing the meaning of the book
- extend and clarify children's language, understanding of, and thinking about the book
- explain some vocabulary
- prompt children to use vocabulary as they talk about the book (McGee & Richgels, 2003)

In order to achieve these goals, teachers carefully plan interactive read-alouds. They preview the book to consider what concepts children may not understand and how to connect what children do know with these unfamiliar concepts. They also select eight to ten vocabulary words that are important for the story and that may be unfamiliar to children to explain during the read-aloud. Exemplary teachers plan questions they might ask children to prompt discussion about critical events in a story or information book. However, they are careful during reading not to make interactive read-alouds like an oral quiz. Chapter 2 (Figure 2.8) presents several high-cognitive demand comments and questions that teachers can use during interactive read-alouds.

Interactive read-alouds are more powerful when the books are related—for example, related to a theme the class is exploring. Reading related books provides more opportunities for children to hear vocabulary words in different contexts and to expand concepts. **Vocabulary prop boxes** can be used to further enhance vocabulary and concept development for related books. For example, the books *The Carrot Seed* (Krauss, 1945) and *Jack's Garden* (Cole, 1997) are about gardening. A vocabulary prop box for these two books might include seeds, a trowel, a small rake, a portion of a garden hose, a watering can, plastic insects, a variety of plastic flowers, and a plastic carrot (Wasik & Bond, 2001). As teachers share these props, they can invite children to "tell me what you know about this" or "tell me how you would use this." As they read aloud, teachers can remind children of the objects in their prop box. For example, when reading *The Carrot Seed,* a teacher paused to ask a question:

TEACHER: How did the little boy plant the seed?

CHILD 1: He dug a hole.

TEACHER (TO SAME CHILD): Tell me more.

CHILD 1: He dug a hole in the ground and he put the seed in.

TEACHER: How did he dig the hole?

CHILD 2:   With a shovel like this. [The child demonstrates the action of digging.]

TEACHER: Kind of like the [trowel] that I showed you." (Wasik & Bond, 2001, p. 249)

This teacher used a clarifying and extending prompt ("Tell me more") to encourage the children to expand their sentence (child l responded to the teacher's questions with "he dug a hole" and expanded this sentence to "he dug a hole in the ground and he put the seed in" after the prompt).

Informational books sometimes prompt more conversation and questions than do simple stories (Smolkin & Donovan, 2002). When reading information books, teachers will want to make explicit the connections among ideas. Books dealing with science concepts often include, for example, cause and effect relationships—how animals catch their prey or why animals hibernate in the winter. Teachers can make these connections explicit by helping children understand that a spider can catch an insect *because* its web is sticky.

After reading books aloud, effective teachers make sure they make those books available in the classroom book center. Children are especially interested in browsing through a book immediately after it has been read aloud. Children develop stronger literacy skills when *they* have access to and engage with books on their own (Neuman, 1999) and are supported in this activity by frequent teacher read-alouds.

Concept-about-Story Activities

We saw in Chapter 3 that even preschoolers begin to understand how stories work. Preschool teachers can support their students' developing more complete and more sophisticated concepts of story. They can plan special **concept-about-story activities** (Tompkins, 1998; McGee & Tompkins, 1981). These activities are designed to help children learn five important concepts about stories, such as that all characters in stories have problems and do many things to try to solve their problems. (These concepts are presented in Figure 7.5.) Activities to help children learn about story problems include having them retell stories using props or having them predict different ways in which a character might solve a problem. Figure 7.5 also lists concept-about-story activities, including dramatizing, retelling, drawing, and painting.

Concept-about-story activities build children's **literary awareness.** Literary awareness operates at the level of whole texts. It involves conscious attention to character and plot development in a well-crafted story. Fully developed literary awareness is beyond most preschoolers, but skillful teachers will help preschoolers to take the first steps toward such awareness, mostly through well-planned gesturing and commenting during interactive read-alouds. Teachers can ask questions and make comments that help children identify settings, characters, and characters' motivations. They can help children predict events and think about causes and effects.

FIGURE 7.5   Activities for Developing Concepts about Stories

Story Concept	Example Activities
1. Characters are the animals and people in the story.	a. Have children draw, paint, or make characters in clay. b. Make a three-page book by having children draw and dictate what a character looks like, does, and says. c. Make a book of "Story Characters I Know." Have children draw and dictate characters' names.
2. Stories take place in different places, times, and types of weather, called settings (Lukens, 1986).	a. Have children identify different places characters go in the story. b. Have children identify changes in weather in the story. c. Have children decide whether settings are real or make-believe. d. Make a list of "Story Places I Have Visited."
3. Characters in stories have problems; they do many things to try to solve their problems.	a. Compose a "Problem Book" by listing the problems of story characters and children's characters. b. Act out the story using story props. c. Have children suggest other methods of solving the character's problem. d. Use a story line to retell the story. e. Use a flannel board to tell the story. f. Play a guessing game in which the teacher describes a problem and children guess the name of the character.
4. Some events in stories happen over and over and some words in stories are said again and again (Tompkins & McGee, 1989).	a. Use story line to retell the story, emphasizing repeating words. b. Act out story, emphasizing repeating events and words. c. Make a list of repeated events. d. Make a big book of the story. e. Compose a story using the structure but adding new content (Tompkins & McGee, 1989).
5. Stories have a beginning that tells about characters, a middle that tells what characters do to solve problems, and an ending that tells the problem's solution (Tompkins, 1998).	a. Make a four-page booklet with one page each for title, beginning, middle, and end; children should draw pictures and dictate the story. b. Make a "The End" book. Children can dictate endings to favorite stories. c. Use three shoe boxes to make a story train as shown here. Make pictures of the events in the beginning, middle, and end of the story. Have children put pictures in the train and tell about the story.

Adapted from McGee, L. M., & Tompkins, G. E. (1981). The videotape answer to independent reading comprehension activities. *The Reading Teacher, 34,* 430–431. Reprinted with permission of the International Reading Association.

Storytelling and Drama

Storytelling and dramatizing are favorite preschool activities. Young children's play often includes extended episodes of fantasy play in which they become their favorite characters in stories or movies (Wolfe & Heath, 1992). Miss Leslie's literary prop boxes are a simple way to encourage children to engage in story drama during their play. **Text and toy sets** can also be used to stimulate dramatic play about books (Rowe, 1998). Text and toy sets are realistic, small-scale toys and other props that are placed in a special box or basket in the book center along with related books. First, teachers read aloud several books on a related topic. Then, children help find the toys in the classroom to place in the book's box or basket. These toys prompt children to enact scenes from books they have read or create new related events in fantasy play.

However, teachers can extend children's vocabulary and language more effectively by modeling storytelling, retelling, and drama by using props. Folktales and fairytales are particularly effective for storytelling activities. Instead of reading a book, teachers tell the story. Simple props make remembering the story much easier. For example, having a pig and a wolf puppet enhances telling the *Three Little Pigs* story especially when accompanied by a bundle of straw, a stick, and a pile of plastic bricks along with a big plastic cooking pot (McGee, 2003).

After telling the story, teachers can share props with the children to involve them in a second telling. If every child has one or more props, teachers can take the lead in retelling the story and demonstrating for children how to manipulate their props. For example, props that children can use in retelling the *Three Little Pigs* story might be as simple as laminated pictures of three pigs, a wolf, a bundle of straw, a bundle of sticks, a pile of bricks, and a big black pot gathered together in a zip-lock bag. Each child can manipulate these props and join in saying the repetitive phrases ("not by the hair of my chinny chin chin" and "I'll huff, and I'll puff, and I'll blow your house down"). After several days of retelling with the teacher, children enjoy retelling the story to each other when the props are placed in the book center.

Another kind of storytelling is when the teacher offers to write a story dictated by a child in the room. Later, that child invites others to join in as he or she acts out the story earlier dictated (Paley, 1990). The teacher invites children to dictate their stories as they arrive for their school day. She sits where she is accessible to all the children. As children tell their stories, the teacher repeats each dictated sentence as she writes it down. She wants the storyteller to be able to correct her if she makes a mistake or to revise if a new idea comes to mind. She questions any part of the story that she is not certain she has gotten correctly. "The child knows the story will soon be acted out and the actors will need clear directions. The story must make sense to everyone: actors, audience, and narrator" (Paley, 1990, p. 22). During the day the teacher talks about the stories, always looking for and voicing connections.

Acting out the stories at the end of the school day is equally social and open to change (Paley, 1990, p. 25). To play out the story, the teacher reads the dictation, and the storyteller and selected classmates dramatize it. Children are free to comment on the dramatizing, and their comments often result in revision in the dramatization. "Intuitively the children perceive that stories belong in the category of play, freewheeling scripts that always benefit from spontaneous improvisations" (1990, p. 25).

Dramatic-Play-with-Print Centers

Another way to expand children's vocabulary and language development is through themed dramatic play. In children's pretend dramatic play, they take on new roles and try out using language in ways that are different from their everyday talk. They become police captains, superheroes, and fairy princesses. Teachers can support children's dramatic play at the same time as encouraging pretend reading and writing. Police captains write reports, superheroes read messages, and fairy princesses get invitations to balls. **Dramatic-play-with-print centers** are specially planned dramatic play centers that encourage children to engage in themed play that offers potential for pretend reading and writing (Neuman & Roskos, 1997). Teachers can plan dramatic-play-with-print centers around themes and activities that are familiar to children and that have the potential for pretend reading and writing (Neuman & Roskos, 1997). For example, children are familiar with having their hair cut. From their experience visiting hair salons or barbershops, children are likely to have seen customers reading magazines in the waiting area and stylists writing bills and appointments. Therefore, teachers can easily capitalize on children's knowledge by setting up a hair salon–barbershop dramatic-play center enriched with literacy materials such as magazines, pads of paper, small cards, and a large appointment book. To arrange dramatic-play centers enriched with print, teachers

- Select play themes that are familiar to children and have literacy potential.
- Separate the center from the classroom with movable furniture, such as bookcases, screens, or tables.
- Label the center with a sign posted prominently at children's eye level.
- Select dramatic-play props related to play themes, for example, empty food boxes, a toy cash register, plastic bags for a grocery store or plastic food, trays, and wrapping paper for a fast-food restaurant.
- Select literacy props related to play themes, for example, coupons and pads of paper for the grocery store and an appointment book, appointment cards, patient's chart, and prescription slips for the doctor's office.
- Arrange the materials within the space to suggest a realistic setting related to the play theme. (Neuman & Roskos, 1990)

Teachers sometimes play with children in dramatic-play centers and model new and more complex ways in which reading and writing can be used (Morrow & Rand, 1991). For example, a teacher in a hair-salon play center may comment, "I'll write you a card so that you can remember your next appointment," as she writes a child's name and date on a small card.

Teachers can make a variety of dramatic-play-with-print centers. Figure 7.6 describes dramatic-play-and-print props that can be used in a shopping mall, a drugstore, and a beauty and barbershop center. Reading books can support and expand children's play in such centers. For example, *Uncle Jed's Barbershop* (Mitchell, 1993) describes not only what happens in a barbershop, but also one man's sacrifice for his family. This book will provide children with many ideas for dramatic play beyond merely pretending to cut hair.

Children's play in dramatic-play-with-print centers is enhanced when teachers introduce children to the materials included in the center and model how to play with these materials. For example, Mrs. Miller carefully prepares her children for centers. On the day that she introduces a center, she uses whole-group time to orient the children to the center. They discuss what happens, for example, at McDonald's. She shows the children the dramatic-play-and-print props, and they discuss how the props might be used. Mrs. Miller and two or three children role-play with the center props. Several children have opportunities to play with Mrs. Miller. Later, while the children play in the center during center time, Mrs. Miller occasionally joins in. She realizes that children will think of many ingenious ways to use props in

FIGURE 7.6   Dramatic-Play-with-Print Centers

	Dramatic Props	Print Props
Shopping Mall Center	1. standing racks for drying clothes 2. hangers and play clothes (hang on racks) 3. cash registers 4. hats, purses, wallets 5. play baby strollers 6. dolls	1. checkbooks and play money 2. signs, such as names of departments, sale signs 3. sales slips 4. pads to write shopping lists 5. tags to make price tags 6. paper bags with store logos 7. credit cards 8. credit application forms
Drugstore Center	1. boxes for counters 2. cash register 3. empty bottles, boxes of various sizes for medicine 4. play shopping carts	1. magazines and books 2. checkbooks and play money 3. prescriptions 4. paper bags for prescriptions 5. labels for prescription bottles
Beauty and Barbershop Center	1. chairs 2. towels 3. play barber kit with scissors, combs 4. telephone 5. hair clips, curlers 6. empty bottles of cologne	1. appointment book 2. checkbooks and play money 3. magazines for waiting area 4. bills

their dramatic play and that they should have plenty of opportunities to create their own unique imaginary worlds. However, she also knows that she can help expand the children's language and increase the complexity of their play by playing along with them (Neuman & Roskos, 1993).

Taking Time to Talk

As surprising as it sounds, many preschoolers have few opportunities to have a one-on-one conversation with their teachers (Dickinson, 2001). Teachers are often busy with the whole class of children so that taking a few minutes each day to talk with each child seems impossible. However, when teachers **sit and stay** in centers for extended periods of time, they can capitalize on numerous opportunities for conversations with children. Effective conversations begin with children's interests and their actions. The best conversations are extended over several turns (where each person takes a turn to talk) and where a topic is explored in depth. Children who are learning English and children with low levels of vocabulary development need more frequent conversations to extend their language skills.

The focus of conversations with children should be on genuine communication rather than on correcting children's language errors. Young children are still acquiring proficiency in language, and attempting to be understood through rephrasing and clarifying are more effective for their language development than repeating a correct sentence. Teachers should include some sophisticated vocabulary in their conversations. One-on-one conversations provide many opportunities to explain words and to use both rare words and everyday words for the same concepts—for example, using the word *infant* as well as *baby*.

As teachers talk with children, they may engage children in conversations about past events or planning for the future. Such conversations require children to use decontextualized language that describes events, objects, and people not present in the here and now of the classroom. Teachers can prompt such conversations by talking about familiar events they have engaged in—going to the dentist, shopping at the mall, or visiting a relative.

The Teacher's Role in Play, Drama, and Conversations: Letting Children Take the Lead

Play and conversation are two of the most important learning activities in the preschool classrooms, and we have already shown many instances of children's reading and writing in their play. We described play with print in Mrs. Miller's McDonald's center and dramatic-play responses to literature facilitated by Miss Leslie's literary prop boxes. We have emphasized that teachers must play an active, involved role in providing literacy support in preschool classrooms. Their role in children's play, however, must also be subtle (Neuman & Roskos, 1997). Teachers can facilitate play; they can influence it; they can even enter children's play; but they must never intrude on it. The difference between the last two items is that entering is on the children's terms, intruding is breaking the spell that children have cast with their play. The roles of a teacher in children's literacy-related play are to create opportunities and then to follow the children's lead.

Supporting Concepts about Print and Alphabet Letter Learning

To become successful readers and writers, children need experiences with print. They need to learn how print works—that it is read from right-to-left and top-to-bottom, that words are separated by spaces, and that written words are read rather than illustrations. Children must also learn to recognize alphabet letters in both upper- and lowercase form, to write them, and to learn how letters work in words. Learning these concepts is not different from learning other early literacy concepts. For most children, learning concepts about print and alphabet letter names occurs as teachers read aloud and as they model writing in meaningful activities. We describe many activities in which teachers demonstrate concepts about print and talk about alphabet letters as they read enjoyable books and compose authentic messages. Teachers can make these concepts more explicit by using written language talk.

Shared Reading

Shared reading is a form of interactive read-aloud using big books or enlarged charts of poems or songs (Parkes, 2000). The text selected for shared reading often includes rhyming words, words with alliteration, or repeated words or phrases making this text highly memorable. After teachers introduce the text to children, they naturally join in saying the text—thus it is called shared reading because the children share reading with the teacher. **Big books** are enlarged copies of children's books. Many publishing companies sell big book versions of some of their most popular children's books. Teachers will want to carefully examine the books to see if they are appropriate for shared reading. Effective big books have a limited amount of text and the print is large enough for children to see when they are seated near, but not next to, the book. Word spaces should also be large enough so that words are easy to isolate.

For reading, teachers will need a sturdy easel large enough to support the big book. The first reading of a big book occurs using the same techniques as used in interactive read-alouds. The focus of the activity is to engage children in talking about the book's meaning and words. Teachers help children predict, connect book ideas to their own experiences, and make comments about characters and their intentions. Because these books are usually short, they can easily be read two or three times.

On subsequent readings teachers can pause to allow children to chime in and say parts of the text. Teachers may want to point out words that rhyme or begin with the same sound (alliteration). As teachers read, they use a pointer to point to each word from left to right across the page of text. Eventually children can take turns pointing to the words (with a teacher's guidance) as the teacher and children chant the story or poem. As children point, teachers can make explicit pointing to the top of the page and the exact place to begin reading. They can make explicit their one-on-one matching and the return sweep each time they read.

Because of their familiarity, children enjoy pretending to reread these books on their own. Small copies of big books should be included in the book center to encourage children's pretend reading.

Shared Writing

Shared writing is an activity in which teachers invite children to compose a message (called **dictation** because the children dictate the message to the teacher who will write it). The teacher helps children compose a message and then dictate a specific word, phrase, or sentence. Shared writing can be used to compose thank-you notes for visitors to the classroom, holiday greeting cards for special classroom friends (e.g., sending a birthday card to an author), or invitations to special classroom events (e.g., a grandparents' tea). Teachers can write the message on large chart paper, invite the children to illustrate the chart, and then send it in a large envelope.

We have found that shared writing with preschoolers is easier when children dictate words or phrases to add to a list. **List making** is effective with young children because each child can contribute several times. Lists can be made quickly, since it only takes a few seconds to write a word in the list. Miss Leslie wrote several lists with her children related to the book *The Little Rabbit Who Wanted Red Wings*. The children dictated a list of animals included in the book, a list of animal features they would like to have, and a list of wishes.

Sometimes young children have difficulty knowing what to say when they are asked to add to a list. Some children may show their confusion by repeating what someone else dictated. We suggest that teachers write what each child contributes even when he or she repeats someone else's responses. Repeated responses provide children with opportunities for paying attention to written language forms. As the teacher and children read and reread their list, they will discover that some words are repeated and that the repeated words look the same.

Another activity calling for shared writing is to compose a **pattern innovation.** Pattern innovations begin as the teacher reads a predictable poem or story. Once the children are familiar with the pattern created by the repeated phrases in the book, they can construct their own innovation on the pattern. For example, *A Dark, Dark Tale* (Brown, 1981) tells the story of entering a scary house, going slowly up the stairs, and looking inside a shadowy cupboard only to find a mouse. It includes the repetitive pattern, "In the dark, dark _____ , there was a dark, dark _____ ." (See the Appendix for a list of other pattern books.)

A group of four-year-olds retold the story using their school as the setting:

Once there was a dark, dark school.
In the dark, dark school there was a dark, dark hall.

Down the dark, dark hall was a dark, dark classroom.
In the dark, dark classroom there was a dark, dark cubbie.
In the dark, dark cubbie there was a SPIDER!

Pattern innovations that are carefully copied on large charts become favorite reading materials for shared reading and pretend reading. Teachers can make these texts into books by typing the text on several pages and illustrating the text with magazine pictures or clip art. These books can be bound and placed in the book center; they often become children's favorites.

Demonstrating Concepts about Print at the Writing Center

When children are exposed to frequent reading and writing experiences, they are eager to become writers themselves. The preschool writing center often becomes a favorite classroom location. Children naturally want to pretend to write and compose messages when their teachers have engaged them in shared writing in which they compose lists, write thank-you notes, and author pattern innovations.

Exemplary teachers know the importance of interacting with children during writing center activities. They introduce new writing center activities during group time and follow a routine as they interact with the children in the center. For example, in December, Mrs. Miller plans several activities related to writing letters to Santa. First, she plans a small-group activity in which she writes a letter to Santa, using suggestions from the children. She places stationery cut from green construction paper and envelopes in the writing center. She also displays words such as *Santa, Dear,* and *Love.*

Teachers who know what motivates and interests young children in their classrooms can create opportunities that will entice many seemingly reluctant readers and writers to participate in activities that lead to reading and writing. Such children may visit a writing center to use the typewriter or letter stamps or to engage in fingerpainting or pudding-writing activities. They may be willing to tell an adult or teacher about a picture that they have drawn, especially if that person is genuinely interested in the drawing. However, teachers must always be able to accept "no" and wait for children to be ready.

The Sign-in Procedure and Other Name Activities

Novice readers and writers who realize that written marks can communicate messages are ready for the **sign-in procedure.** In this procedure, each child writes his or her name each day on an attendance sign-in sheet (Harste, Burke, & Woodward, 1981). This procedure is functional; it should actually serve as the attendance record of the classroom. With young three-year-olds, the procedure may consist of having children place a card with their name on it in a box or on a chart. Later, they may place their name card and a slip of paper (the same size as the name card) on which they have written their names in the attendance box. Eventually, children will sign in by writing their signatures on an attendance sheet. Naturally, three- and four-year-olds' signatures will not be conventional when they first begin the sign-in procedure (recall Robert's early signatures presented in Figure 3.9 in Chapter 3). However, by signing in daily, children gradually refine their signatures into readable names.

Mrs. Miller uses the sign-in procedure because many of the children who come to her classroom have had few writing experiences prior to beginning preschool. Many children do not have crayons and paper in their homes. Before she began the sign-in procedure, few children voluntarily visited the writing center. The sign-in procedure gave the children an opportunity to write each day. As they became comfortable with that very brief writing experience, they gained confidence and began visiting the writing center for more lengthy writing experiences. The children also observed that their writing was useful; Mrs. Miller used the sign-in list to comment on children's absences.

Activities to Promote Alphabet Letter Learning

The sign-in procedure provides many opportunities for teachers to talk about alphabet letters and demonstrate their conventional formation. We do not recommend that preschool teachers engage children in handwriting practice or require children to copy alphabet letters merely for the purpose of learning a letter's correct formation. However, we do recommend that teachers frequently model for children how to write letters and as they model and talk about the strokes they are making (Schickedanz, 1999). This naturally occurs during shared writing as teachers spell words as they write them. However, teachers can also capitalize on other opportunities to introduce and reinforce alphabet letters. For example, one preschool teacher noticed that one child was writing a letter *S* in nearly conventional form in his sign-in signature while most of the other children had not yet mastered this difficult letter. During whole-group, the teacher complimented the writer, "I noticed that Sakeil wrote a very nice *S* today at sign-in." Then she quickly demonstrated how to write the letter on a large chart and invited Sakeil to step up to the chart and also write the letter. Later, the chart was hung in the writing center and all the children were invited to practice writing *S*s. This is an example of a **write on** in which children are invited to write on the chart. Write ons can be used as a part of any shared writing activity. For example, after composing a list of animals found in a story, children can be invited to step up to the chart, find an alphabet letter they would like to write, and then write the letter on the chart (McGee & Richgels, 2003).

Another activity that directs attention to alphabet letters is teaching children to write everyone's name (Cunningham, 2000). Every day the teacher demonstrates how to write one child's name on a large chart paper. Children practice writing the name on small wipe-off boards or on paper attached to a clipboard. As they write, the teacher and children talk about the alphabet letters they are writing. One preschool teacher also reads a special alphabet book coordinated with the name being introduced. For example, on the day that the children wrote Eldric's name, she read *Ellen's Book* (Brown & Ruttle, 1999). This small alphabet book includes pictures of an egg, an elephant, and an elf. In this way, the teacher introduced children to still another literacy concept—listening to the beginning sounds in the words *Eldric, Ellen, egg, elephant,* and *elf.* The next section of this chapter provides more activities that direct children's attention to the sounds in language.

Supporting Children's Development of Phonemic Awareness

Phonemic awareness, that is, conscious attention to individual sounds (phonemes) in words, is essential to learning to read and write (Adams, 1990; Share, 1995). Fully developed phonemic awareness, the sort of awareness that allows children to use the alphabetic principle in reading and writing, entails phoneme-by-phoneme segmentation of words. Most preschoolers do not achieve this level of awareness. However, preschoolers can develop other sorts of phonological awareness that are first steps toward this fully developed phonemic awareness; they can attend to syllables, rhymes, and words with alliteration (the same beginning sounds).

Children seem to develop phonemic awareness from the largest chunks of sounds in words (syllables) to smaller (onset and rime) to even smaller (beginning phoneme) chunks (Goswami, 2001). The **onset** is the sound or sounds before the vowel in a syllable; the **rime** is the rest of the syllable. For example, in the word *plan* the onset is /pl/ and the rime is /an/. The word *plan* and its onset and rime provide a good example of why this unit of sound is easier to detect than a single phoneme. Both the onset and rime in *plan* are composed of more than one sound or phoneme, yet the word seems to naturally divide at the juncture between onset and rime (Goswami, 2001).

Of course, some words have single phoneme onsets (such as the word *pan*, which has as its onset the phoneme /p/) and some words have no onsets (such as the word *out*). Although teachers need to be aware of the distinction between onsets of one or more phonemes, it is *not* something that preschoolers need to learn or that preschool teachers need be concerned about teaching. With experience, preschoolers can learn to detect syllables, recognize and produce rhyming words, and recognize words with the same beginning sounds. This will occur as teachers read nursery rhymes and other texts with many examples of rhyme and alliteration and not as a part of direct instruction. In the last part of the chapter we describe many activities that will allow preschoolers to develop the beginnings of phonemic awareness.

Reading Nursery Rhymes and Other Text with Language Play

Nursery rhymes and other rhyming jingles can be found in literature from around the world. They provide a perfect starting point for drawing children's attention to the sounds of language. In fact, three-year-olds who have had so many experiences with nursery rhymes that they have memorized some of them are far more likely to have high levels of phonemic awareness as five-year-olds than children who have not had many experiences with nursery rhymes (MacLean, Bryant, & Bradley, 1987). Children naturally learn nursery rhymes when they are repeated again and again as a part of whole-group activities in preschool. Many nursery rhymes and jump rope jingles can be quickly recited emphasizing the rhythm created by accented syllables. Using the word *syllables* as children chant the rhyme raises their awareness of this unit of sound in language. Teachers can make syllables even more explicit by chanting and emphasizing the syllables in children's names.

When teachers turn to rhyme, attending to syllables should be eliminated so that children can concentrate on this new unit of sound. Teachers can draw children's attention to the rhymes included in nursery rhymes with **"I can hear" talk.** For example, when listening to the nursery rhyme *Hickory Dickory Dock,* teachers can say, "I can hear 'clock' and 'dock'; they rhyme." Or, with another rhyming book, teachers can say, "I hear *mouse, house*—those two words rhyme *mmmm ouse* and *hhh ouse.*" Simply pausing to notice a few rhyming words during shared or interactive read-alouds is enough to capture some children's attention (Cunningham, 1998). Soon a few children will be noticing rhyming words themselves. Once children begin to notice rhymes, teachers can prepare pictures of rhyming words found in favorite books for small-group or center activities. Children can match pictures of rhyming words in pocket charts. As they do so, teachers can model how to segment the words into their onsets and rimes using more "I can hear" talk: "I hear /k/ /an/ and I can hear /p/ /an/." Preschoolers will not be able to segment the words, but teacher modeling helps draw attention to these salient sound units.

Figure 7.7 shows a poem written by one of the authors of this book to provide an enjoyable, wintertime experience to highlight the rhyming *-old* words. The teacher might say, as part of the shared reading, "I can hear rhymes: *cold, told, sold, hold.*" At a later rereading, she might say, "I can hear /Old/ in *cold,* and I can hear /Old/ in *told,*" and so on. Still later, she might say and show, "I can hear /s/ in *sold.* Here's the /s/ part. And I can hear /Old/ in *sold.* Here's the /Old/ part."

Drawing attention to both the rime and the onset is the bridge from rhyming words to words with alliteration. Many **language play books** contain both rhyme and alliteration as well as other sounds of language. These books are specially designed to highlight sounds in words. *Charlie Parker Played Be Bop* (Raschka, 1992), for example, is a picture book that contains a bit of a story line—about Charlie Parker's cat waiting for him to come home. But its power to captivate listeners is in its rhythm and rhyme, its made-up words, and its imaginative illustrations. Readers and listeners of any age can enjoy its use of the sounds and accents in the made-up words to re-create the feel of be bop music. Preschool teachers can also use it (after more than one reading just for fun) to heighten awareness of sounds in words. After reading the single line of text displayed across two facing pages, "Boppitty, bibbitty, **bop. BANG!**", a preschool teacher might say, "I can hear /b/ in those words!" and repeat all four words, emphasizing their initial *b* sound.

FIGURE 7.7   "I Don't Like the Cold"

I Don't Like the *Cold*
I *told* you I don't like the *cold* !

I'm not *sold* on *cold*—

I *told* you **so!**

Take this **snow** and **go!**

I *told* you **so!**

I'll *hold* out for sun and hot—
not *cold* and **snow**!

I *told* you **so!**

Copyright by Don Richgels.

Teachers can continue making "I can hear" statements about beginning sounds when talking about children's names. If Miguel is chosen as helper for the day, the teacher can say, "I can hear Miguel's /mmmm/." Or she may say, "I can hear /mmmm/ at the beginning of *Miguel*." In a later instance of Miguel's being helper, the teacher might ask, "What sound do you hear at the beginning of *Miguel?*" Still later, the teacher might withhold display of Miguel's name card until she gets a response to "The name of today's helper starts with /mmm/. Who could it be?"

Discussion of the calendar is a routine in many preschool classrooms. This presents another opportunity for teachers' informal, matter-of-fact "I can hear" talk. They might say, "I can hear /mmmm/ in *March.* That's just like the /mmmm/ I hear in *Monday* and in *Miguel*." Often children notice the replication of the syllable *-day* in *Sunday, Monday, Tuesday, Wednesday, Thursday, Friday, Saturday*, and in the word *day*.

Making Rhymes

A next step, following teachers' "I can hear" talk about rhyming words, is to invite children to make rhymes, to involve them in **rhyming games.** From "I can hear rhymes," teachers can proceed to "Let's make rhymes." Many of the same contexts for "I can hear" are suitable for rhyming games. For example, children who discover the repeated *-day* in calendar words *today, Sunday, Monday, Tuesday, Wednesday, Thursday, Friday,* and *Saturday* are prepared to make rhymes from *day*. The teacher might say, "I can make a rhyme: *day—pay!*" She might add other *-ay* words or say, "I can hear /ā/ in *day*, and I can hear /A/ in *pay*."

Rhyming games include inviting children to repeat rhymes the teacher has made and to make their own rhymes. However, because of the difficulty of making rhymes, preschool teachers can expect students to give responses that involve sound similarities but are not rhymes. Teachers' responses can be accepting, while distinguishing among "rhymes with," "sounds like," "sounds the same at the beginning," and "sounds the same at the end." If a student offers *dinosaur* as a rhyme for *day,* the teacher might respond, "*Dinosaur* and *day* sound the same at the beginning. *Pay* and *day* are rhymes. Can you say, 'Pay—day'?"

Reading and Constructing Alphabet Books

Reading many kinds of alphabet books extends children's awareness of letters and alliteration. The best alphabet books for helping children listen to beginning sounds are books with large alphabet letters and pictures of a few items that are familiar to children. A picture of a walrus on the *W* page is not helpful when children call it a seal ("W is for seal!"). As teachers select alphabet books for reading aloud with preschoolers, they should carefully consider whether the illustrations and words used in the book help children's understanding of beginning sounds (Murray, Stahl, & Ivey, 1996). For example, alphabet books with illustrations of a ship on the *S* page are not useful in helping children hear the /s/ phoneme or later in making the connection between the phoneme /s/ and the letter *S*. Making an alphabet wall or book together is one way to call attention to beginning sounds. Children can bring in environmental print or cut pictures from magazines to contribute to this activity.

The Internet includes many web sites featuring alphabet letters (Duffelmeyer, 2002). At www.learningplanet.com/act/abcorder/htm the alphabet letters are spoken aloud and children are invited to click on alphabet letters to indicate which letter comes next in a sequence. All of the alphabet letters are displayed in order so the child does not need to remember letters to play the game. An alphabet chart is presented at www.literacyhour.co.uk/kids/alph_char2.html. Children can click on the letters and a page of an alphabet book is displayed. The alphabet letters are animated at www.enfagrow.com/language008.html. Letters are presented in both upper- and lowercase letters along with an animal whose name begins with that letter. The animal moves across the screen. The alphabet game presented at http://funschool.com is more challenging. Here children must locate alphabet letters hidden in a scary Halloween picture. The sound effects add to the pleasure of this activity. However, children need to already know the alphabet letters in order to play the game. A similar game is found at http://sesameworkshop.org/sesamestreet.

Another Look: The Teacher's Roles

We have presented descriptions of preschoolers and their teachers as they are engaged in language and literacy activities. The children had multiple opportunities to learn, and the teachers used subtle instruction to support that learning. Preschool teachers *infuse the environment with print,* as Mrs. Miller did in her classroom. They *invite children to interact with print,* as the teacher did when she invited children to tell and dramatize their stories. They *demonstrate reading and writing by participating in literacy events,* as Mrs. Miller did when she joined in play in the home center. She pretended to phone someone, and one of the children took a message about the call. Miss Leslie sat in the writing center and said, "I'm going to write. I think I'll draw a picture of Little Rabbit. I want to draw his red wings."

Preschool teachers *model reading and writing strategies,* as Miss Leslie did when she read big books with her children and as Mrs. Miller did when she wrote a letter to Santa with her children. They *plan group activities involving reading and writing,* as Miss Leslie did during interactive read-alouds and as Mrs. Miller did in composing a menu with her children. They *plan individual activities involving reading and writing,* as Miss Leslie did when she prepared storytelling props for the book she used in booksharing and as Mrs. Miller did when she organized graphing activities in the math center. Finally, *they become audiences for children's reading and writing,* as Mrs. Miller did when she listened to her children read their Trash Can compositions.

The real secret to effective early-literacy programs in preschool is to make literacy an everyday routine. As children read, write, and talk about print, teachers can seize opportunities to respond to what children are trying to do (Ballenger, 1999).

Chapter Summary

Preschoolers can be expected to achieve much written language competence. They enjoy storybook read-alouds and discussions, identify signs and labels, play rhyming games, have partial alphabet and sound–letter knowledge, and use some alphabet letters or mock letters to write meaningful words and phrases, including their names. They retell favorite storybooks and informational books and write pretend messages as part of dramatic play. Although most preschoolers do not develop full phonemic awareness, teachers help them to take first steps through enjoyable, informal phonological awareness activities, such as "I can hear" and rhyming games.

Preschoolers acquire concepts about written language when their classrooms are filled with print and when teachers model how to use that print in play. Mrs. Miller's classroom included many games and dramatic-play opportunities in which children used print in entertaining and functional ways.

Well-planned interactive read-alouds and response-to-literature activities support preschoolers' developing literary awareness, story concepts, and concepts of print. Miss Leslie demonstrated effective interactive reading techniques, including making comments and using gestures and voice to interpret stories as she read aloud. She was especially skillful at getting children to participate in interactive reading. She provided story concept activities and literary prop boxes.

Effective preschool teachers use written language talk to demonstrate how to use print and to encourage children's own writing attempts. In shared writing activities, including pattern innovations and list writing, preschoolers learn from their teachers' modeling about written language meanings, forms, meaning-form links, and functions. Finally, preschoolers learn much from play, including play in dramatic-play-with-print centers and in storytelling and playing activities.

Together all the literacy activities in preschool support children's learning in three major areas of literacy development: language and concept development, concepts about print and alphabet letter recognition and writing, and phonemic awareness.

Applying the Information

We suggest two activities for applying the information presented in this chapter. First, make a list of the seven characteristics of literacy-rich classrooms presented in Chapter 6. Then reread this chapter and locate classroom activities from Miss Leslie's and Mrs. Miller's classrooms that are examples of these characteristics. Discuss these examples with your classmates.

Second, make a list of all the literacy learning activities mentioned in this chapter, including interactive reading books, shared writing, writing lists, story concept activities, response-to-literature activities, prop boxes, sign-in procedure, dramatic-play-with-print centers, print puzzles, letter games, "I can read" bags, and storytelling and drama. For each of these activities, describe what children learn about written language meanings, forms, meaning-form links, or functions. For example, as children participated in interactive read-alouds with Miss Leslie, they had opportunities for meaning making by answering questions and retelling the story with storytelling props. As children wrote "Trash Can Books" with Mrs. Miller, they focused on the form of written language. They compared words in environmental print and printed forms and they named letters. Discuss your list with classmates.

Going Beyond the Text

Visit a preschool classroom and observe several literacy activities. Take note of the interactions among children as they participate in literacy experiences. Also note the teacher's talk with children in those experiences. Make a list of the kinds of literacy materials available in the classroom. Talk with the teacher about the kinds of literacy activities he or she plans. Compare these materials, interactions, and activities with those found in Miss Leslie's and Mrs. Miller's preschool classrooms.

REFERENCES

Adams, M. J. (1990). *Beginning to read.* Cambridge: M.I.T. Press.

Bailey, C. (1987). *The little rabbit who wanted red wings.* New York: Platt and Munk.

Ballenger, C. (1999). *Teaching other people's children: Literacy and learning in a bilingual classroom.* New York: Teachers College Press.

Brown, R. (1981). *A dark, dark tale.* New York: Dial.

Brown, R., & Ruttle, K. (Eds.). (1999). *Ellen's book.* Cambridge, UK: Cambridge University Press.

Cole, H. (1997). *Jack's garden.* New York: Mulberry.

Cunningham, P. (1998). Looking for patterns: Phonics activities that help children notice how words work. In C. Weaver (Ed.), *Practicing what we know: Informed reading instruction* (pp. 87–110). Urbana, IL: National Council of Teachers of English.

Cunningham, P. (2000). *Phonics they use: Words for reading and writing.* New York: Longman.

Dickinson, D. (2001). Large-group and free-play times: Conversational settings supporting language and literacy development. In D. Dickinson & P. Tabor (Eds.), *Beginning literacy with language: Young children learning at home and school* (pp. 223–255). Baltimore, MD: Paul H. Brookes.

Duffelmeyer, F. (2002). Alphabet activities on the Internet. *The Reading Teacher, 55,* 631–635.

Gee, J. (2001). A sociocultural perspective on early literacy development. In S. Neuman & D. Dickinson (Eds.), *Handbook of early literacy research* (pp. 30–42). New York: Guilford.

Goswami, U. (2001). Early phonological development and the acquisition of literacy. In S. Neuman & D. Dickinson (Eds.), *Handbook of early literacy research* (pp. 111–125). New York: Guilford.

Hargrave, A., & Senechal, M. (2000). A book reading intervention with preschool children who have limited vocabularies: The benefits of regular reading and dialogic reading. *Early Childhood Research Quarterly, 15,* 75–90.

Harste, J. C., Burke, C. L., & Woodward, V. A. (1981). *Children, their language and world: Initial encounters with print* (Final Report NIE-G-79-0132). Bloomington: Indiana University, Language Education Department.

Krauss, R. (1945). *The carrot seed.* New York: Harper Trophy.

Lukens, R. L. (1986). *A critical handbook of children's literature* (3rd ed.). Glenview, IL: Scott, Foresman.

MacLean, M., Bryant, P., & Bradley, L. (1987). Rhymes, nursery rhymes, and reading in early childhood. *Merrill-Palmer Quarterly, 33,* 255–281.

McGee, L. (2003). Book acting: Storytelling and drama in the early childhood classroom. In D. Barone & L. Morrow (Eds.), *Literacy and young children: Research-based practices* (pp. 157–172). New York: Guildford.

McGee, L., & Richgels, D. (2003). *Designing early literacy programs for at-risk preschoolers and kindergartners.* New York: Guilford.

McGee, L. M., & Tompkins, G. E. (1981). The videotape answer to independent reading comprehension activities. *The Reading Teacher, 34,* 427–433.

McGill-Franzen, A., Lanford, C., & Adams, E. (2002). Learning to be literate: A comparison of five urban early childhood programs. *Journal of Educational Psychology, 94,* 443–464.

Mitchell, M. (1993). *Uncle Jed's barbershop.* New York: Scholastic.

Morrow, L. M., & Rand, M. (1991). Promoting literacy during play by designing early childhood classroom environments. *The Reading Teacher, 44,* 396–402.

Murray, B., Stahl, S., & Ivey, G. (1996). Developing phoneme awareness through alphabet books. *Reading and Writing: An Interdisciplinary Journal, 8,* 306–322.

Neuman, S. (1999). Books make a difference: A study of access to literacy. *Reading Research Quarterly, 34,* 286–311.

Neuman, S., Copple, C., & Bredekamp. S. (2000). *Learning to read and write: Developmentally appropriate practices for young children.* Washington, DC: National Association for the Education of Young Children.

Neuman, S., & Roskos, K. (1990). Play, print, and purpose: Enriching play environments for literacy development. *The Reading Teacher, 44,* 214–221.

Neuman, S., & Roskos, K. (1993). Access to print for children of poverty: Differential effects of adult mediation and literacy-enriched play settings on environmental and functional print tasks. *American Educational Research Journal, 30,* 95–122.

Neuman, S., & Roskos, K. (1997). Literacy knowledge in practice: Contexts of participation for young writers and readers. *Reading Research Quarterly, 32,* 10–32.

Paley, V. G. (1990). *The boy who would be a helicopter: The uses of storytelling in the classroom.* Cambridge: Harvard University Press.

Parkes, B. (2000). *Read it again! Revisiting shared reading.* Portland, ME: Stenhouse.

Raschka, C. (1992). *Charlie Parker played be bop.* New York: Orchard.

Rowe, D. W. (1998). The literate potentials of book-related dramatic play. *Reading Research Quarterly, 33,* 10–35.

Schickedanz, J. (1999). *Much more than the ABCs.* Washington, DC: National Association for the Education of Young Children.

Schickedanz, J., Schickedanz, D., Forsyth, P., & Forsyth, G. (2001). *Understanding children and adolescents.* Boston: Allyn and Bacon.

Senechal, M., LeFevre, J., Hudson, E., & Lawson, E. (1996). Knowledge of storybook as a predictor of young children's vocabulary. *Journal of Educational Psychology, 88,* 520–536.

Seuss, Dr. (1957). *How the Grinch stole Christmas!* New York: Random House.

Share, D. (1995). Phonological recoding and self-teaching: *Sine qua non* of reading acquisition. *Cognition, 55,* 151–218.

Smolkin, L., & Donovan, C. (2002). "Oh, excellent, excellent question!": Developmental differences and comprehension acquisition. In C. Block & M. Pressley (Eds.), *Comprehension instruction: Research-based best practices* (pp. 140–157). New York: Guilford.

Snow, C., Burns, M., & Griffin P. (Eds.). (1998). *Preventing reading difficulties in young children.* Washington, DC: National Academy Press.

Tabors, P., Snow, C., & Dickinson, D. (2001). Homes and schools together: Supporting language and literacy development. In D. Dickinson & P. Tabor (Eds.), *Beginning literacy with language: Young children learning at home and school* (pp. 313–334). Baltimore, MD: Paul H. Brookes.

Tompkins, G. (1998). *Language arts: Content and teaching strategies* (4th ed.). Upper Saddle River, NJ: Merrill.

Tompkins, G. E., & McGee, L. M. (1989). Teaching repetition as a story structure. In D. M. Glynn (Ed.), *Children's comprehension of text* (pp. 59–78). Newark, DE: International Reading Association.

Treiman, R., & Zukowski, A. (1996). Children's sensitivity to syllables, onsets, rimes, and phonemes. *Journal of Experimental Child Psychology, 61,* 193–215.

Wasik, B., & Bond, M. (2001). Beyond the pages of a book: Interactive book reading and language development in preschool children. *Journal of Educational Psychology, 93,* 243–250.

Wells, G. (1986). *The meaning makers: Children learning language and using language to learn.* Portsmouth, NH: Heinemann.

Whitehurst, G., & Lonigan, C. (2001). *Emergent literacy: Development from prereaders to readers handbook of early literacy research* (pp. 11–29). New York: Guilford.

Wilkes, A. (1989). *My first cookbook.* New York: Alfred A. Knopf.

Wolf, S., & Heath, S. (1992). *The braid of literature: Children's worlds of reading.* Cambridge: Harvard University Press.

Supporting Literacy Learning in Kindergarten

KEY CONCEPTS

explicit focus on print
academic agenda
alphabetic reading
invented spelling
fully developed phonemic
   awareness

direct instruction
functional and contextualized
   experiences with written
   language
"What Can You Show Us?"
   activity

preparation
previewing
student demonstrations
applications
word frames
phoneme segmentation

phoneme deletion
"Rounding Up the Rhymes"
  activity
spelling pattern
vowel
reading-new-words activity
writing-new-words activity
say-it-and-move-it activity
Elkonin boxes
classroom print

specials schedule
birthday chart
shared reading
choral reading
text reconstruction
pointer reading
journals
extended sign-in procedure
writing the room
shared writing

interactive writing
language experience
  approach
Words for Today activity
dramatic-play-with-print
  center
sign making
dramatizing information
  from nonfiction

The Kindergarten Context: What's New Here?

In this and the next two chapters, we discuss the context for instruction and learning in terms of how it is different from that presented in the preceding classroom chapters. In this case, we distinguish between the preschool context discussed in Chapter 7 and the unique kindergarten context.

In the last twenty-five years, there has been a shift toward a more academic kindergarten experience. No longer is kindergarten viewed as merely a socialization for school, a year to get used to how to behave for teachers and with other children. Many children have already been away from home and in the organized, long-time company of large numbers of their age cohort for several years before coming to kindergarten. Kindergarteners are expected to recognize and write numerals, count, and understand the number line. The academic agenda also includes knowledge in a variety of mandated social studies and science curriculum units (e.g., the neighborhood or the life cycle). Expectations about literacy learning in kindergarten also have changed.

What Kindergartners Learn about Literacy

The greatest change from preschool to kindergarten is that kindergartners approach written language with an **explicit focus on print.** The International Reading Association and the National Association for the Education of Young Children, in their joint statement about developmentally appropriate literacy expectations (1998), suggest that kindergartners can recognize and begin to write alphabet letters, match spoken and written words, know rhyming words and beginning sounds in words, know sound–letter correspondences, understand concepts of print, and begin to write some high-frequency words. All of these expectations involve an attention to print and a mastery of knowledge of forms and meaning-form links that are not expected of preschoolers (see Chapter 7). In addition, the IRA-NAEYC joint statement suggests that kindergartners can "enjoy being read to and themselves retell simple narratives or informational texts [and] use descriptive language to explain and explore" (p. 200). We would elaborate on these suggestions and add to this list by describing kindergartners' abilities to write their first and last names; identify initial and final sounds in spoken words; know sounds associated with many letters, especially consonants; use sound–letter correspondences in invented spellings; and participate in read-alouds with increasingly complex comments and answers to teachers' questions.

The Teacher's Role

The constraints inherent in this new academic kindergarten context often are not limited to content. Frequently, kindergarten teachers feel less independence than in the past, in terms of not only what they teach, but also how they teach it. Teachers' manuals and children's practice booklets and work sheets accompany mandated curricula in many kindergartens.

We feel that it is possible for kindergarten teachers who are knowledgeable about the characteristics of young children as they emerge into literacy to turn this academic expectation to their advantage. Furthermore, we believe that it is possible and desirable for kindergarten teachers to maintain the child-centered approach that has always been part of their outlook, even while addressing the new **academic agenda.** Kindergarten teachers can still be attentive to and responsive to individual children's interests and abilities; they can still be flexible.

Teachers can be flexible by presenting models of conventional reading and writing, but expecting kindergartners to respond in unique ways. For example, a teacher may model a handwriting method and give children many opportunities to write (in a sign-in routine, at a dramatic-play-with-print center, or at a writing center), but not require conformity to that handwriting model or drill and practice in that method. A kindergarten teacher may offer shared reading experiences with big book stories or chart-paper poems, opportunities for individual children to tell the class what they know on a big book page or on a poster at the easel, and follow-up experiences with little books and individual reading and writing activities, but not require learning all the words in the big book or poem as sight words.

Most important of all is for kindergarten teachers to provide models (theirs and children's) and to provide children with opportunities for the unique kind of exploration that we have argued is characteristic of experimenters (see Chapter 4). Then children will show what they know, what they are working on, and what scaffolding they can benefit from. When teachers let the children shape the task, children can achieve goals that will surprise even the most academically oriented parents and administrators.

The IRA and the NAEYC (1998) suggest that the kindergarten teacher's role is to

> encourage children to talk about reading and writing experiences; provide many opportunities for children to explore and identify sound–symbol relationships in meaningful contexts; help children to segment spoken words into individual sounds and blend the sounds into whole words (for example, by slowly writing a

word and saying its sound); frequently read interesting and conceptually rich stories to children; provide daily opportunities for children to write; help children
build a sight vocabulary; [and] create a literacy-rich environment for children to
engage independently in reading and writing." (p. 200)

In Chapter 6, we shared our vision of a literacy-rich environment. In the following section, we specify characteristics of that environment in kindergarten.

The Kindergarten Setting: Space and Materials

As with all teachers, an important part of being a kindergarten teacher is arranging
the classroom and gathering materials. Figure 8.1 presents our design for a well-
appointed and well-arranged kindergarten classroom. One whole-group area in
this classroom is the large, open, carpeted area in front of a bulletin board. Teachers often use an area like this when they conduct opening-of-the-day activities,
such as their calendar activity.

In our exemplary classroom, the bulletin board holds a Helpers' Tree on
which the names of each day's two helpers are displayed (on apple-shaped cutouts
taken from an apple basket containing every child's name); a tooth graph (on
which the names of children who lose teeth are written); a calendar; a specials
schedule and hook for displaying a sign that tells each day's special class (gym,
music, art, or library story); and a weather chart with yes and no options for reporting whether it is sunny, cloudy, windy, rainy, or snowy.

A pocket chart hangs from a nearby stand. This large vinyl chart has several
horizontal pockets running the width of it in which words on cards can be placed
to make sentences or lines from poems. Also near to the carpeted whole-group area
is an easel used for displaying big books, chart paper, and an erasable marker
board.

This classroom has a second whole-group area where children can sit at
tables near a chalkboard. There are five centers in the classroom: blocks and make-
believe play, home and restaurant, computing, writing, and reading. In addition,
children play in the whole-group centers when they are not being used for group
activities. Play props are stored in bins and low cupboards in these centers and in
the home center's kitchen furniture.

The writing center looks much like the one in the preschool classrooms
described in Chapter 7. There is a large, round table where children are able to see
others' work and to share their own work. There is also a smaller table with a typewriter and space for one or two children to write without interruption or distraction. On low shelves, there are many kinds of writing tools and paper; picture
dictionaries; several letter-stamp sets and ink pads; several laminated cards, each
showing the alphabet in uppercase and lowercase letters; and a file box filled with
cards on which children have written words for future reference, some of which
are illustrated. On the countertop above the shelves are pigeonhole mailboxes, one
for each child. They hold unfinished writing and letters to kindergartners from
classmates or the teacher.

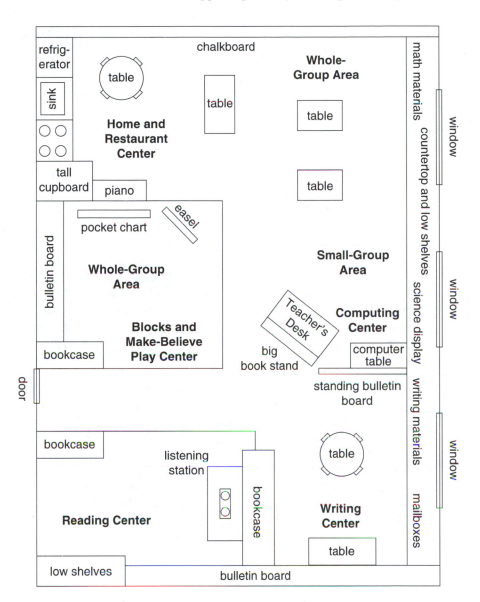

FIGURE 8.1 A Kindergarten Classroom

In the reading center, children's books stand on low, deep shelves and lie on low cupboard tops, where they are easily accessible. These include story and informational picture books, often chosen to complement a unit of study; class-made books (such as a book of bear stories written from children's dictation on bear-shaped pages during a bear unit); big books that the class has read; and multiple standard-sized copies of some of the big books. There are soft cushions on which the children can make themselves comfortable when they read. The cushions can be stacked out of the way when the reading center is used for a small-group area. The listening station is set up on a small table in the reading center, with chairs for four children to use a tape player with headsets.

Talking and Writing Together in Mrs. Poremba's Classroom

The space and materials just described provide the setting for kindergarten teachers to support literacy development in a flexible, child-centered way. This flexibility and response to individual children is critical—a kindergarten class is likely to include some children from each of the descriptions given in Chapters 3 through 5—some novices, some experimenters, and some conventional readers and writers.

Mrs. Poremba is an exemplary kindergarten teacher. In the examples from her classroom that follow, some children are learning to recognize alphabet letters, whereas others can read words and notice spelling patterns. Still others can read poems independently. Mrs. Poremba plans activities that allow all children to show what they know. (For a detailed account of a year in Mrs. Poremba's classroom see Richgels, 2003.)

Counting Days of School

It is the seventieth day of kindergarten, and the kindergartners have emptied the yellow *ones* cup that is attached to the bulletin board below their calendar of its ten loose drinking straws, made of them a seventh bundle of ten straws and put it in the blue *tens* cup along with six previous bundles. Mrs. Poremba has added a *70* to the number line that is stretched across the top of the bulletin board. She is about to circle the *70*, using a blue marker. The kindergartners are familiar with this routine, which has been repeated every tenth day of school since the beginning of the year. Mrs. Poremba asks, "Sarah, do you know why I need a blue marker today?"

"Because it's a bundle number," answers Sarah.

Mrs. Poremba confirms that she uses the blue marker to remind everyone that today the kindergartners use the blue cup.

Talking about One Hundred

Ian asks, "When will we get to 100?"

Mrs. Poremba answers, "That's a very good question. Actually, I have that figured out. And we should arrive at the number 100 sometime in the month of February, probably during the first week of February."

Eric, who will soon be moving and attending a different school, says, "We're not gonna be here in February."

Mrs. Poremba responds, "Well, actually we will. I know that you're going to be going to your new school in February, but kindergarten at [our] school will still be going on in February. We'll actually be in kindergarten past the day of *100*. So that will be nice. We're going to have a special 100 Day celebration, actually."

The children talk about this party, and Eric has an idea: "Maybe I can come here, because I'm going to afternoon at my other school."

Shared Writing of a Reminding Note

This leads to an invitation. Mrs. Poremba asks, "On the 100th day celebration, Eric, would you like to come back and visit us?" Eric and his classmates agree that this is a good idea. Mrs. Poremba makes a literacy connection; she makes explicit the reminding function of written language: "Well, Eric, if we remember to send you an invitation to invite you to come to our 100th day of school party, we'll mail it to you in the mail. I'll write it down in my book so I remember."

But then, Mrs. Poremba has an even better idea for making this function clear to the children: They compose together such a reminder. "You know what I could do right now? I'm going to write it down right now to remind myself." She says, "I'm going to remember the 100th day by writing *100*," and she does so on a slip of paper displayed for the whole class to see (see Figure 8.2). Then she says, "I'm going to write a word next to it."

"*Day,*" predicts a kindergartner.

The kindergartners know this word from their 70 days of calendar work so far in kindergarten. Several of them read as Mrs. Poremba writes: "'Day.'"

Mrs. Poremba reads the whole message so far: "'100 day.'" She asks, "What else could I write down to remember?"

"Party!" say several kindergartners. "Eric," suggest others.

"Write down *party?*" asks Mrs. Poremba. "The word *party?*"

One kindergartner already knows how to begin: "*P! P!*"

100 day

prty

Eric D.

Invtsn

FIGURE 8.2   Shared Writing: A Reminding Note

Mrs. Poremba echoes this, *"P?"*, and she writes *p*. Then she cues the kindergartners for another letter by saying *"Parrrrr—"*

"R," say several kindergartners.

"Is there an *R* in it?" Mrs. Poremba responds as she writes *r*.

A kindergartner suggests the next letter: *"D."* And this kindergartner is right. It is difficulty to enunciate the /t/ in *party*. Often the word ends up sounding more like "pardee." One kindergartner even isolates a /d/ phoneme; he says, "Duh."

Mrs. Poremba emphasizes the /t/: *"Par-tee."*

Now several kindergartners say, *"T!"*, and Mrs. Poremba writes *t*.

Now a kindergartner suggests the last letter: *"Y."*

"You think we need a *Y* in it?" responds Mrs. Poremba. The kindergartners have seen *Y* for /E/ all year, in words on their weather chart (*windy, snowy, sunny, cloudy, rainy*) and in other words (e.g., *muddy, frosty*) they have written together on a Words for Today sheet posted next to the weather chart.

But this is a difficult concept. One kindergartner says, *"No—E!"*

But Mrs. Poremba is writing *y* and reading, *" 'Par-ty.' "*

Now Eric suggests, "You should write my name on there, 'cause—"

"We need your name on there also?" responds Mrs. Poremba. The kindergartners are very familiar with one another's names by December 13, and they quickly lead Mrs. Poremba through the writing of *Eric D.* "Why do we need the *D?*" asks Mrs. Poremba. The kindergartners explain that it distinguishes this Eric from another Eric in their class.

"Anything else we need to write down to remind us about inviting Eric to our 100 day party?" asks Mrs. Poremba. "Do you think this will remind us?"

"Write *invitation*," suggests a kindergartner. And others take this up: *"Invitation!" "Invitation!"*

Mrs. Poremba responds, "Write *invitation*? That's a big word. How would I write that?"

A kindergartner says, *"I."*

Eric is thinking about his invitation. He suggests, "Everybody can sign that card if they want."

Mrs. Poremba says, "And we can all sign it when we send it to you? That's good." She writes *In* and reads, *" 'In—' "*

A kindergartner says the next syllable, "Vuh."

And Mrs. Poremba repeats it: "Vuh."

Several kindergartners provide the next letter: *"V!" "V!"* And another notices something about *In*: "Hey, that's part of Ian's name!"

Mrs. Poremba writes *v* and reads, *" 'In-vuh,' "* and says the next syllable: "Tay."

"T!" "T!" "T!" several kindergartners say.

Mrs. Poremba writes *t* and continues, "-tay-shhhhun."

Several kindergartners suggest, *"S!" "S!" "S!"*

Mrs. Poremba responds, *"S?"* and writes *s*. Then she asks, "What would be on the end? *-shunnn?"*

"N!" "N!" "N!" several kindergartners say.

"Do you hear an *N* on the end?" Mrs. Poremba writes *n* and reads, " 'In-vi-ta-tion.' "

When Tara contends, "That's not a long word," Mrs. Poremba repeats a spelling strategy that the kindergartners have heard before and that accounts for this shortened spelling: "We wrote down the big sounds in the word. We wrote down the big sounds that we hear." Then she points to and reads the whole message (see again, Figure 8.2), pointing to each word as she reads it: "So we have, '100 day party. Eric D. Invitation.' "

Kaitlynn suggests that they add Zack's name " 'cause Zack's not going to be here on February."

Zack objects, "What do you mean?"

It turns out that Kaitlynn thinks that Zack will be six years old by then and so won't be in kindergarten anymore.

Mrs. Poremba clarifies that kindergartners can be five, six, or seven years old, and Zack says, "I'll be in kindergarten then!"

Mrs. Poremba says, "But this will help us to send [Eric] an invitation. Where could I put this that will help us to remember to write him—"

"On your desk!" suggests a kindergartner.

Mrs. Poremba thinks that might not be such a good idea, and she and the class settle on hanging it on an overhead line on which they display art work. It remains there until February 4, when the class does write an invitation to Eric, who shares in their 100th day celebration on February 14.

Lessons from This Shared Writing Episode

This case study contains many examples of literacy in action in a kindergarten classroom. This writing activity was unplanned, but it shows that Mrs. Poremba is prepared for it by being on the lookout for opportunities to demonstrate meaningful uses of writing and to involve her students in writing processes. This episode began in a routine number activity, counting and recording the days spent so far in kindergarten. It turned into a writing activity that had the authentic purpose of reminding. The words (meanings) came from the students; Mrs. Poremba asked, "What else could I write down to remember?" and "Anything else we need to write down to remind us about inviting Eric to our 100 day party?" With this real-life writing piece, Mrs. Poremba demonstrated two kinds of form. By frequently directing her students' attention to the print as she created it, she modeled letter formation. By accepting a list of key ideas (*100 day party—Eric D.—invitation*) rather than a complete sentence (*Remember to send Eric D. an invitation to the 100 Day party*), she demonstrated an acceptable, workable format for a reminder. Finally, the spellings came from the students, demonstrating that Mrs. Poremba knew that in December of their kindergarten year, they had several strategies for spelling. They could dictate the spelling of Eric's name because they see it on his name collar and on name cards every day. Many of them could listen to salient sounds in *party* and *invitation* and match those sounds with letter names. Those who had not mastered this strategy benefited from watching it in action as their classmates suggested spellings and

Mrs. Poremba reinforced them. After a kindergartner suggested a letter, she always repeated it or asked about it (e.g., "Is there an *R* in it?") as she wrote. In this way, she directed other kindergartners' attention to the sound–letter correspondence. This asking, coming after the students' suggestion, was not to call into question the correctness of the suggestion, but rather to confirm the authority of the student. Her pointing and reading as the message took form further emphasized sound–letter correspondences for those who were still learning them.

At the end, Mrs. Poremba reinforced what she and her students had demonstrated about functions, meanings, and meaning-form links. She enlisted the kindergartners in helping her preserve this reminder, posting it in a prominent place so that it could serve its purpose nearly two months in the future. Zack demonstrated that he knew the meaning of this message when he objected to being included in it, and Mrs. Poremba helped others to explore and resolve the mistaken notion behind Kaitlynn's suggestion to include Zack. Responding to Tara's observation about the length of *Invtsn*—that it doesn't look so long for a word that Mrs. Poremba had introduced as a big word—Mrs. Poremba made explicit an invented spelling strategy the students had used before ("We wrote down the big sounds that we hear"). Earlier a kindergartner had demonstrated that Mrs. Poremba's expectation that her students can listen to individual sounds in words was well-founded; that kindergartner had heard a /d/ in *party* because there really is one in the way many people (including this group of kindergartners) pronounce that word. This is phonemic awareness in action. Sometimes Mrs. Poremba goes along with unconventional letter matches for the very real sounds kindergartners hear in words (later we will see her accept a kindergartner's spelling of the last syllable of *little* with an *O*). However, for this message, which would be posted for a long time, Mrs. Poremba elicited the correct letter *T* in *prty* by over-enunciating "par-tee." Mrs. Poremba also knew what her kindergartners could not do at this time in the school year; she did not expect fully conventional spellings for all the words in this reminder. She knew that her kindergartners were not able yet to produce letter matches for all the sounds in *party*; *prty* is a more conventional spelling than *prde* would have been, but it is not as conventional as *party*. More important, the product of this writing episode was readable; it would be able to serve its purpose when the time for the 100th day celebration drew closer.

In three of the remaining sections of this chapter, we describe how kindergarten teachers can support students' learning about meaning making, forms, meaning-form links, and functions of written language in their reading, writing, and play. First, however, we devote a section of this chapter to kindergartners' most important work in the area of meaning-form links—their gaining phonemic awareness and knowledge of sound–letter correspondences.

Helping Children Attend to Sounds in Words

Learning to read and write requires conscious recognition of the individual sounds in words (Adams, 1990; Share, 1995). When children can segment phonemes in words, they can begin to associate letters with those phonemes and thus perform

alphabetic reading and **invented spelling,** both phonics-guided processes. In Chapters 3 and 7, we saw that **fully developed phonemic awareness** is beyond the ability of most novices, and therefore of most preschoolers. These achievements, however, are a mark of being a literacy experimenter (see Chapter 4). In this section, we describe ways kindergarten teachers can support their students' becoming experimenters and making these achievements.

The "What Can You Show Us?" Activity

Kindergarten teachers must go beyond the matter-of-fact modeling of phonological awareness that we described, for example, in the "I can hear" teacher talk (see Chapter 7). They must take the additional step of frequently and explicitly focusing children's attention on print. Explicitness does not mean, however, that kindergarten teachers must engage in the sort of **direct instruction** of phonemic awareness that uses heavily scripted lessons and focuses on isolated sounds and words (e.g., Lindamood & Lindamood, 1969; McGuinness & McGuinness, 1998).

Our work with children and teachers shows us that many kindergartners are capable of acquiring phonemic awareness from **functional and contextualized experiences with written language** (McGee & Purcell-Gates, 1997). Functional experiences are those that serve a real purpose in the everyday home and classroom lives of children. Contextualized experiences are those that use whole texts. The immediate focus may be on words and on letters and sounds within those words, but those words are found, for example, in the text of a big book the class is reading, in a poem they are rereading with the goal of eventually doing a choral reading, or in a list of facts generated from a discussion of a social studies or science topic of study.

The fact that some kindergartners may need additional help in the form of direct instruction does not justify depriving them of functional, contextualized literacy experiences. Those experiences benefit all children in ways besides their promoting phonemic awareness. They also, for example, demonstrate the functions of written language, foster the message concept, and provide enjoyment of literature. And functional, contextualized literacy experiences provide a context for practice, application, and strengthening of phonemic awareness skills that some children may need to acquire in other, direct-instruction activities.

Nor does the fact that some kindergartners need additional help in the form of scripted, direct instruction justify subjecting all children to such instruction. Much of direct instruction is so divorced from actual reading and writing of authentic texts for real purposes as to be counterproductive for those students who already have phonemic awareness, or are on their way to acquiring it in other, more functional and contextualized ways.

One way of providing functional, contextualized support for acquiring phonemic awareness is the **"What Can You Show Us?" activity** (Richgels, Poremba, & McGee, 1996). The four elements of this activity are preparation, previewing, student demonstrations, and applications.

Preparation involves the teacher's choosing or composing and displaying a text that is relevant to ongoing events or units of study. Figure 8.3 shows a letter

Dear Kindergarteners,

   It is fall!

Fall is apple time.

We picked an apple

on a tree.

   Yum! Yum!

   Love,

     Uncle Wally

FIGURE 8.3   A Letter from Uncle Wally

Mrs. Poremba wrote as a pretend message from Uncle Wally. He and Aunt Edith are large, floppy, stuffed dolls who reside in the reading center. The letter was written on chart paper and displayed on the classroom easel.

Previewing is the creating of an opportunity for students to look at the text before working with it as a group. As children enter her room at the beginning of a day when there is a new poem or letter on the easel, Mrs. Poremba invites them to begin looking at the chart: "You might want to visit the easel during your sign-in time today. There is a new poem there for you."

Student demonstrations are the core of "What Can You Show Us?" Before she reads the displayed text, Mrs. Poremba invites children to come to the chart and point out something they know. Children take turns stepping up to the easel and talking about a variety of letters or words or even trying to read the poem on their own. The other children are appreciative of whatever their fellow students can teach them about the text.

In October, Erin participated in the "What Can You Show Us?" activity by reading a word in a chart-paper letter from the class's imaginary Uncle Wally (see below). Richgels, Poremba, and McGee describe the benefits of student demonstrations:

This gives children the opportunity to engage with the text based on their current interests and abilities. Children may identify letters or words, or even try to read the text on their own. The teacher learns about students' interests and abilities, and the children come to appreciate what their fellow students can teach them about the text. The teacher is observer, helper, and commentator. It is very important for him or her to hold back and let students do the teaching, and to make positive, affirming comments about whatever students demonstrate. (p. 635)

With the applications step, the teacher extends and applies what students have done in their demonstrations. **Applications** occur during what is now the teacher's first reading of the text (remember that the teacher has not yet read the text when students do their demonstrations), during later rereadings, and during reading of related texts. Richgels, Poremba, and McGee (1996) include an example of applications using such a related text, the label print on a can of chicken with rice soup, which Mrs. Poremba and her students discussed after a shared reading of Maurice Sendak's poem *Chicken Soup With Rice* (Sendak, 1991). The authors summarize,

> The children read words and phrases by using letter names, letter sounds, co-occurrence of words in the two texts, and context clues. Again, they learned from one another as well as from their teacher. Poremba performed an active, though not imposing, role. She had intended to highlight the word *chicken* and the S sound–letter correspondence during her sharing a favorite poem and a related piece of environmental print, but . . . it was a child who first identified the word *chicken* and . . . the children went beyond the S sound–letter correspondence in their exploration of meaning-form links. (p. 641)

The following examples are from "What Can You Show Us?" lessons in Mrs. Poremba's class, using Uncle Wally's letter (see Figure 8.3), a similar letter from Aunt Edith, and two poems. In October, Erin is at the easel doing a student demonstration with Uncle Wally's letter. She points to the word *is.*

MRS. POREMBA: You're pointing to that *i-s,* Erin. Tell us about it.

ERIN: It's *is!*

MRS. POREMBA: That's the word *is?* (Erin nods, and Mrs. Poremba points to the word and reads.) "Is."

Mrs. Poremba calls on Eric to come to the easel. Unlike Erin's focus on the whole word *is,* Eric's focus is on a letter that he recognizes.

MRS. POREMBA: (to the class) Watch Eric.

ERIC: There's a *Y* for Freddy (pointing to the first letter in *Yum*).

MRS. POREMBA: Oooh. There's a *Y* for Freddy. What do you mean "a *Y* for Freddy"? Does Freddy have a *Y* somewhere in his name?

ERIC: Yeah, and he has an *F* (pointing to the first letter in *Fall*).

Ten days later, the class reads another letter, this time from imaginary Aunt Edith. Now Mayra, who speaks almost no English at this point in the school year (Spanish is her first language), shares what she knows about letters.

MRS. POREMBA: Mayra has something she would like to teach you. . . .

MAYRA: A *W* (pointing).

> **MRS. POREMBA:**   A *W!* (pointing to the same *W* that Mayra had pointed to).
>
> **MAYRA:** *W.*
>
> **MRS. POREMBA:**   That's a *W.* Thank you, Mayra, for showing us the *W.* Thank you.

Mayra bows and makes the American Sign Language sign for "Thank you" that Mrs. Poremba has taught the class (Bornstein, Saulnier, & Hamilton, 1983; Children's Television Workshop, 1985; Rankin, 1991; Riekehof, 1978). Then Eric shows what he learned from Mayra.

> **ERIC:**   (pointing from his place on the floor to another *W* in Aunt Edith's letter) "And there's another *W!*"

In February, when children are invited to show what they know about a new poem, Freddy makes a connection with a familiar word. He uses one of Mrs. Poremba's **word frames** (window-shaped cutouts with handles that can be placed around a word to isolate it from the other words in a text) to show the word *Little.*

> **FREDDY:**   It starts like—(He goes to the wall and points to the word *Library* in the "Library Story" sign posted there for that day's special class.)
>
> **JASON:**   *Library* has the same two letters.
>
> **ANOTHER CHILD:**   And *Lisa* (his sister's name).
>
> **MRS. POREMBA:**   Okay now, Freddy, you touch the *L* and the *i* right there and I'll get the *L* and the *i* right here. Freddy, that's very interesting. What about the rest of the word, Freddy?
>
> **FREDDY:**   No.
>
> **MRS. POREMBA:**   . . . Freddy noticed the *L* and the *i* at the beginning of that word—the same thing as in *Library.* Freddy, that was important.

Freddy's and his classmate's recognition of the beginning similarities in *Little, Library,* and *Lisa* is indeed important. Mrs. Poremba's affirmation of student demonstrations includes explicit talk about letters and sounds. Her talk appropriately goes beyond the "I can hear" talk we suggested for preschool teachers (see Chapter 7). While preschoolers typically cannot achieve full phoneme awareness and sound–letter correspondence knowledge, kindergartners usually are capable of such achievements. Reinforcing their focus on print can result in their associating letters with sounds and doing the sort of **phoneme segmentation** and **phoneme deletion** required for explicit work with onsets and rimes. Children's work with phonemes and teachers' supportive talk in such contexts is the stuff of phonics. Note the phonics learning and phonics instruction in the remaining examples of "What Can You Show Us?" in Mrs. Poremba's classroom.

Later in February, Ian reads the word *Lincoln* in a poem about that president.

> MRS. POREMBA: How do you know that says *Lincoln?*
>
> IAN: *L* (pointing to the *L*).
>
> MRS. POREMBA: So the *L* in the beginning of the word helped you to read it to be *Lincoln.*

In March, during the applications step of "What Can You Show Us?" with a poem about leprechauns, Lauren uses a word frame to show that she can read *old* in the words *gold* and *told.*

> MRS. POREMBA: Lauren, what did you want to show us?
>
> LAUREN: There's the word *old* (putting her frame around the *old* part of *gold*).
>
> MRS. POREMBA: She found the word *old* inside of—(Lauren moves her frame to *old* in *told*) oh!
>
> LAUREN: And there.
>
> MRS. POREMBA: Look, there's *told,* but if you cover up the *t,* you just have the *old* part left. And there's *gold;* cover up the *g* and *old* is left. Isn't that interesting?
>
> ANOTHER CHILD: Old—gold!

Then Lauren shows the *an* part in *man.*

> LAUREN: An!
>
> MRS. POREMBA: Oh and you saw the *an* word inside of *man.* Thank you, Lauren!

"Rounding Up the Rhymes"

"Rounding Up the Rhymes" (Cunningham, 1998) is a contextualized activity that promotes awareness of beginning phonemes and rhyming words. First, children listen to a poem and chime in with the rhyming words. The teacher writes those words on cards for display on a pocket chart. The next day, kindergartners can analyze spelling patterns, using knowledge of letter names, vowel letters, and onsets and rimes. After rereading the text, with the children again chiming in with the rhymes and finding them on the cards in the pocket chart, the teacher says, "Now we know that all these words rhyme. Our job today is to look very closely and see which ones have the same spelling pattern" (p. 91). Part of using this step of "Rounding Up the Rhymes" is helping children to understand words such as **spelling pattern** and **vowel.** With frequent use of "Rounding Up the Rhymes," children begin to remember that the vowels are *a, e, i, o,* and *u,* and that the spelling pattern is the part of the word from the first vowel to the end.

The teacher picks up a pair of rhyming word cards from the pocket chart, explains or reminds the children what *spelling pattern* and *vowel* mean, and invites children to identify the letters in the spelling pattern in the rhyming words, for example, *o-l-d* in *gold* and *told.* Then the teacher underlines the *-old* part of each word, and the teacher and children decide that *gold* and *told* have the same spelling pattern, and they rhyme. "We emphasize that we can *hear* the rhyme and *see* the spelling pattern" (p. 91). Then the teacher replaces those word cards and moves on to another pair of rhyming words from the pocket chart. If some rhyming pairs have different spelling patterns (e.g., *snow* and *go*), they are discarded. Finally, when the teacher and students have underlined spelling patterns in several pairs of rhyming words, they move to an application activity that involves using the word card words to read and write additional words. For the **reading-new-words activity,** the teacher writes words that rhyme with and have the same spelling pattern as the words of an already displayed pair (e.g., *sold* and *fold* to go with *gold* and *told*), elicits the children's telling what letters to underline in the new words, displays them in the pocket chart under the original pair of words, and helps the children to read the new words using the spelling pattern.

For the **writing-new-words activity,** the teacher mentions a word the children might want to write and gives an example of a sentence in which it might be needed. For example, if one of the already displayed rhyme pairs is *dog* and *log,* the teacher might say, "What if you wanted to write *fog,* like in 'I saw *fog* on the way to school today'?" Then the teacher leads the children through a reading of all the rhyme pairs in the pocket chart, adding *fog* after each, until they find the pair that rhymes with *fog:* "*gold, told, fog; man, can, fog; dog, log, fog!*" When they notice that *fog* rhymes with *dog* and *log,* the children can use the underlined spelling pattern in the two displayed words to help the teacher to spell the new word on a word card for display.

Like "What Can You Show Us?," "Rounding Up the Rhymes" is suitable for groups of children who have varying abilities. It

> has something for everyone. Struggling readers and writers whose phonemic awareness is limited learn what rhymes are and how to distinguish rhymes from beginning sounds. Other children whose phonemic awareness is more developed may learn spelling patterns and also that words that rhyme often share the same spelling pattern. Our most advanced readers and writers become proficient at the strategy of using words they know to decode and spell unknown words. This proficiency shows in their increased reading fluency and in the more sophisticated nature of the invented spellings in their writing. (Cunningham, 1998, p. 93)

Kindergarten teachers can extend other preschool activities we suggested in Chapter 7. They can add more explicit teacher and student talk about letters, sounds, and word parts. Preschoolers, for example, might create a "Charlie Parker Be Bop" stanza patterned on the text of a page from the word play picture book *Charlie Parker Played Be Bop* (Raschka, 1992):

> Elephant, elephant, elephant, el,
>
> Tambourine, tambourine, tambourine, tam,
>
> Pencil, pencil, pencil, pen,
>
> Dinosaur, dinosaur, dinosaur, di!

Preschoolers enjoy inventing such stanzas. For them, the game—and the phonological awareness benefits—is in the hearing and the repeating of the stanzas.

Kindergarten teachers might extend this activity by writing the stanza on chart paper and using that displayed text for explicit talk about the spellings of the words and word parts. For example, with the last line of the stanza, the teacher identifies the letters as he writes the first *dinosaur* word, invites the children to repeat the letters as he writes and spells aloud *dinosaur* the second time, and then has the children tell him how to spell *dinosaur* as he writes it the third time. Then he reads what they have, "Dinosaur, dinosaur, dinosaur," and says, "Now we have to write just the *di* part." He moves his hand below the last *dinosaur* word they have written as he stretches out his reading of it, "Diiiii-noooooo-ssssaurrr. Which is the *di* part?" He might have to underline the *di* part in the first three words. Then the children tell him how to spell *di.*

The examples we have given so far—"What Can You Show Us?," "Rounding Up the Rhymes," and "Charlie Parker Be Bop" stanzas—are functional and contextualized activities. They include explicit teacher and student talk about sounds, letters, and word parts that will help most kindergartners to achieve phonemic awareness, alphabetic reading, and invented spelling. They involve all participants in enjoyable, meaningful experiences with written language.

Some children may benefit from additional more direct instruction. Many phonemic awareness training methods are adopted from research tasks. Some involve children's clapping or other rhythmic activity to coincide with spoken words or syllables (e.g., Lundberg, Frost, & Petersen, 1988). Some involve **say-it-and-move-it activities,** in which children move poker chips or other such tokens as they pronounce syllables or individual phonemes in words (Elkonin, 1973).

Yopp (1992) describes several singing activities, performed to the tunes of traditional children's songs, that help children to isolate, blend, or substitute sounds in words. She suggests first using these as strictly oral activities, especially with preschoolers or beginning kindergartners, who may lack alphabet knowledge and for whom the use of written letters may be a distraction from the intended work with sounds. Then, as children learn alphabet letters—often during the kindergarten year—written words or letters may be used.

Ball and Blachman (1991) concluded that their study of phonemic awareness training in kindergarten "supports the notion that phoneme segmentation training that closely resembles the task of early reading may have more immediate effects on reading . . . than instruction that does not make this connection explicit. . . . It may be . . . that the most pedagogically sound method of phoneme awareness training is one that eventually makes explicit the complete letter-to-sound mappings in segmented words" (p. 64). They suggest using blank tokens for say-it-and-move-it phoneme awareness activities and then introducing tokens with letters written on them as children learn to identify the letters.

Griffith and Olson (1992) describe a say-it-and-move-it activity borrowed from Clay (1985) that can be changed in a similar way as children learn the alphabet. Students are given a picture, below which are **Elkonin boxes,** that is, boxes arranged in a horizontal matrix, one box for each phoneme in the pictured word.

As the teacher slowly pronounces the word, the children move tokens into the boxes. She says "mmmmmmmaaaaaaannnnnn" for *man,* for example. The children move a token into the first box while she is pronouncing the phoneme /m/, move another token into the second box while she is pronouncing the phoneme /a/, and, finally, move a third token into the third box while she is pronouncing the phoneme /n/. As children learn the alphabet, rather than moving tokens into boxes, they can write letters in the boxes.

We suggest that whenever teachers use these direct-instruction activities, which use isolated words and rather prescribed sequences of teacher talk and student behavior, they keep in mind ways to reestablish connections to children's classroom and home lives and to whole texts—in other words, ways to make them more functional and contextualized. The words used for Elkonin box work, for example, can come from a displayed big book text or chart-paper poem, and after doing the Elkonin box work, the teacher and students can return to that text and highlight the words there. Or the Elkonin box words may be used in a subsequent piece of writing that is meaningful to the children, such as a class letter to parents that tells about a current unit of study. The letter is composed on chart paper, reproduced by word processor on the classroom computer, and taken home the same day.

The activities that we have described in this section are only a part of the kindergarten literacy agenda. There are other contexts for supporting kindergartners' learning about phonics besides those described. In addition, there is much more besides phonics-related knowledge that kindergartners must achieve. In the sections that follow, we describe experimenters' learning about meaning making, forms, meaning-form links, and functions of written language in additional kindergarten reading, writing, and play contexts.

Kindergarten Experiences with Reading

We return to Mrs. Poremba's classroom to describe additional kindergarten reading experiences. These include classroom print reading and shared reading of big books and other enlarged texts.

Using Classroom Print

The exemplary kindergarten setting is filled with print. An important part of the teacher's role in this classroom is to invite children's responses to that print that reveal their current understandings about written language. This practice allows the teacher always to validate those understandings and at times to give children support for expanding those understandings.

A guiding principle of using **classroom print** is that it is always appropriate if presented to children in a supportive way. Teachers ask, "What can you read here?" and then accept the child's interpretation of that task. Some children will identify the object on which the print is found. When asked to read a toothpaste box, they may reply "toothpaste." Teachers celebrate their reading, saying, "Yes, it is a *toothpaste* box and it says *toothpaste* right here" (pointing to the appropriate word). Other children may identify letters (replying, "C-R-E-S-T"). Teachers celebrate this reading by saying, "Yes, you're right, and it says *Crest.*" Still other children may identify words (replying, "Crest"), and others may read connected text (replying, "Tartar control Crest"). In each case, teachers recognize children's reading as valid.

Mrs. Poremba includes classroom print in a variety of ways in her units and activities. During a unit about taking care of the environment, children were examining bottles, cans, and other packaging that Mrs. Poremba had collected in a recycling bin. She had told the class about using the recycle symbol, a triangular shape formed from three interlocking arrows with a number in the center, to determine which numbered items their trash collectors would accept for recycling. Jason noticed a similar symbol on an empty cottage cheese carton. This was a symbol used by the dairy to indicate a real dairy product, an oval formed from two interlocking curves with the word *REAL* printed in the center. It was very similar in appearance to the recycle symbol. Jason asked, "Does this mean anything?" He knew that this symbol should have meaning, that it did not appear on packaging randomly—in effect, that it was readable.

Some classroom print in Mrs. Poremba's room is presented in a more organized manner. Several charts provide information that children use frequently. An example is the **specials schedule,** at the top of which are the words "Today we have:". Underneath are a hook and an envelope. The envelope contains four laminated signs, one each for art, music, gym, and library story, to hang on the hook. On the envelope is the word *Specials.* Each sign has a word telling the special class and a picture: a gym shoe for gym, a paintbrush for art, a musical note for music, and a book for library story. In early October, Mrs. Poremba posted a specials schedule beneath the specials envelope. Information is organized in this schedule by column, color, and picture. Across the top is the word *Specials.* Heading the left column is the word *Morning;* heading the right column is the word *Afternoon.* Each column has five cells, one for each day; in each is the name of the day of the week, the name of the special class that day, the time of the class, and the same picture symbol for that class as on the special signs. The day names are color coded: pink for Monday, yellow for Tuesday, green for Wednesday, blue for Thursday, and orange for Friday.

As part of beginning-of-the-day activities, one of the two helpers posts the specials sign for that day. For a time after introducing the specials schedule, Mrs. Poremba directed the helper's attention to the appropriate column, cell, and picture. By the middle of the year, children knew the schedule, and helpers seldom needed to consult it, but if they forgot what day it was, Mrs. Poremba said, "You can look at the schedule. Today is Tuesday," and, if necessary, "That's in a yellow rectangle."

The specials schedule is a resource for self-scheduled practice using informational print. In October, Jeff and Tara were reading the specials schedule together during free-choice time. Tara pointed to the appropriate columns and cells on the schedule and said, "On Tuesday we have library; on Tuesday, they have gym, the afternoon class. On Wednesday we have gym and they have library story."

Shared Reading

An important way in which kindergartners learn from each other is through planned group-literacy experiences. In this section we describe **shared reading** (Holdaway, 1979). With this technique, teachers read aloud from charts or big books (with large-sized print so that children can look at the print as teachers read). Then the children and the teacher read together (the shared reading portion of the activity). Finally, children read with a partner or alone.

Shared reading guides children's learning about print so that they gradually learn more conventional concepts. They can develop concepts about print, such as the concept of a written word, directionality (left-to-right orientation), and knowledge of sound–letter relationships and spelling patterns in word families. Some children learn to read some words by sight. Shared reading also demonstrates meaning-making strategies, such as predicting, connecting with real experiences, and making inferences. Mrs. Poremba frequently uses the shared reading technique with a poem that she has written on chart paper and displayed on the easel.

Step One: Orienting Children to Print.   Before Mrs. Poremba reads a new poem to them, she orients the children to print. She has already emphasized the poem's line-by-line structure by printing the poem on the chart in two colors of ink, alternating colors for each new line. Mrs. Poremba always invites children to study a new chart-paper text on their own before the class gathers to read it as a group.

During a whole-class time, Mrs. Poremba continues to orient children to the text of a poem. She points out the names of the author and illustrator. When the author is unknown, Mrs. Poremba discusses what "Author Unknown" means. At this point in shared reading, Mrs. Poremba may do the student demonstrations step of "What Can You Show Us?" Earlier in this chapter, we saw examples of Ian's and Lauren's demonstrations of what they knew in the texts of a poem about Abraham Lincoln and a poem about leprechauns.

Step Two: Teacher Reading.   The teacher reading portion of shared reading ensures that students attend to meaning. As teachers read, they invite children's comments and questions and model using meaning-making strategies. Mrs. Poremba maintains the interactive talk of the orienting-children-to-print portion of shared reading as she reads a poem, a story, or other text aloud to the class and as she and the children read together. When she reads, she stops to comment about character or plot, to invite predictions, to remark about illustrations, and to accept and acknowledge students' comments and questions. Sometimes she points out a familiar or an unusual word; comments about punctuation, especially a question mark or an exclamation point; or reminds the class of a student's earlier observation during their orientation talk.

Step Three: Teacher and Children Reading Together.   In shared reading in kindergarten, poems, letters, stories, and informational books are read many times. Sometimes, when a poem has become familiar enough, Mrs. Poremba's class reads it aloud together, while she directs with a pointer on the chart-paper text. She knows that it is important for children to look at the print during this reading. Before such a **choral reading,** she says, "Where will you look to find the first word of the poem?" and makes sure children are looking there.

Step Four: Response Activities. The final step of shared reading involves response activities with the text. The purpose of these activities is for children to attend to print on their own without the support of a teacher. In kindergarten, many of these activities take place in pairs or small groups; some are done by individuals.

A pocket chart provides opportunities for response activities that focus on print. After reading a poem about November, Mrs. Poremba wrote the poem on long strips of posterboard, one strip for each line of the poem. She placed these strips in the pocket chart, one strip per pocket, and the class read the poem one line at a time. Then she invited students to step up to the pocket chart, choose a line of the poem, read it, and remove that strip from the chart. When all the strips were removed, Mrs. Poremba returned them to the pocket chart and repeated the activity until every student had had a turn choosing and reading a line of the poem.

On another day, this opportunity to attend to print with a now familiar poem was extended through a **text reconstruction** activity. Mrs. Poremba assigned students to small groups. Each group had all the words of the poem on separate word cards and a large piece of lined posterboard. Their job was to work together to reconstruct the poem by placing the word cards onto the lines on the posterboard.

The pocket chart with the poem displayed on strips was still available as a model for students who wanted one during their text reconstruction. As some children worked in their small groups to reproduce the poem, they used the model from the pocket chart to match words. Some children were able to locate words using picture clues, such as a drawing of blades of grass on the word card for *grass* in the line "No green grass."

As an individual activity with the November poem, Mrs. Poremba's students made their own books, each page of which contained a line from the poem and a pop-up illustration. Because they had listened to Mrs. Poremba read the poem, had read the poem together, and had done a small-group activity with the poem, all the children could read their November poem books when they took them home.

Another individual response activity, **pointer reading,** provides opportunities for the student to focus on print and for the teacher to assess the student's print-related knowledge. An example of pointer reading occurred in May after Mrs. Poremba's class had observed the three-week-long process of chicken eggs' incubating and hatching in their room. A chart-paper poem/song used during this unit began, "Cluck Cluck Red Hen" and followed the pattern of "Baa Baa Black Sheep." During free-choice time, Zack was singing this song while visiting the brooder box that contained the class's newly hatched chicks. Mrs. Poremba noticed this and invited Zack to the easel. She pointed out that he was singing what was written on the chart paper, which the class had read together many times. She invited him to point with a pointer as he read the text. She watched and listened, nodding as he read, even when his pointing did not always match his reading. Her role was audience, not instructor; she did not correct him. When he finished reading, both Mrs. Poremba and Zack were smiling broadly. She said, "You did it! Very nice, Zack!"

Zack's reading attracted Alyssa, Tara, and Elise, each of whom took a turn pointing to and reading the poem. These three varied in the accuracy of their pointing, with only Elise pointing perfectly; all three had an appreciative, fully attentive audience in Mrs. Poremba.

Even when Zack's, Alyssa's, or Tara's pointing sometimes digressed from their reciting or singing of the poem, they were able to recover, that is, to find a place in the poem where they could identify a word with confidence and proceed. Their self-correcting using sight words or beginning sound–letter correspondences demonstrated significant growth from what they had been able to do in individual reading activities at the beginning of the year. Their confidence and the number of reading strategies now in their repertoires made pointing and reading a chart-paper poem a viable free choice for them in May. Mrs. Poremba was aware of this when she seized the opportunity presented by Zack's singing to the chicks and by the girls' interest in what Zack was doing at the easel.

Shared Reading with Big Books

Big books (see Chapter 6) are excellent texts for shared reading. Big books can be effective in extending kindergartners' literacy knowledge, especially in helping them to appreciate written language forms, to understand the relations between what a reader says and what is written in a book, and to become increasingly influenced by a book's text in their pretend reading. Big books make text especially accessible to children who are taking these steps (Martinez & Teale, 1988; Trachtenburg & Ferruggia, 1989).

Early in the year Mrs. Poremba reads the big book *Bears, Bears Everywhere* (Connelly, undated). This is a pattern book with the title repeated on every page, followed by a three-word phrase, the last word of which rhymes with *where*. Mrs. Poremba's orienting the children to *Bears, Bears Everywhere* demonstrates that a picture book's illustrations are as important as the text. She helps children to use both illustrations and text to answer questions about the book. One of these questions concerns a topic the class has been exploring. They have already made a large poster from index cards on which were written facts about bears dictated by the children. Also, Mrs. Poremba had asked parents to write bear stories their children dictated at home and send the stories to school. When Mrs. Poremba read these to the class, she always asked if they were real or pretend stories. Now, with *Bears, Bears Everywhere,* she asks the same question, and the answer can be found in the cover illustration of bears that are behaving more like humans than like bears.

MRS. POREMBA: I want you to look at the cover of the book and get your ideas for what this book is about.

CHILDREN: (loudly and all together) Bears!

MRS. POREMBA: Turn and tell a friend.

CHILDREN: (whispering to one another) Bears. Bears.

MRS. POREMBA: I have a thinking question for you right now. . . . I want you to think about whether this book will be about pretend bears or real facts about real bears. Don't say it, just think.

After a short pause, many children answer.

MRS. POREMBA: Can you turn and share your idea with a friend?

Children whisper their predictions to one another, but some loud *nos* and *yeses* can be heard as children disagree with one another. One child suggests that the illustration might be showing real bears who are in the circus.

MRS. POREMBA: Now there's an idea—I hadn't thought of that. Why don't we read and then we'll get more ideas about whether these are real bears or pretend bears, bear facts, or pretend things about bears.

Now Mrs. Poremba shifts the focus to the print on the cover of the book. She helps the children to concentrate on where to begin reading, how to spell the first sound in *bears,* and how a written word looks (by counting words in the title).

MRS. POREMBA: Where could I look to find the name of the story?

CHILDREN: B! B!

MRS. POREMBA: What do you mean *B?*

CHILD: The title page.

MRS. POREMBA: Well that's one place to look.

CHILD: The cover.

MRS. POREMBA: The cover? Okay . . . and I noticed that some of you said the letter *B* because that's the very first letter in the word (pointing) *Bears.* Here's another one (pointing to the *B* at the beginning of the second word *Bears*). This story is called (pointing) *Bears, Bears Everywhere!*

CHILD: Bears, bears everywhere?

MRS. POREMBA: I'll read it again—first of all, how about if we count the words in the title, so we know how many words there are. (with some children reading and counting along) "Bears"—one. "Bears"—there's two. "Everywhere"—three words in the title.

CHILD: No, how about that top one (referring to writing above the title)!

MRS. POREMBA: Up here it says "CTP Big Book"—that's the name of the store, or the company, I should say, that printed this book.

CHILD: There's some down there.

MRS. POREMBA: Down here it says, "Author, Luella Connelly"—she wrote the words—and . . . the other words here say, "Illustrator Neena (hesitating) Chawla Koeller."

CHILD: That's hard.

MRS. POREMBA: That's a lot—she's the person who did the pictures. She's the illustrator.

CHILD: Two people worked on it!

MRS. POREMBA: (confirming) Two people worked together to make this book.

CHILD: Teamwork!

MRS. POREMBA: (confirming) Teamwork, teamwork—that's a very good idea!

During her first reading of the big book *Bears, Bears Everywhere,* Mrs. Poremba points out where to look when reading; contrasts the spellings of two similar words, one of which is familiar to some of the children; and demonstrates meaning-making strategies. She weaves these and other activities—many of them suggested by the children's questions and comments—into a rich interaction about a simple story. As she reads a page about bears in pairs, for example, she first establishes a focus on meaning by asking the children to look at the illustration and call to mind what the story might be about. Then she points to the text as she reads.

MRS. POREMBA: I want you to look at the pictures and get some ideas. (pause) I want you to put your eyes right down here and I'll start reading (pointing to the text at the bottom of the page).

Mrs. Poremba reads, and the children laugh. Next, Mrs. Poremba responds to a child's question, capitalizing on the opportunity to expand their understandings about the meaning of the word *pair.*

CHILD: Pairs?

MRS. POREMBA: I wonder what it means—bears in pairs?

JASON: Two together make a pair.

MRS. POREMBA: Oh, there are two together. So this isn't the kind of *pear* that you buy at the store and eat, like a fruit. This is a different way to use the word *pair.* Jason said that a pair is when two things are together. Look at your shoes. Like a pair of socks.

CHILDREN: Pair of earrings . . . pair of shoelaces . . . eyes . . . ears . . . arms . . . pair of legs . . . pair of elbows!

MRS. POREMBA: So things that come in twos are pairs.

Still later, for a page about bears on chairs, Mrs. Poremba shifts to form and meaning-form links. She calls attention to the picture of bears on chairs and asks what the bears are doing. Then she takes a moment from the big book reading to demonstrate with her writing how written language works. Mrs. Poremba uses a small, erasable marker board that she keeps near her big book easel. In this case, she reads the page about bears on chairs, but stops before the word *on*.

MRS. POREMBA: What's this word (pointing)?

Several children respond at once with their guesses, including "Sitting in chairs," "Zero," and "No."

MRS. POREMBA: Does anyone know what O-N spells? . . . Let me show you.

CHILD: (still working on her own) On chairs.

MRS. POREMBA: (writing on the erasable board) Here is how you spell *no*. How do you spell it?–with *N* first and then–

ERIC: Oh I get it! I get it. The *O* has to be on that side and the *N*'s on that side.

MRS. POREMBA: Yes when the *O* is on this side and the *N* is second, that's the word *on*.

TARA: It's like a pattern! (The children are used to finding patterns in the shapes on which the numbers of the calendar are written.)

MRS. POREMBA: It *is* kind of.

CHILDREN: (reading) On. On. On. On chairs! It's "On chairs"!

Mrs. Poremba then reads the page and comments, "Some of you have been writing *on* in your sign-in sheets."

Still later, when Mrs. Poremba points to the word *lair,* Tara says, "Just like the Blairs!" One of the class's favorite books is *Somebody and the Three Blairs* (Tolhurst, 1990), a parody of the Goldilocks and the three bears story.

Over the next several days, the children frequently reread *Bears, Bears Everywhere* together. They also read their own little-book versions of this book to one another and take them home to read to their families.

Often, children who at first say that they cannot read are willing to read a big book page after a group reading and discussion. They become enthusiastic about the big books and want to return to them again and again (Combs, 1987).

Shared reading in the examples from Mrs. Poremba's class was the vehicle for teaching and learning about all aspects of written language. For example, children learned about meaning making when Mrs. Poremba asked them to think about what a book or a page might be about from studying a book cover or page illustration. They learned about form when she asked them where to start reading a poem or where to find the title of a big book and when they worked together to reconstruct a poem from word cards. They taught one another about meaning-form links when they pointed out print-to-speech matches (e.g., Zack's, Alyssa's, Elise's, and Tara's finger-point reading). They learned about functions of written language, that it can provide information (e.g., "Author Unknown," "CTP Big Book") and entertain (e.g., a poem about bears in pairs, on chairs, in lairs, etc.).

It is important to keep in mind that shared reading is only one kind of reading aloud to children that takes place in Mrs. Poremba's classroom. Mrs. Poremba frequently reads aloud quality literature, including poems, stories, and informational books. The purposes of these readings are to promote children's enjoyment, to enrich children's vocabularies, to find out more about a topic of study (such as dinosaurs or recycling), and to extend children's experiences with literature. During these interactive read-alouds, Mrs. Poremba focuses on meaning—responding to children's questions and comments and encouraging their predictions. Therefore, her attention to print in shared reading is balanced by her attention to meaning in a variety of other kinds of reading activities.

Kindergarten Experiences with Writing

Many of the activities and contexts we have already described include opportunities for kindergartners to experiment with writing. They write during the response activities that are part of shared reading and during applications in "What Can You Show Us?" They write at the writing center, computer center, and play center, and in a corner with a clipboard and before the class at the easel. In this section, we describe additional kindergarten writing activities: journal writing, the extended sign-in procedure, and shared writing.

Journal Writing

Kindergartners enjoy writing in **journals** both about self-selected topics and about topics suggested by their content study. Figure 8.4 presents a journal entry written by a kindergartner after he had played in a doctor dramatic-play-with-print center. Figure 8.5 presents Tara's journal entry on the day Mrs. Poremba's class witnessed a chick's hatching.

Another teacher included journal writing in a unit about Pilgrims. As a part of the unit, the class "gathered around a small box and talked about what they would put in it to take to the New World where there would be no stores" (Fallon & Allen, 1994, p. 547). They acted out being Pilgrims and living on a cramped ship. Each day the teacher read aloud books about the *Mayflower*, and children wrote in journals as if they were traveling on the ship.

Kindergarten journals often become places where children dictate content information of personal interest. Marina dictated about a caterpillar that she brought to school on a stick. "A calipitter [sic] likes to climb on his stick. He's fuzzy. . . . And he gots short hair and its [sic] thick. I don't know how many legs he's got because he won't turn over on his back" (Fallon & Allen, 1994, p. 548). Journals are also places where teachers provide individual help with invented spellings (Freppon & Dahl, 1991). As teachers sit with children writing in journals, they help children listen for the big sounds in words and celebrate children's successes in inventing spellings.

FIGURE 8.4 A Kindergartner's Journal Entry

FIGURE 8.5 Tara's Journal Entry ("9 chicks hatched. May 11, [year]")

The Extended Sign-in Procedure

A variation on kindergartners' daily journal writing is their writing more than their names as part of signing in at the beginning of their school day. We call this the **extended sign-in procedure.** In Mrs. Poremba's classroom, this is part of an attendance-taking routine. Each child goes to an assigned table where he or she shares a sign-in sheet with three other children.

With each class, Mrs. Poremba's sign-in procedure evolves differently over the course of the school year. In late September one year, a few children wanted to write something other than their names on their sign-in sheets. They decided to copy words from the print in the classroom (e.g., labels on objects—*chair, desk, clock;* words on bulletin boards—*green, writing center, oval*). These children asked Mrs. Poremba for their own sign-in sheets (recall that up to now, sign-in sheets were shared by four children sitting at a table together). She provided new sheets for these children for their signing in and copying interesting words from the classroom. She celebrated this writing during a whole-class gathering, showing it to the rest of the class and congratulating the writers. Soon everyone wanted his or her own sign-in sheet.

Then one day there was a new Halloween bulletin board above the writing-center table. Several children wanted to sit at the writing center and copy onto their sign-in sheets the words labeling the Halloween pictures on the bulletin board, more children than could sit at the writing-center table. Several children pulled chairs up to make a second row of writers at the table. Mrs. Poremba gave these children clipboards for their sign-in sheets so that they, too, could write. Then everyone wanted a clipboard, and soon the entire class had clipboards and pencils and sign-in sheets, freeing them to wander around the room copying whatever print they found, not just the print on the new Halloween bulletin board. Figure 8.6 shows Meagan's sign-in sheet from this day. She copied "Color Cats" and color words from a color-word bulletin board; "big blocks" from a label in the block center; "bat," "pumpkin," and "witch" from the Halloween bulletin board; and "Please," "Thank you!" and a smiley face from the sign-in sheet itself! She used dashes to mark spaces between some of the words she copied.

This activity became known as **writing the room.** By midyear, Mrs. Poremba had added the sentence "Today is _____ ." As the year progressed, children used their clipboards and sign-in sheets to write down what was important to them in the morning's opening activities (calendar and weather report), to copy parts of a new poem displayed on chart paper on an easel in the large-group area, or to remember something special about the day, such as a classmate's birthday.

Children were free to complete the "Today is" sentence as they wished. For example, on March 15, Ian noted that "Today is 120," that is, it was the 120th day of school. The next day, Tara noted that "Today is Gym."

Another year Mrs. Poremba used her classroom computer, connected to a large overhead monitor, to post sign-in questions. Each day the kindergartners saw a question on the monitor as they entered the classroom. This allowed them to begin talking together about the question and how they would answer it even before they saw the same question on their sign-in sheets and wrote their individual answers there. This also motivated them to think of their own questions, which

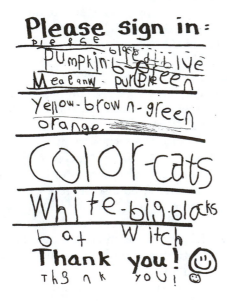

FIGURE 8.6   Meagan's Writing the Room Sign-in Sheet

might appear on the screen the next day or the day after. One kindergartner's question, for example, was "Do you like salami?" (Richgels, 2003).

Shared Writing

Shared writing and a similar activity, **interactive writing,** are instructional activities designed to resemble shared reading (Fountas & Pinnell, 1996). Teacher and students compose a text together. Students suggest ideas, the teacher models writing processes, and the students participate in both the writing and the subsequent reading and rereading of the text. It is similar to writing in the **language experience approach** (Nelson & Linek, 1999; Stauffer, 1980; Van Allen & Van Allen, 1982), which also involves creation and subsequent learning from student-composed texts. Shared writing differs from language experience writing, however, in two ways. While language experience texts are usually accounts of class experiences, shared-writing texts are more varied. They may, for example, be lists, signs, letters, reminders, labels, poems, or extensions of favorite storybooks. While the language experience composing process is strictly limited to the teacher's acting as scribe for student dictation, shared writing involves greater interaction. This may take the form of the teacher's making connections (for example, between words in the text and other words children know, such as their names or words that appear in familiar classroom print), the students' contributing to the actual writing, and the teacher's using the writing process for related word study (for example, about beginning letters and sounds or about spelling patterns) as she writes the text one word at a time (Pinnell & Fountas, 1998). Shared-writing texts can be used for later shared reading.

Mrs. Bellanger and her class wrote the following shared-writing text about the human heart:

> We have a heart.
> Our heart is a muscle that pumps blood.
> It is as big as a fist.
> Animals have hearts, too.
> Hearts are usually found in the chest.

Then they read and reread it several times. Mrs. Bellanger placed it in the science center and invited children to read it to a friend during center time.

We have seen Mrs. Poremba and her class engage in shared writing to compose a note reminding themselves to invite Eric D. to the class's 100th-day party (see Figure 8.2). Their **Words for Today activity** also involved shared writing (see Figure 4.15). At the beginning of the year, as part of the class's opening-of-the-day routine, Mrs. Poremba wrote weather words the children suggested. She used this as an opportunity to model alphabet letter formation, letter identification, and spelling strategies. Usually children would repeat words from the classroom weather chart for Mrs. Poremba to write. By midyear, they often suggested weather words not on the weather chart (e.g., *foggy*) or even nonweather words (e.g., *Easter*). As Mrs. Poremba wrote these words, she would ask children to identify letters or hear big sounds in order to spell. In February, she changed the activity by giving one of the two daily helpers the option of writing the Words for Today. As children wrote, Mrs. Poremba would ask them to listen to the big sounds or to find the word somewhere in the room.

It is Wednesday, April 20, the 141st day of school in Mrs. Poremba's kindergarten class. As part of opening-of-the-day activities, the kindergartners, sitting on the carpet before a large bulletin board, have just had a weather report from Steven, one of today's two helpers. Steven has never before been the writer of Words for Today, and although he at first hesitates, he decides to take the opportunity to be the writer. He knows that his classmates not only will suggest words, but also will help him to spell them. Even without being asked, two classmates retrieve the month and year cards from the calendar to serve as models for Steven's writing the date at the top of the Words for Today paper posted on the bulletin board next to the weather report chart. He calls on Alyssa for the first word.

"A little chilly," suggests Alyssa.

Steven seems a bit taken aback. He presses his lips into a straight line and looks sideways at Mrs. Poremba who is sitting in a chair off to the side of this activity. She says nothing, so Steven turns to the Words for Today sheet and immediately writes *r*. He stops and looks back at the group and Mrs. Poremba, but he keeps his right hand with its marker positioned on the paper.

"What word are you writing?" asks Mrs. Poremba.

"*A little*," answers Steven.

"You're writing *a little* first? Okay. What letter did you write first?"

"*R*."

"Okay. Where do you hear the *R*, so I know how you were thinking?"

Steven says, "Ah-ah." He is beginning to say the letter name *ahr*. He holds his mouth in the open position, like its position when saying the word *a*.

Mrs. Poremba says, "Uh [as when saying the word *a*]. Oh, I see."

"Little," prompts a kindergartner.

"Can you help him with the word *little*?" asks Mrs. Poremba.

Little is part of a posted poem that the children have read many times during the year when one of them reports having lost a tooth. Perhaps that is the source for two kindergartners' spelling for Steven: "*L-I-T-T—*" "*L-I-T-T—*"

Steven begins writing.

"Does that help, Steven?" Mrs. Poremba asks about Steven's classmates' coaching.

He nods and writes *Litt*. Consistent with his earlier calling *a little* one word, he leaves no space between his *r* and his *L* (see Figure 8.7).

"Litt-le," says Mrs. Poremba. "What do you hear on the end, Steven? Uhllll."

Steven writes *O* and turns to Mrs. Poremba. He now has written *rLittO*.

"Little?" she says. "Now would you like to work on *chilly*? Does anybody know anything about the *ch-ch* sound in *chilly*?"

"C! C!" says a kindergartner.

"Actually, there's two letters together to make the *ch-* sound."

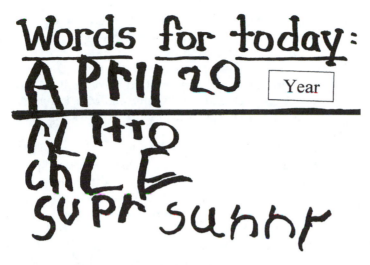

FIGURE 8.7   Steven's Words for Today

Steven is looking directly at Mrs. Poremba, and he immediately answers, "*C-H!*"

Others echo this. Kaitlynn says, "I have a *C-H* in my name, in my middle name!" and, indeed, Kaitlynn Rochelle does. Steven turns to his paper and writes *ch.*

"Okay," says Mrs. Poremba, "chilll-y. What else do you hear, Steven?"

Steven stands still, thinking.

"You have the *ch-*. Now you need the *lll* part. Chilll-y."

This time Steven immediately responds, "*L?*"

"Mmm hmm, that would make sense," answers Mrs. Poremba while Steven writes *L.* "What would you like on the end of *chilly*?"

"*E,*" answers a kindergartner, and Steven immediately writes *E.* He calls on Jeff next.

"Super sunny," suggests Jeff.

Ian has some helpful knowledge. He says, "I think, I know, I know, I know that *super* start—that it, *super* has a *U* and it has *S,* but first is the *S.*"

"The *S* is first? And then the *U* in *super*?" responds Mrs. Poremba. Ian nods, and Steven turns to his paper and writes *S.* He hesitates. "Sooo—" says Mrs. Poremba. "What comes after the *S,* Ian?"

"A *U,*" answers Ian. And Steven writes *U.*

"Sooo—" says Mrs. Poremba.

Steven turns to Mrs. Poremba, his lips already together to pronounce /p/.

"Now you have the *su-* part; now you need to do the *-per* part," she says.

"*P,*" says Steven without hesitation.

"Mmm hmm."

Steven turns and writes *P.*

"That's a good choice. What do you hear on the end of *superrr*?"

A kindergartner provides the sound: "Rrrrr."

Steven names the letter: "*R.*" He writes *r*.

"Mmm hmm. You have the *super* part; now you need to do the *sunny* part."

Steven copies *sunny* from the weather chart next to his Words for Today paper. He leaves a space between *SUPr* and *sunny,* and Mrs. Poremba emphasizes that they are two words: "Steven, can you show us where *super* ends right there, and where *sunny* begins?"

Steven points with his marker.

"Good job." Mrs. Poremba asks the class, "Do you see the space in between those two words that helps us to know that that's two different words?"

When Steven reads his writing, he points to *rLitto* and reads, "'A little chilly.'" Then he hesitates at *chLE*. Classmates prompt him with "Super sunny," but he knows that *chLE* isn't that.

"Which word are you thinking about right now?" asks Mrs. Poremba.

Steven points to *chLE* while a classmate prompts, "*Ch-ch-ch*."

"Oh, the *ch-* part," says Mrs. Poremba.

"'Chilly.'" "'Chilly.'" read two kindergartners, and Steven echoes that.

"That's the *chilly* part," says Mrs. Poremba. "Good."

Steven points to *SUPr,* and two classmates read, "'Super.'" "'Super.'"

Steven then reads, "'Super sunny,'" pointing to each word in turn.

"Great job!" says Mrs. Poremba.

Steven smiles with pride and relief.

His classmates have had their clipboards and sign-in sheets with them during opening-of-the-day activities. They have recorded different parts of what they have seen and heard in those activities. Mrs. Poremba now directs, "What I'd like you to do is to turn and show somebody something on your writing." The carpeted area is abuzz as everyone has something to read to a classmate. Elizabeth has copied Steven's first words as he wrote them, but on a single line of her sign-in sheet: *rLittchLE.* Elise has written all of the words for today, but with some modifications: *A LittLE ChiLY SUOPr SUNNy.*

Words for Today is a routine, with a history on which Steven and his classmates could rely as they tried new, sometimes daunting tasks. Words for Today has intersected with other routines, such as the weather report and sign-in writing. Steven and his classmates have collaborated, and Mrs. Poremba has given just the right amount of support and only at needed points, usually with unobtrusive questions, not answers. The result is that all the kindergartners have remained involved; they have shown what they know and have learned new things about word writing and reading. In less than ten minutes, they have accomplished a great deal, both collectively and individually, both with writing and reading.

Kindergarten teachers can use journal writing, extended sign-in writing, and shared writing to teach students about meaning making (for example, Tara's "Today is Gym" message), forms (for example, Meagan's concept of word, shown by the dashes she made between words she copied), meaning-form links (for example, Steven's *L* in *chilly*), and functions of written language (for example, Tara's recording of a significant class event, "9 chicks hatched"). As examples in this section show, writing opportunities are not limited to planned lessons. They arise during routine activities as well, such as weather chart work and Words for Today in Mrs. Poremba's classroom. Making use of such opportunities is one way to vary activity within a routine. In this way, a routine can provide the structure and security that children often desire, while at the same time support their learning as teachers affirm existing understandings and provide scaffolding for next steps.

Kindergarten Experiences with Play

Play is one of the most important activities in a kindergarten classroom. We described in Chapter 7 how one of the many benefits of play in preschool is its serving as a context for literacy learning. The same is true of play in kindergarten, and many of the methods for encouraging preschool literacy-related play are equally suitable for kindergarten. In the academic context of today's kindergartens, it is important for teachers to remember the benefits for their students of having plenty of space, materials, and time for free play. In this section, we describe some of the literacy-related uses of play in Mrs. Poremba's kindergarten.

Dramatic-Play-with-Print Centers

An example of play-related writing occurred when Deborah was taking orders at the **dramatic-play-with-print center's** pizza parlor. This was a popular play scenario for both boys and girls. Deborah chose it as a play activity for at least a small part of the free-choice time several times a week. Like most of her classmates, when taking a customer's order, she always wrote a line of mock cursive for each item in the customer's order. She took a pizza order from one of the authors of this book: seven lines of mock cursive for "extra large . . . thin and crispy . . . green olives . . . sausage . . . extra cheese . . . root beer . . . large." Later, however, when delivering the order, Deborah used a different writing strategy, one she had never before used during pizza parlor play. "Wait—you need your receipt," she said, and she used the numerals and symbols on the toy cash register to copy "¢25¢" and "$5" on the back of the paper she had used for writing the order (see Figure 8.8).

Sign making was another use of written language during play times. In December, Mrs. Poremba turned the block center into a dramatic-play-with-print shoe store. In response to a letter asking for help stocking the store, parents sent old shoes, slippers, and boots; shoehorns; and foot sizers. The children arranged the footwear on shelves and set up a checkout counter. They also wrote signs and their own paper money.

Frequently, children in Mrs. Poremba's room wanted to continue a play project from one free-choice time to another. At the beginning of the day, on April 20, Eric, Zack, Jeff, Jason, and Ian were playing at a table with dominoes and little plastic, brightly colored bears and bunnies. They made towers or enclosures with the dominoes and arranged the animals on the towers and in the enclosed spaces.

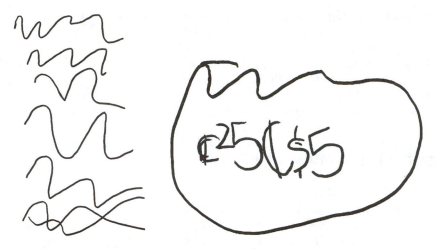

FIGURE 8.8   Deborah's Pizza Parlor Writing ("Extra Large," "Thin and Crispy," "Green Olives," "Sausage," "Extra Cheese," "Root Beer," "Large" and a Receipt)

Now it is time to go to the carpeted area for opening-of-the-day routines, but they want to preserve their domino creations for a later free-choice time. Eric has already made a sign and left it by his domino creation. He has used a nearby model. The class has begun a unit about chick hatching. Yesterday, Mrs. Poremba made a sign and posted it above their incubator. It is the word *Yes* beside a drawing of two eyes and the word *No* beside a drawing of a hand hovering over three eggs in a tray. The message is clear: The kindergartners may look at but not touch the incubator and its eggs.

Eric's sign is his name and the word *NO* beside a drawing of a hand. Next to their domino creations, the other boys have left torn scraps of paper, on which each has written his name. Ian adds *NO* to his sign (see Figure 8.9).

"Can we save all this?" Jeff asks Mrs. Poremba.

"Yes, you're welcome to save it," says Mrs. Poremba, "but you need to know that at the end of the day, when it's time to go home, it will all have to be cleaned up and put away by that time."

Ian points to his domino structure and tells Mrs. Poremba, "Here's a little bunny house. I'm not finished with it yet."

"Okay," replies Mrs. Poremba.

Ian begins walking away while telling her that he has more ideas for his structure.

Mrs. Poremba stops him. "Ian, I noticed you wrote a *no* on your sign. What did you mean by the *no*?"

"Like *no touch.*"

"Ah. Okay. Is there something else that you could put on the sign so we know for sure what you mean by your *no*?"

NO B   **FIGURE 8.9   Ian's, Jeff's, and Jason's Signs**

Jeff takes this as a suggestion for him, too. He says, "I'll put, I'll put *no, tuh, touch*—"

"That's a great idea," says Mrs. Poremba.

"—*T*," Jeff finishes.

"That's a great idea," Mrs. Poremba repeats.

"I'll put *T* at the end," Jeff adds.

Ian responds, "I'll put *no D*. I'm gonna put *no D*."

Jeff sticks to his plan: "I'm putting *no T*."

Both boys begin writing. Jeff writes *NOT*. Ian adds a *D*, removed by a space from his *NO*. (See Figure 8.9.)

Kaitlynn happens by. She reads Ian's sign, " 'No dominoes?' "

Ian doesn't stop with *NO D*. He is looking at a nearby domino box. He looks then writes a letter, looks then writes another letter.

Jason returns to the table. "What're you doin'?" he asks.

Jeff answers, "We're writing *no touch, no touch.*"

Kaitlynn clarifies, "No. Ian's writing *no dominoes.*"

Jeff argues, "No, he's writing *no touch.*"

Ian settles it, "No, I'm writing *no dominoes.*" He reaches the right edge of his paper with *NO DOMIN*. He asks me, "Dr. Richgels, what does this spell?"

"Well, so far, you've got 'No dah-minnn.' "

"That's good enough," Ian decides.

Kaitlynn echoes my "nnnn" and then reads, " 'Domin.' "

Jason decides to add *NO B* below his name on his sign (see again Figure 8.9). He reads it as " 'No dominoes.' "

A bit later, I notice that Ian has written *oes* beneath his *DOMIN* (see Figure 8.9). "Oh, you decided to write more, huh, Ian?" I say.

He points and reads, " 'Dominoes.' "

"Mmm hmm."

Ian reads his whole message, " 'No dominoes.' " Then he puts away his pencil and joins the group.

Similar playful explorations of written language forms and functions can occur in the computer center (Shilling, 1997). This is especially so when teachers model and make available to children such uses for the computer as sign making, greeting card making, and basic word processing.

Dramatizing Informational Books

Dramatizing information from nonfiction is a playful and powerful learning opportunity. After reading several informational books about bees, Mrs. Holcomb invited her kindergartners to play about being bees. "Now I would like you to pretend that you are bees looking for a flower. When I ring the bell, stop buzzing and land on a petal of a flower." After the teacher rang the bell, she said, "Suck up the nectar. All right, now brush some of the pollen to the back of your legs. . . . Now, you have the nectar in your honey stomach and the pollen on your back legs. . . . Fly home" (Putnam, 1991, p. 463).

Mrs. Poremba directed a similar play episode as part of her chick-hatching unit. Her students had read many informational books and posters about chick development and hatching. As the children anticipated their first chick's hatching, they applied what they had learned from their reading.

> MRS. POREMBA: Let's pretend that we are a chick that's been in the egg twenty-one days. You are SO crowded, your legs and your wings and your head and your back and your beak are ALL crunched together. . . . Okay, the first thing you do is you SLOOOOOWLY move your head up and you're going to poke your air sack on the top of your egg to take that breath of your first air. Poke your air sack. Okay. Take your breath. Do you like that air?
>
> CHILDREN: Yes. Uh huh.
>
> MRS. POREMBA: But you know what? That took a lot of work. So now you're tired again. . . . Ohhhh. Now a little bit of a rest. Now we're going to take

our head and get your egg tooth up, part of the end of your beak. And we're going to make our very first pip in the shell—and that's very hard work. Find your place to pip.

CHILDREN: Pip, pip, pip. Peep, peep, peep.

MRS. POREMBA: Did you get a pip in your shell?

CHILDREN: Yeah. Yes.

MRS. POREMBA: Go back to sleep. You are so tired. This is HARD work hatching. Okay, now let's look at our picture to see what we need to do next.

Play provides a rich context for extending children's understandings about written language. As children listen along with tapes in the listening center, they extend their understandings about stories. As they dramatize informational books, they show their understandings of the meanings of words such as *pollen, nectar, honey stomach, air sack, pip,* and *egg tooth.* Copying numbers, for example, copying 25 from a toy cash register, extends children's knowledge of written language forms. Using seven lines of mock cursive to write seven phrases in a pizza order allows children to test a meaning-form link hypothesis—that written language must relate to spoken language. Sign making is a functional activity—making a sign "No Touch" means that children expect written language to be heeded.

Another Look: The Teacher's Roles

We have described kindergartners and their teachers as they participated in activities using reading and writing. The children had rich and numerous opportunities to learn about written language. In particular, Mrs. Poremba played at least six roles in supporting her kindergartners' language and literacy learning.

First, she *followed children's leads.* Mrs. Poremba invited children to tell what they knew as they read big books and sign-in questions. She said, "Tell us about that," demonstrating that children had something important to teach each other. Their information—what they knew about print—became part of each day's lessons. Mrs. Poremba also followed children's leads as she changed her sign-in procedures after noticing that children wanted to use the sheets for a new kind of writing—writing the room. She observed children as they talked and as they read and wrote. Each day she provided opportunities for children to show what they were learning about.

Second, Mrs. Poremba *planned routines that included functional reading and writing.* She used sign-in questions to foster reading for information and other beginning-of-the-day activities to orient children to their daily schedule and the weather. She expected that children would read and write as a part of these activities.

Third, Mrs. Poremba *modeled reading and writing strategies in ways that supported children's own reading and writing.* During shared reading, she demonstrated reading from print, knowing where to begin reading, and paying attention to titles as a clue for meaning. She pointed to words as she read and provided opportunities for children to practice pointing as they read. During shared writing, she modeled listening for the big sounds and finding words in the room, and she expected children to use these strategies when they wrote Words for Today.

Fourth, Mrs. Poremba *drew explicit attention to print.* She demonstrated by writing on a small, erasable board the differences between *no* and *on,* she elicited talk about print as she wrote the sign-in question, and she oriented children to print before and during shared reading by using the "What Can You Show Us?" activity.

Fifth, Mrs. Poremba *gradually shifted the responsibility for reading and writing to the children.* In the beginning of the year, children were expected to write only their names on their sign-in sheets. By the middle of the year, they might use their sign-ins as a personal journal-like record of the opening-of-the-day events. In the beginning of the year, Mrs. Poremba wrote the weather words, but by the middle of the year, she offered children the option of writing themselves. By the end of the year, the children were writing Words for Today.

Finally, Mrs. Poremba *planned individual and group activities involving reading and writing.* She planned shared reading activities, including special small-group- and individual-related activities, such as text reconstructions and pop-up books. She planned ways to make group learning more effective, including giving children a model for their text reconstructions.

Chapter Summary

Kindergartners are expected to recognize and begin to write alphabet letters, match spoken and written words, know rhyming words and beginning sounds in words, know sound–letter correspondences and use them in invented spellings, understand concepts of print, write their first and last names, begin to write some high-frequency words, and enjoy and participate in read-alouds. Many of these expectations are in the area of meaning-form links, and their achievement depends on a related achievement—fully developed phonemic awareness. Kindergartners meet these expectations and continue to develop in all areas of written language acquisition when classrooms are filled with print, when teachers and children model reading and writing, and when children participate in functional and con-textualized written language experiences.

Kindergartners' literacy learning is supported through classroom routines using print. Routines such as journal writing, "What Can You Show Us?," and the extended sign-in procedure encourage children's reading and writing and provide opportunities for teachers and children to talk about written language. Shared reading is a rich context for literacy learning; teachers orient children to print, read with children, and plan response activities. Shared reading is used with poems, songs, letters, stories, and informational texts presented on charts and in big books.

Shared writing is another context for language and literacy development in kindergarten. Teachers and students compose texts together. Students suggest ideas, teachers model writing processes, and the students participate in both the writing and the subsequent reading and rereading of the text. Finally, play is a critical component of the kindergarten curriculum. Children learn about written language in dramatic-play-with-print centers and during computer play.

Applying the Information

We suggest two activities for applying the information. First, make a list of the seven characteristics of literacy-rich classrooms from Chapter 6. Then reread this chapter and identify classroom activities appropriate for kindergartners that are examples of each of these seven characteristics. Discuss with your classmates why these activities fit the characteristics.

Second, make a list of all the literacy-learning activities described in this chapter, including group and individual activities. For each activity, describe what children learn about written language meanings, forms, meaning-form links, or functions. For example, children who participate in text reconstruction activities with a pocket-chart text as a model are learning about written language forms as they match words by matching letters. Children who pointer read a familiar poem are learning about meaning-form links as they adjust their pointing using what they know about sounds and letters.

Going Beyond the Text

Visit a kindergarten and observe several literacy activities. Take note of the interactions among the children and between the teacher and the children as they participate in literacy experiences. Make a list of the kinds of literacy materials and describe the classroom routines in which children read and write. Talk with the teacher about the school's academic expectations for kindergarten. Find out how the teacher meets those expectations. Compare these materials, interactions, and activities with those found in Mrs. Poremba's classroom.

REFERENCES

Adams, M. J. (1990). *Beginning to read.* Cambridge: M.I.T. Press.

Ball, E. W., & Blachman, B. A. (1991). Does phoneme segmentation training in kindergarten make a difference in early word recognition and developmental spelling? *Reading Research Quarterly, 26,* 46–66.

Bornstein, H., Saulnier, K. L., & Hamilton, L. B. (Eds.). (1983). *The comprehensive signed English dictionary.* Washington, DC: Gallaudet University Press.

Children's Television Workshop. (1985). *Sign language ABC with Linda Bove.* New York: Random House.

Clay, M. M. (1985). *The early detection of reading difficulties* (3rd ed.). Portsmouth, NH: Heinemann.

Combs, M. (1987). Modeling the reading process with enlarged texts. *The Reading Teacher, 40,* 422–426.

Connelly, L. (undated). *Bears, bears everywhere.* Cypress, CA: Creative Teaching Press.

Cunningham, P. (1998). Looking for patterns: Phonics activities that help children notice how words work. In C. Weaver (Ed.), *Practicing what we know: Informed reading instruction.* (pp. 87–110). Urbana, IL: National Council of Teachers of English.

Elkonin, D. B. (1973). Reading in the U.S.S.R. In J. Downing (Ed.), *Comparative reading* (pp. 551–579). New York: Macmillan.

Fallon, I., & Allen, J. (1994). Where the deer and the cantaloupe play. *The Reading Teacher, 47,* 546–551.

Fountas, I. C., & Pinnell, G. S. (1996). *Guided reading: Good first teaching for all children.* Portsmouth, NH: Heinemann.

Freppon, P., & Dahl, K. (1991). Learning about phonics in a whole language classroom. *Language Arts, 68,* 190–197.

Griffith, P. L., & Olson, M. W. (1992). Phonemic awareness helps beginning readers break the code. *The Reading Teacher, 45,* 516–523.

Holdaway, D. (1979). *The foundations of literacy.* New York: Ashton Scholastic.

International Reading Association & National Association for the Education of Young Children. (1998). Learning to read and write: Developmentally appropriate practices for young children. *The Reading Teacher, 52,* 193–216.

Lindamood, C. H., & Lindamood, P. C. (1969). *Lindamood phoneme sequencing program for reading, spelling, and speech.* Austin, TX: Pro-Ed.

Lundberg, I., Frost, J., & Petersen, O. (1988). Effects of an extensive program for stimulating phonological awareness in preschool children. *Reading Research Quarterly, 23,* 263–284.

Martinez, M., & Teale, W. H. (1988). Reading in a kindergarten classroom library. *The Reading Teacher, 41,* 568–572.

McGee, L. M., & Purcell-Gates, V. (1997). Conversations: So what's going on in research in emergent literacy? *Reading Research Quarterly, 32,* 310–327.

McGuinness, C., & McGuinness, G. (1998). *Reading reflex: The foolproof phonographix method for teaching your child to read.* New York: Free Press.

Nelson, O. G., & Linek, W. M. (Eds.) (1999). *Practical applications of language experience: Looking back, looking forward.* Boston: Allyn and Bacon.

Pinnell, G. S., & Fountas, I. C. (1998). *Word matters: Teaching phonics and spelling in the reading/writing classroom.* Portsmouth, NH: Heinemann.

Putnam, L. (1991). Dramatizing nonfiction with emerging readers. *Language Arts, 68,* 463–469.

Rankin, L. (1991). *The handmade alphabet.* New York: Scholastic.

Raschka, C. (1992). *Charlie Parker played be bop.* New York: Orchard.

Richgels, D. J. (1995). A kindergarten sign-in procedure: A routine in support of written language learning. In K. A. Hinchman, D. J. Leu, & C. K. Kinzer (Eds.), *Perspectives on literacy research and practice, 44th yearbook of the National Reading Conference* (pp. 243–254). Chicago: National Reading Conference.

Richgels, D. J. (2003). *Going to kindergarten: A year with an outstanding teacher.* Lanham, MD: Scarecrow.

Richgels, D. J., Poremba, K. J., & McGee, L. M. (1996). Kindergartners talk about print: Phonemic awareness in meaningful contexts. *The Reading Teacher, 49,* 632–642.

Riekehof, L. L. (1978). *The joy of signing: The new illustrated guide for mastering sign language and the manual alphabet.* Springfield, MO: Gospel Publishing House.

Sendak, M. (1991). *Chicken soup with rice: A book of months.* New York: HarperCollins.

Share, D. (1995). Phonological recoding and self-teaching: *Sine qua non* of reading acquisition. *Cognition, 55,* 151–218.

Shilling, W. A. (1997). Young children using computers to make discoveries about written language. *Early Childhood Education Journal, 24,* 253–259.

Stauffer, R. (1980). *The language experience approach to teaching reading* (2nd ed.). New York: Harper and Row.

Tolhurst, M. (1990). *Somebody and the three Blairs.* New York: Orchard.

Trachtenburg, P., & Ferruggia, A. (1989). Big books from little voices: Reaching high risk beginning readers. *The Reading Teacher, 42,* 284–289.

Van Allen, R., & Van Allen, C. (1982). *Language experience activities* (2nd ed.). Boston: Houghton Mifflin.

Yopp, H. K. (1992). Developing phonemic awareness in young children. *The Reading Teacher, 45,* 696–703.

KEY CONCEPTS

sight words	point of difficulty	grand conversations
literacy centers	teaching for strategies	make-a-word activities
talk-through	leveled texts	phonograms
interactive writing	dynamic ability groups	word sorts
word study	linking to the unknown	Daily Oral Language (DOL)
guided reading approach	coaching	words for the week

word wall

vowel digraphs

vowel diphthongs

partner reading

take-home books

independent reading level

instructional reading level

fluency

predictable books

transitional texts

decodable texts

effective literacy instruction

reading-writing connections

writing conferences

drafts

flexible groupings

varied materials

scope and sequence of skills

multiple-purpose teaching

instructional density

minilessons

expectations

classroom management

telling

explicit phonics teaching

whole language approach

balanced instruction

coherence

process writing instruction

planning, drafting, revising, and editing

interactive journals

response journals

writers' journals

science journals

home-school journals

targeted instruction

What's New Here?

The "what's new" in first grade is the expectation that by the end of the year all children will be reading and writing conventionally. They are expected to comprehend stories and informational texts, learn the meanings of new words, learn a few hundred sight words, and use sound–letter relationships to identify unknown words. They are expected to learn the spellings of some words and to use sound–letter relationships and other strategies to spell words. They are expected to write a variety of kinds of compositions for a variety of purposes (to inform, to interact with others, to entertain).

But how do children get to these end points? Many children will begin first grade already reading and writing conventionally. The print-rich environment and literacy instruction provided for them in preschool and kindergarten were sufficient for them to make the transition from experimenters to conventional readers and writers. Children who begin first grade already reading and writing often make tremendous gains in reading during first grade. They often end their first grade year reading on a third grade level or above (Dahl et al., 1999).

Other children will enter first grade as experimenters. They have sufficient knowledge about and experience with written language to make the transition to conventional reading and writing during first grade. For them, beginning to read and write conventionally will be relatively easy as they participate in instructional activities such as those we describe in this chapter (Snow, Burns, & Griffin, 1998). For other children, this transition will take careful attention from a highly knowledgeable teacher. Children who begin first grade with knowledge and experiences of written language like those of novice readers and writers need carefully planned instruction in order to become conventional readers and writers by the time they are seven years old. We expect that most children will become early conventional readers and writers by age seven (IRA/NAEYC, 1998).

We know a great deal about what children need to learn in order to begin reading conventionally (Adams, 1990; Juel, 1991). The hallmark of conventional reading is orchestrating all sources of information so attention is free to focus on meaning. Experienced conventional readers pay attention to print; they look at and read every word in a text. However, the print seems transparent; readers' attention is on the meaning they are constructing rather than on the print. Attention is free to focus on a text's meaning when readers automatically and fluently recognize words, know their meanings, and chunk those meanings into phrases, sentences, and larger chunks. That is, readers recognize and access the meanings of words quickly (in less than a fraction of a second) "by sight" and chunk them together into phrases without consciously having to decode words or "sound them out." **Sight words** are words that readers recognize instantly.

As most children acquire sight words, an amazing thing happens quite unconsciously. As they read more and more text, they go beyond just learning specific words. They automatically relate letter sequences in frequently encountered words to spoken word parts. Knowing the pronunciations of word parts allows them to decode very complicated words they have never before encountered. They can do so very quickly, seemingly without stopping to "sound out." For example, for older readers, the letters *con, tempt,* and *ible* in the word *contemptible* automatically trigger pronunciation of /kun/, /tempt/, and /ibl/ even when they have never encountered the word *contemptible* in their reading before.

Readers use many more strategies than merely decoding or using phonics to figure out unknown words. It is critical to keep in mind that the purpose of instruction in beginning reading and writing is not merely to develop sight words or strong decoding and spelling abilities (although these are important); it is to foster active readers and writers who have a wide variety of strategies, which they use to engage in deep thinking. Table 9.1 summarizes the wide variety of strategies and understandings that we expect children at the end of first grade to have acquired.

TABLE 9.1   Reading and Writing Outcomes for First Grade

By the end of first grade, children

Read and retell familiar narrative and informational text

Use strategies (predicting, rereading, imagining, questioning, commenting) for comprehension

Select to read and write for a variety of purposes

Have an awareness of a wide variety of literary elements found in narratives, informational texts, and poetry (character, setting, problem, event, sequence, lining, rhyming, repetition)

Write personal, narrative, informational, and poetic text

Have an interest in and strategies for learning meanings of vocabulary

Acquire sight words and spell words

Use a variety of strategies for decoding and spelling (including strategies that build from phonemic awareness, maintain fluency, detect and correct errors, solve problems with words using multiple sources of information, and link to current knowledge, including the use of consonants, short vowels, long vowels, and high-frequency phonograms)

Use punctuation and capitalization

Engage in independent reading and writing

Based on IRA/NAEYC, 1998; Fountas & Pinnell, 1996; and Bear, Invernizzi, Templeton, & Johnston, 2000.

Reading and Writing Instruction in Five First-Grade Classrooms

How do teachers help students to attain these strategies and understandings? In this section, we share examples from five first grade teachers. Mrs. Tran uses the guided reading approach to first grade reading instruction. Mrs. Walker uses a variety of techniques for teaching reading, many of them centered on the shared reading of a pattern story. Mr. Schultheis exemplifies good first grade writing instruction. Mrs. Duthie's and Mrs. Zickuhr's teaching includes examples of mini-lessons to support first graders' informational text writing and poetry writing.

Guided Reading Instruction in Mrs. Tran's First Grade

Mrs. Tran teaches twenty first-grade children in a large urban district. The majority of the children in her classroom have home languages that are not English; the classroom includes six different home languages. We describe six components of Mrs. Tran's instruction: **literacy centers, talk-through** as an introduction to children's guided reading, teaching for strategies while children are reading, **interactive writing,** teaching for comprehension, and **word study.** Mrs. Tran's literacy program also includes multiple daily read-alouds, shared reading, independent reading, and writing workshop.

The **guided reading approach** (Fountas & Pinnell, 1996) to reading and writing instruction is based on strategies used in Reading Recovery (Clay, 1993), a specialized program for struggling first grade readers, and components of a nonability, multileveled instructional program (Cunningham, Hall, & Defee, 1998), especially the use of word walls and word study.

There are three critical characteristics of the instruction used in the guided reading approach. First, a major emphasis is placed on developing strategic readers as active problem solvers who are expected to take initiative in solving their own reading difficulties. Important teaching occurs at the **point of difficulty** (Askew & Fountas, 1998) while children are reading. Children are expected to work at difficult points in reading by monitoring and discovering new information for themselves. Children make new discoveries as they search for and use information in the text, check one source of information with another, and link to what they already know. **Teaching for strategies,** helping children develop strategies they use during reading and writing, is an important focus of instruction in the guided reading approach.

A second critical component of the guided reading approach is using sets of **leveled texts** that begin with easy texts that are highly repetitive with few words. Gradually children read more difficult texts that include more words and more complex, literary and informational language. Reading Recovery uses over a dozen levels of text difficulty in the first grade. Fountas and Pinnell (1996) recommend using sixteen levels of text difficulty in first through third grade, and Gunning (1998) has identified thirteen levels of text difficulty from first through early second grade. Lists of texts at several levels of difficulty can be found in Fountas and Pinnell (1996) or Gunning (1998), and many school districts have developed their own lists of leveled texts. Many texts at the easiest levels of difficulty can be purchased through publishers such as Wright Group, Rigby, Sundance, or Scholastic. Table 9.2 presents a description of eight levels of text difficulty and example books for each level (based on Peterson, 1991; Gunning, 1998).

TABLE 9.2   Levels of Text Difficulty

Level	Description	Example
1. Picture or Phrase	Each page includes a single word or phrase with close relationship to illustrations.	*Colors* (Birningham) Crown *1 Hunter* (Hutchins) Greenwillow *Count and See* (Hoban) Macmillan *Have You Seen My Cat?* (Carle) Scholastic
2. Sentence Pattern	Each page includes a repetitive sentence with some new content. From close to some relationship with illustration as difficulty increases. Number of different words in pattern increases with difficulty.	*I Went Walking* (Williams) Harcourt *Spots, Feathers, and Curly Tails* (Tafuri) Greenwillow *Things I Like* (Browne) Knopf *Five Little Ducks* (Raffi) Crown *Bears on Wheels* (Berenstain) Random House *It Looked Like Spilt Milk* (Shaw) HarperCollins
3. Sight Word	Includes one sentence per page; most words are high-frequency, but a few content words. Most words strongly related to illustrations. Up to thirty-five different words and may be one hundred words in text.	*Blue Bug Goes to School* (Poulet) Children's Press *All By Myself* (Mayer) Golden Books *Go Dog Go* (Eastman) Random House *Just Like Daddy* (Asch) Simon and Schuster *Pardon? Said the Giraffe* (West) HarperCollins *A Dark, Dark Tale* (Brown) Dial *Cookie's Week* (Ward) Putnam *Marmalade's Nap* (Wheeler) Knopf
4. Easy Beginning	Text of 100 to 150 words, with many high-frequency words and some content words. Less repetition and more words per page. Up to fifty different words.	*The Carrot Seed* (Kraus) HarperCollins *One Monday Morning* (Shulevitz) Scribner *Peanut Butter and Jelly* (Wescott) Dutton *Sheep in a Jeep* (Shaw) Houghton Mifflin *Titch* (Hutchins) Macmillan *More Spaghetti I Say* (Gelman) Scholastic
5. Moderate Beginning	Text of 150 to 200 words, with more content words, but the majority are still high-frequency words.	*Are You My Mother?* (Eastman) Random House *Hattie and the Fox* (Fox) Harcourt *Henny Penny* (Galdone) Clarion *George Shrinks* (Joyce) HarperCollins *Where Are You Going Little Mouse?* (Kraus) Greenwillow *Hop on Pop* (Seuss) Random House

(continued)

TABLE 9.2   Continued

Level	Description	Example
6. Difficult Beginning	Varied vocabulary, longer text, more detailed information and complex plots. Most vocabulary in reader's listening vocabulary.	*Mouse Soup* (Lobel) HarperCollins *Do Like Kyla* (Johnson) Orchard *Kiss for Little Bear* (Minarik) HarperCollins *More Tales of Amanda Pig* (Van Leeuwen) Dial *Elephant and the Bad Baby* (Vipont) Putnam *Clifford, the Big Red Dog* (Bridwell) Scholastic
7. Early Transitional	Some vocabulary not in reader's listening vocabulary. May have short chapters and some unfamiliar concepts.	*Henry and Mudge* (Rylant) Simon and Schuster *Frog and Toad Together* (Lobel) HarperCollins *Fox in Love* (Marshall) Dial *Three Little Pigs* (Galdone) Clarion *The Art Lesson* (de Paola) Putnam *Bear's Picnic* (Berenstain) Random House
8. Later	Vocabulary beyond reader's listening vocabulary, complex plots and unfamiliar concepts.	*Nate the Great* (Sharmat) Dell *Cam Jan and the Mystery of the Dinosaur* (Adler) Dell *The Chalk Box Kid* (Bulla) Random House

Based on B. Peterson, 1991; and T. Gunning, 1998.

A final component of the guided reading program is small **dynamic ability groups** (Fountas & Pinnell, 1996). In dynamic ability grouping, a small number of children who have similar reading abilities are selected to read together. Texts are carefully selected to match the needs of the small group of readers. Teachers read twenty to thirty minutes with the small group of readers at least four times per week. However, many teachers meet twice daily with some small groups of children who are struggling to make progress. In the following section, we describe Mrs. Tran's first grade classroom and her use of the guided reading approach.

Literacy Centers.   In order to provide time for instruction of small guided reading groups, Mrs. Tran prepares several activities for children to work on independently, which she places in seven centers in her classroom. Mrs. Tran plans these activities carefully so they present a range of challenges to the variety of learners she has in her classroom. Mrs. Tran expects that the children will work together without teacher support in the centers, capitalizing on peer support for learning (MacGillivray, 1994; Sipe, 1998). Figure 9.1 lists the materials found in Mrs. Tran's seven literacy centers and describes activities that are typical for each center. Mrs. Tran changes the materials and activities included in the centers weekly or biweekly. During September and early October, she demonstrates how to work in the centers, showing children how to find and replace materials and sustain their

FIGURE 9.1 **Mrs. Tran's Literacy Centers**

Listening Center. Tape recorder, multiple headphones, and approximately one hundred audiotapes of children's literature, including commercially available tapes as well as tape recordings of parents of present and past students, the principal and other teachers, and other guests reading books aloud. Sentences from the informational book or storybook that is read aloud are placed on sentence strips. Children select a sentence after listening to the book and illustrate it.

Big and Little Book Center. Small easel with four or five recently read big books, small children's chair, pointer, and small tubs of books for each child in the classroom, with copies of five or six books or poems read during shared or guided reading. Children take turns being the teacher and pretending to direct a shared reading experience. They also reread poems and books from their book tubs.

Library Center. Cozy corner created by shelves with nearly 300 books, including books Mrs. Tran has recently read aloud, books included in a social studies or science unit, and books by favorite authors and illustrators. Children browse through books and use props to retell stories (during this week, the retelling props are spoon puppets for versions of *The Three Billy Goats Gruff* and transparency props for retelling *Where's Spot?* on an overhead projector, which sometimes is located in this center).

Writing Center. A large, round table with shelves stocked with a variety of writing tools and materials. This week, Mrs. Tran has included letter writing as a part of the writing center. She has posted several examples of letters children may use.

Letter and Word Center. An easel, a small table for writing, and shelves to hold letter and word games and puzzles. Mrs. Tran writes words on chart paper each day and places the paper on the easel for children to copy if they wish. This week, Mrs. Tran has written her name and invited children to write her name several times on the chart paper. This week, small clipboards are available for children to copy the names of other children in the class (located on sentences strips and clipped on a ring in the center). Children are also challenged to write ten words included on the word wall, using letter tiles.

Computer Center. A large table with two computers, word-processing packages, reading and other games, and Internet access. This week, children are challenged to write a grocery list. Food ads from the newspaper and alphabet books with food are located at the computer center.

Specials Center. This center is for special activities that occur in the classroom. This week, three parents have volunteered to read aloud with children. Other specials include art projects, cooking activities, and science experiments.

---

activity in a center for twenty minutes. She shares a classroom aide, who assists in supervising the children as they work in the centers for an hour three mornings a week, with three other first grade teachers in her building.

Mrs. Tran assigns four or five children with mixed abilities to a center group; each center group is assigned to three centers a day. The membership in the groups changes every month so that children work with a variety of others throughout the school year. Mrs. Tran's schedule includes a large block of uninterrupted time for reading instruction, during which the children spend one hour and twenty minutes in centers while Mrs. Tran teaches three guided reading groups. In early November, the children are divided into five groups, and Mrs. Tran reads with each group four or five times a week. A reading specialist works in Mrs. Tran's classroom four mornings a week, and she works with another guided reading group. The reading specialist returns to the class in the afternoon to conduct a final guided reading group lesson. Altogether, most children read with a teacher in a guided reading group once a day, but some children work with a teacher twice a day for three days a week.

Talk-Through to Introduce Guided Reading.   The guided reading approach uses the talk-through activity to prepare children to read a particular text (Clay, 1991b; Fountas & Pinnell, 1996). Keep in mind that guided reading prepares children to read text on their own without teacher support during reading. Talk-through is intended to orient children to the text: to text meaning, repetitive patterns, particular words that might not be decodable, or phonics and other strategies for identifying unknown words and monitoring meaning prior to reading. Talk-through can provide much support for children's reading or minimal support. Teachers carefully gauge how much support to provide in talk-through, given their awareness of the reading abilities of particular children and the level of challenge presented in a particular text.

In this lesson in early November, Mrs. Tran is working with six children who are just beginning to read conventionally. Mrs. Tran carefully selects an instructional level text to use with this group and decides how much support to provide during talk-through. She considers what the children already can do. She knows that these children have acquired a few sight words and can track print at the word-by-word level in pattern sentence books by using some initial consonant sounds to monitor their finger-pointing. They know many consonant sound–letter associations, are beginning to learn vowel associations, use initial and sometimes final consonants in their invented spelling, and are developing a strong concept of written words. Mrs. Tran's goals for this group are to develop a larger store of high-frequency sight words, practice monitoring reading by using initial and final consonant cues to cross-check, and practice using the strategy of linking new with known.

After careful consideration, Mrs. Tran decides to use *Where's Spot?* (Hill, 1980) as an introduction to the guided reading text *Where's Tim?* (Cutting, 1996). *Where's Spot?* is familiar to the children, employs the same repetitive language pattern found in *Where's Tim?*, and includes many of the same positional words she intends children to learn (for example, the words *under* and *behind*). Further, Mrs. Tran plans to use the pattern in *Where's Spot?* during a writing process lesson within the next few weeks. Mrs. Tran reads through both books in order to make decisions about what to include in her talk-through activity.

Mrs. Tran knows that the words *no, he, the, is,* and *in,* which are found in the text of *Where's Tim?*, are familiar to these children. These words along with left-to-right pointing should anchor their reading. She will introduce the **linking to the known** strategy by having children try to figure out the word *Tim* in the title by using what they already know about short vowels. Later, she will work with the short-*i* vowel in further word study.

Before the talk-through, Mrs. Tran reads *Where's Spot?* to the children, asking questions and inviting children to make comments. She quickly rereads the story a second time. Then she introduces the guided reading book *Where's Tim?*, using the talk-through. Figure 9.2 presents her talk-through introduction to this text.

FIGURE 9.2   Talk-Through for *Where's Tim?* (Cutting, 1996)

T: We're going to start today by reading this book. (Several children make overlapping comments: "Where's Spot?" "I know that book." "I like that book.")

T: How many words are in the title?

c: Two.

T: Yes (points), one, two (reads and points to the words) *Where's Spot?*

(Mrs. Tran and children discuss the author and read the book together, stopping frequently to talk about the story. She reads the story twice and stresses the positional words, such as *under* and *behind*.)

T: Now, today for guided reading we are going to read this book (passes out copies of book for each child), and it is also a book about someone searching. This man is searching. He can't find someone. I wonder who he is searching for?

(Mrs. Tran and children make guesses about who the man might be searching for.)

T: How many words in the title? Let's count them together. One, two. The title is *Where's* (pauses). Um, who are they searching for? Does anybody know anything that will help me figure out the name of the person this man is searching for?

c: It starts like Tamika.

T: Yes it starts with the sound (Mrs. Tran pauses and many children offer sounds, most of which are /t/. Mrs. Tran confirms the /t/ sound).

T: Anything else that could help us? What about this vowel? Does anyone know anything that might help us? (Children offer a variety of vowel sounds, and Mrs. Tran helps the children blend /t/ /i/ /m/.)

T: Now let's look through the book. Find the title page. (Mrs. Tran observes as children locate the page.) Let's look and see where the man is searching for Tim.

(Children discuss each page and where the man is looking. Mrs. Tran stresses the positional words that will be read on each page, especially *under* and *behind*.)

T: (page 5) Where is the man looking on this page? (Some children suggest the bathtub.) Yes, he is looking in the room where we find the bathtub. He is looking in the *bathroom*. Put your finger on the word *bathroom*. (Mrs. Tran makes sure everyone is on the correct word.)

T: (page 8) There's Tim! Why he's *fast asleep,* isn't he? Who can find the word *fast*. How would you check if this word was *fast?* (Children discuss cross-checking the *f* and *t* sounds.) Ok. Now use your pointing fingers and read the book softly to yourself.

Notice how she calls attention to the connection to the earlier book she read aloud; establishes the repetitive pattern; focuses on locating the words *under, bathroom,* and *behind;* has children figure out the surprise ending; and models the linking with the known strategy as they read the title. Following the talk-through, the six children read the book independently. They read quietly, but aloud, and Mrs. Tran listens to all the children as they read, noting children's tracking of print, cross-checking, and linking to the known.

As children are reading aloud, Mrs. Tran observes and notes one or two teaching points she will make with the children during the next part of the lesson. She decides to refocus on the vowel sound in the word *Tim* and use a small, dry erase board to have children use the phonogram *im* to build more words such as *dim, him, rim,* and *slim.* Mrs. Tran has children reread portions of the entire text several times; she integrates teaching during the rereading. She prepares a printed version of the text without the picture cues which goes in a special binder and is available in each child's independent reading tub. After rereading the illustrated text once or twice and participating in the instructional activity focusing on reading and spelling words with the *im* phonogram, the children read the print-only version. Finally, children choose one or two stories from the binder that they have recently read during guided reading to reread.

Teaching for Strategies during Guided Reading. Keep in mind that a critical component of the guided reading approach is to foster active readers who solve by themselves the problems they encounter while reading. Teachers are aiming for readers who have self-extending reading strategies (Clay, 1991a). That is, eventually readers acquire a sufficient number of strategies that enable them to actually get better at reading with minimal teacher support. Rather than solve reading problems before reading by providing children with all the sight words they will need, teachers in the guided reading approach intentionally leave problems for children to solve on their own during the very first reading of a text. In this way, children must use strategies to solve their own reading difficulties (Askew & Fountas, 1998; Schwartz, 1997).

Mrs. Tran has already taught several strategies to this particular group of children and uses prompts to encourage children to employ these strategies while they are reading. Mrs. Tran demonstrates a strategy several times during talk-throughs and then uses prompts and comments to encourage and reinforce strategy use when children are at a point of difficulty in their reading. This group of children has some strategies firmly under control, such as moving left to right and matching word-for-word while reading. Mrs. Tran demonstrated "reading with her finger" and often praises children for carefully reading with their fingers during guided reading (Fountas & Pinnell, 1996). When children have difficulty, she prompts for this strategy by asking, "Are there enough words? Were there too many words? Try rereading it again."

These children sometimes use other strategies, such as cross-checking picture and meaning cues with initial consonants and noticing mismatches between words they attempt and the way they appear in print. Mrs. Tran demonstrated the strategy by reading text that makes sense but does not match the initial consonant and talking about how to cross check. When children have difficulty reading, she may provide several prompts for the strategy, such as asking, "Where's the tricky word? What did you notice? What letter did you expect at the beginning? Would _____ fit there?"

Children in this group are beginning to make more than one attempt at a word before asking for help. They are beginning to use the strategy of backing up and trying again. In this lesson, Mrs. Tran demonstrated a more complex strategy of linking to known information to figure out an unknown word during the talk-through. Later, she will use prompts such as, "Can you find something you know about here? Does it look like _____ ? Do you know a word like this? Do you know a word that starts with those letters? Do you know a word that ends with those letters? What do you know that might help?"

Other groups of children in Mrs. Tran's classroom are learning more sophisticated strategies, such as using decoding a new word by analogy (using a familiar phonogram to identify a new word, such as using *ham* to figure out *scram*) or decoding multisyllabic words by using several analogies (such as using *ex* and *fan* to figure out *Mexican*). Other strategies focus on expanding vocabulary knowledge, such as calling to mind related concepts for words that are only somewhat familiar. Still other strategies focus on meaning, such as inviting children to predict and confirm, pause and build a mental picture, assess whether a character's action is expected or unusual, and connect story events or characters to life experiences and acquaintances.

Coaching. When Mrs. Tran encourages her students to use strategies that she has already taught, she is using a teaching strategy known as **coaching.** She observes her students so that she knows to what extent they are able to put what she has taught into practice. Some students will have internalized those strategies and will be able to use them in the self-extending reading that is the goal of guided reading. But Mrs. Tran's observations also show her which students need the sorts of prompts quoted in the previous section. This teaching of specific strategies, giving students opportunities to use them, observing who can and cannot do so, and prompting those who are not yet self-extending readers is the essence of coaching.

The International Reading Association (IRA), in a position statement about excellent reading teaching, captures the essence of coaching.

> Excellent reading teachers . . . are skilled at observing children's performance and using informal interactions to call children's attention to important aspects of what they are learning and doing. They often help children with a difficult part of the task so that the children can move forward to complete the task successfully. . . . Excellent reading teachers know where their children are in reading development and they know the likely next steps. They help children take these steps by providing just the right amount of help at just the right time. (2000, p. 239)

This may seem to be a daunting prescription. Taylor et al. (2002) observed that even the most accomplished teachers of reading used coaching more often for word identification skills and strategies than for comprehension processes. We agree that the best context for teachers to begin to develop a coaching style of teaching is in helping students with word recognition as they read extended texts.

Interactive Writing.   Mrs. Tran uses interactive writing as part of her guided reading program. She may use a guided reading lesson. Or she might use it prior to or after reading a particular text. Mrs. Tran has decided to use an interactive writing activity using the pattern found in *Where's Spot?* with another small group of children. Mrs. Tran is particularly concerned about these three children in her classroom because of their need to develop many foundational concepts. These children do not have a firm grasp of identifying and writing all alphabet letters and are just beginning to control the left-to-right print orientation. They need many experiences with rhyming words and words with similar beginning consonants.

This group has already heard Mrs. Tran read *Where's Spot?* several times. Mrs. Tran has made a pocket chart of the text from this book for shared reading experiences. The children have practiced using a pointer to reread the story from the pocket chart, pointing to the words from left to right. They have participated in many pocket-chart extensions, such as matching words on word cards to words on the pocket chart.

Now Mrs. Tran has decided they will use interactive writing to compose pattern writing. The children decide to compose a pattern story called *Where's Mrs. Tran?* For this lesson, the children will only write the title of the story together during the interactive lesson. Mrs. Tran guides the children by having them repeat the title (*Where's Mrs. Tran?*) and count the number of words. She writes three lines on chart paper from left to right, emphasizing that they will write the three words in the title across the paper on these lines.

Mrs. Tran reminds the children of the first word in the title that they will write. She tells the children they will use the strategy of finding the word and copying its spelling. She asks the children, "Where could we look? Where do we know to find this word?" Mrs. Tran recognizes that an important reading and writing strategy for children at this stage is to draw on resources such as familiar stories, poems, and charts to read and write words (Sipe, 1998). The children find the word *Where's* both on the book *Where's Spot?* and on their pocket chart. Then the children spell the word, saying its letters left to right. Mrs. Tran briefly discusses the apostrophe. She invites first one child and then another to come to the chart and write the first four letters in the word *Where's*. Mrs. Tran quickly writes the remaining letters on the chart as the children tell her the letters. She has children remember the second word in their title and again has children think of where they could find the word. They locate five different places in the classroom where Mrs. Tran's name is written. Again, they name the letters, and children are selected to write them on the chart. Figure 9.3 presents the interactive writing result of *Where's Mrs. Tran?*

FIGURE 9.3   Interactive Writing of *Where's Mrs. Tran?*

Mrs. Tran uses interactive writing with all the groups in her classroom. Depending on what the children know, Mrs. Tran adjusts what she expects children to write, the amount of support she provides, and how much text will be written in one lesson. In some groups, children write sight words quickly and spend more time discussing how to write words with complex vowel spelling patterns or adding suffixes, such as consistent spelling of *ed* and *s*. In other groups, children focus on writing the beginning, middle, and final sounds in words.

Teaching for Comprehension.   The guided reading approach uses leveled texts, and many first graders begin reading picture and phrase- or sentence-level books, which are not difficult to understand. These books, of course, have meaning, but their meanings are obvious from the illustrations. Not much interpretation—going beyond the literal words of the text—is needed to enjoy and understand these texts. While children are having a heavy dose of these kinds of texts, they should also be engaged in comprehension activities from teacher read-alouds. Children should be encouraged to ask questions, make predictions, insert comments, and draw conclusions during teacher read-alouds. Children may be part of small or large groups that have **grand conversations** about a book their teacher has read aloud (McGee, 1996). Grand conversations are directed by children's comments and questions rather than by a teacher's asking of questions. Teachers begin the conversation by asking, "What did you think?" or "Who has something to say about the book?" Improved understandings result from the comprehension work that emerges during a grand conversation (see Figure 12.7).

However, first graders are also expected to move beyond reading easy books. They will read sight word-level, beginning-level, and transitional-level books that have more complex story structures and detailed information with unfamiliar vocabulary. Meaning in these books goes beyond what is illustrated, and children can be encouraged to interpret them beyond the literal level. Grand conversations about these books in guided reading activities support children's deep thinking. Similarly, there are many comprehension activities that extend children's understandings of what they have read. Children can retell stories or information in journals, act out stories or draw diagrams of information, or compose new endings for old favorites.

Word Study.   Mrs. Tran uses twenty minutes daily to engage in word study with the entire class (Bear, Invernizzi, Templeton, & Johnston, 2000; Pinnell & Fountas,

1998). Word study involves looking carefully at how words are put together, learning sound–letter relationships useful for reading and writing words, and building new words from known words. Mrs. Tran also has a word wall and uses this wall daily as part of her word study program. Mrs. Tran began the year with **make-a-word activities** (Cunningham & Cunningham, 1992). She selected two familiar word families from **phonograms** that she knows are frequently found in words first graders encounter, such as *ack, ail, ain, ame, eat, est, ice, ide, ick, ock, oke, op, uck, ug,* and *ump.* (Figure 9.4 presents thirty-seven phonograms that are most frequently found in English spellings; Adams, 1990, pp. 321–322.) Each child is given a card with the phonogram written on it, several cards with individual consonants, and a folder that had been stapled to hold the cards. Mrs. Tran says, "I have the word *eat;* now what do we need to make the word *beat?* Who can show me?" She emphasizes the sound of the letter *b* by elongating it. The children use their letters and phonogram cards to spell words while Mrs. Tran or the other children pronounce them.

Mrs. Tran uses word-building activities in her letter and word center. She writes several words on a sheet of writing paper and challenges children to write additional words when they are in the center. Figure 9.5 presents a word-building activity that Sindy completed in the letter and word center. She composed the words *bat, mat, rat, sat,* and *vat* using the pattern Mrs. Tran provided in her word *cat.* Then Sindy went on to build words from another pattern, one that Mrs. Tran did not suggest. She wrote *Mom* and *Tom.*

Mrs. Tran will increase the difficulty of making words by introducing consonant blends and digraphs. Later she will select a set of letters that can be used to spell single- and multisyllable words (Cunningham, Hall, & Defee, 1998; Gaskins et al., 1997). For example, children might have the letters *d, p, r, s, e,* and *i* and use these letters to spell a variety of words, including *is, rid, red, dip, ride, rise, rider, pride,* and finally, *spider* (Cunningham & Cunningham, 1992, p. 109).

Later in the year, Mrs. Tran will also introduce **word sorts** (Bear, Invernizzi, Templeton, & Johnston, 2000). Children will collect and sort words according to particular spelling patterns. For example, children may collect words that have the long-*a* sound in them over several days. All the words will be collected and placed

FIGURE 9.4   Thirty-Seven Phonograms That Are Most Frequently Found in English Spellings

ack	ail	ain	ake	ale	ame	an
ank	ap	ash	at	ate	aw	ay
eat	ell	est	ice	ick	ide	ight
ill	in	ine	ing	ink	ip	ir
ock	oke	op	ore	or	uck	ug
ump	unk					

From Adams, 1990, pp. 321–322.

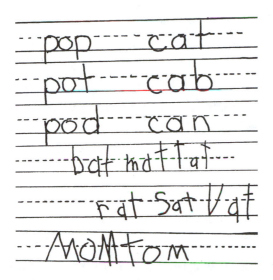

FIGURE 9.5   Sindy's Word-Building Activity

on cards. Then children can sort the words to discover all the patterns used to spell long *a*, such as in the words *fade, rage, fail, raise, pale, paste,* and *straight.*

Mrs. Tran's Balanced Reading Program.   Mrs. Tran has crafted a balanced reading program that supports and extends the literacy learning of children who began first grade with a wide range of knowledge about literacy. Mrs. Tran uses multiple instructional contexts as ways to support children who might otherwise be at risk for literacy failure. For many children, she uses a mixture of shared reading and interactive writing to provide opportunities for children to gain foundational concepts about print, the alphabetic principle, and phonemic awareness. However, these children are also engaged in guided reading experiences in which they acquire sight words, develop strategies, and build vocabulary as they read text at increasing levels of difficulty. Mrs. Tran's word study extends children's reading and writing experiences through systematic examination of words. Finally, Mrs. Tran provides many opportunities for children to gain fluency by reading and rereading favorite books and poems. She carefully selects books for individual children, which she places in small tubs for each child in the room. Children read these materials at the beginning of every day and during some center activities. Mrs. Tran also provides time for children to browse through a variety of books, most of which will be beyond their reading level. She reads several books aloud daily and places these books in the library center.

Reading in Mrs. Walker's First Grade

Mrs. Walker is a first grade teacher in a suburban public school. She is especially effective at meeting the needs of her thirty students. The following example is from November, when Mrs. Walker provided multiple reading and writing experiences, including daily oral language, word wall, reading aloud, shared reading, partner reading, reading extensions and follow-ups, and self-selected books.

Daily Oral Language.   An important daily routine in Mrs. Walker's class is **Daily Oral Language (DOL)** (Vail & Papenfuss, 1982). It involves a three-line text that Mrs. Walker writes on the chalkboard and into which she has inserted errors in spelling, punctuation, and usage. Today's DOL text is

> jimmy he CAN wach
> the car jast lik his dad
> what can you do

Mrs. Walker first asks children to read the text; then they determine whether the information in the text is true.

> **MRS. WALKER:** Let's find out if that [sentence is] true first. Jimmy, can you wash the car like your dad? (Jimmy nods.) He can!
>
> **JIMMY:** I can wash it better!

Then the children offer suggestions about how to correct the text.

> **LAURA:** (about CAN) You put all capitals. . . .
>
> **MRS. WALKER:** There's no real reason to have all capitals here, although I'm still seeing a lot of capital letters in some of [your] journals. . . .
>
> **KASEY:** We don't need the *he.*
>
> **MRS. WALKER:** Okay, when we have that *he,* it's just like we said "Jimmy Jimmy," isn't it?

Robert suggests a period after *do.*

> **MRS. WALKER:** Think about this—"What can *you* do?" (with question intonation and emphasis on *you*)
>
> **CHILD:** It's a question!
>
> **MRS. WALKER:** I'm asking you something, aren't I? I'm asking you what you can do. So does it need a period? What does it need, Robert?
>
> **ROBERT:** A question mark. . . .
>
> **KARA:** You need a *e* in *like.*
>
> **MRS. WALKER:** Is this how I spell *like?*
>
> **CHILDREN:** No! No!
>
> **MRS. WALKER:** L-I-K, actually if I were sounding it out, that sounds pretty good—/l/, /I/—but if I wouldn't put the *e* on it, it would be /l/, /i/. Sometimes—

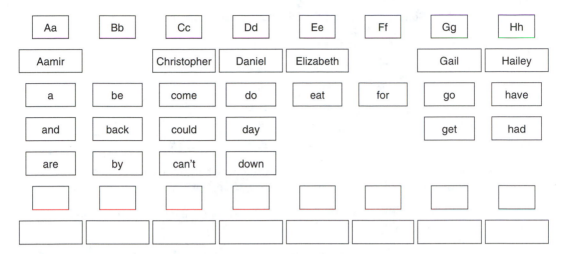

FIGURE 9.6   Portion of a Word Wall

CHILD: Like "Lick a stick!"

MRS. WALKER: Sometimes we put an *e* on the end, and the *e* helps the other vowel say its name—/l/, /I/.

Eventually, they find all the errors, and the text is now written correctly on the chalkboard.

Word Wall.   After daily oral language, Mrs. Walker introduces six **words for the week:** *am, on, look, who,* and *can't.* These are words that the children will encounter during today's shared reading activity and that they will practice reading and spelling throughout the week. Later, these words can be added to a **word wall** (Cunningham, 1995; Wagstaff, 1997–1998). Figure 9.6 presents an example of a word wall.

During the week, the children practice reading and writing the words. Mrs. Walker uses the word wall daily for a variety of activities as part of her phonics and spelling instruction. For example, the children might use the words on the wall to find words with short-*a* and -*i* sounds. Other times, Mrs. Walker might add words to the wall when an occasion arises, such as when several children need the same high-frequency words (e.g., *they, where,* or *this*) in their writing. She may add words from social studies and science units, and later in the year, she may add words with suffixes such as *s, es,* and *ing.*

Mrs. Walker makes decisions about the nature of words to include on the word wall, in her daily oral language activities, and for word family study based on her knowledge of what the state and school system require first graders to know, the scope and sequence of skills taught in her basal reading series, and from observations of children as they read and write. Figure 9.7 presents a general scope and sequence of phonics skills that children would be expected to learn in first through third grade.

FIGURE 9.7   **Some Phonics and Spelling Generalizations 1–3**

1. Each of the consonant letters corresponds to one sound, as in the words:

bag	hair	nest	toe
dog	jar	pipe	violin
fan	kite	queen	wig
	lamp	rug	box
	milk	sun	zebra

2. Consonant clusters or blends are composed of two or three consonant sounds blended together (e.g., *bl, cr, dr, fl, gl, pr, sm, st, scr, str, thr, nt*)

3. The consonant digraphs are comprised of two consonants that correspond to a single sound in the words:

church   shoe   phone   thumb   whistle

4. The vowel letters take several sounds, such as:

long	**short**	**r-controlled**	**l-controlled**
ape	apple	her	hall
eagle	egg	sir	talk
ice	igloo	fur	
oboe	octopus	can	
unicorn	umbrella	care	

5. Some consonants have more than one sound associated with them, as in the following:

   When the letter *g* is followed by the letters, *e, i,* or *y,* the *g* usually takes the soft sound, as in the letter *j* (*gym*). Otherwise, it takes the hard sound, as in the word *gum.*

   When the letter *c* is followed by the letters *e, i,* or *y,* the *c* usually takes the soft sound, as in the letter *s* (*cycle*). Otherwise, it takes the hard sound, as in the letter *k* (*cake*).

6. **Vowel digraphs** are two or more vowel letters that together represent a single sound, as in the words:

say	seat	light	goal	blue	caught	boot	foot
sail	feet		stow	flew	awful		
weigh	field		hoe				
great							

7. **Vowel diphthongs** are vowel pairs that make a blended sound, as in the words:

oil   toy   mouse   cow

FIGURE 9.7   Continued

8. Some vowel digraphs and diphthongs have two sounds associated with them, as in the words:

cow	boot
blow	foot

9. When a word has the CVVC pattern, the vowel usually takes the long sound (*feet*).

10. Many phonograms illustrate the short, long, and other vowel patterns in CVC, CVCe, CVVC, and CVCC words, such as in the words (this generalization may be used to teach vowel sounds and spelling patterns):

cat	bake	sail	rock
sat	make	mail	lock
fat	take	tail	dock

Read Aloud.   Later in the morning, Mrs. Walker reads the picture book *Just Me and My Dad* (Mayer, 1977). As she reads, she talks about both the print and strategies for meaning making. She begins by calling attention to words in the title.

> **MRS. WALKER:** This one has 1-2-3-4-5 words in the title.... Some of these words are in the morning sentences or in the morning graph question (pointing to the two texts still on the board from the opening routine). ...
>
> **KIMBERLY:** I know some of them.

Kimberly reads *My, Dad, Me,* and *and.*

> **MRS. WALKER:** So the only one you don't know is the first one. "Blank me and my dad." J-U-S-T is in our morning sentence right here (pointing to the Daily Oral Language text)—remember that's the one I put the wrong vowel in? (The children had changed *jast* to *just*.)
>
> **SEVERAL CHILDREN:** Just!

Mrs. Walker calls on Nicholas, and he reads the whole title.

> **MRS. WALKER:** What do you think this little boy and his dad are doing in this story?

Mrs. Walker points to the cover picture, which shows a Mercer Mayer creature and his dad fishing. She reminds the children of their responses to the morning question ("Have you ever gone fishing with your dad?") and suggests that they might have some ideas about what will happen in the story. She encourages children to use an important meaning-making strategy.

MRS. WALKER: What's a good question we could ask ourselves? Good readers always ask themselves a question before they start reading. What do you want to know about this book? What are you wondering about?

CHILD: I wonder where they go camping.

DAVID: I wonder what kind of fish they are going to catch.

Mrs. Walker reads the story of the boy and his dad going camping. The story contains a pattern of events: The boy starts an activity (e.g., taking the dad for a canoe ride, cooking their fish), but it goes wrong (e.g., he launches the canoe too hard and it gets a hole in it, a bear steals their dinner), and the dad fixes it (e.g., takes them fishing, cooks eggs instead). The story is not limited to this pattern, however; other events occur (e.g., the dad takes a snapshot of the boy with the fish he caught). It is told with humor, some of which comes from its being told from the boy's perspective. For example, he says he gives his dad a big hug to make him feel better after they tell scary stories, but we know that the boy is the one who needs to feel better. The illustrations are Mercer Mayer's usual richly detailed, entertaining pictures. Mrs. Walker's students noticed and commented on the details (e.g., "There's always a spider on each page," "And a grasshopper!").

Shared Reading.   Today's shared reading is carefully planned to complement the DOL sentences, and the story *Just Me and My Dad*. Mrs. Walker has chosen the first grade story *Just Like Daddy* (Asch, 1984). This simple pattern story about father and son bears who go fishing with their mother has been reproduced in the basal reader that Mrs. Walker uses. The pattern in *Just Like Daddy* is that the boy tells about performing a series of acts (yawning a big yawn when he gets up, having breakfast, getting dressed, picking a flower, baiting a hook) and each time adds the phrase "Just like Daddy." The twist that ends the story is that the boy catches a big fish "Just like Mommy" (Daddy is pictured with a much smaller fish).

The sentences in this story are shorter than those in *Just Me and My Dad;* the vocabulary is more regular; the pattern is more obvious; and the structure of the story is simpler (everything leads to the one joke of Mommy's big catch, in contrast to the multiple funny mishaps that befall the boy in *Just Me and My Dad*). There is an almost one-to-one correspondence between the illustrations and what the text tells. This story is typical of texts that provide the best kind of support for beginning readers.

Mrs. Walker combines the first two steps of shared reading (the teacher's reading and then the children's reading together) in order not to give away the joke at the end of the story. Instead of a big book, all the children have their own basal readers, which include this story. Mrs. Walker reads a page from her basal reader, and then the class rereads the same page together. They talk about the story and the illustrations as they go.

Partner Reading and Teacher Support.   Next is **partner reading.** Mrs. Walker assigns each child a partner, and each pair has one book. The partners take turns: one reads while the other looks on and, as Mrs. Walker explains, "gets to be the teacher and help with any words they don't know."

Mark and Jacob are partners; they find a corner of the room, and Mark reads first. This text is easy for him; he reads fluently, with expression and no mistakes. Jacob follows Mark's reading with his eyes. When it is Jacob's turn, he works harder than Mark did, but with Mark's help he is able to finish the story with comprehension. He substitutes words that make sense in the story. He reads "jacket" for *coat*, "Mom" for *Mommy*, and "put on my worm on my hook" for *put a big worm on my hook*. Later, when reading with Mrs. Walker, Jacob will use cross-checking to read the words correctly.

Most pairs of children read the story two or three times to each other and then begin working on reading extension activities that Mrs. Walker has planned. However, some children may need Mrs. Walker's more explicit help (Turpie & Paratore, 1995). For these children, Mrs. Walker would gather a small group of children together for extra teaching and rereading of the story. Mrs. Walker would guide children's discussion of particular vocabulary words, support their use of phonics and other decoding strategies in reading portions of the story, and supervise their rereading of the story several times. Then Mrs. Walker would prepare the children for writing a story extension: a summary, retelling, or pattern sentence. She would demonstrate such composing strategies as elongating words and listening for big sounds (much like Mrs. Poremba in Chapter 8), rereading, using word spaces, and finding words in the classroom.

Extension activities may make use of Internet sites associated with children's books. Many children's book authors have their own web sites, which students can visit to learn more about the authors and sometimes to communicate with them. Slanina (2001) lists several teacher friendly web sites, including Eric Carle's (www.eric-carle.com/), Tomie dePaola's (www.tomiedepaola.com), and Jan Brett's (www.janbrett.com) web sites and a general information site about children's book authors and illustrators (http://falcon.jmu.edu/schoollibrary/biochildhome.htm). A popular Internet-related storybook extension is based on the children's book *Flat Stanley* (Brown, 1964). The book's title character is flattened but otherwise unhurt when a bulletin board falls on him. Being two dimensional enables Stanley to have many adventures, including flying as a kite and being sent through the mail. Teachers have created whole units of study around students' mailing their own Flat Stanley reproductions around the world and back (Hoewisch, 2001). They learn about the geography of the places where their Flat Stanleys travel, they correspond with recipients (sometimes famous people) of their Flat Stanleys (the correspondence is often accompanied by photos of the recipients with Flat Stanley). Schools can share their Flat Stanley projects with one another at http://flatstanley.enoreo.on.ca.

Self-Selected Reading. As a balance to whole-group shared reading, Mrs. Walker makes sure that each child engages in daily independent reading at his or her reading level. One kind of self-selected reading she plans is what she calls **take-home books.** Each child has a basket of books that Mrs. Walker carefully selects to match the child's current reading level. These are copies of poems, big books, and other little books suitable for children's independent reading. Each child's basket contains a dozen or more choices from which children select a book to take home.

Children practice reading these books at home and to each other or to an adult. For many children, the take-home books are predictable texts. Since many children who are struggling to make the transition to conventional reading often do not read on their own (Lysaker, 1997), Mrs. Walker's careful selection of books ensures that children practice reading appropriate text independently on a daily basis (Martinez et al., 1997).

The take-home books play a critical role in Mrs. Walker's first grade literacy program. For many children, the take-home books provide opportunities to practice reading and rereading books at their independent reading level. Books at children's **independent reading level** are books that they can read with full comprehension and less than 5 percent errors in word recognition. In contrast to take-home books, Mrs. Walker selects books for partner reading that are at most children's **instructional reading level.** In order to be successful in reading these texts, children need much instructional support such as provided by Mrs. Walker's DOL, read-aloud books, and shared reading. Reading books at the instructional level provides children with opportunities to encounter new words, discuss meanings, and try out reading strategies. In contrast, reading books at the independent level provides children the practice they need to consolidate sight words and develop fluency. **Fluency** is the ability to read with natural intonation. As children mature in reading, their reading rate increases along with their fluency. Even more important, reading books at an independent level is enjoyable, and children are naturally motivated to engage in reading for longer and longer time periods.

For some children in Mrs. Walker's class, the take-home books provide reading challenges. Reading *Just Like Daddy* was very easy for Mark during partner reading; he read it accurately and with full comprehension. In order to stretch his reading abilities, Mark needs more challenging texts. Mrs. Walker selects more difficult books for Mark's take-home reading.

The take-home books can be accompanied by a journal for parents to write their observations about the home reading (Morningstar, 1999). Teachers may write a letter to parents explaining the range of different reading behaviors and texts that are expected in first grade. The teacher might invite parents to read along with their children and then listen to their children read. Parents are invited to make comments about the strategies their children seem to be using or points of discussion about a text's meaning. Parents who have used this journal are often surprised at the amount of growth children make in achieving success with new levels of text difficulty, strategy use, reading accuracy, and reading rate.

We have seen that Mrs. Walker selects stories from a basal reader anthology and uses other predictable books. There are many different types of texts that support first graders as they move from emergent reading (as experimenters do) into and beyond early reading. First, **predictable books** (books that have many repetitive phrases and words) are appropriate to help children acquire advanced concepts about print including one-on-one matching along with decoding (usually using the beginning letters of words). However, to develop more sophisticated decoding strategies and acquire a solid set of high-frequency words, children need to read

transitional texts (Brown, 1999/2000). These texts are leveled by both predictability and decodability. At the easy levels, the texts are highly predictable. As the texts get harder, they include less predictability but increase in the number of words that use familiar vowel patterns. Thus, children gain more control over the alphabet system. **Decodable texts** do not usually include predictable patterns. Instead, they are leveled by the order in which phonics patterns are taught and then appear in the decodable books. Teachers carefully select the texts that match the needs of their readers (Hiebert, 1999), and readers' needs change as they acquire more reading power. Today, predictable texts, transitional texts, and decodable texts can be located in basal readers or through other commercial companies.

Mrs. Walker's Balanced Reading Program. It is important to note that Mrs. Walker has carefully constructed a balanced reading program. She provides many opportunities for children to extend strategies for comprehending and interpreting a wide variety of texts. She reads aloud in ways that engage children in predicting, confirming, and hypothesizing. Children extend their knowledge of vocabulary and understandings of stories, poems, and informational books in Mrs. Walker's read-alouds and in shared reading. Children also extend their strategic approaches to reading and writing during pattern writing and other extension activities. Mrs. Walker provides other opportunities for children to extend strategies for decoding and spelling through her word wall activities. She plans instruction that is systematic and intensive (Strickland, 1998) based on the individual needs of children. Mrs. Walker also provides opportunities for extensive amounts of reading in shared reading, partner reading, and take-home books. Later we will describe Mrs. Walker's writing workshop, in which children have multiple opportunities for shared and independent writing.

Writing in Mr. Schultheis's First Grade

We have already shown ways that Mrs. Walker and Mrs. Tran capitalize on writing to strengthen reading instruction. Both teachers plan pattern writing experiences as a way to extend children's reading of predictable stories and poems. In this section, our emphasis will be on writing instruction as we look at Mr. Schultheis's first grade classroom. Wharton-McDonald (2001a) describes Mr. Schultheis's teaching as a case study of **effective literacy instruction.** Just as our descriptions of Mrs. Tran's and Mrs. Walker's reading instruction included teaching and learning of writing, so also will this account of Mr. Schultheis's writing instruction include teaching and learning of reading.

Mr. Schultheis's daily schedule embodies the integration of reading and writing and the rest of the curriculum; that is, it demonstrates the multiple opportunities that he creates for students to engage in meaningful reading and writing, for them to show him what they know and can do, and for him to scaffold their progress. Students' desks are in clusters, and books in a bin at each cluster are available for the independent reading that starts each day. Students choose books that interest them and that they can read comfortably. Mr. Schultheis describes this independent reading as " 'a warm up' for students who perhaps had not done any reading since they left school the previous afternoon" (p. 117).

Next on the schedule is whole-class discussion, which may connect upcoming activities with learning from the previous day and give students a common vocabulary and the same beginning point for thinking about a new topic. "Thus, this block of time might include a preview of a book students would be reading with a partner, an introduction to [a] new writing topic, and/or a review of a spelling pattern that students would be working with independently or with a partner later" (p. 117).

Then, during reading and writing blocks, students work in small groups, with partners, or individually. Mr. Schultheis joins them for guided reading or to give targeted instruction about a student's current draft of a writing piece. He told Wharton-McDonald that he saw writing as an integral part of reading development. " 'It gives [students] an opportunity to tell about what they have learned. And at the same time as I go around [conferencing with students], I'm monitoring what they're working on *within* their writing. I'm working on *skills.*' " (2001a, p. 123, brackets and emphasis in original). In their study of exemplary first grade literacy instruction, Morrow et al. (1999) quote a teacher whose view of **reading-writing connections** is similar to Mr. Schultheis's: " 'I can often tell children's reading level when I review their writing. Writing helps them with decoding skills and subsequently with reading.' " (p. 466).

Wharton-McDonald notes that during **writing conferences,** Mr. Schultheis

> constantly pushed students to improve. He frequently asked them to read to him what they had written. Then he would ask, "How could we make that sound better?" He used the analogy of a skeleton, asking students to "fill out" the bones of the story. In all of his conversations with students, the emphasis was on writing pieces that were interesting, coherent, and true to the ideas the students brought to the table. (2001a, p. 124)

Mr. Schultheis helps students with both large aspects of form, such as beginnings, middles, and ends, and smaller aspects, such as grammar, spelling, punctuation, and capitalization. These are not required in first drafts; he said, "The first part of writing is getting your writing down. Then we go back and make sure the skills have been incorporated" (p. 123). For later **drafts,** students have the help of classmates, Mr. Schultheis, dictionaries, signs, and word lists. And Mr. Schultheis allows some pieces to end without subsequent drafts; Wharton-McDonald observes that "sometimes children just need to get their ideas out and *write*—without getting bogged down in the steps of revision" (p. 124).

During Mr. Schultheis's reading and writing blocks, **groupings are flexible;** he forms groups with the specific purpose of addressing needs that members of the groups display in their daily reading and writing. **Materials are varied.** For example, Wharton-McDonald describes Mr. Schultheis's sitting with three students as they read a trade book together, then joining two students reading a phonetically regular basal reader selection, and then monitoring two other children's reading of finished, published pieces written by classmates.

A mid-morning break gives children options such as playing with board games, putting together puzzles, or playing at the sand table. The reading and writing blocks both before and after this break are sometimes punctuated by a return to whole-class discussions. Wharton-McDonald observes that Mr. Schultheis followed a **scope and sequence of skills,** but that it was an internal reminder of what to teach in first grade, developed from his twenty-one years of experience; it was not a published list, such as provided by a basal reading series. And he did not follow it in a step-by-step progression. Instead, he "regularly cycled back to review, integrate, and expand upon skills he had taught earlier" (Wharton-McDonald, 2001a, p. 121). This is just one example of how thoroughly Mr. Schultheis knows the content he teaches.

Wharton-McDonald also notes that Mr. Schultheis's teaching always served **multiple purposes.** Figure 9.8, for example, shows how he taught about the phonics generalization that *oa* spells /O/ while at the same time developing vocabulary. This is an example of the **instructional density** of Mr. Schultheis's teaching, or teaching more than one thing at a time.

Informational Writing in Mrs. Duthie's First Grade

Mrs. Duthie teaches first grade in New York state and has written extensively on her experiences helping first graders read and write informational texts (Duthie, 1996). She has discovered, like other teachers, that informational reading and writing is

FIGURE 9.8 Mr. Schultheis Combines Phonics and Vocabulary Instruction

Mr. Schultheis*:	How about something that Mom puts in the oven—a kind of meat?
Student 1:	Meat loaf!
Mr. Schultheis:	I was thinking of something else, but that's a good one, too.
Student 2:	Roast beef!
Mr. Schultheis:	Yes. Roast. Put that on your list. (*Students write.*) How about something that comes in a bar?
Student 3:	Soap!
Mr. Schultheis:	What happens when you put wood in water?
Students:	Float!
Mr. Schultheis:	Now, I like that word that Amy thought of—What was that?
Students:	Loaf!
Mr. Schultheis:	Put that on your lists. (*Students write.*) How about something that Charlie made in the story we read yesterday [referring to the Tomie dePaola book *Charlie Needs a Cloak;* dePaola, 1973]?
Students:	Cloak.
Mr. Schultheis:	And what's the difference between a coat and a cloak?

*Wharton-McDonald uses *Andy,* Mr. Schultheis' first name, here; we continue our usual reference to the teachers in this chapter by Mr., Miss, Mrs., or Ms. and their last names.

From Wharton-McDonald, 2001a, p. 121.

inspirational to all children, but especially to those children who naturally select this kind of text for their independent reading and writing (Caswell & Duke, 1998). Mrs. Duthie's classroom library has a special section for informational books, and she makes a special effort to read informational big books as part of shared reading experiences, as well as stories and poems. The class learns about as many informational book authors and illustrators as authors and illustrators of stories and poems. Her children keep personal lists of the call numbers of books in the library for quick reference (informational books about cats are found under 636.8 and dinosaurs under 567.9).

Mrs. Duthie uses **minilessons** to teach about informational writing. First, she shares one or more informational books that have a special feature. Children talk about these special features and sometimes construct a group drawing or composition that includes the feature. For example, Mrs. Duthie showed *Oil Spill!* (Berger, 1994) to illustrate labeled drawings, *Jack's Garden* (Cole, 1995) to illustrate cutaway drawings, and *Water* (Asch, 1995) to illustrate cross-sectioned drawings.

As a part of minilessons about informational writing, children can learn how to put information into sets or groups, write about one part at a time, or lead with a question. They may discover and use captions, headings, tables of contents, and indexes. They may experiment with many different kinds of informational writing beyond that found in informational books. Figure 9.9 presents a first grader's want ad.

Want Ad

Cat wanted

I want a Sianmese

cat by

Saturday. Be fluffy

and cute. Call

Will

739-6305

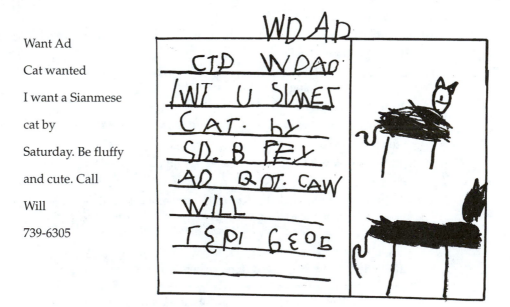

FIGURE 9.9   A First Grader's Want Ad

Poetry Writing in Mrs. Zickuhr's First Grade

Poetry reading and writing is an important part of literature enjoyment and literacy instruction in another first grade teacher's room. In Mrs. Zickuhr's room, children respond to poems through choral reading, collecting poems, drama, art, music, talking, and writing. Mrs. Zickuhr teaches several minilessons about poetry as a part of process writing. With one, she stresses the importance of feelings in writing and responding to poetry.

Cullinan, Scala, and Schroder (1995) agree with Mrs. Zickuhr:

> Students need to experience enjoying poetry before they begin to look at the technical aspects of poetry forms. Children often become so caught up in the rules and regulations that they lose the pulse and emotion of what they want to say. Meaningful poetry must touch us personally. It dies when that element is missing. (p. 38)

She reads a poem about which she feels strongly, shares her feelings about it, and invites the students to respond in small groups. Another minilesson is about topic selection ("Poetry has to hit a person right in the heart or it won't work"). Another is about form. Mrs. Zickuhr suggests that after writing a draft, her young poets should think about structure: "Just like buildings have architecture—some are tall and thin, some are short and wide—poems also have to be built according to a design which works." She finds that first drafts often look proselike, so she has students read their poems aloud and add slashes for line breaks where they naturally pause. Another minilesson is about endings, that they can hold the rest of the poem together, surprise the reader, or make the reader think.

As inspiration, Mrs. Zickuhr reads poems that make use of sounds, such as the sound "vroom" found in the poem "The Go-Go Goons" from *Street Poems* (Froman, 1971). Children use these ideas in their own poetry compositions. Figure 9.10 shows a poem about motorcycles written by Mike, one of Mrs. Zickuhr's first

Motorcycle	Modrigl
Fast, too loud	fast, to lode
Racing, driving, vrooming	rasirg, Driveihg, vroming
I like motorcycles	I like modrsigls
Bike	Bike
	By Mike

FIGURE 9.10   Mike's Poem

graders. Mike's use of *vrooming* shows that he benefited from Mrs. Zickuhr's read-ing "The Go-Go Goons" to his class.

Exemplary First-Grade Literacy Instruction

Mrs. Tran, Mrs. Walker, Mr. Schultheis (Wharton-McDonald, 2001a), Mrs. Duthie, and Mrs. Zickuhr are exemplary teachers. The test of exemplary teaching, of course, is exemplary learning, and we have shown the work of children in these classrooms. First graders like Sindy (see Figure 9.5) generate new words using phonograms; other first graders write their own informational texts and poems (see Figures 9.9 and 9.10). So what is exemplary teaching versus merely adequate first grade literacy instruction?

Exemplary Teaching Means Lots of Instruction

Three outcomes distinguish high-achieving classrooms from lower-achieving classrooms: higher reading achievement (most students in the high-achieving class-rooms reading at or above grade level at the end of the year), higher writing achievement (most students in the high-achieving classrooms writing coherent stories longer than one page and with good punctuation, capitalization, and spelling), and student engagement (Pressley et al., 2001). Like many first-grade teachers nowadays, exemplary teachers use a mixture of direct instruction, process writing instruction, small-group instruction, and independent reading and writ-ing. They provide positive reinforcement, demonstrate caring and dedication, and realize the importance of parents' contributions. Several factors, however, differ-entiate exemplary teachers from typical teachers (Pressley et al., 2001). They inte-grate skills instruction with holistic literacy activities, often in the form of minilessons provided at opportune times. Still, their teaching is not skills-driven, but instead emerges as children are engaged with excellent children's literature and write authentic narratives and essays. Exemplary teachers provide a great deal of instruction in all settings and serving multiple purposes. Minilessons about phonics rules occur with vocabulary development activities; spelling practice occurs with class dismissal routines. During minilessons, teachers scaffold stu-dents' learning, so that they "provided just enough support to enable a student to begin to make progress on a task but not so much as to be doing the task for the stu-dent" (p. 57). They have high **expectations** of their students and let them know it. Finally, they have good **classroom management** skills, as shown by routines for daily tasks, much advanced planning for instruction but paired with flexibility (as when teaching minilessons in response to needs as they arise), efficient time man-agement, and effective use of volunteers, aids, and visitors.

More effective teachers help children learn. They provide multiple strategies for decoding and explicit comprehension strategy instruction. They give coaching as children write, use checklists (such as an editing checklist) to make children accountable for using what they have been taught, and by the end of first grade, expect children to use strategies to find the conventional spelling of words. Their students devote more time to "doing academically rich processing" (Pressley et al., 2001, p. 67) such as reading and writing and less time on such nonacademic activities as illustrating a story.

The best teachers facilitate students' being on task most of the time, use a coaching style of teaching, frequently engage students in practicing sight words, frequently ask higher-level comprehension questions, and have students write in response to reading (Taylor et al., 2002). An example is a teacher's saying to a group after Mara has read aloud, "I noticed that Mara got stuck and skipped it and read around it and then came back to it. That's good thinking" (p. 25). Other examples include one teacher's giving a general prompt when a child was having difficulty identifying a word: "What could give you a clue on that word?" (p. 25), and another teacher's giving more specific prompts: "Whoah, back up there. Frame the [word] with 'i-n.' What is the first sound? What is the second sound? What's the word?" (p. 26).

One way of looking at the value of such coaching is to compare it with another teaching style, **telling,** in which teachers merely dispense facts and do not tell what to do with them or how to use them. The most accomplished teachers very seldom use telling; the least accomplished teachers frequently use it (Taylor et al., 2002). Importantly, while this matter of style distinguishes more accomplished teachers from less accomplished teachers, **explicit phonics teaching** does not. A majority of teachers—both the most and least effective teachers—frequently give explicit phonics instruction (Taylor et al., 2002).

How Explicit Phonics Instruction Is Delivered

Explicit phonics instruction is best delivered in the coaching style. Coaching occurs in child-centered classrooms with an emphasis on meaning making with connected text, with wide use of children's literature, and with emphases on reading and writing as means for learning and solving problems and on student collaboration (Dahl & Scharer, 2000). With such an approach, teachers teach letter patterns in words, but also teach phonics strategies, that is, how to use knowledge of letter patterns while reading. They ask children to tell about how they put those strategies to use in identifying words during their reading or in spelling words during writing. In addition, teachers give real-time demonstrations of the strategies, using the students' own writing and reading, and they emphasize both the working of the strategies and the resulting meanings of the texts (Dahl et al., 1999).

For example, Mrs. Spencer coached the children in a small group to use the strategy of rechecking a mistaken reading of a word by looking at the word again:

MRS. SPENCER: Reread and see if you can check yourself. Point to the words. Some of you said, "I do like flies." If that word was *do* (points to *like*) what would you expect it to start with?

RANDY: *D.*

MRS. SPENCER: O.K. What does it start with?

RANDY: *L*. Oh! *Like*.

MRS. SPENCER: That's what good readers do—stop and see if it makes sense. (Dahl & Scharer, 2000, pp. 587–588)

Balanced Instruction

The term **balanced instruction** is a good description of what teachers like Mrs. Spencer do. Mr. Schultheis is representative of such teachers' rejection of being typed as either skills-oriented or whole language teachers. He said, "We need to be able to say that we don't *have* a program that everybody's going to [succeed with], but that we're going to make adjustments and provide a program that is going to best meet the child's need" (Wharton-McDonald, 2001a, p. 116, brackets and emphasis in original).

In balanced instruction, systematic phonics teaching is not isolated or separated from text reading. Phonics in exemplary classrooms does not consist of a systematic phonics lesson followed by text reading merely for practice. Instead, teachers provide targeted, coached phonics instruction *during* text reading and writing. They carefully monitor their students to determine which ones need phonics minilessons and when they need them, for example, "a minilesson on the sound 'h' makes as a student struggle[s] to spell the word 'heart'" (Pressley et al., 2001, p. 56).

Exemplary Writing Instruction

In adequate first grade classrooms, children's writing pieces usually consist of two or three sentences and rarely exceed a page. Children write mostly personal narratives, stories that describe a typical sequence of events (first this, then that), and daily journal entries that tend to be repetitive (such as, "I like to . . . I like to . . . I like to . . . "). Their writing often lacks coherence, that is, it is a collection of unconnected sentences. They write left to right, usually with spaces at word boundaries, but they use capitals and periods intermittently. In contrast, students in exemplary classrooms usually write a page or more and in many genres. Besides personal journal entries and personal narratives, they write in science, math, and response journals. They write letters, informational texts, and stories about fictional characters. Their stories, in general, are coherent. Specifically, their plotting includes beginnings, middles, and ends; their characters are consistent; and their structures conform to story grammar. **Coherence** is demonstrated not just in stories, but in all genres. The first grade students of exemplary teachers can remain on topic for a page or more and write with consideration of their intended audiences. Finally, they use capitals and periods consistently and accurately, and they frequently use question marks and exclamation marks (Wharton-McDonald, 2001b). Figure 9.11 gives examples of these differences.

	Struggling Writer
Typical Classroom	 I Pa9 BaYS1 I played baseball.
Exemplary Classroom	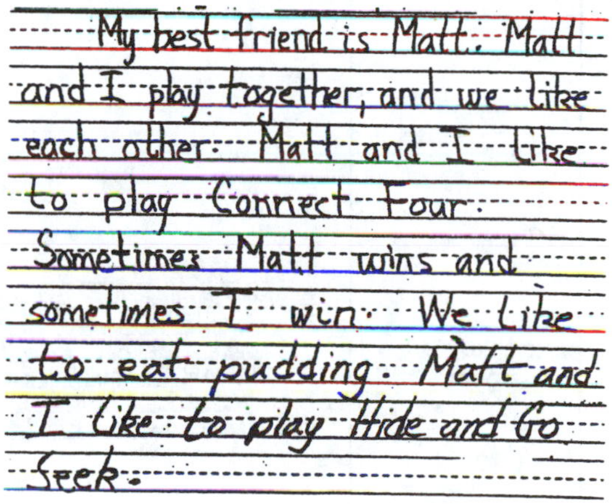 My best friend is Matt. Matt and I play together, and we like each other. Matt and I like to play Connect Four. Sometimes Matt wins and sometimes I win. We like to eat pudding. Matt and I like to play Hide and Go Seek. My best friend is Matt. Matt and I play together and we like each other. Matt and I like to play Connect Four. Sometimes Matt wins and sometimes I win. We like to eat pudding. Matt and I like Hide and Go Seek.

FIGURE 9.11   First Grade Writing in Typical and Exemplary Classrooms

From Wharton-McDonald, R., *Teaching Writing in First Grade* in **LEARNING TO READ.**
Reprinted with permission by the Guilford Press: New York.

(continued)

	Average Writer
Typical Classroom	*[handwritten sample]* I like to play with my dog.
Exemplary Classroom	*[handwritten sample]* Yesterday my stomach hurt. After I ate lunch I rode my bike with my friend. When our tires went together I fell off my bike and scraped my knee and elbow. On Thursday night I was wiggling my tooth and it came out. Then I got one dollar. Some days are lucky. Some days are not lucky.

FIGURE 9.11   Continued

	Strong Writer
Typical Classroom	I slept over my nanny's. We went on a boat. I loved the waves.
Exemplary Classroom	My best friend is my brother, we go to camp to together. We go swimming off the dock. Our Grampa takes us fishing in a boat. We ride our bikes at the campgrounds. We Get up early in the morning and go for a ride to get chocolate milk and donuts. Then, we go for a ride around the lake. We go for a boat ride to Sand Island and play on the island. We have campfires at night and roast marshmallows.

FIGURE 9.11　**Continued**

How do the exemplary teachers elicit the sort of writing shown in Figure 9.11? One way is by thoroughly integrating writing and reading instruction. "[E]xemplary teachers see reading and writing as tightly interwoven processes, each supporting and being supported by the other" (Wharton-McDonald, 2001b, p. 90), and they use the same teaching strategies and approaches for teaching both reading and writing. Exemplary teachers use **process writing instruction,** but compared to adequate teachers, they more regularly teach writing processes and expect follow-through in students' **planning, drafting, revising, and editing.** One purpose of writing in their classrooms is to improve decoding skills, and one purpose of reading is to encounter models of good writing. Compared to adequate teachers, exemplary teachers are themselves more aware of and make their students more aware of multiple purposes for students' writing (Morrow et al., 1999; Wharton-McDonald, 2001b).

Journal Writing. One manifestation of this multiplicity in exemplary first grade classrooms is the wide range of content in journals: **interactive journals** contain students' communications with teachers and classmates, **response journals** contain their responses to literature, **writers' journals** contain their process writing work, **science journals** include records of their science thinking and experimenting, and **home-school journals** contain messages to and from parents. Journal writing fosters better writing in three ways. First, writing in personal journals strengthens students' writing fluency and expression by allowing them to express themselves in writing without concern for spelling, punctuation, or other aspects of writing mechanics. One exemplary teacher explains, " 'I want [my students] to understand that they have wonderful ideas in their heads, and sometimes if you can't express [them], people will never hear your good ideas; so in order to do that, you need to write [them] down in a journal' " (Wharton-McDonald, 2001b, p. 73, brackets in original). Second, although they do not correct students' journal writing, exemplary teachers use journal entries for diagnosis of writing ability. They note strengths and weaknesses, and then use minilessons in order to reteach skills that are weak. Third, journals foster authentic communication. Exemplary teachers see journals as a means of gaining understanding of children's lives; they respond in students' interactive journals. They also encourage student-to-student communication (Wharton-McDonald, 2001b).

Writing in multiple genres in exemplary classrooms is partly due to greater integration of reading and writing and content teaching and learning. For example, Wharton-McDonald (2001b) reports,

> [F]irst grade students wrote reports about ocean animals or birds in conjunction with units on these topics. The students did research for the projects, reading informational texts at appropriate reading levels and taking notes to prepare for writing the reports. Report writing demands the integration of information from multiple sources. These students were able to accomplish this with targeted instruction from their teachers. (pp. 76–77)

Targeted Instruction.   What is this **targeted instruction?** In general terms, teachers scaffold students' work by themselves knowing the subjects well, by observing students closely, by responding to students' ongoing work, and by providing minilessons when needed. More specifically, instruction is about specific writing skills and strategies, about the forms of writing, and about writing processes. Explicit instruction about skills and strategies takes place in fifteen-minute lessons to small groups. Exemplary teachers determine the content of these short lessons (which skills and strategies to teach) by knowing the prescribed writing curricula of their districts and by knowing their students. In other words, they know the big picture of what they are expected to teach by the end of first grade, and they know the little picture of what their students' current writing products show they need to learn at any particular time (Wharton-McDonald, 2001b).

In these short, focused lessons, the teacher models the skill or strategy (for example, writing a paragraph as a set of sentences related to one another because they develop a single idea, and marking the start of a paragraph by indenting) and provide examples of it from books. Then students immediately have the opportunity to implement the skill or strategy in their own writing, with the teacher giving individual scaffolding as needed (for example, the teacher observes students writing and notes who is independently writing single-idea paragraphs with indentation and who needs to be reminded of the model, asked to tell a single idea, and helped to write an opening sentence about that idea and one or two other sentences about the same idea).

Two types of input help first graders to write the longer, more coherent pieces that are found in exemplary classrooms: input about forms and input about processes. With regard to forms, exemplary teachers explicitly teach that there are units beyond the sentence. They address the structure, content, and meanings of whole pieces of students' writing. This includes teaching about different genres, which can serve as vehicles for longer pieces, and teaching about story grammar. Story grammar provides both the structure upon which to hang parts that make stories longer (e.g., beginning, middle, end) and the mechanisms that propel a story to greater length (e.g., setting and character introduction, problem or conflict, solution or resolution). One way to teach about these forms is through reading: Students of exemplary teachers do not just write in many genres, they also regularly read and have read to them books in many genres (Wharton-McDonald, 2001b).

Input about processes includes guidance in developing independence and self-regulation and guidance in conferring with classmates. For example, students of exemplary teachers learn "strategies for choosing a topic, monitoring their progress in a piece, and evaluating completed works and works in progress" (Wharton-McDonald, 2001b, p. 85). Teachers accomplish this in the same way that they teach about paragraphing or other skills and strategies. They model the processes, give immediate opportunity for students to try out the processes, and observe and scaffold students' use of the processes. Teachers think aloud about topics they might write about next, discuss one of the possible topics, write on a large paper displayed on an easel a map or web of ideas that they want to include in a piece, and then give students a chance to do the same. Similarly, for conferring with classmates, exemplary teachers introduce peer conferences by modeling conference processes and having students role-play conferences. Wharton-McDonald (2001b) observes that, unlike in typical classrooms where peer conferences have a rote quality, peer conferences that followed such modeling and role playing "were not just another step in a meandering process. They had purpose and moved students' writing forward" (p. 87).

High Expectations.   We have described many ingredients of exemplary teaching, including teaching specific writing skills and strategies, teaching about forms and processes, and teaching by modeling and scaffolding. An equally important ingredient is having high expectations for students' work.

> Many teachers believe that students in first grade simply need opportunities to pick up a pencil and put it to paper. They are satisfied when children end the year writing a sentence or two. After all, what can you expect from 7-year-olds? . . . [However,] research indicates that when it comes to writing, first graders will give you what you ask for. If the teacher is satisfied with a single sentence and a picture, then that is exactly what most students will be producing at the end of the year. If, on the other hand, students are taught the attitudes, skills, and strategies of writing—and are expected to apply them—then, in fact, they become writers. (Wharton-McDonald, 2001b, pp. 89–90)

Summary: Effective First-Grade Literacy Instruction

Studies of exemplary first-grade literacy instruction (Morrow et al., 1999; Pressley et al., 2001) suggest the following recipe for effective teaching: knowledge, balance, expectation, opportunity, and support. Teachers must have thorough knowledge of what they will teach their students. In fact, they must know more about phonemes or punctuation or paragraphing than they will ever teach, because they always must have in mind the big picture, only parts of which are ever embodied in any student's performance or in any one of the teacher's specific minilessons. Teachers must have balance in order to hold many students' varying abilities and needs in mind at one time, to teach more than one thing at a time, and to use more than one approach to instruction. Teachers must expect much of their students while providing the instruction about literacy skills and strategies that will enable them to meet those expectations. They must give students opportunities to apply and practice what they have taught immediately following the teaching and frequently thereafter, and they must use those student application and practice sessions as opportunities for their own learning, that is, for determining what their students can and cannot do, which students need real-time coaching, and which skills and strategies need additional emphasis in later minilessons. Coaching and minilessons are two of the most effective forms of support that teachers can give their students.

In this chapter's case studies were many examples of teachers' knowledge. Mrs. Tran knows that her first graders know most of the sound–letter correspondences for English consonants and some for English short vowels. She can rely on this when she helps them to read the word *Tim* by sounding it out, letter-by-letter (see Figure 9.2). She also knows that first graders need strategies for reading beyond the first consonant when trying to identify unknown words, and that awareness of phonograms and word families can be a big part of such strategies. She can teach them to sound out a phonogram (for example, *ed*) as a first step to knowing that phonogram by sight. She knows it is worth spending the time on such teaching strategies because the resulting automatic recognition of the phonogram will enable reading of a whole list of unknown words, that phonogram's word family (for example, *bed, fed, Fred, led, red, sled, sped*). Her students will be able to use the general strategy of looking beyond an unknown word's first consonant or consonants and the specific knowledge of that phonogram in order to be able quickly to read a whole family of words. This is part of the strategic, self-extending reading she wants her students to achieve.

Moreover, Mrs. Tran keeps in mind numerous English phonograms and word families. She will want her students eventually to know most of them, but she knows that some are easier than others. For example, *im* is relatively easy because it has a single-letter short vowel spelling and its individual phonemes are easy to emphasize during teaching (both can be stretched into continuous pronunciations: "ihhhhhh-mmmmm"); *ide* is more difficult because it has a double-letter long vowel spelling (and the two letters are not even adjacent!) and its individual phonemes are difficult to emphasize during teaching (/I/ when stretched out becomes /ah/ plus /E/, and /d/ cannot be stretched out without introducing an extraneous, distracting "uh" sound: "duh"). This is much more phonology than first graders ever have to know in order to learn to read, but it can guide a first grade teacher's search for opportunities to teach specific phonograms and word families. It can inform their choosing to teach first the easier ones, as Mrs. Tran did when she taught *im* in *Tim, dim, him, rim,* and *slim* following the class's reading of *Where's Tim?*

We saw balance in Mr. Schultheis's teaching phonics and vocabulary in the same minilesson (see Figure 9.10). Teachers must also balance the sometimes competing demands of many children, of different constituencies (students, parents, administrators, the public), and of multiple curricula (literacy, math, science, social studies). Balance also means using a variety of instructional approaches and materials. We saw, for example, that Mrs. Walker used a trade book (*Just Me and My Dad,* Mayer, 1977) and a basal reader selection (*Just Like Daddy,* Asch, 1984) in the same lesson, that she balanced a read-aloud of the trade book with a shared reading of the basal selection, and that these group reading activities were followed by individual extensions activities. The common theme for all of this day's reading and writing was parents' and children's shared activities.

Figure 9.11 is striking evidence of the power of high expectations, but so are many of the other examples of students' work in this chapter. Sindy (see Figure 9.5) could generate word families because Mrs. Tran had taught about word families and then provided a challenging word family activity in the Letter and Word Center. Mike could write a personal poem (see Figure 9.10) because Mrs. Zickuhr believes that first graders can be poets and because she provided Mike's class with models, formats, and even powerful vocabulary that they could use in their poetry writing.

Mr. Schultheis's schedule allowed students immediate opportunities to practice and apply what he taught them. Whole-class discussions included minilessons about reading and writing processes that students then put into practice in the reading and writing block that followed. Mr. Schultheis used that block to observe and coach. Recall that he told Wharton-McDonald that while conferring with students, he was able to monitor what they could do and work with them on skills.

Mr. Schultheis was not the only teacher featured in this chapter whom we saw using minilessons to give targeted support for students' reading and writing. Mrs. Tran taught a minilesson about the phonogram *im* in connection with story reading. Mrs. Walker incorporated a minilesson about long vowel sounds and final silent *e* in her class's Daily Oral Language activity. We saw that Mrs. Duthie taught minilessons about features of informational texts, and Mrs. Zickuhr taught minilessons about feelings and topics in poetry writing.

Chapter Summary

First grade marks an important time in children's schooling. They are expected to begin "really" reading and writing; at the end of first grade, society expects children to have made great strides toward conventional reading and writing. We have shown that there are many ways in which this journey is taken.

We have described conventional reading as reading from print, but attending to meaning. Similarly, we could describe conventional writing as writing words, but attending to message. Acquiring knowledge about the alphabet, phonemic awareness, and print concepts forms a foundation for the later acquisition of sight words and strategies for identifying unknown words and extending understanding.

First graders gain this knowledge when their teachers carefully observe their students and provide targeted instruction. We described Mrs. Tran's guided reading methods, including her use of talk-through before guided reading, guided reading lessons, teaching for strategies, teaching for comprehension, and use of interactive writing. We saw that Mrs. Walker used a variety of techniques, including Daily Oral Language, word wall work, shared reading, and reading extensions. Mr. Schultheis's literacy instruction used flexible groups and varied materials. His teaching frequently served multiple purposes, and he constantly integrated reading and writing. Mrs. Duthie and Mrs. Zickuhr used minilessons to teach reading and writing of informational texts and poetry. All five teachers featured in this chapter demonstrate characteristics of exemplary literacy instruction. Such instruction is balanced, there is a lot of it, and it can often be characterized as targeted coaching.

Applying the Information

We suggest two applying-the-information activities. First, make a list of the seven characteristics of a literacy-rich classroom presented in Chapter 6. Then reread this chapter to locate an activity that is consistent with each of these characteristics. Discuss your examples with a classmate.

Make a list of all the literacy-learning activities described in this chapter. For each of these activities, describe what children learn about written language meanings, forms, meaning-form links, or functions.

Going Beyond the Text

Visit a first grade classroom and observe several literacy activities. Make a list of all the print and literacy materials in the classroom. Take note of the interactions among the children and between the children and the teacher during literacy activities. Talk with the teacher about his or her philosophy of beginning reading and writing. Compare these materials, activities, and philosophies with those of Mrs. Walker, Mr. Schultheis, and Mrs. Tran.

REFERENCES

Adams, M. (1990). *Beginning to read: Thinking and learning about print.* Cambridge: MIT Press.

Asch, F. (1984). *Just like Daddy.* New York: Simon & Schuster.

Asch, F. (1995). *Water.* New York: Harcourt Brace.

Askew, B., & Fountas, I. (1998). Building an early reading process: Active from the start! *The Reading Teacher, 52,* 126–134.

Bear, D. R., Invernizzi, M., Templeton, S., & Johnston, F. (2000). *Words their way: Word study for phonics, vocabulary, and spelling instruction (2nd ed.).* Upper Saddle River, NJ: Merrill.

Berger, M. (1994). *Oil Spill!* New York: Harper-Collins.

Brown, J. (1964). *Flat Stanley.* New York: Harper Trophy.

Brown, K. (1999/2000). What kind of text—for whom and when? Textual scaffolding for beginning readers. *The Reading Teacher, 53,* 292–307.

Caswell, L., & Duke, N. (1998). Non-narrative as a catalyst for literacy development. *Language Arts, 75,* 108–117.

Clay, M. (1991a). *Becoming literate: The construction of inner control.* Portsmouth, NH: Heinemann.

Clay, M. (1991b). Introducing a new storybook to young readers. *The Reading Teacher, 45,* 264–273.

Clay, M. (1993). *Reading Recovery: A guidebook for teachers in training.* Portsmouth, NH: Heinemann.

Cole, H. (1995). *Jack's garden.* New York: Greenwillow.

Cullinan, B. E., Scala, M. C., and Schroder, V. C. (1995). *Three voices: An invitation to poetry across the curriculum.* York, ME: Stenhouse.

Cunningham, P. (1995). *Phonics they use: Words for reading and writing* (2nd ed.). New York: Harper-Collins.

Cunningham, P., & Cunningham, J. (1992). Making words: Enhancing the invented spelling-decoding connection. *The Reading Teacher, 46,* 106–115.

Cunningham, P., Hall, D., & Defee, M. (1998). Non-ability-grouped, multilevel instruction: Eight years later. *The Reading Teacher, 51,* 652–664.

Cutting, J. (1996). *Where's Tim?* Illus. by J. van der Voo. Bothell, WA: Wright Group.

Dahl, K. L., & Scharer, P. L. (2000). Phonics teaching and learning in whole language classrooms: New evidence from research. *The Reading Teacher, 53,* 584–594.

Dahl, K. L., Sharer, P. L., Lawson, L. L., & Grogan, P. R. (1999). Phonics instruction and student achievement in whole language first-grade classrooms. *Reading Research Quarterly, 34,* 312–341.

dePaola, T. (1973). *Charlie needs a cloak.* Englewood Cliffs, NJ: Prentice-Hall.

Duthie, C. (1996). *True stories: Nonfiction literacy in the primary classroom.* York, ME: Stenhouse.

Fountas, I., & Pinnell, G. (1996). *Guided reading: Good first teaching for all children.* Portsmouth, NH: Heinemann.

Froman, R. (1971). *Street poems.* New York: McCall.

Gaskins, I., Ehri, L., Cress, C., O'Hara, C., Donnelly, K. (1997). Procedures for word learning: Making discoveries about words. *The Reading Teacher, 50,* 312–327.

Gunning, T. (1998). *Best books for beginning readers.* Boston: Allyn and Bacon.

Hiebert, E. (1999). Text matters in learning to read. *The Reading Teacher, 52,* 552–565.

Hill, E. (1980). *Where's Spot?* New York: Putnam.

Hoewisch, A. (2001). Creating well-rounded curricula with *Flat Stanley:* A school-university project. *The Reading Teacher, 55,* 154–168.

International Reading Association (IRA). (2000). Excellent reading teachers: A position statement of the International Reading Association. *The Reading Teacher, 54,* 235–240.

International Reading Association (IRA) and the National Association for the Education of Young Children (NAEYC). (1998). Learning to read and write: Developmentally appropriate practices for young children. *The Reading Teacher, 52,* 193–216.

Juel, C. (1991). *Beginning reading.* In R. Barr, M. Kamil, P. Mosenthal, & P. Pearson (Eds.), *Handbook of reading research* (vol. 2) (pp. 759–788). New York: Longman.

Lysaker, J. (1997). Learning to read from self-selected texts: The book choices of six first graders. In C. Kinzer, K. Hinchman, & D. Leu (Eds.), *Inquiries in literacy theory and practice* (pp. 273–282). Chicago: National Reading Conference.

MacGillivray, L. (1994). Tacit shared understanding of a first-grade writing community. *Journal of Literacy Research, 26,* 245–266.

Martinez, M., Roser, N., Worthy, J., Strecker, S., & Gough, P. (1997). Classroom libraries and children's book selection: Redefining "access" in self-selected reading. In C. Kinzer, K. Hinchman, & D. Leu (Eds.), *Inquiries in literacy theory*

and practice (pp. 265–271). Chicago: National Reading Conference.

Mayer, M. (1977). *Just me and my dad.* Racine, WI: Golden Books.

McGee, L. (1996). Response-centered talk: Windows on children's thinking. In L. Gambrell & J. Almasi (Eds.), *Lively discussions: Fostering engaged reading* (pp. 194–207). Newark, DE: International Reading Association.

Morningstar, J. (1999). Home response journals: Parents as informed contributors in the understanding of their children's literacy development. *The Reading Teacher, 52,* 690–697.

Morrow, L. M., Tracey, D. H., Woo, D. G., & Pressley, M. (1999). Characteristics of exemplary first-grade literacy instruction. *The Reading Teacher, 52,* 462–476.

Peterson, B. (1991). Selecting books for beginning readers. In D. E. DeFord, C. Lyns, & G. Pinnell (Eds.), *Bridges to literacy: Learning from Reading Recovery* (pp. 111–138). Portsmouth, NH: Heinemann.

Pinnell, G., & Fountas, I. (1998). *Word matters.* Portsmouth, NH: Heinemann.

Pressley, M., Allington, R. L., Wharton-McDonald, R., Block, C. C., & Morrow, L. M. (2001). *Learning to read: Lessons from exemplary first-grade classrooms.* New York: Guilford.

Schwartz, R. (1997). Self-monitoring in beginning reading. *The Reading Teacher, 51,* 40–48.

Sipe, L. (1998). Transitions to the conventional: An examination of a first grader's composing process. *Journal of Literacy Research, 30,* 357–388.

Slanina, A. M. (2001). Twenty-five web sites for the language arts teacher. *The Reading Teacher, 55,* 170.

Snow, C., Burns, S., & Griffin, P. (1998). *Preventing reading difficulties in young children.* Washington, DC: National Academy Press.

Strickland, D. (1998). *Teaching phonics today: A primer for educators.* Newark, DE: International Reading Association.

Taylor, B. M., Pearson, P. D., Clark, K., & Walpole, S. (2002). Effective schools and accomplished teachers: Lessons about primary-grade reading instruction in low-income schools. In B. M. Taylor & P. D. Pearson (Eds.), *Teaching reading: Effective schools, accomplished teachers* (pp. 3–72). Mahwah, NJ: Lawrence Erlbaum.

Turpie, J., & Paratore, J. (1995). Using repeated reading to promote reading success in a heterogeneously grouped first grade. In K. Hinchman, D. Leu, & C. Kinzer (Eds.), *Perspective on liter-*

acy research and practice (pp. 255–264). Chicago: National Reading Conference.

Vail, N. J., & Papenfuss, J. F. (1982). *Daily oral language*. Racine, WI: D.O.L. Publications.

Wagstaff, J. (1997–1998). Building practical knowledge of sound–letter correspondences: A beginner's word wall and beyond. *The Reading Teacher, 51*, 298–304.

Wharton-McDonald, R. (2001a). Andy Schultheis. In M. Pressley, R. L. Allington, R. Wharton-McDonald, C. C. Block, & L. M. Morrow (Eds.), *Learning to read: Lessons from exemplary first-grade classrooms* (pp. 115–137). New York: Guilford.

Wharton-McDonald, R. (2001b). Teaching writing in first grade: Instruction, scaffolds, and expectations. In M. Pressley, R. L. Allington, R. Wharton-McDonald, C. C. Block, & L. M. Morrow (Eds.), *Learning to read: Lessons from exemplary first-grade classrooms* (pp. 70–91). New York: Guilford.

Supporting Literacy Learning Beyond First Grade

KEY CONCEPTS

social construction of
   meaning
writing workshop
guided reading
book club
reading workshop
schema
make inferences

mental images
determine the importance
   of information
synthesize ideas
think-alouds
explicit comprehension
   strategy instruction
text-to-self connections

anchor chart
prewriting
planning cluster
drafting
revising
editing
publishing
minilesson

status of the class	multiple character perspective	poetry festival
writing block	literature discussion	inquiry units
conference groups	grand conversation	idea circles
legibility	running records	recording grid
reading workshop	leveled texts	content-specific vocabulary
response journals	instructional level	Internet workshop
reading block	strategy sheet	homophones
reading conferences	character cluster	homographs
story retelling	word cluster	word sorts
readers' theater	word walls for specific books	word hunts
literary opposites	list, group, and label activity	making big words
question-making activity	reading log	word-part word wall
long questions	choral reading	word pool

What's New Here?

This chapter describes instruction that moves children into and beyond transitional reading and writing. While many of the same kinds of instructional activities we described in Chapter 9 continue to be important during this phase of reading and writing, teachers can expand reading and writing activities to capitalize on children's new competencies.

Increasing Expectations for Traditional Skills, Child-Centered Classrooms, and New Competencies

In second and third grade, children are held accountable for mastering an ever-increasing number of academic skills in all subject areas. However, child-centeredness does not have to end in the primary grades. Student choice continues to be an essential component in the reading and writing program. As we will demonstrate, second and third grade teachers continue to weave opportunities for children's own active exploration of reading and writing with instruction that is directed at helping children achieve the school's expectations for second and third grade literacy.

An important aspect of the context beyond first grade is that a class as a whole usually has achieved a critical mass of literacy competence. Teachers can rely on this competence to integrate learning in content areas with instruction in reading and writing. All students can work together with increasing independence on tasks that require literacy competence. All can function in heterogeneous cooperative-learning groups, using strategies for problem solving and content learning as well as reading and writing.

Activities like these have a characteristic that we can call **social construction of meaning** (Wells & Chang-Wells, 1992). They involve both a social component and a process of revision. In social construction of meaning, children work together to create an understanding, by which we mean that they interact with others in order to construct compositions and understand literature. As a result, children become a community of learners (Miller, 2002).

A Balanced Reading and Writing Program

The balancing act of teachers in second grade and beyond continues with many of the same struggles faced by first grade teachers. Perhaps the biggest struggle to achieve balance in the second grade and beyond is meeting the very diverse needs of children. Some children will begin second grade reading and writing far above grade-level expectations. They are transitional readers capable of reading more complex picture storybooks, informational books, and easy chapter books independently.

Other children will begin second grade as early readers. However, these children will have in place many literacy skills and strategies. They are on their way, but will need continued teacher support and extended practice to move into and beyond the transitional text levels.

Some children will not yet have accomplished what we expect in first grade. They may be reading only at the beginning stage of early reading. They will need considerable teacher support and extensive amounts of practice in texts at their instructional level to enhance their early literacy skills and strategies.

Teaching for strategies within the context of rich reading and writing experiences with narrative, poetic, and informational text is another component of balancing the literacy program in second and third grade. Teachers must balance the amount of time used for instruction, guided practice, and independent reading and writing. Teachers continue to provide direct instruction in reading and writing strategies during instructional lessons. They also provide children with opportunities for guided practice using strategies in reading and writing activities. However, strategy development is only a part of competent reading and writing. Competent readers and writers are motivated and knowledgeable about a variety of text genres (Dowhower, 1999; Guthrie & McCann, 1996). Therefore, strategy instruction is embedded in rich conversations about literature (Taberski, 2000).

Components of a Balanced
Reading and Writing Program

The balanced reading and writing program includes time for children to read independently and with teacher guidance books of their choice (regardless of text difficulty), books at just the right level of text difficulty, and more challenging books. Effective reading programs also include daily read-alouds in which teachers share books that are more difficult than those that children can read with guidance or alone. The writing program is connected to the reading program so that children use what they are learning about genre and other characteristics of text features in their own writing.

We recommend that teachers use a **writing workshop** approach. In this approach, teachers provide minilessons about how to write and children write on self-selected or teacher-selected topics. We recommend three approaches that teachers can use to organize and manage their reading programs for transitional readers including: (1) guided reading programs, (2) book clubs, and (3) readers' workshops. In the **guided reading** approach (Fountas & Pinnell, 1996), small groups of children who are reading on similar reading levels meet with the teacher for reading instruction two to four times a week. In the **book club** approach (Raphael & McMahon, 1994), also called literature circles (Short & Pierce, 1998), small groups of children select books that they would like to read and discuss together. In the **reading workshop** approach (Taberski, 2000), children confer with the teacher about books they are reading.

Most exemplary second and third grade teachers will include all three kinds of reading approaches in their reading programs. At this grade children need opportunities for guided reading instruction, but they also benefit from learning how to talk more independently about books with their peers as is done in literature circles (Frank, Dixon, & Brandts, 2001). Book clubs can sometimes be used as a part of science and social studies instruction when groups of children read about related topics together. Finally, children need extensive practice reading books that are just right for their reading level, which is provided in the readers' workshop approach. Effective teachers provide time for children's independent reading of books that are carefully selected for them, opportunities for learning in guided reading groups, and additional reading experiences in book clubs.

Shared Reading and Reading Aloud

Shared reading and reading aloud to children play a critical role in the reading and writing program. Shared reading is particularly useful in demonstrating strategies such as how to read or write a particular text feature, like how an author crafts the first sentence in a story or the main idea sentence in an exposition, and how to decode unfamiliar words or figure out a word's meaning. Reading aloud is used to demonstrate comprehension and vocabulary strategies.

Explicit Teaching of Decoding and Vocabulary in Shared Reading

Shared reading in second and third grade takes a different form than shared reading in kindergarten or first grade. At the second and third grade levels, teachers use enlarged copies of short text (for example, using an overhead projector to show a paragraph the teacher and children will read together) or multiple copies of longer texts. Texts used in shared reading are frequently more difficult than most children can read either independently or with guidance.

Shared reading is especially useful in helping children learn strategies for decoding words. Although as first graders, children learned to apply phonics as a word-solving strategy, in second and third grades they need multiple strategies for both decoding and figuring out a word's meaning. For example, a third grade teacher used *Golem* (Wisniewski, 1996) to demonstrate how to decode difficult words and to infer their meanings. She borrowed copies of the book from other teachers and the library so that pairs of children had a copy of the book to examine as she read aloud. She read the first page of the story and paused at several difficult words including *Protestant, ignorant, matzoh, incited,* and *vicious.* Each time she modeled how to stop and look all the way through the word, break the word into parts, and use familiar word parts to decode the word. She modeled rereading the entire sentence saying the new word. She also modeled how to read the surrounding text to look for clues that would help her infer the word's meaning.

At the end of shared reading lesson, she guided the children in summarizing the steps in the decoding and word meaning strategy and wrote them on a chart. Over the next several days, the teacher used the chart as she taught guided reading lessons and conducted conferences with individual children.

Explicit Teaching of Comprehension during Reading Aloud

Miller (2002) describes a systematic approach to explicit instruction in comprehension. Across a year's time she uses read-alouds to introduce children to major categories of comprehension strategies including: using schema, creating mental images, inferring, asking questions, using special strategies for informational books, and synthesizing.

Systematic: What Strategies to Teach.   In general, proficient readers call to mind what they already know about actions and events about which they are reading and connect them to ideas in the text in powerful ways (Pressley & Block, 2002). That is, they use relevant **schema** to elaborate on and **make inferences** about what they are reading. They create vivid **mental images** and ponder the significance of certain words or events. They **determine the importance of information** and **synthesize ideas.** However, many proficient readers are not aware of using these strategies because they have become so automatic (Sinatra, Brown, & Reynolds, 2002). In addition, proficient readers seem to automatically adapt their general strategies to meet the needs of specific texts. For example, they activate schema that are relevant to a particular text.

Figure 10.1 presents a list of comprehension strategies that are appropriate for transitional readers. These strategies are intended to help children make high-level inferences and interpretations of stories they read and to construct sophisticated understandings of informational books.

Explicit: How to Teach Strategies.   In order to teach strategies, teachers must become more consciously aware of their own use of strategies so they can describe them explicitly. Such descriptions are called **think-alouds** because they are

FIGURE 10.1 Reading Strategies

Using schema

Text-to-self connections

stopping to think about big ideas and making connections to my life

Text-to-text connections

comparing characters in different or the same texts

Text-to-world connections

stopping to think about big ideas and connecting to events in life

Schema for story elements

considering characters and their enduring qualities

determining the relationship between character traits and problems, plot, and theme

moving from what happens, to how, and why it happens

Activating, building, and revising schema

Creating mental images

Creating images from readers' schema and words in the text

Changing images to incorporate new information

Inferring

Inferring the meaning of words

Predicting

making more than one prediction and using text as support

Stopping to think what happened and why it happened (from what to why)

Stopping to think why the character acted as he/she did (from what to why)

Inferring answers to questions (when the answers are not in the text)

Asking questions

Asking "I wonder why"

Asking questions before, during, and after reading

Determining whether questions can be answered in text, in schema, or from outside source

Using special strategies for informational text

Noticing and remembering when we learn something new

Using informational text features

Distinguishing important from unimportant information

Synthesizing

Retelling what's important and makes sense, but does not tell too much

Moving from literal level to inferential level

I'm thinking that, now I'm thinking, I used to think—but now I'm thinking

Adapted from Miller, D. (2002). *Reading with meaning: Teaching comprehension in the primary grades*. Portland, ME: Stenhouse; Taberski, S. (2000). *On solid ground: Strategies for teaching reading K–3*. Portsmouth, NH: Heinemann.

demonstrations of thinking done aloud. Explicit instruction involves four stages (Pearson & Gallagher, 1983):

1. Teacher modeling and explanation of a strategy
2. Guided practice in which the teacher participates with the children as the strategy is jointly used

3. Independent practice in which children practice using the strategy on their own with feedback from the teacher

4. Application of the strategy in which children use the strategy in their reading when it is called upon.

Teacher modeling usually takes the form of thinking aloud as teachers say aloud what they are thinking. Guided practice can take place during whole-group discussions and then can be applied during smaller group activities. Finally, teachers find out how frequently children use the strategies on their own by asking them questions during conferences.

Teacher modeling includes telling children what to do, why it is important to do it, and how to do it. Most teachers use sophisticated language for strategies in **explicit comprehension strategy instruction.** For example, Miller (2002) starts strategy instruction by telling what the strategy is that she will be demonstrating and why it is important: "Thinking about what you already know is called using your schema, or using your background knowledge. Schema is all the stuff that's already in your head, like places you've been, things you've done, books you've read—all the experiences you've had. . . . When you use schema, it helps you use what you know to better understand [what you read]" (p. 57). She identifies and explains the strategy she wants children to learn, "Today we are going to talk about one way [you use schema]: using schema to make connections from our reading, or the text, to ourselves. We'll call these **text-to-self connections.**"

Next, Miller demonstrates using the strategy, "Let me show you what I mean. I'm going to read a story to you; its title is *The Relatives Came* by Cynthia Rylant. I'll read for a while, then I'll stop and think out loud to show you how I use my schema, or what I already know, to make connections from my life to the story" (pp. 57–58). She reads the book, then stops at a page and puts the book down in her lap signaling she will be talking about the book rather than reading. She says, "[T]his page made me laugh. You see right here, where I read to you 'It was different going to sleep with all that new breathing in the house'? I understood exactly what Cynthia Rylant meant. That's because at the same time I was reading I was making a connection to when I was a little girl, remembering how my family and all my cousins and aunts and uncles would visit my grandparents in their farmhouse on old Route 92 near Oskaloosa, Iowa. Sometimes it was so hot and sticky at night that we'd all pile down to the living room—just like this picture. We'd sleep together on the black carpet with the pink and red roses" (p. 58). Next Miller (2002) makes explicit that she has modeled using the strategy, "Do you see how using my schema helped me understand just how the people in the book feel?" (p. 58).

Strategy instruction helps children reflect on how and why strategies help to make them better readers. One student reflected that "[I]f we connect to a word, like mailman or cat or soccer ball, that doesn't really help us, but if we connect to a bigger thing, like if it's on almost all the pages and it's what the book is really about, like an idea or something, then it can help you" (p. 61). Miller makes what she calls an **anchor chart** that summarizes children's reflections about using strategies.

Writing and Reading Workshop, Book Clubs, and Guided Reading

Children in the second grade and beyond benefit from their kindergarten and first grade writing experiences using the beginnings of a process approach to writing. In second and third grade, children continue using writing processes as they develop greater writing sophistication.

Writing Workshop

As we showed in Chapter 9, first graders use at least three writing processes: planning, revising, and sharing. Some first grade teachers introduce children to all five writing processes in their writing workshop. That is, most descriptions of writing processes describe five writing processes: prewriting, drafting, revising, editing, and sharing or publishing. However, it is misleading to think of these processes as occurring linearly or sequentially; rather, they are interactive, and they often occur simultaneously (Tompkins, 2003).

One writing process is called **prewriting.** This process includes a writer's search for a topic, identification of audience and purpose, and collection of ideas about which to write. Many young children plan by talking to a friend or to their teacher, by writing a list of ideas, by role-playing an experience, by listening to or reading literature, or by simply thinking. The purpose of rehearsing and planning during prewriting is to generate ideas and formulate plans for writing.

Teachers demonstrate planning strategies in minilessons. One second grade teacher demonstrated how to use a cluster to plan for writing a mystery. His class brainstormed a list of all the elements found in mysteries, such as clues, scary characters, frightening events, and spooky settings. Then the teacher demonstrated using this list to write a cluster of ideas as a prewriting strategy. Figure 10.2 presents a **planning cluster** one second grader wrote to identify the characters, setting, and clues for her Campout Mystery.

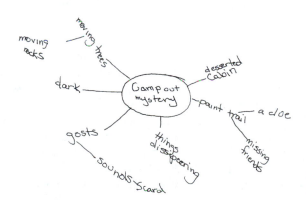

FIGURE 10.2   Cluster for Planning the Campout Mystery

Another writing process is called **drafting.** In this process children commit their ideas to paper. First drafts of conventional readers and writers can be short, sometimes consisting of only a few words. More accomplished readers and writers write longer first drafts and more consciously consider the necessity of writing details.

A third writing process is **revising;** it consists of children's rethinking what they have written. In revising, children reread their drafts; add or delete words, phrases, or sentences; and move sentences. The focus of these activities is the ideas and content of the writing. In another writing process, **editing,** children focus on misspellings and errors in capitalization, punctuation, and usage. Children gradually learn to edit their own writing. The last writing process, **publishing,** consists of sharing writing with an audience.

Many teachers use the author's chair for informal classroom sharing as one way of publishing. Other ways of sharing children's published writing include having a "Share Fair" once a month, in which child-authors read to their parents or to other classrooms of children, write letters to members of the community, construct birthday cards to authors and illustrators, publish a class newspaper or literary magazine, bind books for a nursing home or children's ward of the hospital, and send compositions to children's magazines that publish children's writing. Many sites on the Internet provide outlets for publishing student writing.

Writing Workshop Format.   Most teachers use a routine format for their writing workshop that includes the following:

- (Five to ten minutes) **Minilesson** on a writing or illustrating technique; literary elements; features of informational text; organizational patterns such as sequence or compare and contrast; rehearsal strategies for gathering and organizing information; revision strategies; or editing strategies
- (Three to four minutes) **Status of the class** (Atwell, 1987), in which each child very briefly states what he or she will do during workshop
- (Twenty to thirty minutes) **Writing block,** in which children write while the teacher conducts large and small group conferences
- (Five to ten minutes) Whole-group share by one or two children who read their compositions and lead discussion (from Duthie, 1996, p. 56)

Minilessons and Conference Groups.   Minilessons are short whole-class lessons in which teachers demonstrate particular writing strategies, patterns that can be used in writing, or a special feature of text (Calkins, 1986), and **conference groups** serve as collaborative learning groups. Writers' conference groups can be used to provide additional time and support for small groups of children to try out various strategies introduced in minilessons. They can also be used to teach children knowledge related to literary and written language conventions, such as letter writing, using similes or metaphors, and sequencing of events, as well as proper use of capital letters, periods, commas, quotation marks, and even colons.

Figure 10.3 presents an editing checklist that would be useful for second graders. To develop such a list, teachers plan a minilesson focusing on just one editing skill, such as listening for sentences. The teacher demonstrates this strategy

FIGURE 10.3   An Editing Checklist

☐ I have reread my writing to a writing partner.

☐ I have listened for sentences.

☐ I have a capital letter at the beginning of each sentence.

☐ I have a period, question mark, or exclamation mark at the end of each sentence.

☐ I have a capital letter for every time I used the word *I*.

☐ I have a capital letter for every person's name.

☐ I have checked spellings of the word wall words.

using her own writing. Later, in a writers' conference group, children practice the strategy using a selected piece of their own writing. Then the teacher adds the strategy to a class list of editing strategies. The list grows longer as children learn more and more strategies. Often teachers will ask children to come to a writers' conference group and bring a draft of their writing with the editing checklist completed for that composition.

Using Computers in Writing Workshop.   Second and third grade classrooms usually include at least one microcomputer. We suggest using computer time for word processing, exploring graphics, and conducting Internet inquiry projects.

Students can do some of their writing on computers, using a word-processing program, but it is not practical for them to do all their writing that way. Most students can do much of their planning and drafting with paper and pencil, rather than with a word processor. They are adept at making revisions with cross-outs, arrows, and brackets and cut-and-paste (see Figure 10.4). Then students can sign

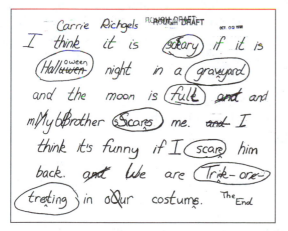

FIGURE 10.4   Carrie's Writing in Writing Workshop (A Rough Draft and One Page from the Published Story)

up for word processor time to do final drafts, to run spelling checks, to add graphics, and to print final copies of their pieces for publication in the classroom. They appreciate the ease of making changes with the word processor and the clean look of their computer-printed final copies.

Writing Fluency and Handwriting.   By second and third grade, children can write their ideas more fluently. They are less likely to focus on spelling and more likely to focus on the ideas they want to write. Because they also know more about spelling patterns, they will be able to spell unfamiliar words relatively quickly. They will also have many more strategies for finding the words they want to write. By this time, their handwriting will be fairly automatic and readable. Most children's letter formation, through practice, will have become conventional.

Handwriting instruction is beneficial in this phase of writing, because children are more likely to expect other children to read what they have written. Instruction in handwriting should focus on **legibility** rather than on imitation of examples; it should provide children with language with which to talk about their handwriting and letters, and it should be connected with publishing children's writing.

There are four aspects of legibility that young writers need to learn. First, letters should conform to expected formations as defined by the writing program. Expected formations, especially of capital letters, differ from one handwriting program to another. The second aspect of legibility is that letters should be of uniform size, proportion, and alignment. Third, letters and words should be evenly spaced. Fourth, letters should have a consistent slant. The time to be concerned about legible handwriting is when writing is for an audience. Just prior to binding children's writing into a hardbound book is an opportune time for handwriting instruction.

Reading Workshop

Reading workshop is an approach to reading instruction that uses a format similar to that of writing workshop. Children select their own reading texts with teacher guidance, and instruction takes place in a variety of places including during teacher read-alouds and conferences. Reading workshop includes five components.

1. Teacher reads aloud to children and conducts a minilesson demonstrating a reading strategy.
2. Teacher holds a status-of-the-class discussion in which each child states the text(s) he or she will read or what will be accomplished on a response project.
3. Children read during a twenty- to thirty-minute **reading block;** they may also work on a response project.
4. Teacher holds conferences with individuals and small groups of children.
5. Two or three children share from a book they are reading or present a response project.

Teachers begin readers' workshop by reading aloud to students. Through read-alouds, teachers demonstrate reading strategies by talking aloud in minilessons.

Reading Workshop Format.   Teachers may demonstrate reading strategies; provide information about authors, illustrators, styles of illustration, genres, or literary conventions; model response activities, including ways of writing in a response journal; and provide information about record keeping, such as how to record in a log the titles and authors of books read during readers' workshop. Students read independently for extended periods of time as a major part of the readers' workshop. The purpose of the reading block is to develop reading fluency, to create interest in reading, and to enhance children's reading ability.

An important weekly response activity is writing in **response journals.** Children are encouraged to reveal parts of the book that are memorable, surprising, or unusual, or to describe related personal experiences or connections they made to another book or poem (Barone, 1990; Kelly & Farnan, 1991; Taberski, 2000). Students are usually not required to write an entry in their response journal for every book they read, but may be required to write responses two or three times a week.

While children are reading and responding to books during reading block, teachers hold **reading conferences** with students about the books they are reading. During these conferences, teachers talk with students about their books, listen to students read, and discuss response-journal entries and other response projects. Teachers use conferences to teach strategies and make assessments of students' progress and needs. As a last part of readers' workshop, students share their response projects and talk about books they are reading. Small groups of students act as audiences for response activities such as dramatizations and readers' theatre productions.

Response Activities.   **Story retelling** is a proven strategy for improving children's comprehension and fluency (Gambrell, Pfeiffer, & Wilson, 1985). Children recall the main characters and critical events in a story in the order in which they appeared and with sufficient detail so that someone not familiar with the story will get the gist from the retelling. They naturally use the story's rich vocabulary and complex sentence structure as they retell the story thereby expanding their own language and vocabulary.

Having children write retellings in response journals is an effective response activity. Teachers may introduce written retellings by having children write on each page of a little book an event that occurred in the beginning, middle, and end of the story (Tompkins, 2003). Eventually, children expand their retellings, as shown in the retelling of *There's an Owl in the Shower* (George, 1995) found in Figure 10.5.

Readers' theatre is another response activity that benefits children's reading fluency. Children who have read the same book can form a readers' theatre group. **Readers' theatre** is a simple form of dramatization in which players read their lines rather than memorize them (Trousdale & Harris, 1993; Wolf, 1993). Players usually sit on stools but may stand in groups. There are few props and only the simplest of costumes. To begin readers' theater, teachers can write their own script from a simple story or informational text. They demonstrate how dialogue from stories is translated into dialogue in script form and how narrative in text is translated into a narrator's words in a script. Eventually, students compose their own readers' theater scripts from a picture or informational book they have selected. Because children

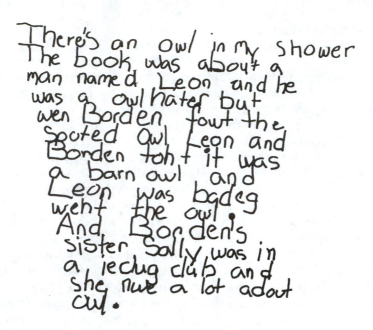

There's an owl in my shower
The book was about a
man named Leon and he
was a owl hater but
wen Borden fowt the
Spoted Owl Leon and
Borden toht it was
a barn owl and
Leon was bqdeg
weht the owl.
And Borden's
sister Sally was in
a iedug club and
she nue a lot adout
cwl.

FIGURE 10.5   Retelling of *There's an Owl in the Shower*
(George, 1995)

need not memorize lines, they are free to work on interpretation as they read the script aloud, they feel less anxiety, and, overall, there is less emphasis on the performance than in traditional drama.

Once children (or the teacher) have composed a readers' theater script, teachers read it aloud during rehearsal. Then players experiment with reading the script by varying their voices and rate of speaking. The teacher assists students who are having difficulty (Hoyt, 1992). Even the least able readers can participate in readers' theater. They are helped by the repeated reading of the scripts that occurs as a natural part of rehearsal. In fact, rereading is another proven comprehension booster and fluency enhancer (Stahl & Kuhn, 2002).

Readers' theater works just as well using nonfiction books as an alternative to content-area textbooks. It "gives the words on the page a voice, and the students in the classroom an active role in internalizing and interpreting new knowledge" (Young & Vardell, 1993, p. 405).

Book Clubs

One way to organize instruction about narratives is to use **book clubs.** With this approach, a small group of students reads a common literature selection. The book club, depending on the teacher's goals and the children's instructional needs, may read its text without the teacher's guidance. Or, children may be guided by the teacher as they read the selection. The following are elements of the book club approach:

- Children or teachers select a book or text set (text sets are five to ten books around a topic or theme).
- Teachers model comprehension strategies, teach literary elements, provide examples of what to talk about during book discussions, and teach lessons on various response activities in whole-group lessons.
- Children read the book or text sets with or without teacher guidance.
- Children participate in literature discussions with or without the teacher.
- Children participate in response activities.
- Teachers hold conferences with individual and small groups of children, focusing on extending children's responses; assessing, modeling, and guiding comprehension strategy use; and expanding strategies for identifying vocabulary meanings and reading unknown words.

Fostering Deep Thinking in Book Clubs. Using quality literature in book clubs is so critical because it calls for deep thinking. Literature invites multiple interpretations, via which readers go beyond the literal to make varied and personal connections with literature (Sipe, 2002).

One teacher used read-alouds to teach children the idea of **literary opposites** (Temple, 1991), that literature has characters and events that are opposites. Stories have greedy characters and more generous ones, events that happen at night contrasted with events that occur in the daytime, or strong girls who rescue weak men. Finding opposites often leads children deeper into stories (Temple, 1991).

A third grade class used literary opposites to explore character traits and themes in *Rumpelstiltskin* (Zelinsky, 1986). They noticed that the miller and his daughter were poor, the king was rich, but the miller's daughter became rich when she was queen. They thought Rumpelstiltskin, the miller, and the king were greedy, but thought the miller's daughter was generous and giving. They noted that the miller's daughter and the king were tall and beautiful and handsome; Rumpelstiltskin was small and ugly. They noted that, at night, the miller's daughter was with Rumpelstiltskin, and during the day, she was with the king.

After listing these and many other opposites in the story, their teacher initiated a **question-making activity** (Commeyras & Sumner, 1995). In this activity, children construct questions that will lead to long discussions about literature. The teacher modeled asking questions that could be easily answered and did not generate much talk versus questions that generated many different ideas and opinions. Good questions are those that have no single correct answer, create many different ideas, and take a long time to discuss. This class called these kinds of questions **"long questions."**

The teacher invited children to suggest long questions to use for talking about *Rumpelstiltskin.* The children posed the following questions with the teacher's guidance:

If the miller was poor, why did he give a daughter to the king?

What kind of father was he to lie to the king in a way that might harm the daughter?

Why would the daughter fall in love with a king who demanded she spin gold or be killed?

Why are the king and Rumpelstiltskin so alike in character, but not looks? Did the miller's daughter think about this?

Another approach to help children perceive multiple perspectives on a story is the **multiple-character perspective** approach. Here, teachers select books that have characters who are in conflict, such as Nyasha and Manyara in *Mufaro's Beautiful Daughters: An African Tale* (Steptoe, 1987). Children discuss the story from first one character's, and then the other character's perspectives, focusing especially on the character's conflicting goals, motivations, intentions, and actions. Differing themes which emerge from discussions of the differing goals, motivations, intentions, and actions of characters can be critically compared and contrasted (Shanahan & Shanahan, 1997).

Literature Discussions in Book Clubs.   The heart of the book club approach is the actual book clubs (Goatley, Brock, & Raphael, 1995). To start a book club, the teacher provides multiple copies of a book, previews it for the class, and then signs up a club of children who are interested in that book. Children read assigned portions of the book with or without teacher guidance and then have a literature discussion. Teachers often participate in the literature discussion groups, providing alternative interpretive perspectives and challenging children to think more critically. Teachers and children may describe strategies used during reading. However, children may also have very productive literature discussions without the involvement of the teacher (Almasi, 1995).

A critical component of the book club approach is **literature discussion** (Almasi, 1995), or **grand conversation** (McGee, 1995). Small groups of children gather with or without a teacher to talk about a book they have read. The expectation is that children will talk about things they thought were important, issues of concern, or things they do not understand. Grand conversations are not dominated by teacher questions (Scharer, 1996). Instead, conversation is shared between the teacher and children. Grand conversations can be initiated by having children identify topics or "seeds" that they would like to talk about at length (Villaume et al., 1994), or teachers can generate a list of possible discussion questions from which children select a few for discussion (Vogt, 1996).

Guided Reading

Guided reading is different from book clubs in that guided reading groups are comprised of groups of children who are on similar reading levels. The text selected for guided reading lessons is slightly above the independent reading level of the members of that group. Teachers can use sets of books that have been leveled for difficulty or basal reading materials (Fawson & Reutzel, 2000). Guided reading provides teachers with another opportunity to coach children in using strategies introduced in whole-group read-alouds or shared reading. However, teachers can personalize instruction to the particular needs of the children in the group and to the text they will be reading.

Selecting a Group of Children, Books, and Strategies. Guided reading groups include four to six children who are reading on similar reading levels. Teachers use **running records** of **leveled texts** (Brabham & Villaume, 2002) to determine children's reading levels (see Chapter 9 for an explanation of leveled texts and Chapter 12 for an explanation of running records). One teacher, Sharon Taberski, who works in a multiage first and second grade classroom, uses four guided reading groups (Taberski, 2000). As the year progresses and her children accelerate their learning, she alters the composition of the groups. She takes short running records of her children's reading during individual conferences which she uses to make judgments about children's group membership as well as about the strategies she will teach during guided reading.

Once the members of the group are identified and their level of reading is determined, teachers select books at the children's **instructional level** to use in guided reading. Teachers consider both the nature of children's current reading and the text selected for instruction to make decisions about strategies to teach. Transitional readers need to practice with strategies that will get them deeper into the meaning of stories and strategies for learning from informational text. They also need to practice using strategies for figuring out how to read unfamiliar multisyllable words and for finding the meaning of unknown words.

Books for transitional readers are usually at level 14 to above level 20 according to Reading Recovery levels and approximately levels J through M according to Fountas and Pinnell (1996). Many commercial publishers produce leveled easy "I Can Read" books and level 2 books in these series are usually appropriate for early transitional readers.

Instruction during Guided Reading. Most teachers use readers' workshop (having children read books at their independent level and having conferences with individual children) along with guided reading. Therefore, they usually can only meet with two or three guided reading groups each day. Most groups meet with the teacher two to four times a week for twenty to thirty minutes each lesson. Guided reading usually begins with an introduction to the text that they will be reading. For transitional readers, this introduction is usually short and differs according to the kind of text they will be reading. Introductions to short picture books (such as commercial leveled books) involve reading the title, the back of the cover, and predicting what the story will be about. Then the teacher introduces the strategy she wants the children to practice during guided reading.

A Guided Reading Lesson to Teach a Comprehension Strategy. Transitional readers need to learn how to infer character traits and be able to see how a story's problems, its plot, and possible themes are related to these traits (Taberski, 2000). *Fox and his Friends* (Marshall, 1982) is a perfect text for helping transitional readers learn how to use this strategy. First, the teacher reminds children about this strategy (usually strategies are introduced first in whole-class read-alouds or shared reading). In this case, the teacher has decided to use a **strategy sheet** to help children use the strategy during reading. A strategy sheet is a simple graphic that children fill in as they read. In this case, the teacher decides to use a **character cluster** as a strategy sheet (Taberski, 2000). The character cluster strategy sheet is a simple graphic organizer with a circle in the center of the sheet in which the children write the character's name. Around the circle they write information about the character which indentifies the character's traits.

To prepare for reading, the teacher usually decides how much text the children will read. She also plans a focus for the discussion after reading depending on their purpose for reading. Transitional readers can read several pages of text, but in this case the teacher wants the children to decide where to stop reading when they think they have discovered information about Fox. Now the children read, stop when they find information about Fox, and fill in a character trait on their strategy sheet. When all the children are finished, the teacher leads a discussion about the traits children have discovered. As they talk, the teacher has children reread portions of the text aloud to support their ideas. During the discussion, the teacher asks for clarifying information and occasionally provides information about what she was thinking while reading.

Next the teacher asks the children to use what they have discovered about Fox to predict a problem that will occur in the story. After children predict and justify their ideas, they read further in the story looking for information about another character, Louise. The cycle of setting a purpose, reading, and discussion is repeated. As the children leave guided reading, the teacher asks them to finish reading the book on their own and to fill in the strategy sheet finding out about both Fox and Louise as they continue reading. They are to bring the book and strategy sheet to guided reading when they next meet. For example, Figure 10.6

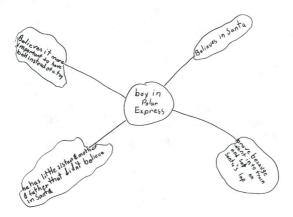

FIGURE 10.6   Character Cluster for *The Polar Express* (Van Allsburg, 1985)

presents a character cluster written by a third grader for the main character, the boy, in *The Polar Express* (Van Allsburg, 1985). This child noticed the boy's altruism (although she did not have the sophisticated vocabulary to label this concept) when she said, "[I]t was more important to have the bell instead of a toy." She also clearly identified the boy as a believer and as brave, two character traits strongly implied in the text. She was able to find two details from the text as support for one character trait (the boy was brave "because he went on the train" and "he sat on Santa's lap").

A Guided Reading Lesson to Expand Vocabulary.   In second grade and beyond, children encounter an increasing number of words in their reading that are not included in their listening vocabularies. They need to learn independent strategies for learning the meanings of these new words. A group of third graders used a **word cluster** during guided reading to practice the strategy of noticing words and inferring their meanings from clues in the text. Figure 10.7 presents a word cluster for the word *polar* constructed by one member of the guided reading group. The teacher introduced the cluster and the children talked about what they knew about the word before reading *The Polar Express* (Van Allsburg, 1985). Then as they read the story, the children added more concepts. Fran's cluster includes "it's a train" and "it's big and black" because she noticed the train on the cover of the book. These ideas reflect her understanding of the story but not the meaning of the word *polar*. After reading the story and discussing how *polar* was used in the story (to describe the polar ice cap and the polar sky), Fran became more aware of the word's meaning. When she spontaneously said, "Hey, polar bear! It's like a *polar bear*. They must live at the North Pole," she finally made the connection between the word *polar* and its referent *North Pole.*

The group discussion surrounding the construction of word clusters (and other strategy sheets) is more important to children's growth as readers than being able to complete a cluster. When we look at the content of Fran's cluster, we are not

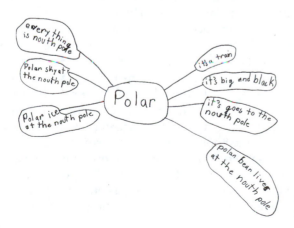

FIGURE 10.7   A Word Cluster for the Word *Polar*

particularly impressed with her understanding of this word. However, her contributions to the discussion of the word's meaning during guided reading were important and helped the other children develop more sophisticated understandings. Effective teachers realize that having children complete strategy sheets is not the goal of instruction. Rather, these sheets are tools for coaching children to be active thinkers while they are reading.

Another way to stimulate children's active thinking about words and their meanings is to construct **word walls for specific books.** As children in a guided reading group read a book together, they can select interesting and important story words to place on a special word wall. After gathering the words on the wall, teachers can help children extend their understandings of these words using a **list, group, and label activity** (Tompkins & McGee, 1993).

A group of third graders reading *Keep the Lights Burning, Abbie* (Roop & Roop, 1985) gathered several vocabulary words from the story into a list and constructed a *Keep the Lights Burning, Abbie* word wall. The word wall included the words *Puffin, medicine, lighthouse, trimmed, wicks, towers, pecked, scraped, waded, henhouse, dangerous, weather, whitecaps, steered, ruffled, Hope, Patience,* and *Charity.* Next, pairs of children selected three to five words from the word wall to form a group. Then they described how the words were alike (the label portion of the activity). They wrote the words on a transparency along with the label for their group of words. Then, using the overhead projector, they shared their group of words and title with the guided reading group. One pair of children grouped the words *scraped, waded, trimmed, pecked,* and *steered* with the title "things you can do." Another pair of children grouped *pecked, ruffled,* and *henhouse* with the title "words related to hens," while a third pair of children gathered *weather, whitecaps,* and *dangerous* with the title "words related to a storm."

Keeping the Other Children Involved in Meaningful Reading.   While the teacher is working with a small group of children in guided reading (or conferring with several children), the other children are occupied mainly with reading. The books they read independently are carefully selected to extend their reading progress (Taberski, 2000). Teachers guide children as they select several books on their independent reading level to place in special book bags for independent reading. Teachers confer with children once or twice a week during which children read aloud a short portion of the text from one of the books they have been reading and talk about the book. From these conferences, teachers monitor that children are reading books that are just right to practice and consolidate reading strategies that they are learning. Children keep track of books they have read by recording the title and author of each book they read in a weekly **reading log.** Children also read books from their guided reading group, sometimes using strategy sheets. They are also expected to respond to some books they read by writing a retelling of a story or listing facts they have learned from an informational book. Children select response activities during conferences with their teacher. However, the goal for transitional readers is to move beyond just reaching a general level of comprehension. Reading narratives does not merely involve finding the meaning—the one, true meaning of a story. Instead, teachers work toward helping children perceive multiple possible meanings (Wolf, Carey, & Mieras, 1996).

Reading and Writing Poetry

Poetry is an important literary genre that all too often is neglected in elementary school. However, teachers have discovered that poetry "not only [is] accessible to primary children, [but] can be *the* genre that excites children and motivates them to read and write" (Duthie & Zimet, 1992, p. 14).

Enjoying Poetry: Developing Fluency

Choral reading is ideal for demonstrating the joy of poetry and providing opportunities to develop reading fluency (Trousdale & Harris, 1993). Poetry is meant to be read aloud again and again. First, teachers read a poem aloud, perhaps displaying the poem on an overhead projector. Children are invited to respond to the poem by discussing interesting words, phrases, and events in the poem. A copy of the poem is distributed to the children, and the teacher rereads the poem again. Children are invited to reread favorite lines or phrases, using different voices, such as loud or soft, fast or slow, for effect. Finally, the teacher guides the children in a choral reading, in which the children read the poem aloud.

Choral reading uses several different reading methods that make it a unique experience (Trousdale & Harris, 1993). One method of choral reading is to use call and response. Here, a leader reads a line or two of the poem and the remainder of the group rereads the line or lines as a response. Another method of choral reading is to use a solo and chorus arrangement. One child or the teacher may read particular lines of the poem and the remainder of the children read other particular lines. This arrangement is good to use with poems with repeating refrains. Another way to arrange choral reading is to use two or more parts. Two groups of children may alternate reading every other line of the poem, or several groups of children may read specific stanzas of the poem, and all the children may read the concluding stanza. A combination of approaches is also effective. A group of children could read the first stanza, two groups of children could read the next stanza, and so on. Choral reading provides for more than enjoyment; it offers meaningful rereading opportunities that extend fluent reading (Dowhower, 1987).

Establishing a poem-a-day routine is another way to create interest in poetry (Durham, 1997). Teachers read at least one poem at either the beginning or the end of the day as a regular and daily routine. Children can be invited to select poems for the day. Teachers can establish a special shelf in the classroom library for poetry books or have a decorated box in which ten to fifteen poetry books are kept. Children can fill out a poetry request form with their name, the poem's title, the book title, and the page number (Durham, 1997). Teachers can use the request forms to select poems for reading aloud. Children may ask to read their own poem for the day. Reading poems daily prepares children for more concentrated study of poems.

Poetic Elements

Writing workshop is an excellent place to begin a poetry unit or to prepare for a **poetry festival** in which children present to their parents or other classrooms of children their favorite poems and poems they have written (Durham, 1997). During minilessons in a poetry-writing workshop, children can learn that not all poems have rhyme, but many do. They can learn effective sound elements, such as repetition, alliteration (repeating beginning sounds), rhyme, and assonance (repeating vowel sounds). They can learn about using invented words, focusing on a single image, and saying common things in uncommon ways. Finally, children can learn about lining, shape, and special uses of punctuation, capitalization, and spaces (Duthie & Zimet, 1992). Together the teacher and children discuss the impact of using the poetic element in the poem. For example, children notice that indentations in the poem's lines make the shape of stair steps in the poem "Descent" (Merriam, 1989, p. 36) and different-length lines and special indenting create the shape of a wiggly snake in "The Serpent's Hiss" (Merriam, 1989, p. 48). A third grader composed the poem "Tree House," making use of line length and indenting to create a tree-shaped poem appropriate to the topic of his poem.

> *Tree house*
> *Just you and me house*
> *Kick up your feet house*
> *Tree house*
> *Free*
> *House*

Poetry and Technology

There are many online resources for teaching poetry (Roberts, 2002). Children enjoy visiting www.poetryteahers.com to read funny poetry, download a readers' theatre of a favorite poem, and even learn how to write poems. This site invites children to submit their poems to a poetry contest. At www.night.net children can listen to poetic songs and play games. At www.gigglepoetry.com children meet Bruce Lansky and can read poems, take a poetry class, and submit their own poems in another contest. An unusual site for writing poetry is http://home.freeuk.net where children can use clicking and dragging to arrange words and compose poems.

Reading and Writing Informational Text

Like poetry, informational text is often neglected in the primary reading and writing program (Duke, 1998), but just as some children find their way into reading and writing through poetry, other children find their way into reading and writing through informational books.

Comprehension of Informational Books

Reading informational books should be part of guided reading, book clubs, or reading workshop. A combination of reading and writing workshop is effective in expanding children's knowledge of the special features of informational text (Duthie, 1996). We recommend that teachers share one or two informational books during each minilesson. The books they select will have one or more special features of informational books such as an index, a glossary, a cut-away drawing, a diagram, or a caption. Teachers may focus on one or two of these features and how the features provide supporting information related to the content of the book. Over time, as teachers read more and more informational books, showing more and more features, children will develop a sophisticated understanding of the variety of ways in which information is presented in them.

During reading workshop conferences or guided reading, teachers guide children's viewing of illustrations and reading of tables of contents, indexes, and text for a variety of purposes. Careful reading of informational text includes making explicit how the information is organized in a text. Some authors use sequence, such as found in how-to books; other authors use narrative; and still others ask and answer questions.

Inquiry Units

Reading and writing informational texts is an important part of content-area learning. Children need to learn how to search for specific information, evaluate whether information is relevant for their topic or question, and integrate and summarize information across several texts (Schmidt et al., 2002). **Inquiry units** involving the study of particular topics in social studies and science, using hands-on experiences, a variety of informational texts, and reading and writing activities, increase children's reading and writing abilities as well as their understanding of scientific and social concepts (Morrow et al., 1997).

Observe and Personalize. During the first phase of inquiry, the observe and personalize phase, children observe objects and events from the natural world. For example, in a unit on birds, children can observe a variety of birds in zoos or museums. They can examine different kinds of bird nests, feathers, and bird bones. They can observe and record behavior at a bird feeder. Observations are extended by browsing through informational books that provide facts and present drawings related to the observations. As children gain more knowledge of birds, they generate questions that they might use for later searches. Teachers gather questions on large charts posted in the room. Questions are added, deleted, and revised as children continue observing in the natural world and in information resources.

Search and Retrieve. In the next phase, search and retrieve, children participate in **idea circles** (Guthrie & McCann, 1996), in which they extend their concept knowledge. They learn and practice locating sources that will provide information on a specific topic or question. For example, children who are studying garden flowers would participate in an initial discussion about flowers. As the children share information, the teacher would write headings related to the different kinds of information that children share. For example, a teacher would write the following headings: height, spread, color, foliage, and fragrance. As a part of the discussion, the teacher would take opportunities to expand children's vocabulary. He might introducing the words *fragrance* and *foliage* as children talk about a flower's *smell* or the different kinds of *flowers* and *leaves* (Wray & Lewis, 1996, p. 64). Later these headings would be used in an activity in which children search for and select information about flowers from informational texts.

Then the teacher and children would gather a variety of resource books, including children's informational books, adult informational books, and pamphlets about gardening. The teacher would prepare a **recording grid** with the headings he had gathered during the class discussion. Over several days, each child would fill in the recording grid with information about one or two flowers of their choice. To begin the work, the class would brainstorm a list of flowers, which the teacher would record on a chart. Then the teacher would demonstrate searching through informational texts to find information about a particular flower. He would show the children how to find the name of the flower in an index or table of contents.

Comprehend, Integrate, and Communicate.   In the final phase, comprehend and integrate, children work on more complex questions, often questions they generate for themselves. For example, third graders were answering the questions, "What are the body parts of your bird, and how do these body parts help this bird to survive?" (Guthrie et al., 1996, p. 326). Children selected birds of choice, located information about body parts, and wrote explanations for how the body parts allowed the bird to adapt to its environment through breeding, feeding, and protecting itself. Here, children needed to read carefully in order to detect critical information relevant to the question, integrate information across different texts, and find meanings of specialized vocabulary they were encountering. Children capitalized on knowing how to read graphs, diagrams, and other illustrations. They learned how to break up the question into parts, gather information, and then put the parts back together. In the final phase, children communicated their information in reports, group-authored books, charts, and informational stories.

Writing Informational Texts

Minilessons in writing workshop can focus on the special informational book features. However, there are a variety of other kinds of informational writing opportunities that extend children's learning including science learning logs, math journals, and diaries of people in history.

Teachers can utilize the special features of computer word-processing and graphics programs to help children compose unique kinds of text. For example, a third grade teacher combined learning about computer graphics with newspaper writing. Children read and analyzed newspapers to discover their special features.

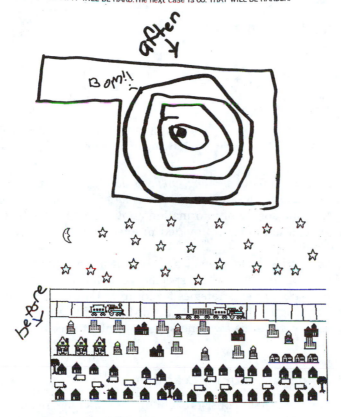

FIGURE 10.8   A Page from Two Children's Newspapers about the Oklahoma City Bombing

At the same time, they explored a graphics and word-processing program on the computer. Figure 10.8 presents a page of two children's newspapers about the Oklahoma City bombing. In their multimedia composition they used a drawing to create the bomb, graphics to create a picture, and word processing to write their text.

Content-Specific Vocabulary

Informational texts have much **content-specific vocabulary,** words that have specific scientific meanings and that do not appear in everyday conversation (Leu & Kinzer, 1999). Informational books intentionally introduce scientific terms which are used to explain phenomena. For example, *Bald Eagle* (Morrison, 1998) provides

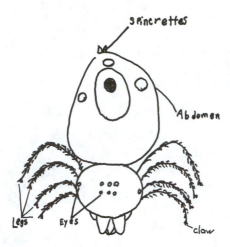

FIGURE 10.9   A Third Grader's Labeled Drawing of a Spider

definitions and illustrations of *nestling, prenatal down, natal down, egg tooth, eye shield, fledgling, thermal soaring, kettle, eyrie,* and *embryo.* Most informational books provide more than one source of information about content-specific vocabulary. Definitions are embedded in text, provided in glossaries, and illustrated in diagrams and drawings.

Teachers can demonstrate strategies such as using multiple sources to find and cross-check definitions of content-specific vocabulary. Children can be encouraged to demonstrate other strategies for locating information about content-specific vocabulary. Figure 10.9 presents a third grader's labeled drawing of a spider, which demonstrates his awareness of the content-specific words *abdomen* and *spinnerets.*

Internet Workshop and Inquiry Learning

Internet workshop (Leu, 2002) consists of children's searching, reading, and using information from the Internet around a topic of inquiry. It is a natural partner with reading and writing across the curriculum as a part of inquiry units. The purpose of the Internet workshop is simultaneously to help children learn more about how to use the Internet and develop the special reading strategies needed for this kind of text as well as to help them learn to evaluate and integrate Internet information with other sources of information. Internet workshop includes five steps:

1. Teachers locate a site on the Internet with content related to a unit of inquiry
2. They design an activity to support children's search through the site to find specific information (including finding links to other sites)
3. They help children evaluate and critique the information they find at the site using what they know about who authored the site
4. Children complete the activity
5. Children share the results of their activity and discuss strategies they used to search, read, evaluate, and use the information they found

There are hundreds of excellent sites that can be used for Internet workshop including sites designed specifically for children. For example, students can learn more about New York City by visiting www.sdcoe.k12.ca.us/score/abuela where several links are posted for finding information about the Statue of Liberty. They can visit www.acs.ucalgary.ca/dkbrown/authors.html to find a list of authors' web sites they can visit. Jan Brett's web site has a wealth of information about her life, her books, and her activities as well as fun activities for children to download (Karchmer, 2000). Another enjoyable children's literature web site is www.sags. k12.il.us.library/Caldecott_Clues.htm. Here clues about Caldecott books are posted weekly and children are invited to e-mail in their guesses of the books' titles. Another site with extensive information is www.enchantedlearning.com/ subjects. At this site children can explore habitats and learn facts about animals living in those habitats. The text at this site is very engaging and provides an excellent model for children's own informational writing. Another excellent site is www. kids-learn.org/stellaluna/project.htm where children are invited to search for information about bats. A similar site for finding facts about bats and their homes is http://members.aol.com/bats4kids/homes.htm.

Learning Conventions

There are a variety of written language conventions that second and third graders are expected to know. They learn about punctuation, capitalization, and grammar; and they develop more sophisticated strategies for decoding and spelling unfamiliar words. Children practice handwriting, study spelling patterns, and acquire an ever larger vocabulary of words they spell conventionally. We have already described teaching capitalization, punctuation, grammar, and handwriting as part of the writing process. This is because the most powerful way to teach conventions is at the point of need. The time to teach how to use commas is when children need to use commas in their writing.

Word Study

Word study continues to be an important component of the reading and writing program in second and third grade. Word study should develop children's concepts about the orthographic structures of words and help them to use those structures to decode and spell multisyllabic words. Children in second and third grade are generally at a variety of levels of decoding and spelling understanding (Bear, Invernizzi, Templeton, & Johnston, 2000). Therefore, word study activities should be geared to those levels of understanding.

Most second and third grade spellers benefit from activities focusing on the variety of long-vowel and other vowel spellings. Knowing how to change word spellings when adding suffixes is also a critical skill acquired at this time. For example, children learn that words having a CVC pattern require doubling the final consonant before adding the suffix, as with *hop* and *hopping.* Also important is learning to differentiate the appropriate spellings of homophones and homo-graphs. **Homophones** are words that sound alike but are not spelled alike, as in *bear* and *bare*. **Homographs** are words that are spelled alike but do not sound alike, such in the words *bow* (weapon used to shoot arrows) and *bow* (to bend from the waist). Again **word sorts** are appropriate. For example, children can sort words that take *s* or *es* or *ies* as their plural spellings (Fresch & Wheaton, 1997). Other activities include **word hunts,** in which children search for words with specific pat-terns in books, magazines, and newspapers.

A critical part of word study is learning strategies for decoding multisyllabic words, which are increasingly encountered in second and third grade reading.

One way to help children develop an intuitive sense of syllables and how to break words apart is to use the **making big words** approach (Cunningham & Hall, 1994). Making big words begins with a big word's letters (for example, the letters *p i c k p o c k e t s*, p. 83). Teachers help children make one syllable words that high-light a variety of familiar word parts such as the words *pet*, **sit**, *tick*, and *sock*. Then children build multisyllable words again focusing on the use of multiple familiar word parts in these words including *picket, pocket*, and *cockpit*. Finally, they build *pickpockets*. Throughout the activity, the teacher and children discuss the words' meanings. Teachers can keep a list of familiar word parts (such as *ick, ock, et,* and *it*) that can be used to decode and spell big words on a spelling **word-part word wall.**

Spelling Programs

Spelling is an important part of the literacy program beyond first grade. Children need to learn to spell many words to use in their writing, to become aware of alter-native spelling patterns, and to develop strategies for spelling unknown words (Wilde, 1992). We describe here a spelling program for second and third grades that has four features:

1. A large number of words that children are expected to learn to spell come from the children's needs, for example, from their own writing and reading, from current and upcoming content-area units, and from current events.
2. There is a balance between individualization and whole-class work. Students work with spelling lists that include personal words, which only they are expected to learn, and words that the whole class is expected to learn.
3. There is a balance between words that follow generalizations (e.g., *sight* words) and high-frequency words that do not follow generalizations (e.g., *said*). The teacher may have a master list of high-frequency words and gener-alizations (see Bear et al., 2000).
4. Children are involved in identifying words to learn and in discovering spelling generalizations or rules.

With these features in mind, we suggest a program using a three- or four-week spelling cycle. At the start of each spelling cycle, the teacher and the children generate a **word pool** of seventy to eighty words from content units, high-frequency words, or words that follow spelling patterns. Children keep their own lists of words.

In some activities, the whole class works with words from the word pool for understanding, not for spelling. For example, children may categorize the words or make word clusters, resulting in adding related words to the word pool. In other activities, the class works together to discover spelling rules or devices to help remember spellings. Children may divide the pool into words that follow spelling generalizations, words that do not follow spelling generalizations (most high-frequency words do not), proper nouns, long words, and short words. Word groupings should highlight features of the words that will aid in learning to spell them.

Small groups of children choose fifteen to twenty words from the word pool to create a list of words to study and learn to spell for the first week. Each child is expected to add one or two personal challenge words to the group list that are unique to that child.

The children learn the words from their group's list. They test each other on Friday. Then groups generate new lists for the next week, still using the pool of seventy to eighty words that began the unit. The cycle continues through several weeks. Three or four weeks seem long enough to make good use of the original pool of words, but not so long that it gets boring.

Chapter Summary

Second grade and third grade are an exciting time for children and their teachers. The great strides that students make as they become able to move beyond transitional reading present teachers with great challenges, opportunities, and satisfactions.

In writing workshop, children use five writing processes: prewriting, drafting, revising, editing, and sharing. Teachers model a variety of writing strategies for each of these processes in minilessons and provide guided practice in conference groups. Similarly, teachers demonstrate reading strategies in minilessons during reading workshop. Children read extensively and respond to books they have read.

The book club and guided reading approaches involve small groups of children reading and discussing a book together. Teachers extend children's understanding of narratives by inviting retellings and helping children discover literary elements by using activities such as constructing character clusters. They extend children's vocabulary knowledge with activities such as list, group, and label. Choral reading allows children to enjoy poetry and provides opportunities for the rereading that is so important for comprehension and fluency development. Teachers extend children's understanding of poems in writer's workshop by calling attention to poetic elements.

Children read and write informational texts in content units in science and social studies. They learn organizational patterns found in expository text. As part of idea circles, children locate, retrieve, and comprehend informational text. They pay particular attention to the content-specific vocabulary they encounter in informational books and learn strategies for independent vocabulary learning. Word study continues in second grade and beyond, extending children's abilities to spell and decode multisyllabic words. A program for learning the spellings of words is also critical.

Applying the Information

We suggest two activities for applying the information. Make a list of the seven characteristics of a literacy-rich classroom presented in Chapter 6. Then reread this chapter to locate one activity from those presented that is consistent with each of these characteristics. Discuss your examples with a classmate.

Next, make a list of all the literacy learning activities described in this chapter. For each of these activities, describe what children learn about written language meanings, forms, meaning-form links, or functions.

Going Beyond the Text

Visit a second or third grade classroom and observe several literacy activities. Write a list of all the print and literacy materials in the classroom. Take note of the classroom layout and the interactions among the children and between the children and the teacher during literacy activities. Talk with the teacher about his or her philosophy of literacy instruction. Compare these materials, activities, and philosophies with those presented in this chapter.

REFERENCES

Almasi, J. (1995). The nature of fourth graders' sociocognitive conflicts in peer-led and teacher-led discussions of literature. *Reading Research Quarterly, 30,* 314–351.

Atwell, N. (1987). *In the middle.* Portsmouth, NH: Heinemann.

Barone, D. (1990). The written responses of young children: Beyond comprehension to story understanding. *The New Advocate, 3,* 49–56.

Bear, D., Invernizzi, M., Templeton, S., & Johnston, F. (2000). *Words their way* (2nd ed.). Saddle River, NJ: Prentice Hall.

Brabham, E., & Villaume, S. (2002). Leveled texts: The good and the bad news. *The Reading Teacher, 55,* 438–441.

Calkins, L. M. (1986). *The art of teaching writing.* Portsmouth, NH: Heinemann.

Commeyras, M., & Sumner, G. (1995). *Questions children want to discuss about literature: What teach-ers and students learned in a second grade class-room* (NRRC Reading Research Rep. No. 47). Athens, GA: University of Georgia and University of Maryland, National Reading Research Center.

Cunningham, P., & Hall, D. (1994). *Making big words.* Torrance, CA: Good Apple.

Dowhower, S. (1987). Effects of repeated reading on second grade trasitional readers' fluency and comprehension. *Reading Research Quarterly, 22,* 397–414.

Dowhower, S. (1999). Supporting a strategic stance in the classroom: A comprehension framework for helping teachers help students to be strategic. *The Reading Teacher, 52,* 672–688.

Duke, N. (1998, December). 3.6 minutes per day: The scarcity of informational texts in first grade. Paper presented at the annual meeting of the National Reading Conference, Austin, TX.

Durham, J. (1997). On time and poetry. *The Reading Teacher, 51,* 76–79.

Duthie, C. (1996). *True stories: Nonfiction literacy in the primary classroom.* York, ME: Stenhouse.

Duthie, C., & Zimet, E. (1992). "Poetry is like directions for your imagination!" *The Reading Teacher, 46,* 14–24.

Fawson, P., & Reutzel, D. (2000). But I only have a basal: Implementing guided reading in the early grades. *The Reading Teacher, 54,* 84–97.

Fountas, I., & Pinnell, C. (1996). *Guided reading: Good first teaching for all children.* Portsmouth, NH: Heinemann.

Frank, C., Dixon, C., & Brandts, L. (2001). Bears, trolls, and pagemasters: Learning about learners in book clubs. *The Reading Teacher, 54,* 448–462.

Fresch, M., & Wheaton, A. (1997). Sort, search, and discover: Spelling in the child-centered classroom. *The Reading Teacher, 51,* 20–31.

Gambrell, L., Pfeiffer, W., & Wilson, R. (1985). The effects of retelling upon reading comprehension and recall of text information. *Journal of Educational Research, 78,* 216–220.

George, J. (1995). *There's an owl in the shower.* New York: HarperCollins.

Goatley, V. J., Brock, C. H., & Raphael, T. E. (1995). Diverse learners participating in regular education "Book Clubs." *Reading Research Quarterly, 30,* 352–380.

Guthrie, J., & McCann, N. (1996). Idea circles: Peer collaborations for conceptual learning. In L. Gambrell & J. Almasi (Eds.), *Lively discussions! Fostering engaged reading* (pp. 87–105). Newark, DE: International Reading Association.

Guthrie, J., Van Meter, P., McCann, A., Wigfield, A., Bennett, L., Poundstone, C., Rice, M., Faibisch, F., Hunt, B., & Mitchell, A. (1996). Growth of literacy engagement: Changes in motivations and strategies during concept oriented reading instruction. *Reading Research Quarterly, 31,* 306–332.

Hoyt, L. (1992). Many ways of knowing: Using drama, oral interactions, and the visual arts to enhance reading comprehension. *The Reading Teacher, 45,* 580–584.

Karchmer, R. (2000). Using the Internet and children's literature to support interdisciplinary instruction. *The Reading Teacher, 54,* 100–104.

Kelly, P. R., & Farnan, N. (1991). Promoting critical thinking through response logs: A reader-response approach with fourth graders. In J. Zutell & S. McCormick (Eds.), *Learner factors/teacher factors: Issues in literacy research and instruction* (pp. 227–284). Chicago: The National Reading Conference.

Leu, D. (2002). Internet workshop: Making time for literacy. *The Reading Teacher, 55,* 466–472.

Leu, D., & Kinzer, C. (1999). *Effective literacy instruction* (4th Ed.). Columbus, OH: Merrill.

Marshall, E. (1982). *Fox and his friends.* New York: Scholastic.

McGee, L. (1995). Talking about books with young children. In N. Roser & M. Martinez (Eds.), *Book talk and beyond* (pp. 105–115). Newark, DE: International Reading Association.

Merriam, E. (1989). *Chortles.* New York: Morrow.

Miller, D. (2002). *Reading with meaning: Teaching comprehension in the primary grades.* Portland, ME: Stenhouse.

Morrison, G. (1998). *Bald eagle.* Boston: Houghton Mifflin.

Morrow, L., Pressley, M., Smith, J., & Smith, M. (1997). The effect of a literature-based program integrated into literacy and science instruction with children from diverse backgrounds. *Reading Research Quarterly, 32,* 54–76.

Pearson, P., & Gallaher, M. (1983). The instruction of reading comprehension. *Contemporary Educational Psychology, 8,* 317–345.

Pressley, M., & Block, C. (2002). Comprehension instruction: Research-based best practices. New York: Guilford.

Raphael, T., & McMahon, S. (1994). Book club: An alternative framework for reading instruction. *The Reading Teacher, 48,* 102–116.

Roberts, S. (2002). Taking a technological path to poetry prewriting. *The Reading Teacher, 55,* 678–687.

Roop, P., & Roop, C. (1985). *Keep the lights burning, Abbie.* Minneapolis: Carolrhoda.

Scharer, P. (1996). "Are we supposed to be asking questions?": Moving from teacher-directed to student-directed book discussions. In D. Leu, C. Kinzer, & K. Hinchman (Eds.), *Literacies for the 21st century: Research and practice* (pp. 420–429). Chicago: National Reading Conference.

Schmidt, P., Gillen, S., Zollo, T., & Stone, R. (2002). Literacy learning and scientific inquiry: Children respond. *The Reading Teacher, 55,* 534–548.

Shanahan, T., & Shanahan, S. (1997). Character perspective charting: Helping children to develop a more complete conception of a story. *The Reading Teacher, 50,* 668–677.

Short, K., & Pierce, K. (Eds.). (1998). *Talking about books: Creating literate communities.* Portsmouth, NH: Heinemann.

Sinatra, G., Brown, K., & Reynolds, R. (2002). Implications of cognitive resource allocation for comprehension strategies instruction. In C. Block & M. Pressley (Eds.), *Comprehension instruction: Research-based best practices.* New York: Guilford.

Sipe, L. (2002). Talking back and taking over: Young children's expressive engagement during storybook read-alouds. *The Reading Teacher, 55,* 476–483.

Stahl, S., & Kuhn, M. (2002). Making it sound like language: Developing fluency. *The Reading Teacher, 55,* 582–584.

Steptoe, J. (1987). *Mufaro's beautiful daughters.* Boston: Houghton Mifflin.

Taberski, S. (2000). *On solid ground: Strategies for teaching reading K–3.* Portsmouth, NH: Heinemann.

Temple, C. (1991). Seven readings of a folktale: Literary theory in the classroom. *The New Advocate, 4,* 25–35.

Tompkins, G. (2003). *Literacy for the 21st century* (3rd ed.). Columbus, OH: Merrill.

Tompkins, G., & McGee, L. (1993). *Teaching reading with literature: From case studies to action plans.* Columbus, OH: Merrill.

Trousdale, A., & Harris, V. (1993). Missing links in literary response: Group interpretation of literature. *Children's Literature in Education, 24,* 195–207.

Van Allsburg, C. (1985). *The polar express.* Boston: Houghton Mifflin.

Villaume, S., Wordon, T., Williams, S., Hopkins, L., & Rosenblatt, C. (1994). Five teachers in search of a discussion. *The Reading Teacher, 47,* 480–487.

Vogt, M. (1996). Creating a response-centered curriculum with literature discussion groups. In L. Gambrell & J. Almasi (Eds.), *Lively discussions!: Fostering engaged reading* (pp. 181–193). Newark, DE: International Reading Association.

Wells, G., & Chang-Wells, G. L. (1992). *Constructing knowledge together: Classrooms as centers of inquiry and literacy.* Portsmouth, NH: Heinemann.

Wilde, S. (1992). *You kan red this! Spelling and punctuation for whole language classrooms, K–6.* Portsmouth, NH: Heinemann.

Wisniewski, D. (1996). *Golem.* New York: Clarion.

Wolf, S. A. (1993). What's in a name? Labels and literacy in readers' theatre. *The Reading Teacher, 46,* 540–545.

Wolf, S., Carey, A., & Mieras, E. (1996). "What is this literachurch stuff anyway?" Preservice teachers' growth in understanding children's literary response. *Reading Research Quarterly, 31,* 130–157.

Worthy, J., & Prater, K. (2002). "I thought about it all night": Readers' Theatre for reading fluency and motivation. *The Reading Teacher, 56,* 294–297.

Wray, D., & Lewis, M. (1996). "But bonsai trees don't grow in baskets": Young children's talk during authentic inquiries. In L. Gambrell & J. Almasi (Eds.), *Lively discussions! Fostering engaged reading* (pp. 63–72). Newark, DE: International Reading Association.

Young, T., & Vardell, S. (1993). Weaving readers' theatre and nonfiction into the curriculum. *The Reading Teacher, 46,* 396–406.

Zelinsky, P. O. (1986). *Rumpelstiltskin.* New York: Dutton.

11 Diverse Learners

KEY CONCEPTS

at-risk learners
utterance length
utterance complexity
vocabulary variety
decontextualized language
phonemic awareness
name reading and writing
alphabet letter naming

concepts of print
phonological awareness
story retelling
socioeconomic status (SES)
minority status
limited proficiency with
    English
knowing how to "do school"

preventative early literacy
    instruction
facilitative early literacy
    instruction
Reading Recovery
children with special needs
individualized educational
    plan (IEP)

repeated reading
diverse cultural backgrounds
ethnicity
social class
cultural discontinuity
culturally responsive
    instruction
participation structures

constructivist models of
    instruction
scaffolding
balance of rights
diverse language
    backgrounds
mainstream dialect
nonmainstream dialects

English language learners
additive approaches
subtractive approaches
shared language
character clues
extended discourse
classroom
    conversations

Learners at Risk

Teachers are concerned with supporting all children's literacy growth, and most children do succeed in becoming reflective, motivated readers and writers with thoughtful instruction. That is, all children are unique and they approach literacy tasks with their own special styles and unique knowledge. Yet most children develop a range of expected knowledge within a reasonable time frame when they are given adequate opportunities and instruction. For young children, this time frame and range of expected knowledge is wide and allows for much individual variation. However, teachers also recognize that some children seem to struggle to acquire literacy even within literacy-rich classrooms and with a wide variety of instructional experiences. We call these children **at-risk learners.** At-risk learners need teachers who are especially observant and adept at modifying instructional techniques. Effective teachers are aware of the variety of special literacy-intervention programs that have been successfully used to accelerate the literacy learning of at-risk learners.

Characteristics That Put Children at Risk

Ideally, teachers would know ahead of time which children are most likely to experience difficulty learning to read and write so that they could provide targeted instruction. Unfortunately, that is not always possible. Still, with careful attention to characteristics that put children at risk of failure, we can at least reduce the likelihood of such failure for a large number of children. Visual impairments, hearing impairments, severe cognitive impairments, and extreme developmental delays are likely to result in low levels of reading and writing achievement. These risk factors are usually identified and addressed by specialists.

What early childhood and primary grade teachers can address are risk factors related to language development and to early literacy experiences. That is, classroom teachers can assess children's language development and the quality of their early reading and writing experiences, and they can provide instruction that responds to identified needs. Fortunately, such instruction is usually the same sort of instruction provided for all children, the sort we have described in this book. It is targeted, child-centered, developmentally appropriate instruction about meaning making, forms, meaning-form links, and functions of written language. It is instruction that serves everyday, real-life purposes and occurs in everyday, real-life contexts.

The difference when risk of failure is present—and almost all teachers will have at least some students at risk—is that the children at the center of child-centered instruction have been identified as having gaps in their language development or early literacy experiences. Targeted instruction for these children merely means that as soon as they are found to have language development and literacy experience risk factors, their teachers make doubly sure that they receive the support for language development and the experiences with print that children without such risk factors have been receiving all along at home and in school from interactions with print, parents, peers, and teachers (McGee & Richgels, 2003).

Risk Factors Related to Language Development.   Normal language development is a complex and multifaceted process (see Chapter 1), and there is considerable variation in how individual children experience that development. Still, before they are four years old, most children acquire competence with sounds of their language (phonology). They learn the meanings of and use in appropriate ways thousands of words (semantics). They master the sentence structures of their language; they can make and understand statements, commands, questions, and negatives with ease (syntax). They learn how to put all this knowledge to use to accomplish important goals in their daily lives (pragmatics).

Within the wide range of normal language development, some specific accomplishments serve as guides. Steady preschool growth in **utterance length, utterance complexity,** and **vocabulary variety** prepare children for successful literacy learning; lack of accomplishment in those areas makes literacy success difficult (Walker et al., 1994; Scarborough, 1991). Utterance length is how many morphemes a child uses, on average, in a turn at talking. Utterance complexity is how many and what kinds of phrases and clauses a child uses to make a number of different kinds of sentences. Vocabulary variety is the number of different words, especially rare words, that a child understands and uses (Dickinson & Sprague, 2001).

Two special abilities with language are involved in early reading and writing, and so lacking them almost always puts children at risk of failing to learn to read and write. One is the ability to use language without the support of immediate context. Children must be able to use **decontextualized language,** as when they talk about things not in the present time or place, if they are to be able to read text written by a non-present author where the words alone provide the only clues to the author's intended message (Dickinson & Smith, 1994). Similarly, they must be able to create texts that future, non-present readers will be able to understand with only the texts to go by. The second special language ability is being able consciously to recognize phonemes and manipulate them (**phonemic awareness**). When they are beginning to read and write in an alphabetic language such as English, children must be able to match sounds with letters. This entails being able to focus on individual phonemes in the stream of speech, a special consciousness that is required for literacy learning but is not required for speaking or for understanding speech (Adams, 1990; National Reading Panel, 2000; Snow, Burns, & Griffin, 1998).

Risk Factors Related to Early Literacy Experiences. High-quality literacy experiences at home and in preschool—experiences like those we have described in this book—increase the likelihood of children's success at learning to read and write (Purcell-Gates, 1996). They give children example, opportunity, motivation, materials, means, and feedback necessary for learning what written language is all about, how it works, and what it can do for them. If teachers can determine what sorts of previous literacy experiences children have had and, especially, what they have lacked, then the teachers can ensure that they make adjustments for those needs. Fortunately, all children can benefit from the literacy activities teachers might plan as compensation for children who lack early reading and writing experiences. Still, it is important for teachers to know which children are at risk so that the teachers can closely monitor those children's responses to the planned compensatory activities.

We will describe in Chapter 12 how teachers can assess children's early literacy knowledge to determine who have and who lack important early literacy experiences and how teachers can monitor children's response to subsequent instruction. For now, we point out that merely asking parents about their children's early experiences usually does not produce sufficiently reliable information (Senechal et al., 1998). So teachers must assess children's knowledge in a few significant areas, where knowledge is an indicator that a child has had the associated experience and lack of knowledge is an indicator that the child has not had the experience. Those areas are **reading and writing of** the child's own **name** (Bloodgood, 1999), as an indication of experience handling writing instruments and focusing on some alphabet letter forms and on the meaningfulness of print; **naming of some alphabet letters** (Hiebert, 1981), as an indication of experience focusing on written language forms at the letter level; **concepts of print** (Clay, 1985; Yaden et al., 2000), as an indication of book handling experience; **phonological awareness** (Lonigan et al., 1998), as an indication of experience with rhymes and other play with sounds; and **story retelling** (Morrow, 1985), as an indication of experience listening to and talking about storybooks.

Risk Factors Related to Family and Community. Three family and community related risk factors that often overlap and interact are **socioeconomic status (SES), minority status,** and **limited proficiency with English.** Children from families with high and middle SES are usually more successful at learning to read and write than children from families with low SES (Lonigan et al., 1998). Poverty is among the factors most predictive of poor literacy achievement (Snow, Burns, & Griffin, 1998). Socioeconomic status, however, is not simply a family factor. Schools and neighborhoods whose populations are mostly low SES are associated with children's low literacy achievement. This may be due to a number of related factors which may include poor literacy resources, such as little publicly displayed print; few public spaces for reading; and poorly provided public libraries in low SES neighborhoods (Neuman et al., 2001). They also may include poor quality school libraries, low numbers of books in classrooms, and high numbers of fellow students who are also at risk in low SES schools. The significance of this last factor is that children from low SES families attending schools with high percentages of children from high and middle SES families are higher literacy achievers than children from low SES families who attend low SES schools.

Minority status is another factor related to risk for failure at learning to read and write. In particular, literacy achievement of non-white children is lower than that of white children (National Center for Educational Statistics, 1996).

Limited English proficiency is another risk factor; Spanish speakers, the largest group of English language learners, have low reading achievement. However, this factor, like SES and minority status, is not simple. Generally, Spanish speaking children's reading scores are low even when they are taught and assessed in Spanish and when their families have high motivation for their succeeding (Goldenberg & Gallimore, 1991). All three of these factors compound: high percentages of children who are non-English speaking are also non-white and living in poverty (McGee & Richgels, 2003).

Mismatch with School Culture as a Risk Factor. An easily overlooked risk factor is a child's having different dispositions and ways of interacting with others than are expected in school, ways that interfere with a successful transition from home life to classroom life. Schools are social settings with their own special ways for students to enter the group and be accepted and their spoken and unspoken rules about interacting with classmates and teachers. Knowing these ways and rules is sometimes referred to as **knowing how to "do school."** When some children do not know how to "do school" because their home ways are in conflict with these school ways (Comber, 2000; Gee, 1996), teachers may mistakenly perceive them as having behavior problems or low levels of literacy knowledge (McMillon & Edwards, 2000). Unless the mismatch between home and school ways is alleviated, this perception can become a self-fulfilling prophecy.

This is not the only misunderstanding to adversely affect children's prospects for success at learning to read and write. Unfortunately, the very use of the term *risk factor* implies negative consequences for characteristics that are not by themselves causes of failure. It is true that a preventative efficiency might be attained by identifying groups in which there are children who are more likely to need help than children in other groups. However, we risk harming those very children if their group membership blinds us to the benefits of the rich cultural capital and specialized funds of knowledge they bring to diverse classrooms (Neuman et al., 2001) or if it lulls us into providing fewer opportunities for their active problem-solving (McGee & Richgels, 2003).

Teachers can avoid shortchanging children considered at risk for low literacy achievement if their teaching is guided by the principle that good literacy practices are good literacy practices—regardless of the type of student. **Preventative early**

literacy instruction, that is, early literacy instruction intended to prevent the failure that some children seem at risk of experiencing, is not qualitatively different from **facilitative early literacy instruction,** that is, early literacy instruction intended to support children who seem already on the way to literacy success. Both are the sort of literacy instruction we describe throughout this book. It is targeted instruction because it is based on what teachers know about students' current and developing understandings of meaning making, forms, meaning-form links, and functions of written language. It is designed keeping in mind what children show that they can do with appropriate coaching, and it is predicated on teachers' high expectations for all of their students.

Observation is the basis for teachers' decision making about how to support all children's literacy development (Dahl et al., 2001). At-risk learners, however, are more likely than other children to experience school failure if their teachers do not use observations to plan instruction targeted at children's demonstrated needs. Teachers who support at-risk learners are sensitive to children's responses to instructional settings and techniques. They make hypotheses about the difficulties that children experience and plan modifications in their instruction to overcome these difficulties. They are patient and understanding of children's unwillingness to take risks and fear of failure (Allen & Carr, 1989). They are watchful for small signs of success and help children celebrate their new accomplishments.

Teachers who are aware of intervention programs may be able to adapt some of those programs' procedures to meet the observed needs of at-risk learners in the regular classroom. The best-known program is **Reading Recovery,** designed by Marie Clay in New Zealand (Clay, 1985) and implemented widely in the United States. Reading Recovery materials are organized from easier to more difficult according to repetition and language patterns. Easier texts have fewer words, more repetition, and spoken language patterns. More difficult texts have more words, less repetition, and literary language (Peterson, 1991). Children are taught to use several reading strategies, including using the meaning (does that make sense?), language patterns (does that sound right?), and orthographics (do you expect to see that letter?). Thirty-minute daily lessons have five components: reading familiar stories, taking a running record, working with letters, writing a message or story, and reading a new book (Pinnell, Fried, & Estice, 1990). Reading Recovery has survived a good deal of controversy (e.g., Barnes, 1996–1997a, 1996–1997b; Browne et al., 1996–1997) and even has inspired change in more traditional reading remediation programs (Spiegel, 1995).

At-Risk Revisited

Our definition of at-risk learners focuses on children who have difficulties learning in a literacy-rich classroom with many opportunities to read and write. Other definitions of at-risk learners include children from backgrounds with historically high drop-out rates and low achievement levels: children with special needs, children from low socioeconomic or minority backgrounds, and English language learners.

Many children who have special needs, have diverse cultural backgrounds, and speak English as a second language are at-risk learners. Of course, not all of these children are at-risk learners, but there are many reasons to give special attention to these diverse learners. The remainder of this chapter describes issues related to supporting the literacy learning of children with special needs, from diverse cultural backgrounds, and from diverse language backgrounds.

Special-Needs Learners

Children with special needs include children with challenging social and emotional behaviors, pronounced differences in learning styles or rates, or deficits in hearing, vision, or mobility (Truax & Kretschmer, 1993). Despite being singled out as having special learning difficulties, most special-needs children develop literacy knowledge in patterns that are similar to those found in all children's literacy understandings. For example, one researcher examined the literacy development of young children who were prenatally exposed to the drug crack or cocaine (Barone, 1993). The children were asked to reread a favorite storybook, write a story, and spell words once a month over a year. During this time, the children's emergent readings became more advanced and their writing evidenced more sophisticated concepts about written language. In a similar study, profoundly deaf preschoolers with delayed receptive language were found to have understandings of written language that were developmentally appropriate (Williams, 1994).

Therefore, we could conclude that the most effective way to support special-needs children's literacy learning is similar to the way in which we support all children's learning. Many special education professionals recommend the use of holistic, integrated approaches to reading and writing instruction similar to the activities and approaches proposed in the preceding chapters (Cousin, Weekley, & Gerard, 1993; Truax & Kretschmer, 1993).

Supporting Special-Needs Children's Literacy

Many educators argue that *all children* acquire literacy when they pursue topics of personal interest, interact with others who share similar interests, and make connections between known and new information. Of course, children with special needs "may vary from their age peers, making connections in their own time and in their own ways; but the steps in the learning process" are similar (Truax & Kretschmer, 1993, pp. 593–594). Effective teachers carefully observe children, including special-needs children, and make adjustments in activities and instruction to meet their needs. Adapting instruction to serve special-needs learners often means careful observation of children as they participate in reading and writing activities in order to make modifications that will allow all learners to take small risks and reap large rewards (Salvage & Brazee, 1991).

The early childhood classroom is an especially supportive environment for young children with developmental or learning differences. Here, children select activities that promote growth in all areas and levels of development. Because teachers spend less time in whole-group instruction and more time with small groups and individual children, accommodating instruction for the special-needs child is usually not difficult.

Children with developmental or learning differences in elementary school are placed in regular classrooms when special education teachers feel they can benefit from instruction and activities planned for non-special-needs children. With some adjustments, children with special needs can benefit from instruction along with other children in the regular classroom.

Figure 11.1 shows the writing of a mainstreamed autistic child. His teacher met with him while his classmates were at the computer lab. The writing processes that produced this piece were no different from what other students would use. The difference was the amount of one-on-one coaching the teacher needed to provide. She helped the student to compose his idea and listen for sounds in the words. When he had finished writing, she reread the piece and showed him all the sounds he had captured. The product looks no different from what we expect of most first graders.

All special-needs children from the age of three who have identified developmental or learning differences have an **individualized educational plan (IEP)** developed by a team of specialists and the child's parents. Teachers should ask for a copy of the plan and quickly become familiar with it so that they can prepare activities to help the child achieve the goals outlined in the IEP.

Modifying Instruction for Children with Developmental Delays. One of the most effective techniques for supporting the literacy learning of children with developmental delays is to provide instruction that is compatible with the child's developmental level, rather than with the child's age. A second effective technique is to provide social experiences that involve interacting with other children on similar social developmental levels, rather than with children of similar ages. Many of the techniques that we have described for younger novice readers and writers or experimenters with reading and writing are appropriate for older children with developmental delays.

FIGURE 11.1 Interactive Writing of "I Had Chicken Fingers for Lunch."

More formal techniques for teaching children with developmental delays to read and write are similar to techniques that support all children's learning to read and write (Dixon, 1987; Sindelar, 1987). Special educators suggest that if children are to become effective readers, they need to read whole texts (not isolated words); however, children with developmental delays may need more practice and may take a longer time than other children. There are several ways for teachers to help children read whole texts and give them the extra practice they need to become good readers. Teachers can read stories first as children follow the text. The method of **repeated reading** provides practice with whole texts (Dowhower, 1989; O'Shea & O'Shea, 1987). In this method, children repeatedly read stories (or parts of stories) that are about fifty or one hundred words in length until they can read the selection with only three to six errors. Children begin the repeated readings only when they understand the story.

Modifying Instruction for Children with Emotional, Learning, and Language Disabilities.   The writing process is an effective approach in helping emotionally and learning-disabled children successfully communicate their feelings (D'Alessandro, 1987). Daily writing encourages children by implying that they have something meaningful to communicate. A process approach to writing deemphasizes spelling and mechanics, which can be significant stumbling blocks for special-needs children. By focusing on ideas, the writing process supports these children's self-esteem.

As the children brainstorm ideas, teachers can record their ideas on a chart. Then teachers can help the children cluster their ideas into groups. Teachers can demonstrate how to use the cluster by writing a group-collaborated composition that in turn may also be used in reading instruction. During revision, teachers need to be especially careful, because too much revision can be frustrating, causing the child to discard a good composition. The most effective motivation for revision occurs when children discover that they have difficulty reading their own compositions as they present their work in the author's chair (D'Alessandro, 1987).

There are many ways in which teachers can help special-needs children become more actively involved in reading and writing. Two ways in which children are active during reading are by making predictions about what they are going to read and by drawing conclusions about what they have already read (Norris, 1988). Pattern books are effective for supporting active reading and writing of learning-disabled children. These books have predictable sequences that make it easier for children to draw inferences as they predict what will happen next.

Avoiding Reductionist Teaching

Opponents of integrated, holistic approaches to literacy learning argue that children learn better when instruction is systematic and explicit (Dolman, 1992; Shapiro, 1992). Because of the tendency of many special-needs children to be easily distracted from completing tasks, teachers have been encouraged to break tasks into smaller or easier-to-complete components and to use tasks that are highly structured. One activity that might seem to make learning to write letters easier is to have children copy only three letters several times. Although learning-disabled children might learn to form the three letters from this activity, they will not learn how letters operate within the written language system, which is much more important than merely learning to form a few letters. We recommend that teachers rarely use drills on isolated written language tasks with any child, and especially not with children who may have trouble figuring out the complexities of reading and writing.

Learners from Diverse Cultural Backgrounds

Children from **diverse cultural backgrounds** may be distinguished by their ethnicity, social class, or language (Au, 1993). **Ethnicity** is determined by the racial, linguistic, cultural, or religious ties of one's national heritage, and most children from diverse cultural backgrounds are included in groups we call African American, Hispanic American, Asian American, or Native American, although people usually identify their ethnicity more precisely with a country of family origin, for example, Puerto Rican, Haitian, or Vietnamese. **Social class** is related to socioeconomic level as reflected in parents' occupations and family income. Children from diverse cultural backgrounds may speak a nonmainstream dialect of English or a language other than English (we discuss the influence of diverse language backgrounds in the next section of this chapter).

Cultural Influences on Learning

Some cultural groups have different ways of helping children learn. In some Native American communities, children are expected to learn by observing adults as they perform tasks; this implies that little verbal interaction takes place. Children who expect to learn from watching adults may not learn well in writing centers, in which teachers expect children to learn by talking with each other as they write. In other communities, children learn cooperatively with other children; the emphasis is on developing a group understanding and performance rather than on individual achievement. Children from these communities may have difficulty in reading groups, in which teachers expect only one child at a time to answer a question.

Culture also influences how children are socialized into being readers and writers. That is, all cultural groups share attitudes and beliefs about the uses and values of literacy and have preferred literacy practices. In general, children from mainstream backgrounds are socialized to use language and literacy within a tradition that places a large responsibility on the primary caregiver, usually the mother (Faltis, 1993). Mainstream mothers often talk with babies from birth and share books with their young children, asking questions that call for labels and clarifications. They include their children in dinner-table talk that supports their recounting of their daily activities or telling stories.

In contrast, Mexican American families recently immigrated to the United States often distribute caregiving among family members and close friends (Heath, 1986). In general, children are expected to observe adults' actions and conversation. In a working-class African American community, children observe parents and other adults as they read aloud and talk together about the meaning of texts (Heath, 1983).

There is considerable variation among families in the ways in which they socialize their young children into language and literacy use. However, we do have evidence of distinctive methods used by particular cultural groups to socialize children to become readers and writers. In mainstream cultural groups, children are expected to share in the construction of meaning with a parent during storybook reading and to construct stories on their own. Children from Mexican and African American backgrounds are less likely to be included in storybook reading experiences and are more likely to learn by observing rather than by participating in language activities.

Differences between mainstream and other cultural groups in how they socialize their children into language and literacy use provide an example of **cultural discontinuity** (Au, 1993). Cultural discontinuity means that there may be a mismatch between the literacy culture of the home and that of the school (which usually represents mainstream practices and values). Children who experience a cultural discontinuity are more likely to have learning difficulties in school. This is one possible explanation for the difference in achievement between children from mainstream and from other cultural backgrounds.

If teachers are to support the literacy learning of children from diverse cultural backgrounds, they need to be sensitive to the possibilities of cultural discontinuities as well as knowledgeable of how to change the classroom to better fit the learning of all children (Gee, 1996). Instruction that supports all children's learning and capitalizes on their cultural ways of learning is called culturally responsive instruction (Au, 1993).

Culturally Responsive Instruction

Culturally responsive instruction is instruction that is "consistent with the values of students' own cultures and aimed at improving academic learning" (Au, 1993, p. 13). We describe two examples of culturally responsive instruction. In these examples, teachers develop instructional strategies that are compatible with the learning styles of their children and at the same time help their children learn to operate more successfully with the learning styles usually associated with schools. This kind of instruction is called *culturally responsive*. The first example of instruction is from Au and Kawakami's (1985) description of the Kamehameha Early Education Project (KEEP); the second presents learning in school and in the community at the Warm Springs Indian Reservation (Philips, 1972).

KEEP: The Talk Story Lesson.   Teachers in a special school in Honolulu for children of Polynesian Hawaiian ancestry studied carefully the kinds of interactions or talk used by Hawaiian children. They researched talk in the community and talk in the classroom. These teachers discovered that their Hawaiian children engaged in interactions resembling "talk stories." In talk stories, many speakers participate together, jointly speaking—often at the same time—to create a narrative. There are few times in a talk story when only one child is speaking. Leaders in talk stories are skillful in involving other children, rather than in carrying the conversation alone. This way of interaction is not compatible with interaction that teachers tradition-ally expect during reading instruction.

Once teachers recognized that children who "spoke out" during reading group time were not being disruptive, they began to consider ways of using this type of interaction to foster reading growth. They decided that they would plan the questions they asked, but allow children freedom in the way they answered ques-tions. They allowed more than one child to respond at a time. The teachers tape-recorded reading lessons to examine whether allowing children to talk in what seemed to be a disruptive manner helped children to learn better. They found that 80 percent of the children's responses in "talk story" reading lessons focused on the story. In contrast, only 43 percent of the children's responses in a traditional lesson focused on the story (Au & Kawakami, 1985).

Learning on the Warm Springs Reservation.   The second example of culturally sensitive instruction comes from a study of Native American children's learning in school and in their community (Philips, 1972). On the Warm Springs Indian Reser-vation, Native American adults work together to solve problems. Leadership is assumed by many adults who have special skills or knowledge, rather than by an appointed leader, and adults choose whom they follow. Adults participate in group activities only when they feel they will be successful, and they participate at the level at which they feel comfortable. Children are observers in community meetings, but are often included in conversation.

These cultural ways of interacting are very different from the behaviors usu-ally expected in school. In school, teachers expect children to follow their direc-tions, to speak when asked a question, and to participate willingly in classroom activities. In contrast, Native American children expect to choose their own leader and make decisions about whether to participate in an activity. It is not surprising that Native American children do not volunteer to answer questions and often refuse to speak when called on in whole-class discussions.

One reason for the lack of participation by Native American children in whole-class recitation activities in school is that the **participation structures** in classrooms and in the community differ. Participation structures include the dif-ferent rules for speaking, listening, and turn taking. Native American children are uncomfortable in the participation structures of whole-class recitations and dis-cussions used frequently in school. They are more comfortable in the participation structures of small groups in which children initiate and direct their own activities. These participation structures have patterns of interaction more like those that the children have observed in their community.

Culturally Sensitive Instruction: A Summary

These projects demonstrate how teachers can alter their ways of instruction and help children develop new ways of interacting in the classroom. First, teachers researched not only their children's community, but also their own way of teaching. They were willing to make changes in how they conducted lessons in order to support their students' learning. Second, teachers sought methods of helping their children make the transition from community ways of learning to school ways of learning. Teachers not only helped children learn, but also helped children learn how to learn in school. Tape-recording lessons, visiting community activities, and talking to parents can provide all teachers with valuable information about developing culturally sensitive learning activities for their children.

Culturally Sensitive Instruction in Multicultural Settings

Many classes, especially in urban settings, comprise children from several different cultural backgrounds. For example, a classroom might include Hispanic American children from different Spanish-speaking countries, African American children, and Vietnamese children. In these situations, developing culturally sensitive instruction cannot be a matter of merely matching instruction with cultural features. Instead, teachers employ instructional approaches that are successful with most of the children, and at the same time provide extra support for those children who are struggling. They are willing to depart from familiar approaches to instruction and to experiment with different ways of learning and teaching (Au, 1993). Teachers craft culturally sensitive instruction when they invite collaboration from families and the community, use interactional styles of instruction, strive for a balance of rights, and seek culturally relevant content (Au, 1993; Cummins, 1986).

Community Collaboration. Involving parents from diverse cultural backgrounds in educational activities is an important part of teachers' responsibilities. In mainstream cultures, most parents acknowledge the importance of their involvement in school activities. Mainstream parents are likely to participate in school activities by helping their children with homework, participating in fundraising activities, attending school functions, such as open houses or music performances, attending parent–teacher conferences, and accompanying children on field trips.

Parents from nonmainstream cultures are also concerned about their children's education (Flores, Cousin, & Díaz, 1991). However, their perceptions about their involvement in schools may differ from the school's expectations. For example, many recently immigrated Mexican American families teach their children to be respectful of elders and to be accountable for their actions. However, they rarely work with their children on homework or other school activities. This may be because they assume that the school is responsible for educational matters.

Teachers using culturally sensitive instruction assume that all parents are interested in their children's success in school. They initiate contact with parents early in the school year through telephone calls, notes, and a weekly newsletter to parents. Inviting parents or other family members to school to share a family story is another way of initiating contacts with parents. Teachers communicate with parents often about the progress of their children's learning and provide concrete suggestions about how parents can help their children. Research has shown that nonmainstream parents are effective in supporting their children's learning at home (Goldenberg, 1989).

Instruction through Interaction.   Children from diverse cultural backgrounds learn best when instruction involves children in constructing their own meaning, when higher level thinking strategies are stressed, and when students set their own goals for learning (Cummins, 1986). This style of instruction is consistent with the instruction that we have recommended throughout this book and is called **constructivist models of instruction.** The essential ingredient of constructivist approaches is that children actively construct understandings. At first, children construct understandings with the support of others. The support that teachers provide for children's learning is sometimes called **scaffolding** (Cazden, 1988). The child accomplishes as much of the task as possible, and the adult scaffolds, or assists (see Chapter 1 for a discussion of the zone of proximal development). The constructivist model recognizes that learning begins with what children already know. Children's understandings about concepts are the beginning point of all learning experiences. In this way, children's experiences become a central part of the classroom.

Examples of interactive or constructivist models of instruction in literacy learning include using grand conversations to build understandings about literature, using writing workshop and the author's chair to support children's writing development, and using small, cooperative groups to learn new concepts, vocabulary, and spellings. In each of these teaching approaches, the children and teacher jointly identify topics of interest about which to talk and write, children's talk is acknowledged as an important avenue for encouraging critical thinking, and children learn to value the insights of their classmates.

Balance of Rights.   The concept of balance of rights is similar to an interactive style of teaching in which both the children and the teacher have input into what is learned. **Balance of rights** recognizes that in a classroom there are three dimensions of control over who gets to speak, what topic is discussed, and with whom children speak (Au & Mason, 1981). In mainstream classrooms with conventional recitation lessons or discussion-participant structures, teachers control which children speak, what they speak about, and to whom they speak (usually the teacher). Achieving a balance of rights means allowing children choices about one or more of the three dimensions of interactions (Au & Mason, 1981).

For example, in grand conversations, teachers and children together choose topics of discussion. Children talk about events or characters of interest to them, but the teacher also poses one or two interpretive questions. Children may speak without raising their hands, but the teacher helps quiet children hold the floor or facilitates turn taking when many children want to speak at once. The children listen carefully to one another and react to each other's comments, and teachers encourage such interactions by asking such questions as, "Jane, did you want to comment on what Jeff just said?"

Culturally Relevant Content. Children who perceive that what they are learning affirms their cultural heritage are more likely to become engaged in learning (Ferdman, 1990). Teachers can draw on three sources to provide culturally relevant content in the classroom: multicultural literature that is culturally authentic, children's experiences, and community resources.

Multicultural Literature. Multicultural literature is literature that incorporates people of diverse cultural backgrounds, including African Americans, Hispanic Americans, Asian Americans, Native Americans, and people from other cultures (see Chapter 6). Culturally authentic multicultural literature is usually written by members of a particular culture and accurately reflects the values and beliefs of that culture.

Children from diverse backgrounds need access to literature that includes characters from those backgrounds. Seeing children like themselves in literature increases children's self-esteem and enlightens others about the worth of different cultures. All children need experiences with culturally authentic literature about a variety of different cultural backgrounds.

Teachers must carefully choose the literature they share with children so that the literature does not distort children's concepts about others. Aoki, an Asian American, reported a childhood incident that illustrates this point (Aoki, 1981). She remembered when her teacher read the story *The Five Chinese Brothers* (Bishop & Wiese, 1938) to her class. (While this book is often considered a classic, it portrays Asians as stereotyped characters.) As her teacher showed the illustrations, a few children darted quick glances at her. Aoki began to sink down in her chair. She recalled that other children taunted her by pulling their eyes so that they slanted. This incident makes a point about helping diverse learners, and all children, to develop more positive attitudes and self-esteem—diverse learners need to feel welcome and safe in their classrooms, and they need to believe in their own worth and abilities.

Children's literature offers many opportunities to explore both language differences and cultural heritages with children. There are many literature selections about different cultural groups and heritages that present nonstereotyped characters. As teachers read these selections to children, they can help children explore common heritages, customs, and human qualities. If Aoki's teacher had been sensitive to stereotypical portrayals in children's books, she might have instead shared *Umbrella* (Yashima, 1958). Then the children would have learned to identify with the little girl in the story. Their teacher could have asked them to describe their common experiences.

Using multicultural literature in the classroom should entail more than merely highlighting the heroes or holidays of a culture or reading works of culturally authentic literature (Rasinski & Padak, 1990) as teachers help children see issues from multiple cultural perspectives. The Appendix presents a list of multicultural literature including folk literature, poetry, fantasy, and realistic fiction that reflects the culture of African Americans, Asian Americans, Hispanic Americans, and Native Americans.

Children's Experiences.   Children's experiences provide an important starting point for many kinds of literacy activities. For example, having children write about their experiences is a critical component of process writing and the writing workshop approach (see Chapters 9 and 10). Children identify topics of interest about which they wish to write, and teachers help them shape their writing by teaching minilessons, guiding writers' groups in which children revise and edit their compositions, and offering opportunities for sharing through the author's chair or other kinds of publishing.

Having children talk about events and people in their experiences is a base for guided reading lessons, especially using the experience-text-relationship approach. Teachers identify broad themes related to what children will read and then invite children to talk about their experiences related to these themes.

Community Resources.   The community can provide many rich resources for the classroom. Inviting local storytellers into the classroom is especially useful when teachers have difficulty locating children's literature representative of a child's cultural heritage. For example, a first grade teacher had a few children in her classroom from Cape Verde, an island off the African coast. When she failed to locate literature that included children from this cultural background, she turned to the community liaison in her school for help and learned that the neighborhood included many families from Cape Verde. The community liaison helped the teacher locate a storyteller from the neighborhood, who came to class and shared several stories from Cape Verde. After the storyteller's visit, the children retold two stories, which the teacher recorded in big book format. The children illustrated the big books, and these books became class favorites.

Culturally sensitive instruction is inclusive—it invites participation from children, parents, and the community. It recognizes the value of cultural heritage and children's experiences. It uses children's knowledge as a beginning point for instruction.

Children from Diverse Language Backgrounds

An increasing number of children in school are from **diverse language backgrounds.** They speak a nonmainstream dialect of English or a language other than English in their homes.

Learners Who Speak Nonmainstream Dialects of English

The way we speak English varies according to our social class, gender, occupation, locale, and ethnic background. Variations of a language are called *dialects*. All dialects of a language are understandable by all speakers of a language, but they are sufficiently different from one another to be distinctive (Wolfram, 2002). Many speakers from New York City, for example, have what speakers from other parts of the country consider a dialect, but New Yorkers are easily understood by English speakers from San Francisco, Atlanta, or any other location in the United States.

Dialects are distinguished by differences in pronunciation, word choice, grammatical structure, and communicative style or usage. For example, the words *park* and *car* are pronounced *pahk* and *cah* in Boston or New York and *pawk* and *caw* in New Orleans (Barnitz, 1980). A sandwich on a long roll is called a *hoagie* in Philadelphia and a *Po Boy* in parts of Louisiana. Some people say they must be home by *quarter til 5,* while others say they must be there by *quarter of 5.*

Nonmainstream and Mainstream Dialects.   There is no one variety or dialect of English that is the standard or **mainstream dialect.** This is a difficult concept to accept. As speakers, we are capable of, and unconsciously make, judgments regarding other people's use of language. When we consider their language use to be standard or nonstandard, we are not applying any consistent criteria. Many speakers would label, "I ain't parkin' no car," as **nonmainstream** (or nonstandard) **dialect.** When asked why, they usually say that it violates rules of grammar. Yet they may consider the sentence "None of the cars were parked" to be standard even though it violates a rule of grammar: the use of a singular subject (*none*) with a plural verb (*were*). In other words, although the word *standard* implies otherwise, there are no objective criteria for determining whether a dialect is standard. All speakers have a range of language patterns that they use depending on situation and audience.

Dialects Considered Nonmainstream.   There are many dialects frequently considered nonstandard or nonmainstream by large segments of the population, especially by teachers and other educated groups. Some of these dialects are tied to locale, and others are tied to social class (Labov, 1966). Even though there is not just one African American dialect, many researchers (e.g., Smitherman, 1977) have described a dialect referred to as Black English or as African American Vernacular English. Many African Americans do not use Black English, and many of the features of Black English are found not only in so-called standard English, but also in many other dialects. Nevertheless, an important court case, *King Elementary School Students* vs. *The Ann Arbor, Michigan, School District Board* highlighted the need to recognize children's dialects, and in particular the dialect known as Black English, as an important consideration in children's education (Smitherman, 1977). The court ruled that teachers need to be familiar with children's home language, and to become more sensitive to their special needs. Some Black English-speaking communities have emphasized the linguistic equality of all dialects and thus the linguistic legitimacy of Black English by renaming it Ebonics (Lippi-Green, 1997).

Nonmainstream Dialects and Attitudes. We not only make subjective judgments about whether speakers have standard or nonstandard speech patterns, but we also make other kinds of judgments based on our assessment of their language. Sometimes people unconsciously think that speakers of a different dialect might not be very intelligent or may have a low social status. Such judgments are especially harmful when teachers make them about children (Gee, 1996). Children who speak dialects that their teachers consider nonstandard are more likely to be identified as having cognitive lags, needing language therapy, and needing special remedial reading and writing instruction (Bartoli, 1986). They are more likely to be placed in lower ability groups for instruction and to receive lower achievement scores than are their peers. This is an injustice. We must understand why it occurs so that we will not perpetuate it.

There are three reasons that children who speak dialects considered nonstandard are more likely to be included in remedial or lower ability groups. The first reason is related to the unconscious practice of using language patterns to judge the worth of a whole person. Teachers are not exempt from the phenomenon of unconsciously deciding on a person's intellectual capacity by virtue of his or her speech. The second reason is that tests that assess reading and writing do not use these students' dialects. The third reason is that teachers may spend more time helping these students acquire standard or mainstream English than they do helping them learn to read and write.

Literacy Instruction for Children with Nonmainstream Dialects. One of the most hotly debated topics in language education is whether, how, and when children should be taught to speak what is considered standard English. Because language is so closely interwoven with a person's sense of identity and self-worth, using language in a different way can be threatening. However, it is hard to counter the argument that people who speak so-called standard English have more access to educational and economic opportunities.

Teaching Children to Speak English That Is Considered Standard in Their Region. Most experts agree that preschoolers should be encouraged to communicate, whether their language is perceived as standard or as nonstandard (Genishi & Dyson, 1984). Teachers need to be more concerned with what children have to say than with how they say it. The practice of requiring children to speak in complete sentences or to "say it right" is not recommended. As all children get older and as they hear a greater variety of language models, they naturally begin to include in their speech more forms considered standard by most people in their region (Padak, 1981). Reading aloud to young children provides a model of written English, which is actually different from any spoken dialect, yet is often the standard against which people compare their so-called standard dialects (Feitelson et al., 1993).

Children in elementary school should have opportunities to use language in many different situations. Role-playing activities can provide children with opportunities to use a variety of language patterns. For example, they may practice interviewing a community leader, a minister, and a senior citizen as preparation for data gathering in a social studies unit. Children in elementary school are capable of discussing how different kinds of language are appropriate in different situations.

Children's literature provides rich models for language growth. Children enjoy hearing and saying many kinds of language found in literature. There are many fine examples of literature in which a dialect considered nonstandard contributes to the authenticity and enjoyment of the story. These selections can be used to demonstrate the variety and richness of language. As children explore language variety through literature, they can also explore language that most consider standard (Cullinan, Jaggar, & Strickland, 1974). Children naturally use the language of literature as they retell stories, role-play story actions, and write stories of their own.

Teaching Reading and Writing.   No special techniques are necessary to introduce written language to preschoolers who speak with a dialect considered nonstandard. All children, whether in preschool or in elementary school, learn about reading and writing when written language is presented in meaningful activities.

In more formal reading and writing programs in the elementary school, teachers need to be knowledgeable of how children's dialects are reflected in their reading and writing. For example, children who speak with a dialect considered nonstandard will use that language as they read aloud—they may translate the text into their own speech patterns. Similarly, they may use their language as a basis for writing—what children write may reflect their oral language patterns. Teachers of children who speak with a dialect considered nonstandard should recognize that children translate text into their own oral language patterns. As children read the text, they may translate it into their spoken language. These translations from text language to spoken language are expected based on what we know about dialects considered nonstandard (Bryen, 1982). Teachers who are sensitive to children's language recognize dialect translations as positive indications that children comprehend as they read.

Children's dialects are reflected in what and how they write. Figure 11.2 presents a story written by a boy whose dialect is considered nonstandard by many

FIGURE 11.2   Darryl's Story: "The Spooky Halloween Night"

The Spooky Halloween Night

One there was a mummy named Eddie Mcdevitt he was so dume at he dump his head in the can in then he chod his head off and then he went and to his house and then he went outside and chod his arm off then the cops came and chase him away and then he tuck some lade and kidl here in then she came alive and chod his bode off and then his spirt comed in kill everybody.

From "Research Update: A Focus on Oral Language and Writing from a Multicultural Perspective," by T. R. Meier and C. B. Cazden, 1982, *Language Arts, 59,* p. 507. Copyright © 1982 by the National Council of Teachers of English. Reprinted with permission.

(Meier & Cazden, 1982, p. 507). Even when we are sensitive to Darryl's dialect, we know that he has several problems with writing. His story lacks the details that make writing vivid, although it is certainly startling. He has many misspelled words (over a fourth of the text), and most of the sentences are ineffective. Although teachers do not need to know a great deal about dialects to see Darryl's weaknesses, they may need this knowledge to see his strengths (Meier & Cazden, 1982). For example, Darryl's use of *in* for both the words *in* and *and* may reflect that he says the word *and* like the word *in*. Similarly, the deletion of the letters *ed* on some of his past tense verbs reflects that the pronunciation rules of his dialect include simplification of past tense verbs (that is, dropping the pronunciation of the final sounds /t/, /uhd/, or /d/).

There are many more important strengths to this story that reflect what all children learn, and specifically, what Darryl is learning, about good stories. His story has a beginning, complications, and an ending all centered on a single character, Eddie Mcdevitt. Darryl's story also contains features of a "trickster tale" (Smitherman, 1977). This is a special kind of story told by African Americans that usually involves an African American male who triumphs over adversaries through cunning and unusual feats (Meier & Cazden, 1982). Although he lacks a head or a body, Eddie lives on at the end of the tale. Teachers who are sensitive to children's language recognize what children bring to writing and are in a better position to build on children's strengths. Writing may be the most effective way to help children gain control over language considered standard.

Dialects and Dictation.   Although many teachers are sensitive to their children's language and they view *oral* language diversity as valid, they wonder what to do when writing down children's dictations. Should teachers translate children's speech into standard text or should they write what children say? Figures 11.3 and 11.4 present a kindergartner's dictated story and a first grader's dictated retelling of *There's Something in My Attic* (Mayer, 1988). These child-authored texts include

They was hiding eggs in the grass.
When they went to bed the Easter Bunny come.   **FIGURE 11.3   Natasha's Story**

FIGURE 11.4   Latosha's Retelling

There was a little girl.
She had a dream about a ghost.
She got off the bed and her dad put her back in the bed.
He say, "Go to sleep."
She got off her bed and went upstairs to her attic.
The little girl tooks a rope and catch the ghost.

some language that many consider nonstandard. Many teachers are concerned that parents will object to such a text, since it is not regarded as standard English. They wonder if children's reading of such texts will somehow be harmful.

There are at least three arguments for writing what children dictate, although words should be spelled conventionally and not as children pronounce them (Jaggar, 1974). First, the main reason for writing down children's dictations, such as stories about their art work, is so that children can realize that what they say is what is written. Children whose dictations are not written as they are dictated may not discover this concept. Second, one of children's most valuable reading strategies is their understanding of what language is like. Therefore, teachers will want to write what children say in dictations so that children can use this strategy as a method of reading. Finally, writing what a child says demonstrates acceptance of the child; it suggests that teachers find children's ideas important and that they recognize the validity of children's expressions.

One method of helping children build bridges from the oral language patterns they use in dictations to patterns found in written texts is to use more than one language story for some dictation experiences (Gillet & Gentry, 1983). In some dictation exercises, the teacher might prepare an experience story that is similar to the children's dictated story, but in language considered standard. Figure 11.5 presents a language story dictated by six-year-olds that includes some language considered nonstandard. Figure 11.5 also presents a story written by their teacher. This story includes many of the same words used in the children's dictation. The teacher and children read and reread both stories many times. Teachers need to use this technique with care so that the children's stories are as valued as their teacher's stories.

Learners Who Speak English as a Second Language

Children whose home language is not English are **English language learners** and may speak English fluently, a little, or not at all. Their entry into preschool or elementary school may be the first time they are expected to speak English, or they may have had many opportunities to speak English prior to their school experiences. One of the first concerns that teachers voice is how to teach children, especially children who speak little English, to speak and to understand English.

FIGURE 11.5   "The Holiday Memory Book"

Children's Dictated Story

The Christmas Tree and Hanukkah Candles

We put seven ball on the Christmas tree.
We puts some lights on the Christmas tree.
We put a lot of candy cane on the Christmas tree.
We lighted candles for Hanukkah.

Teacher's Story

Holiday Celebrations

We celebrated Christmas and Hanukkah. We decorated a Christmas tree. First, we put lights on the tree. Then we put balls and candy canes on the tree. Last, we lit Hanukkah candles. We enjoyed our celebration of Christmas and Hanukkah.

Teaching Spoken English.   The easiest way to learn to speak English is to participate in meaningful activities (Genishi & Dyson, 1984). The structure provided by familiar objects and activities supports children's language learning. To be effective, the objects must be real and the children must use them in real activities. Just as many toddlers first learn familiar phrases or words associated with repeated activities (called "routines"), so do English language learners first learn familiar phrases and words in English (Urzua, 1980). Many children learn to say "Night night," "go to sleep," and "read books" because these routine phrases are repeated daily as they participate in the activity of getting ready for bed. Preschool English language learners can learn the same phrases as they interact with their teacher and other children in their play with dolls, blankets, beds, and books in the housekeeping center. Many dramatic-play activities, such as grocery shopping, visiting the dentist, and taking a trip to McDonald's, provide rich language-learning experiences. Teachers can join in play and provide models of language. At first, many English language learners will be silent in their play as they internalize the sounds of English and discover the actions of routines. They may switch between using English and using their home language (this practice should not be forbidden; Lara, 1989).

Even in elementary school, props and dramatic play can be used as a bridge to English. All children enjoy a pretend trip to McDonald's that includes such props as bags, hamburger containers, drink cups, and hats for the employees. As part of the McDonald's play, children will learn the English words *hamburgers, French fries, Coke, milk, ketchup, salt,* and *money.* They might learn routine phrases such as "Welcome to McDonald's," "May I take your order, please?" "I'd like a hamburger," or "Give me a Coke." Pictures of familiar activities can also be used to increase English language learners' oral language proficiency (Moustafa & Penrose, 1985).

Teaching Reading and Writing.   Children need not be proficient speakers of English in order to begin reading and writing in English (Abramson, Seda, & Johnson, 1990). In fact, reading and writing instruction supports learning spoken English. Effective strategies for literacy instruction in English include using additive approaches, developing comprehensive input, using shared language, and providing opportunities for extended discourse.

Additive Approaches.   **Additive approaches** build on children's home language and culture (Cummins, 1986) and are in contrast with **subtractive approaches,** which replace children's home language and culture with English and mainstream values. The best approaches to supporting the literacy learning of English language learners are those in the children's home language. But in many classrooms this is not possible. Sometimes children speak many different languages, and at other times, parents request that children receive instruction in English.

All teachers can take an additive approach to their literacy instruction when they allow students to use their home language in some reading and writing activities. For example, a third grade teacher who had several Spanish-speaking children in her class introduced the characters and events in *Mirandy and Brother Wind* (McKissack, 1988) by using simple props to act out important parts of the story. As part of her introduction, the teacher used descriptive phrases from the story and illustrated the meaning of these phrases through her dramatic portrayal of the characters in action. Then the children formed pairs to read the story. Next the children gathered together to have a grand conversation about the story. As part of the conversation, the teacher shared many responses in which she used several of the vocabulary words from the story. These portions of the lesson were all conducted in English. Finally, the class broke into small groups to act out portions of the story, and several children planned their dramatic reenactments in Spanish. Although most groups presented their dramas to the class using English, one group used Spanish in its enactment.

Using a class or school postal system provides another example of how teachers can support children's use of home language in literacy activities. Children can help make mailboxes and establish a routine for delivering and receiving mail. Teachers can encourage children to write to them, to each other, to school personnel, and to famous people (including favorite children's authors). Writing letters and notes can become part of free-time activities, or it can become part of more formal reading and writing lessons. Teachers who have used this system have found that English language learners begin writing in their home language. This practice should be encouraged as a way for children to continue their literacy growth in their home language. Teachers in areas where a majority of children come from families whose first language is not English will welcome this opportunity to demonstrate the value of being literate not only in English, but also in other languages. This cross-cultural literacy can be reinforced by including materials written in languages other than English in the classroom, sending notes home to parents in both the language of the home and English, and posting signs and labels in both the predominant language and English (Ortiz & Engelbrecht, 1986).

Gradually, English language learners begin to write their notes and letters in English to communicate with children who write in English (Greene, 1985). English-language learners may find letter and note writing especially motivating because the emphasis is placed on communicating meaning to friends, rather than on correct conventions. Writing may be a particularly meaningful bridge to literacy in English (Urzua, 1987).

Instruction can also be additive when written language and spoken language are used as mutually supportive systems (Fitzgerald, 1993). For example, teachers can reinforce their spoken questions by writing the questions as well. Before having children read to find answers, teachers write two or three questions on the chalkboard. As children read, they can refer to the written questions as a guide for their reading (Gersten & Jiménez, 1994).

Another way in which spoken and written language support reading is through the use of the language experience approach. Dialogues that emerge from activities such as a pretend trip to McDonald's provide material for reading and writing (Feeley, 1983). After participating in dramatic play about a visit to McDonald's, children can learn to read and write many words found on the environmental print at McDonald's and associated with going to a McDonald's restaurant, such as *McDonald's, restrooms, men, women,* and *push* (Hudelson & Barrera, 1985). The teacher can prepare a story about the children's activities, incorporating English words and phrases used as part of the McDonald's play experience. Children can also dictate or write about their experiences (Moustafa & Penrose, 1985). Photos of the children taken during the activity provide useful support for reading these stories or writing about the experience (Sinatra, 1981). These language stories can be used to help children develop sight words or practice decoding skills. Figure 11.6 presents a story dictated by an English language learner in second grade after he made Play Doh.

In addition to language-experience materials, English language learners need frequent and early experiences with children's literature both to read and as a support for their writing (Hough, Nurss, & Enright, 1986). Pattern books are particularly effective as first reading materials for all children, including English language learners. Pattern books are especially useful in developing English language learners' sense of syntax as well as giving them experience with new vocabulary. Chap-

---

FIGURE 11.6   English Language Learner's Dictation

Lim Makes Play Doh

I can use two cup flour.
I put one cup salt.
I am mix with spoon.
I am measure with water and flour.
I put spice in bucket.
I put two tablespoon oil in bucket.
We put color in bucket.

ter 9 describes how pattern books can be used to encourage children's reading and writing. Wordless picture books are also useful to stimulate dictation and writing.

Finally, additive approaches invite participation from parents and the community. Teachers make every effort to communicate with parents despite language differences. School systems provide community liaisons—people who know the different school communities and are native speakers of the languages spoken in the various communities. English language and bilingual teachers are also useful resources and may be able to locate bilingual parent volunteers to help communicate with parents or to work in classrooms. Teachers make sure that all notes and newsletters sent to parents are written in the home language. They check with community liaisons or school volunteers to find ways of showing respect to parents during parent–teacher conferences or telephone conversations. They invite parents or other community members to school to share family stories or traditions, to read books related to their culture, or to demonstrate special skills.

Shared language. Effective teachers of English language learners realize that students can be easily overwhelmed by too many changing instructional techniques. These children need repeated use of familiar instructional routines and activities using shared language. **Shared language** refers to vocabulary that is used repetitively when talking about a reading or writing task (Gersten & Jiménez, 1994). For instance, one teacher who taught many children with limited knowledge of English repeatedly used a few familiar words when talking about literature. She taught her children the components of a *story grammar* (see Chapter 2 for a description of a story grammar and its components), and her students understood the English words *character, goal, obstacle, outcome,* and *theme.* The students knew how to look for **character clues** because the teacher frequently asked questions such as, "What kind of character is he? What are the clues?" (Gersten & Jiménez, 1994) and modeled answer-finding techniques.

Another teacher taught students the vocabulary needed to conduct writers' conferences with partners. Using whole-class minilessons, the teacher taught children to talk about "'favorite part,' 'part you didn't understand,' 'part you'd like to know more about,' and 'part you might like to work on'" (Blake, 1992, p. 606). Through modeling, the teacher showed children the kinds of language that he expected them to use and the kinds of information that he expected them to talk about in a writer's conference.

These teachers focused on teaching their children how to participate in highly successful activities. They did not use many different strategies, but instead used only a few strategies routinely. As children gained confidence using these strategies, these teachers gradually added other instructional strategies.

Extended discourse. Mastering English and becoming competent readers and writers of English is possible only when students use English for a variety of purposes in situations that are not anxiety producing (Faltis, 1993). That is, children need opportunities for **extended discourse,** or talking and writing extensively in a variety of settings (with a variety of partners, including the teacher, in small groups, and in whole-class gatherings). Teachers can encourage extended discourse by acknowledging children's input to lessons and by providing models of more complete English-language structure, as in the following example (Gersten & Jiménez, 1994, p. 445).

> TEACHER: What does he hope will happen when he shoots the arrow?
>
> CHILD: The rain (gestures like rain falling).
>
> TEACHER: Right, the rain will fall down.

A kindergarten teacher provided opportunities for extended discourse that use repeated readings of a favorite book, storytelling with flannel-board props, and emergent reading of the favorite book (Carger, 1993). First, the teacher read aloud an engaging picture book that appealed to young Hispanic children. After each reading, the teacher invited individual children to reread the story using the pictures in the picture storybook as prompts (for emergent readings). The teacher accepted the children's attempts at reading using their limited English. Then the teacher reread the story and retold the story in Spanish, using flannel-board props. She invited the children to retell the story once again in English, this time using the flannel-board props.

Instructional Conversations. **Classroom conversations** are beneficial for all students' language and literacy development, but they are especially important for English language learners (Martinez-Roldan & Lopez-Robertson, 1999/2000; Williams, 2001). Teachers do not just ask questions and evaluate students' answers. They ask few known-answer questions. Instead, they establish a focus or direction for the conversation, activate participants' background knowledge, and foster wide participation, such as by encouraging self-selected turns. The goal is shared meaning making with much give-and-take. Teachers are responsive to students' contributions; they validate and expand students' comments. They do not give up on students when their utterances seem limited. In a shared writing activity with four kindergartners, one teacher stayed with Carlos until he revealed the full meaning of a one-word comment about what the teacher had written so far.

> CARLOS: (pointing to a word at the end of a line) *Spot.*
>
> TEACHER: What do you mean, Carlos?
>
> CARLOS: *Spot.* (points again to the last word in a line)
>
> TEACHER: Tell me more. What do you mean?
>
> CARLOS: No room. (pointing to the end of the first line)
>
> TEACHER: (recognizing Carlos's point and that there was no more room on the line to write another word) Oh, I see, Carlos. There is no more room for words on this line, so I will continue writing on the next line. (Williams, 2001, p. 753)

Instructional conversations are more likely to happen in rich contexts and with motivated students. One of the best ways to ensure this is to create thematic units of study that integrate reading, writing, speaking, and listening with content learning in social studies, science, math, and the fine arts (Robb, 1994). Students are motivated because they are involved in selecting topics and generating questions for study. Contexts are rich because they involve academic work across subject areas and invite learning and communicating in more than one modality. Freeman and Freeman (2000) list other benefits of thematic units of study for English language learners. Students hear vocabulary repeated in the contexts of more than one content area. They see the curriculum making sense because it deals with big-picture issues, and so they are more engaged and, ultimately, more successful. This engagement enables teachers to plan lessons and activities adjusted to varied levels of English proficiency.

Debbie teaches in an inner-city school; hers is a multiage, multilingual class of twenty first, second, and third graders, two of whom are of Chinese descent, three are African American, and six are of Mexican descent (Freeman & Freeman, 2000). Inspired by *Moon Journals* (Chancer & Rester-Zodrow, 1997), she wanted to teach a moonwatch unit, but she waited until her students were interested. When a classroom visitor from the zoo led a discussion about bats, the students talked about the creatures' nighttime habits and began to ask about the stars and the moon. Debbie inquired whether they would be interested in studying the moon.

The students designed and decorated moon journals. Each night, they recorded in their journals observations of the moon. These led to discussions and questions (for example, where was the moon on the night of the new moon?). Answering their own questions led to more reading, more discussion, and more writing. Debbie collected a text set of informational, story, and poetry books about the moon.

> All of the readings and activities informed the group and actually increased their interest. As Debbie explained, "I've never before had an inquiry project where there was absolutely 100 percent involvement. Everyone was interested. Everyone participated. Everyone learned." (p. 112)

The students wrote their own moon poems, gathered them in a book, *Moon Images*, and read them to one another on a camp out, which also included moon watching with a telescope.

Issues Related to Teaching Children from Diverse Backgrounds

The models of instruction that we and others (Au, 1993) have proposed for supporting children from diverse backgrounds are called by many names, including constructivist, interactional, socio-psycholinguistic, process oriented, and holistic. They share the underlying principles that learning is more effective when learners actively construct understandings for themselves rather than passively repeat what teachers tell them, when teachers stress processes rather than adultlike products, and when learners engage in meaningful activities that involve reading and writing rather than practice skills in isolation.

However, it is important to keep in mind that children from diverse backgrounds also need instruction that ensures their academic success. "If students from diverse backgrounds are to have access to opportunities in the mainstream culture, schools must acquaint them with the rules and codes of the culture of power, such as the grammar of standard English" (Au, 1993, p. 51). Many children from diverse backgrounds will benefit from explicit teaching of the conventions of writing. One educator put it this way: "Unless one has the leisure of a lifetime of 'immersion' to learn them, explicit presentation [of the rules of the culture of power] makes learning immeasurably easier" (Delpit, 1988, p. 283).

Explicit teaching, however, does not mean that teachers necessarily need to resort to traditional drills and recitation. Instead, teachers can provide explicit teaching within the context of reading and writing activities, as is done during the writing phase of Reading Recovery lessons, during minilessons in the writing workshop approach, or through guided reading lessons. All teachers must strike a balance between allowing children to construct their own understandings and providing direct, explicit instruction (Spiegel, 1992). All good instruction includes both opportunities to explore and explicit teaching.

Chapter Summary

At-risk learners are children who are especially at risk for school failure. At-risk learners include children who struggle to acquire literacy concepts despite quality classroom support.

While it is helpful to be aware of language, literacy, family, and community factors that might suggest a need for preventative early literacy instruction, it is also important to be aware of the rich cultural capital inherent in diversity. Fortunately, early literacy instruction aimed at preventing the failure of at-risk children is not qualitatively different from early literacy instruction for other children. Observant teachers adapt instructional activities to meet the needs of special learners without resorting to reductionist methods of instruction.

Teachers recognize that culture influences the way in which children learn and how they interact with each other and with adults. For example, children of Hawaiian ancestry are familiar with interaction styles in which more than one speaker talks at a time and children from one Native American culture are more familiar with talking in small informal groups than in whole-class recitation. Once teachers recognize the ways in which culture affects how children learn and interact, they are on the way to crafting culturally sensitive instruction. Culturally sensitive instruction is characterized by interactive instruction, a balance of rights, and culturally relevant content. Culturally relevant content includes multicultural literature, resources from the community, and children's own experiences.

Children who speak a nonmainstream or nonstandard dialect of English may be the victims of teachers' unconscious judgments about their academic potential.

To counter this possibility, teachers understand that all dialects, including non-mainstream dialects, reflect an underlying logic and structure. They help children feel comfortable and accepted when using their dialect to communicate while they help children to expand their language use to include the dialect that is considered standard in their region.

Children who speak English as a second language learn spoken English at the same time that they learn to read and write in English. Teachers support this process when they use additive approaches, shared language, and extended discourse. All teachers of diverse learners must strive for a balance between supporting children as they construct their own understandings and providing explicit instruction.

Applying the Information

Julia Felix is a first-year teacher in a large urban school that serves children from a variety of cultural and language backgrounds. This year she will be teaching third grade (or, you may assume that she will be teaching kindergarten). She opens her class list and reads the following names (X = ESL Student) (Faltis, 1993, p. 5).

1.	Brown, Leon	
2.	Cavenaugh, Kimberly	
3.	Cui, Xiancoung	X
4.	Cohen, Daniel	
5.	Evans, Lisa	
6.	Fernandez, Maria Eugenia	X
7.	Freeman, Jeffrey	
8.	Garcia, Aucencio	X
9.	Gomez, Concepcion	X
10.	Hamilton, Jessica	
11.	Mason, Tyrone	
12.	O'Leary, Sean	
13.	Pak, Kyung	X
14.	Petruzzella, Gina	
15.	Quinn, Frank	
16.	Rosen, Chatty	
17.	Rojas, Guadalupe	X
18.	Sandoval, Kathy	
19.	Tran, Do Thi	X
20.	Vasquez, Jimmy	X
21.	Williamson, Amy	
22.	York, Leonard	
23.	Zbikowski, Antonin	

Julie thinks to herself, "I especially want the ESL students to fully join in my class" (Faltis, 1993, p. 6). How will Julie accomplish this task? What suggestions can you make about her room arrangement, the materials she will need, and the modifications she can be expected to make in instruction? Suppose that Julie decides to teach a unit about animals. Make suggestions for materials that she can include in the unit, and plan at least one lesson that will meet the needs of the English language learners in her class.

Going Beyond the Text

Visit a preschool or elementary school that has special-needs children. Observe the children in their classroom as they interact with the other children and during literacy activities. Take note of ways in which the special-needs children are similar to and different from the other children. If possible, talk to a teacher about supporting the literacy learning of special-needs children. Take at least one reading and one writing activity that you can share with a special-needs child. For example, take a children's book and literature props for the child to retell the story; plan a hands-on experience, such as popping corn, that will stimulate writing; or prepare a special book that you can give to the child for his or her own journal. Carefully observe the child's language and behaviors during these literacy activities. Be ready to discuss what this child knows about literacy.

REFERENCES

Abramson, S., Seda, I., & Johnson, C. (1990). Literacy development in a multilingual kindergarten classroom. *Childhood Education, 67,* 68–72.

Adams, M. (1990). *Beginning to read.* Cambridge: MIT Press.

Allen, J., & Carr, E. (1989). Collaborative learning among kindergarten writers: James learns how to learn at school. In J. Allen & J. Mason (Eds.), *Risk makers, risk takers, risk breakers: Reducing the risks for young literacy learners* (pp. 30–47). Portsmouth, NH: Heinemann.

Aoki, E. (1981). "Are you Chinese? Or are you just a mixed-up kid?" Using Asian American children's literature. *The Reading Teacher, 34,* 382–385.

Au, K. (1993). *Literacy instruction in multicultural settings.* New York: Harcourt Brace Jovanovich.

Au, K. H., & Kawakami, A. J. (1985). Research currents: Talk story and learning to read. *Language Arts, 62,* 406–411.

Au, K., & Mason, J. (1981). Social organizational factors in learning to read: The balance of rights hypothesis. *Reading Research Quarterly, 17,* 115–152.

Barnes, B. L. (1996–1997a). But teacher you went right on: A perspective on Reading Recovery. *The Reading Teacher, 50,* 284–292.

Barnes, B. L. (1996–1997b). Response to Browne, Fitts, McLaughlin, McNamara, and Williams. *The Reading Teacher, 50,* 302–303.

Barnitz, J. G. (1980). Black English and other dialects: Sociolinguistic implications for reading instruction. *The Reading Teacher, 33,* 779–786.

Barone, D. (1993). Wednesday's child: Literacy development of children prenatally exposed to crack or cocaine. *Research in the Teaching of English, 27,* 7–45.

Bartoli, J. S. (1986). Is it really English for everyone? *Language Arts, 63,* 12–22.

Bishop, C. H., & Wiese, K. (1938). *The five Chinese brothers.* New York: Coward, McCann and Geoghegan.

Blake, B. (1992). Talk in non-native and native English speakers' peer writing conferences: What's the difference? *Language Arts, 69,* 604–610.

Bloodgood, J. W. (1999). What's in a name? Children's name writing and literacy acquisition. *Reading Research Quarterly, 34,* 342–367.

Browne, A., Fitts, M., Mclaughlin, B., McNamara, M. J., & Williams, J. (1996–1997). Teaching and learning in Reading Recovery: Response to "But teacher you went right on." *The Reading Teacher, 50,* 294–300.

Bryen, D. (1982). *Inquiries into child language.* Boston: Allyn and Bacon.

Carger, C. (1993). Louie comes to life: Pretend reading with second language emergent readers. *Language Arts, 70,* 542–547.

Cazden, C. (1988). *Classroom discourse.* Portsmouth, NH: Heinemann.

Chancer, J., & Rester-Zodrow, G. (1997). *Moon journals.* Portsmouth, NH: Heinemann.

Clay, M. (1985). *The early detection of reading difficulties* (3rd ed.). Portsmouth, NH: Heinemann.

Comber, B. (2000). What *really* counts in early literacy lessons. *Language Arts, 78,* 39–49.

Cousin, P., Weekley, T., & Gerard, J. (1993). The functional uses of language and literacy by students with severe language and learning problems. *Language Arts, 70,* 548–556.

Cullinan, B. E., Jaggar, A. M., & Strickland, D. S. (1974). Oral language expansion in the primary grades. In B. E. Cullinan (Ed.), *Black dialects and reading* (pp. 43–54). Urbana, IL: National Council of Teachers of English.

Cummins, J. (1986). Empowering minority students: A framework for intervention. *Harvard Educational Review, 56,* 18–36.

Dahl, K. L., Scharer, P. L., Lawson, L. L., & Grogan, P. R. (2001). *Rethinking phonics: Making the best teaching decisions.* Portsmouth, NH: Heinemann.

D'Alessandro, M. E. (1987). "The ones who always get the blame": Emotionally handicapped children writing. *Language Arts, 64,* 516–522.

Delpit, L. (1988). The silenced dialogue: Power and pedagogy in educating other people's children. *Harvard Educational Review, 58,* 280–298.

Dickinson, D. K., & Smith, M. W. (1994). Long-term effects of preschool teachers' book readings on low-income children's vocabulary and story comprehension. *Reading Research Quarterly, 29,* 104–122.

Dickinson, D. K., & Sprague, K. E. (2001). The nature and impact of early childhood care environments on the language and early literacy development of children from low-income families. In S. B. Neuman & D. K. Dickinson (Eds.), *Handbook of early literacy research* (pp. 263–280). New York: Guilford.

Dixon, R. (1987). Strategies for vocabulary instruction. *Teaching Exceptional Children, 19,* 61–63.

Dolman, D. (1992). Some concerns about using whole language approaches with deaf children. *American Annals of the Deaf, 137,* 278–282.

Dowhower, S. L. (1989). Repeated reading: Research into practice. *The Reading Teacher, 42,* 502–507.

Ellson, D. G., Barber, L., Engle, T. L., & Kampwerth, L. (1965). Programmed tutoring: A teaching aid and a research tool. *Reading Research Quarterly, 1,* 77–127.

Faltis, C. (1993). *Joinfostering: Adapting teaching strategies for the multilingual classroom.* New York: Merrill/Macmillan.

Feeley, J. T. (1983). Help for the reading teacher: Dealing with the Limited English Proficient (LEP) child in the elementary classroom. *The Reading Teacher, 36,* 650–655.

Feitelson, D., Goldstein, Z., Iraqi, J., & Share, D. (1993). Effects of listening to story reading on aspects of literacy acquisition in a diglossic situation. *Reading Research Quarterly, 28,* 70–79.

Ferdman, B. (1990). Literacy and cultural identity. *Harvard Educational Review, 60,* 181–204.

Fitzgerald, J. (1993). Literacy and students who are learning English as a second language. *The Reading Teacher, 46,* 638–647.

Flores, B., Cousin, P., & Díaz, E. (1991). Transforming deficit myths about learning, language, and culture. *Language Arts, 68,* 369–379.

Freeman, D. E., & Freeman, Y. S. (2000). *Teaching reading in multilingual classrooms.* Portsmouth, NH: Heinemann.

Gee, J. P. (1996). *Social linguistics and literacies: Ideology in discourses* (2nd ed.). Bristol, PA: Taylor & Francis.

Genishi, C., & Dyson, A. H. (1984). *Language assessment in the early years.* Norwood, NJ: Ablex.

Gersten, R., & Jiménez, R. (1994). A delicate balance: Enhancing literature instruction for students of English as a second language. *The Reading Teacher, 47,* 438–449.

Gillet, J. W., & Gentry, J. R. (1983). Bridges between nonstandard and standard English with extensions of dictated stories. *The Reading Teacher, 36,* 360–364.

Goldenberg, C. (1989). Making success a more common occurrence for children at risk for failure: Lessons from Hispanic first graders learning to read. In J. Allen & J. Mason (Eds.), *Risk makers, risk takers, risk breakers: Reducing the risks for young literacy learners* (pp. 48–79). Portsmouth, NH: Heinemann.

Goldenberg, C., & Gallimore, R. (1991). Local knowledge, research knowledge, and educational change: A case study of early Spanish reading improvement. *Educational Researcher,* *20,* 2–14.

Greene, J. E. (1985). Children's writing in an elementary school postal system. In M. Farr (Ed.), *Advances in writing research. (Vol. 1,* pp. 201–296). Norwood, NJ: Ablex.

Heath, S. (1983). *Ways with words: Language, life, and work in communities and classrooms.* New York: Cambridge University Press.

Heath, S. (1986). Sociocultural context of language development. In California State Department of Education (Ed.), *Beyond language: Social and cultural factors in school language minority students* (pp. 143–186). Los Angeles: California State University.

Hiebert, E. (1981). Developmental patterns and interrelationships of preschool children's print awareness. *Reading Research Quarterly, 16,* 236–260.

Hough, R. A., Nurss, J. R., & Enright, D. S. (1986). Story reading with limited English speaking children in the regular classroom. *The Reading Teacher, 39,* 510–514.

Hudelson, S., & Barrera, R. (1985). Bilingual/second-language learners and reading. In L. W. Searfoss & J. E. Readence (Eds.), *Helping children learn to read* (pp. 370–392). Englewood Cliffs, NJ: Prentice-Hall.

Jaggar, A. M. (1974). Beginning reading: Let's make it a language experience for Black English speakers. In B. E. Cullinan (Ed.), *Black dialects and reading* (pp. 87–98). Urbana, IL: National Council of Teachers of English.

Labov, W. A. (1966). *The social stratification of English in New York City.* Washington, DC: Center for Applied Linguistics.

Lara, S. G. M. (1989). Reading placement for code switchers. *The Reading Teacher, 42,* 278–282.

Lippi-Green, R. (1997). What we talk about when we talk about Ebonics: Why definitions matter. *Black Scholar, 27,* 7–11.

Lonigan, C. J., Burgess, S. R., Anthony, J. L., & Baker, T. A. (1998). Development of phonological sensitivity in 2- to 5-year-old children. *Journal of Educational Psychology, 90,* 294–311.

Martinez-Roldan, C. M., & Lopez-Robertson, J. M. (1999/2000). Initiating literature circles in a first-grade bilingual classroom. *The Reading Teacher, 53,* 270–281.

Mayer, M. (1988). *There's something in my attic.* New York: Dial.

McGee, L. M., & Richgels, D. J. (2003). *Designing early literacy programs: Strategies for at-risk preschool and kindergarten children.* New York: Guilford.

McKissack, P. (1988). *Mirandy and Brother Wind.* New York: Knopf.

McMillon, G., & Edwards, P. (2000). Why does Joshua "hate" school . . . but love Sunday School? *Language Arts, 78,* 111–120.

Meier, T. R., & Cazden, C. B. (1982). Research update: A focus on oral language and writing from a multicultural perspective. *Language Arts, 59,* 504–512.

Morrow, L. M. (1985). Retelling stories: A strategy for improving young children's comprehension, concept of story structure, and oral language complexity. *Elementary School Journal, 85,* 647–661.

Moustafa, M., & Penrose, J. (1985). Comprehensible input PLUS, the language experience approach: Reading instruction for limited English speaking students. *The Reading Teacher, 38,* 640–647.

National Center for Educational Statistics. (1996). *NAEP 1994 reading report card for the nation and states.* Office of Educational Research and Improvement. U.S. Department of Education.

National Reading Panel. (2000). *Report of the National Reading Panel.* Washington, DC: National Institutes of Health.

Neuman, S. B., Celano, D. C., Greco, A. N., & Shue, P. (2001). *Access for all: Closing the book gap for children in early education.* Newark, DE: International Reading Association.

Norris, J. A. (1988). Using communication strategies to enhance reading acquisition. *The Reading Teacher, 41,* 668–673.

O'Shea, L., & O'Shea, D. (1987). Using repeated reading. *Teaching Exceptional Children, 20,* 26–29.

Padak, N. D. (1981). The language and educational needs of children who speak Black English. *The Reading Teacher, 35,* 144–151.

Peterson, B. (1991). Selecting books for beginning readers. In D. DeFord, C. Lyons, & G. Pinnell (Eds.), *Bridges to literacy: Learning from Reading Recovery* (pp. 119–147). Portsmouth, NH: Heinemann.

Philips, S. (1972). Participant structures and communicative competence: Warm Springs children in community and classroom. In C. Cazden, V. John, & D. Hyumes (Eds.), *Functions of language in the classroom.* New York: Teachers College Press.

Pinnell, G., Fried, M., & Estice, R. (1990). Reading recovery: Learning how to make a difference. *The Reading Teacher, 43,* 282–295.

Purcell-Gates, V. (1996). Stories, coupons, and the *TV Guide:* Relationships between home literacy experiences and emergent literacy knowledge. *Reading Research Quarterly, 31,* 406–428.

Rasinski, T., & Padak, N. (1990). Multicultural learning through children's literature. *Language Arts, 67,* 576–580.

Robb, L. (1994). *Whole language, whole learners: Creating a literature-centered classroom.* New York: William Morrow.

Salvage, G., & Brazee, P. (1991). Risk taking, bit by bit. *Language Arts, 68,* 356–366.

Scarborough, H. (1991). Early syntactic development of dyslexic children. *Annals of Dyslexia, 41,* 207–220.

Senechal, M., LeFevre, J., Thomas, E. M., & Daley, K. E. (1998). Differential effects of home literacy experiences on the development of oral and written language. *Reading Research Quarterly, 33,* 96–116.

Shapiro, H. (1992). Debatable issues underlying whole-language philosophy: A speech-language pathologist's perception. *Language, Speech, and Hearing Services in Schools, 23,* 308–311.

Sinatra, R. (1981). Using visuals to help the second language learner. *The Reading Teacher, 34,* 539–546.

Sindelar, P. T. (1987). Increasing reading fluency. *Teaching Exceptional Children, 19,* 59–60.

Smitherman, G. (1977). *Talkin and testifying: The language of Black America.* Boston: Houghton Mifflin.

Snow, C. E., Burns, M. S., & Griffin, P. (Eds.). (1998). *Preventing reading difficulties in young children.* Washington, DC: National Academy Press.

Spiegel, D. (1992). Blending whole language and systematic direct instruction. *The Reading Teacher, 46,* 38–44.

Spiegel, D. L. (1995). A comparison of traditional remedial programs and Reading Recovery: Guidelines for success for all programs. *The Reading Teacher, 49,* 86–96.

Truax, R., & Kretschmer, R. (1993). Focus on research: Finding new voices in the process of meeting the needs of all children. *Language Arts, 70,* 592–601.

Urzua, C. (1980). A language-learning environment for all children. *Language Arts, 57,* 38–44.

Urzua, C. (1987). "You stopped too soon": Second language children composing and revising. *TESOL Quarterly, 21,* 279–304.

Walker, D., Greenwood, C., Hart, B., & Carta, J. (1994). Prediction of school outcomes based on socioeconomic status and early language production. *Child Development, 65,* 606–621.

Williams, C. (1994). The language and literacy worlds of three profoundly deaf preschool children. *Reading Research Quarterly, 29,* 124–155.

Williams, J. A. (2001). Classroom conversations: Opportunities to learn for ESL students in mainstream classrooms. *The Reading Teacher, 54,* 750–757.

Wolfram, W. (2002). Everyone has an accent. In B. M. Power & R. S. Hubbard (Eds.), *Language development: A reader for teachers* (2nd ed.) (pp. 225–230). Upper Saddle River, NJ: Merrill.

Yaden, D., Tam, A., Madrigal, P., Brassell, D., Massa, J., Altamrano, L., & Armendariz, J. (2000). Early literacy for inner-city children: The effects of reading and writing interventions in English and Spanish during the preschool years. *The Reading Teacher, 54,* 186–189.

Yashima, T. (1958). *Umbrella.* New York: Viking.

CHAPTER

12 Assessment

KEY CONCEPTS

observation notebook
classroom assessments
anecdotal notes
analyses of anecdotal notes
work samples
captions
scoring rubrics
portfolio conferences
portfolio summaries
essential components of
   reading and writing

screening assessments
monitoring assessments
concepts-about-print tasks
fingerpoint reading
alphabet recognition tasks
alphabet writing task
rhyming word task
alliteration
beginning phoneme task
isolating beginning phoneme
   task

segmenting and blending
   phonemes task
alphabetic principle in
   decoding and spelling
orthographic principle in
   decoding or spelling
letter–sound correspondence
   task
decodable texts
decodable text reading
   task

A Day in Kindergarten

The following is a story of a day in a kindergarten classroom that is similar to several classrooms that we have observed. We use this story as a case study of effective assessment practice. Ms. Orlando and her children are studying travel in a combined literature and content unit. As a part of this unit, Ms. Orlando has read many stories about characters who travel away from their homes and poems about traveling (including imaginary travel of the mind). The children have learned different methods of transportation and are examining ways in which seeds travel.

A Day in Ms. Orlando's Classroom

Ms. Orlando's half-day kindergarten class is divided into four blocks: whole-class gathering, center time, snack and recess or a special class, and storytime.

Whole-Group Gathering. The children are gathered on the rug as the teacher reads Kovalski's (1987) version of *The Wheels on the Bus.* Two other versions of this story are displayed in the classroom library center. Ms. Orlando holds up the book and says, "I'm going to read a new version of *The Wheels on the Bus.* This one is written and illustrated by Maryanne Kovalski. It begins differently from the other 'Wheels on the Bus' stories that we have read before. Listen carefully to find out how this version is different. When I come to the part of the story that you know, join right in and read with me." Then she begins reading, and after several pages all the children are reciting the familiar story along with her. After reading the story, Ms. Orlando and the children talk about how this story is different from the other two versions they read.

Finally, Ms. Orlando says, "Let's sing our version of the song." She finds the chart for "The Wheels on the Bus" song which was dictated earlier in the week. Ms. Orlando says, "Husalina, you can be pointer first." Husalina comes to the front of the group and takes the pointer. The children sing the song as Husalina points across the lines of the text. Then another child is selected to be pointer, and the class sings the song again.

Next Ms. Orlando introduces a new story. She says, "Our new story today is about another character who leaves home and travels to many different places. But instead of reading the story to you, I am going to tell it. The title of the story is *The Runaway Bunny,* and it was written by Margaret Wise Brown (1942)." Ms. Orlando hangs a copy of the front cover of the book on the classroom story clothesline as she reads the title (see clothesline props in Chapter 6).

After telling the story, Ms. Orlando begins a grand conversation by saying, "What did you think about the story?" The children spend several minutes sharing their personal responses. Then Ms. Orlando says, "Little Bunny sure did become a lot of things in this. You might want to draw a picture in the art center about Little Bunny and his mother and all the different things they became. Let's write a list of all the things Little Bunny turned into, and I'll put the list in the art center to remind you what you might want to draw."

Ms. Orlando uses the interactive writing technique with the children to write the list of things Little Bunny turns into. One child offers, "Little Bunny turned into a flower." Ms. Orlando asks the children to tell her which letters she will need. She says, "Flower. FFFFFlower. Everyone say out loud what letter I need to begin spelling the word *flower.*" Many of the children say "F," some children offer other letters, and a few children are silent. Ms. Orlando confirms, "Yes. F. FFF." She calls on Rayshawn, who comes to the chart and writes the letter *f.* Ms. Orlando writes the remainder of the word. She and the children complete the chart, with different children writing each initial letter.

Center Time: Ms. Orlando Teaches a Minilesson and Observes Children.

The children select centers, and Ms. Orlando circulates among the children helping them find materials and making sure that everyone has settled into an activity. (Figure 12.1 presents a description of the activities available in the centers in Ms. Orlando's classroom.) Then she calls five children over to a table where she frequently conducts small-group lessons for a minilesson on phonemic awareness and spelling. She has a collection of environmental print objects and small toys that the children have brought to school in the past two weeks. The objects include toys or print objects that begin with the letters *T, R, V,* or *L,* including a toy rabbit, a box of Tide, a toy train, a bunch of violets, and a box of lima beans. Each of the children has a metal pizza pan and several magnetic letters.

To begin a familiar game, Ms. Orlando holds up an object and emphasizes its beginning sound. She says, "Rrrrice. Now let's listen to the first sound at the beginning of rrrice." She models saying /r/ and several children select the letter *r* and put it on their pizza pans. After spelling several more words, Ms. Orlando says, "Today we are going to change this game a little bit. We are going to spell the beginning and ending of words. Like this (she holds up the toy rabbit). First I listen to the beginning of the word. Rrrrabbit. I hear an *r.*" (She puts the letter *r* on her pizza pan.) "Now I have to listen for the ending. Rabbit /t/ /t/. I hear a *t.*" (She puts the letter *t* after the letter *r* on her pizza pan.) "Now I've spelled *rabbit* with two letters, one for the beginning and one for the ending. Now let's try one together."

Ms. Orlando and the children spell several more words. Then Ms. Orlando says, "I want everyone to visit the writing center today or tomorrow. When you are writing, think about using beginning and ending letters." Then the five children

FIGURE 12.1   Ms. Orlando's Centers

Blocks:	sets of large and small blocks, several toy trucks, several toy cars, road maps, toy road signs, clipboards with paper and pencils (on which children pretend to keep track of mileage)
Art:	assorted art materials (including a variety of papers, crayons, markers, collage materials, scissors, and glue) and materials for making a visor, including paper plates and a pattern (for cutting the plate into a visor shape), elastic, and hole punchers (to punch a hole for the elastic)
Travel— Dramatic Play:	dress-up clothes, including purses and wallets; checkbook, play credit cards, play airline and bus tickets; materials for going to the beach, such as empty bottles of suntan lotion, towels, sunglasses, sand bucket and shovel; travel brochures and other materials, such as maps, blank postcards, paper, markers; materials for an ice-cream stand, including play money, cups, spoons, order pads, and a cash register
Library:	quality collection of literature; retelling props for "Henny Penny" and "The Gingerbread Man"; display of "Wheels on the Bus" books; display of books featuring ways to travel and toy boats, airplanes, trucks, motorcycles, and cars that the children collected; special tub of books, labeled "Traveling Characters," which includes four books each in a plastic bag with an audiotape for the listening center
Letter and Word:	two pieces of chart paper on which Ms. Orlando has printed the letters *T* and *R* in upper- and lowercase letters and markers (children write on the charts practicing letter formations); magazines, scissors, glue, and paper (children cut letters and pictures out of magazines and glue them on the paper); a collection of environmental print items and toys with beginning sounds of /t/, /r/, /v/, and /l/, which the children have gathered, and four grocery store sacks labeled with those letters; picture dictionaries; names of all the children in the class, and other words, such as the days of the week, months of the year, colors, and numbers
Math:	assorted manipulatives and math materials for sorting and counting; toy coins; directions for playing a game with the coins (money madness)
Discovery:	a display of different kinds of seeds the children have collected; several books about seeds and how seeds travel; magnifying glass; directions for an experiment exploring how far a piece of paper can travel when it is shaped like an acorn and when it is shaped like a maple seed, string for measuring, and paper for drawing and writing the results
Writing:	assorted writing materials and tools, blank postcards, paper, envelopes, a variety of stamps (which children use as postage stamps), picture dictionaries, photo album of children in the class with their pictures, first and last names, directory of children's addresses, telephone book, maps

choose centers for the remainder of center time; three of the children begin writing at the writing center.

Ms. Orlando picks up a clipboard on which she has placed six pieces of sticky notepaper with five children's names written at the top of each paper (one extra, blank notepaper is included). Ms. Orlando observes five or six children nearly every day. At the beginning of the year, she divided her twenty-two children into two groups of five and two groups of six children. Then she assigned each group of children to a day of the week. The first group of children is observed on Monday, the second group on Tuesday, and so on. One day a week she does not observe children, but uses the day for more small-group instruction, guests, films, cooking, or other special activities.

Ms. Orlando circulates among the children in the centers. She decides to watch Ishmail as he works in the letter and word center. She observes as he dumps out the bag of *R* and *T* objects that the class has gathered and separates them into two piles. He says "ro-bot," and places the toy in the *R* bag. He says "rrr-ice," and places it in the *R* bag. He says "t-t-tums," and places it in the *T* bag. He says "tr-ain," and places it in the *T* bag. Ms. Orlando writes her observations on one of the sticky notes.

In the library center, Ms. Orlando observes Husalina retell "Henny Penny" using the story clothesline. Husalina includes every event in the story, recalls the characters' names correctly, and repeats the dialogue, "Wanna come? Yes. Tell king sky's falled." Ms. Orlando then observes Cecelia playing in the travel dramatic-play center with Josephine and Barbara. All three girls pretend to write a letter home to their mothers. Ms. Orlando observes their writing and then asks Cecelia to read her letter. Cecelia reads, "Dear Mom, I'm having fun. Cecelia."

Ms. Orlando invites Rayshawn to read the "Wheels on the Bus" chart with her; she is aware that he rarely chooses to reread the classroom charts or retell stories in the library center. Rayshawn points to the text from left to right and across the lines as he recites the words to the song. Ms. Orlando notes that he has memorized the words to the song, but is not matching the words he says with the words in the text.

Storytime.   As center time comes to an end, Ms. Orlando helps the children put away their center activities and get ready for snack and outdoor recess. After recess, she reads a big book version of *Rosie's Walk* (Hutchins, 1968). As she reads, she pauses to invite children to make predictions about what will happen next. She notes that Jasmine, Tuong, and Ishmail catch on to the repetitive pattern and make accurate predictions of the story. After reading, the children share responses.

Ms. Orlando Reflects and Plans

After the children are dismissed, Ms. Orlando takes time to organize her observations and make plans for instruction. First she takes the sticky notes off the clipboard and puts each note in her **observation notebook.** This notebook is divided into sections, one for each child in the classroom. As she places the sticky notes in the notebook, she reflects on what the observations show about each child's understanding about reading or writing. She writes her analysis beside the sticky note in the observation notebook.

Her notes capture what she observed Ishmail and Husalina doing and saying. She indicates that Ishmail segmented the word *robot* into syllables (*ro*) and (*bot*), the word *rice* into its beginning phoneme (*r*) and rime (*ice*), and the word *train* into its onset (*tr*) and rime (*ain*) by segmenting these words in her notes. She indicated in her notes that he matched each of the words with its appropriate letter. Her analysis reflects these observations: "Ishmail segments words between syllables, onset and rimes, and beginning phonemes. He knows the sounds associated with *T* and *R*. He is making the transition from phonological to phonemic awareness."

Ms. Orlando decides to put Cecelia's letter, which she collected from the travel dramatic-play center, in Cecelia's portfolio (a large folder in which she keeps examples of that child's work). She quickly writes a caption for Cecelia's letter and clips it to the letter. The caption includes the date and Ms. Orlando's analysis of what the letter reveals about Cecelia's understanding about writing. Figure 12.2 shows Cecelia's letter and Ms. Orlando's caption.

FIGURE 12.2   Cecelia's Letter and Caption

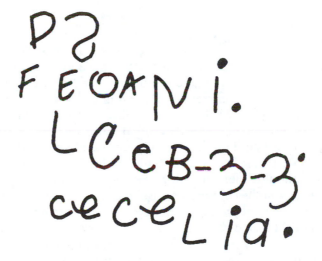

Caption: 11/2   Cecelia is using emerging letter form. Her signature is in the appropriate location for letters. She shows awareness of linearity, hyphens, and periods. Her meaning is appropriate for the situation (pretending her mother misses her) and includes language used in a letter. She uses conventional alphabet letter forms (with one reversal). She relies on contextual dependency.

Text: Dear Mom,
          I'm having fun.
          Cecelia

Then Ms. Orlando thinks back on the day's activities and her observations. She decides that she needs to teach a small-group lesson with Jasmine, Rayshawn, and a few other children on finger-point reading of memorized stories. She plans to teach a minilesson on monitoring fingerpoint reading and plans to include a pocket-chart activity for the "Wheels on the Bus" song.

Effective Classroom Assessment

Ms. Orlando's instructional and assessment practices are highly effective. At the preschool level, effective assessment practices are guided by teachers' understandings about child development in general and literacy development in particular. Assessments gathered from classroom activities that are used to guide instruction are called **classroom assessments.**

Classroom assessment is a critical component of effective teaching; teachers use information from their assessments of children's learning to guide instructional decisions and inform parents about their children's progress in literacy acquisition. Many teachers, like Ms. Orlando, gather information from their classroom assessments of children into portfolios.

Components of a Portfolio

Portfolios are collections of anecdotal notes and analyses, work samples and captions, and work samples and scoring rubrics that have been purposefully selected to show children's current understandings about a variety of literacy concepts (Valencia, 1990). Over time, these collections show children's growth as readers and writers (Barone, 1999). **Anecdotal notes** are written accounts of what teachers observe children doing and saying during literacy activities (Rhodes & Nathenson-Mejia, 1992). They are objective accounts, without evaluation, of what happens. Although brief, they capture enough information about children's actions so that even months later teachers can use them to recall exactly what was done and said. **Analyses of anecdotal notes** are written statements that identify what children know based on their behavior and words. Analyses identify the concepts that children know while anecdotal notes capture what children do. Anecdotal notes and analyses are based on careful and systematic observations of children as they engage in literacy activities. **Work samples** are samples of children's reading and writing activities collected from ongoing classroom experiences. Work samples might include compositions, grocery lists written in a grocery store dramatic-play center, pages from journals, stories or reports, copies of improvised structure stories that children compose collaboratively, or copies of children's signatures from sign-in sheets. These samples reflect the diversity of children's classroom literacy experiences.

Captions are the same as analyses of anecdotal notes; they are written statements that identify the concepts revealed in children's products and their talk surrounding the making of the samples. **Scoring rubrics** are used to evaluate particular kinds of work samples. The next section describes using observation and analyses as a part of the portfolio process, followed by a discussion about rubrics.

Using Observation and Analysis as Assessment Tools.   Observation is one of the most important classroom assessment tools. As teachers observe children interacting with other children and using reading and writing in functional ways, their concepts about written language meanings, forms, meaning-form links, and functions are revealed. Teachers capture this information by writing anecdotal notes. They provide glimpses into what children were doing and saying in an ongoing classroom activity. Teachers use the fewest possible words to describe the classroom setting of an event and children's activities; they include as many of the children's words as possible.

Deciding what to write anecdotal notes about is one of the most critical components of effective assessment (Clay, 1998). Teachers can be guided by their awareness of possible emergent concepts that children might acquire as suggested by developmental sequences (such as the ones we described in Chapters 2 through 5), but they should be cognizant that these developmental sequences provide only a rough guide to any one child's literacy development. Teachers usually choose to write an anecdotal note when they observe an event that reflects a child's current level of understanding about written language or a new level of understanding. For example, suppose that a first grade teacher is concerned about a child's inability to select and sustain interest in a book for independent reading. The teacher observes that the child selects three different books in five minutes and does no more than look quickly through the books at the illustrations. Figure 12.3 presents the teacher's anecdotal note and analysis of this behavior. Several months later, the teacher may observe the same child spending more than fifteen minutes reading *Hop on Pop* (Seuss, 1963) with a friend in the library center. The teacher writes an anecdotal note about this event because the teacher knows that it documents significant growth in the child's ability and willingness to sustain interest in reading. Figure 12.3 also shows the teacher's anecdotal note about this new behavior and analysis of the child's progress.

Observations are only powerful when they are accompanied by thoughtful analysis. Observation merely provides information about observable behaviors and the language that children use as they complete a task or participate in a literacy event. Analysis is when teachers determine the significance of these behaviors and language—they make a statement about the concepts that children are using. This means that teachers must make inferences about the underlying cognitive strategies and understandings that are reflected in the child's language and behavior (Clay, 1998). For example, Ms. Orlando's analyses reveal inferences she made about Ishmail's phonemic awareness knowledge.

Observation and analysis are important tools for all teachers, but especially so for teachers with struggling readers or when children's literacy concepts are not yet conventional. Observation is also important for children from diverse back-

FIGURE 12.3   **Anecdotal Notes Showing Development**

Note 10/15

[handwritten note:]
10/15 Barbara

sits near bookcase
pulls books out at
random, flips through
looking at pictures,
spends 4 minutes
then leaves center

Analysis 10/15

Barbara willingly participates in independent reading. She browses through books looking at pictures. (needs support in selecting books and strategies for sustaining interest)

Note 2/7

[handwritten note:]
2/7 Barbara
searches for and
retells Hop on
Pop
sustains retelling
for over 10
minutes

Analysis 2/7

Barbara enjoys reading books to others. She is comfortable reading books she has memorized and spends long periods of time rereading these books. She selects these books for independent reading. Note progress from unable to sustain interest in books to sustains interest for prolonged periods of time from 10/15.

grounds. For example, one preschool teacher, new to the bilingual preschool program, noticed that her children "did not, for example, know how to hold a book; they did not know letter names nor did they try to write them; they were not accustomed to drawing; [and] their early scribbles did not distinguish between letter-like forms and drawings" (Ballenger, 1999, p. 42). She was concerned that she document the growth these children made as literacy learners although she knew that it would be some time before they would display conventional understandings. She decided to use observations at the writing table to document her children's literacy growth. There she observed four-year-old Giles write his name and then carefully cut out the G. He carried it "around the classroom saying, 'I no cut my G'" (p. 46).

Teachers in kindergarten and first grade will want to use observation and analysis to supplement the assessments of children's conventional reading and writing proficiency that often are required at that level. They are often required to assess children's conventional knowledge about, for example, alphabet letter recognition, phonemic awareness, or letter–sound correspondences. During these phases of literacy development children will display both conventional knowledge, for example, of alphabet letter names, knowing the sounds or phonemes associated with some letters, and being able to name rhyming words. However, they will also display incomplete, not fully developed awareness of these concepts in their reading and writing attempts. The combination of observation, collection of work samples, and careful analyses along with more conventional assessment will provide the most powerful information to guide teachers' decision making about instruction for particular children, especially for those most at-risk for reading failure.

Using Scoring Rubrics as Assessment Tools

Rubrics are assessment tools that show how well children have learned particular features taught in instruction. Rubrics identify key areas or elements that should be included in a high-quality work sample (Skillings & Ferrell, 2000). For example, when evaluating a child's story composition, a scoring rubric would identify the components that should be included in the story (e.g., setting, character names, and problem) as well as indications of quality (e.g., sometimes, usually, or always includes descriptive words).

Scoring rubrics can be even more effective when children and teachers develop the rubric together. Figure 12.4 presents a scoring rubric developed by second graders and their teacher as a part of a poetry writing unit. As a part of the unit, the children learned to use words that appeal to the five senses, lining and shape, alliteration and rhyme, and other poetic elements. They wrote shape poems and developed the rubric to evaluate their poems. To develop the rubric, the teacher asked the children to describe what would be included in an excellent shape poem. The children said that these poems would have good ideas, correct spelling and punctuation, and have good handwriting. Then the teacher guided the children to also think about some of the poetic elements that she had been teaching: the poem's title, the shape of the poem, and if the poem appeals to the five senses. Then the teacher guided the children to discuss what would be included in a poor shape poem and finally an adequate one.

Figure 12.5 presents Lane's shape poem. His poem was judged to be an excellent shape poem because it had a good title, the shape was related to the poem's topic, it appealed to two senses (taste and sight), he used good handwriting, and he spelled words correctly.

Using Portfolios

Portfolios serve several functions in the classroom. They are used to make instructional decisions, help children reflect on what they have been learning, and share with parents information about their children's literacy growth (Hansen, 1996; Porter & Cleland, 1995). For portfolios to be useful, they must be manageable and up-to-date. Most importantly, portfolios help teachers reflect on their own practice (Bergeron, Wermuth, & Hammar, 1997; Kieffer & Faust, 1994).

Using Portfolios to Make Instructional Decisions. We have stressed that teachers' observations and analyses focus on what children *can* do. However, making instructional decisions means that teachers look beyond what children can do and consider the next steps in learning. For example, Ms. Orlando noticed that Rayshawn attempted to point to text while he recited a familiar song. She knows that eventually the children need to be able to match the text word for word. With

FIGURE 12.4   Shape Poem Scoring Rubric

Excellent Shape Poem	Good/Adequate Shape Poem	Poor Shape Poem
best handwriting	good handwriting	sloppy handwriting
all words spelled correctly	most words spelled correctly	many words misspelled
good title	has a title	no title
appeals to two or more senses	appeals to one sense	does not appeal to senses
words written in obvious shape of poem's topic	words written in a shape but not obvious	words written in lines
very interesting ideas	some interesting ideas	no interesting ideas

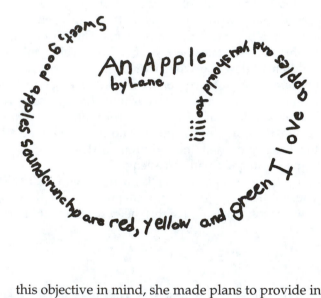

FIGURE 12.5   Apple Shape Poem

this objective in mind, she made plans to provide instruction to nudge children in this direction. Teachers always keep in mind the next step in learning and consider whether they need to plan instruction to help children take that next step.

Using Portfolios to Support Children's Reflections.   One way to encourage children to reflect on their learning is to hold portfolio conferences. **Portfolio conferences** provide opportunities for children to select pieces to include in their portfolios and to reflect on their learning (Bauer & Garcia, 1997). Children talk about reasons for selecting samples to add to a portfolio (most interesting story, best writing, favorite poem, and so on).

After the conferences, teachers prepare **portfolio summaries** (Courtney & Abodeeb, 1999), which summarize the children's literacy growth and achievement toward the literacy goals. To prepare the summaries, they review all their anecdotal notes, children's work samples, and children's performances on any literacy tasks that they have administered.

Using Portfolios to Inform Parents.   Portfolios provide teachers with an excellent resource for sharing information about children's learning with parents. To prepare to share with parents, teachers consider information that parents will find useful and make a list of a few of each child's key new understandings. Then they select eight to ten work samples, anecdotal notes, or checklists to illustrate each child's learning. Finally, teachers think about one or two areas in which the child needs further practice or instruction.

Children may be involved in the parent conferences. If so, teachers help children prepare for the conferences by having them identify two or three things that they have learned and find evidence of this learning in their work samples. During the conferences, children share what they have learned. Teachers extend the conferences by sharing their analyses with both parents and children. The conferences might end with having the children formulate one or two goals for future learning.

Making Portfolios Selective.   Many teachers believe that they need to collect many work samples and anecdotal notes (Roe & Vukelich, 1998). They carefully observe each child once a week, write analyses, and collect one or two work samples for each child each week. However, collecting this much information on each child may not be productive. Portfolios are intended to document children's typical literacy performances and to show how those typical performances change over time (Gronlund, 1998). Therefore, teachers should be selective in choosing to write an anecdotal note or collect a work sample (Sarafini, 2001). Notes and samples need to be collected when teachers notice a change in children's understanding or performance. When they observe the children performing the same way with similar levels of proficiency, they may decide not to take note of this activity or collect this particular sample.

Keeping Portfolios Manageable.   Teachers' time is limited, and collecting and analyzing assessment information is time-consuming. Teachers need to make manageable plans and then make a commitment to follow those plans (Gronlund, 1998). For example, Ms. Orlando takes fifteen minutes four days a week to observe her children. She writes anecdotal notes as she observes in the classroom and analyzes those notes the same day. She realizes that collecting notes on children over time is extremely valuable in helping her to know individual children. All teachers must make decisions about how much time they have to devote to assessment and which assessments will provide them with the information they need. Teachers cannot use all the assessments described in this chapter—they would do nothing but assess! Nevertheless, teachers are responsible for documenting children's growth as readers and writers. Their assessments reflect their commitment to a quality, child-centered program that supports the literacy learning of all children.

Screening and Monitoring Literacy Development

The perspective that we take in this book and in the first part of this chapter is a developmental one. We emphasize that children's conventional reading and writing grows out of their unconventional early literacy concepts (Clay, 1998). However, important reports synthesizing research on reading and literacy development (National Reading Panel, 2000; Snow, Burns, & Griffin, 1998) have outlined key components of literacy that children need in order to become successful and highly proficient readers and writers. *All of the essential components of reading and writing identified in these reports are embedded in our earlier discussion of what children can and do learn as they become self-generative readers.*

Essential Components of Reading and Writing

Figure 12.6 presents a list of the **essential components of reading and writing** for children in the emergent stage of reading and writing (novices and experimenters), early reading and writing, and transitional reading and writing. These components include a focus on meaning (comprehension and vocabulary), form (alphabet knowledge, grammar, and punctuation), and meaning-form links (phonemic awareness, alphabetic principle in decoding and spelling, and orthographic principle in decoding and spelling).

FIGURE 12.6   Overview of Essential Components of Literacy and Assessment Tasks

Reading Phase	Literacy Concept	Assessment Tasks
Novice and Experimenting Readers and Writers (Pre-K and Kindergarten)	• concepts about print	*Concepts about Print* (Clay, 1993) task fingerpoint reading task
	• alphabet recognition and writing	alphabet recognition task alphabet writing task
	• phonemic awareness	rhyming word and beginning phoneme tasks isolating beginning phoneme task *blending and segmenting onset and rime task
	• comprehension and vocabulary	retelling and retelling checklist of read-aloud
	• *alphabetic principle	*developmental spelling inventory and analysis *letter–sound correspondence task *advanced concepts to be assessed if children demonstrate moderate knowledge of alphabet and beginning phoneme

FIGURE 12.6 Continued

Reading Phase	Literacy Concept	Assessment Tasks
Early Readers and Writers (first and second grades)	• phonemic awareness	blending and segmenting onset and rime task
		blending and segmenting phoneme task
	• alphabetic principle in decoding	decodable text reading task/running record/ analysis
		leveled text reading/running record/ miscue analysis/decoding analysis
	• alphabetic principle in spelling	*Elementary Spelling Inventory and Feature Guide* (Bear et al., 2000)
	• comprehension and vocabulary	retelling and retelling checklist of read-aloud
		instructional text reading: questions
	• reading text of increasing difficulty	leveled text reading/instructional level
	• writing longer and more coherent texts for a variety of purposes with increasing use of conventions	samples of writing/analysis
Transitional Readers and Writers (second grade and beyond)	• orthographic principle in decoding	*The Names Test of Decoding* (Cunningham, 2000)
	• orthographic principles in spelling	*Elementary Spelling Inventory and Feature Guide* (Bear et al., 2000)
	• comprehension and vocabulary	retelling of instructional level text/checklist
		grand conversation/response to literature checklist
		instructional text reading/questions
	• fluency	instructional text reading/rate and prosody
	• reading variety of genre of increasing difficulty	leveled text reading (narrative and nonfiction)/ instructional level
	• writing text of increasing complexity in a variety of genres and with increasingly complex conventions	samples of writing/analysis/rubrics

This figure also lists at least one assessment task that teachers can use to screen and monitor children's knowledge of each of the essential components. **Screening assessments** are used to determine children's initial level of concept development. In kindergarten and beyond, they can be used to identify children who have particularly low levels of literacy development and may be at risk for later reading difficulties. These children may need more intensive teaching to accelerate their literacy growth. **Monitoring assessments** are used throughout the year to monitor the children's progress. The assessment tasks we describe are easily administered to individual or small groups of children as a small-group activity or during a conference.

As we discussed earlier in this chapter, we believe it is essential that teachers supplement their assessment of individual children's progress in acquiring the essential components of reading and writing with careful observation, collection of work samples, and analyses. The assessment tasks that we describe in this part of the chapter capture children's acquisition of conventional reading skills and strategies. These end points of literacy development are important, but emerge from children's early unconventional concepts.

Concepts-about-Print Tasks

Concepts-about-print tasks are designed to assess children's understanding of familiar words used to talk about books, awareness of directionality, and understanding of the conventions of written language (Clay, 1993). Teachers can construct their own concepts-about-print test. They select an unfamiliar picture book and ask children to point to the front and back of the book, to the beginning and ending of the story, and to the top and bottom of a page. They have children point to where to start reading (upper left), where to go next (across to the right), and then where to read next (return sweep to the next line of text). Using a big book, teachers can have child locate one word, the first and last letter in a word, a period, and a capital letter.

Another concepts-about-print assessment task is to engage children in fingerpoint reading (Bloodgood, 1999). **Fingerpoint reading** is when children have memorized three to six lines of a familiar poem, song, or portion of a book, and they point to each word as they recite the memorized text. For example, teachers could help children sing and then say the song, "Twinkle, Twinkle Little Star" and then prepare an enlarged version of the song on a chart or in a pocket chart. Children fingerpoint read and teachers observe to evaluate how well children memorize the short text, match their saying of the song to pointing to the words (one-to-one match of the spoken words to the written words), and can use fingerpoint reading to locate a target word. Children who have well-developed concepts about print easily memorize the text, point to each written word as they say the spoken word, and can use fingerpoint reading to locate words such as *star, wonder, up, the,* and *Twinkle.* Children who are developing concepts about print will memorize most of the song easily and attempt to point at each word (although the two-syllable words may disrupt their pointing). They may be able to locate meaningful words and words at the beginning or end of lines of texts. However, they may not be able to locate words such as *the* or words in the middle of lines. Children who have not yet developed many concepts about print may merely sweep their hands across the text without attempting to point at individual words and will not be able to use fingerpoint reading to locate individual words in the song.

Fingerpoint reading is not an assessment of children's conventional reading ability. In fact, this assessment is not appropriate for children who have acquired many sight words and can read easy beginning texts. Instead, this assessment provides information about children who are not yet conventionally reading or who may have only acquired a few sight words. One-to-one matching of spoken language to written language is one of the first strategies early readers acquire and this assessment allows teachers to determine children's progress in achieving this critical emergent reading skill.

Alphabet Recognition Tasks

To assess children's knowledge of alphabet letter names, teachers can prepare **alphabet recognition tasks.** They write (or type) all the uppercase and lowercase alphabet letters in random order on a sheet of paper or on index cards. Children are asked to name the letters, and teachers record the letters that children fail to identify. Preschool and kindergarten teachers are particularly interested in recognizing children's progress in identifying letters correctly.

Teachers may also want to assess which alphabet letters children can write. In the **alphabet writing task,** teachers dictate letters for children to write and assess which letters children know (noting when orientation may be off). For preschoolers who do not yet recognize or write alphabet letters conventionally, teachers can observe children as they pretend to write in the dramatic-play center or writing center (Ballenger, 1999).

Phonemic Awareness Tasks

We recommend a variety of phonemic awareness assessments that progress from easier to more difficult (also see Adams, Foorman, Lundberg, & Beeler, 1998; Yopp, 1995). At the emergent stage, we recommend having children match rhyming word pictures in a **rhyming word task.** Teachers gather pictures of rhyming word pairs (such as *goat* and *boat*) along with a nonrhyming foil (such as *truck*). Children can either point to pictures of the two words that rhyme or to the picture that does not rhyme with the others (Lonigan et al., 1998). Teachers should demonstrate the task with at least two sets of pictures before beginning the assessment. This assessment can be used with small groups of two or three children with careful observation. Ten sets of pictures are sufficient to determine whether the children have a concept of rhyme (finding seven or more rhyming matches) or not (choosing four or fewer matches).

A similar phonemic awareness assessment can be developed for assessing children's awareness of **alliteration** or words with the same beginning phonemes using a **beginning phoneme task.** Teachers gather pictures of beginning phoneme pairs (such as *goat* and *girl*) and a nonalliterative foil (such as *sock*). The words selected for this assessment should have single initial consonants or digraphs (e.g., *bat, fish, soap, ship,* and *chicken*) rather than consonant clusters (e.g., *broom, flower,* and *star*). Again, ten sets of pictures is sufficient to determine whether children have this concept. The pictures used in the beginning phoneme assessment can also be used to assess whether children can isolate and identify beginning phonemes in an **isolating beginning phoneme task.** Here teachers show a picture (such as *goat*) and ask the child to say just a little bit at the beginning of the word (/g/). Demonstration of this task is essential. Again, ten pictures with several different beginning phonemes is sufficient.

The most difficult phonemic awareness task is to blend and segment two- and three-phoneme words into individual phonemes (Yopp, 1988). To prepare a **segmenting and blending phonemes task,** the teacher again selects twenty pictures plus additional pictures for demonstration. Several of the pictures should be of two-phoneme words (e.g., *bee, toe, ape,* and *shoe*) while the others are three-phoneme words (e.g., *sock, bike, house,* and *ship*). The teacher demonstrates the task by perhaps using a puppet. The child completes the task and the teacher determines how many single phonemes the child segments or whether the child is able to say the correct word. Not all children need all of these phonemic awareness assessments we have described. Rather, teachers select the task at which children are most likely to be successful and then try the next more challenging task. Across time, children (especially in first and second grades) will develop more sophisticated phonemic awareness and be able to master the most difficult task we described.

Assessing Alphabetic and Orthographic Principle Use in Decoding and Spelling

One of the essential components of reading is to be able to decode unfamiliar words. Children demonstrate their understanding and use of the **alphabetic principle in decoding and spelling** in a variety of ways—some of which require more sophisticated knowledge and use of letter–sound relationships (phonics) than others. For example, using only the beginning letter to make a guess at an unknown word while reading does demonstrate some level of the alphabetic principle in decoding. Similarly, a child who invents a spelling using only one letter to spell the word is demonstrating a rudimentary knowledge of alphabetic principle. The most advanced level of alphabetic decoding and spelling is sounding out or decoding an entire word, blending each of the letter–sound correspondences in that word or spelling a word with a letter for each of the word's phonemes (fully phonemic spelling).

However, using letter–sound correspondences alone is not the most sophisticated decoding strategy. Employing orthographic principles where children use chunks of letters to pronounce words parts is more efficient especially for reading multisyllable words (Cunningham, 2000). When employing the **orthographic principle in decoding or spelling,** children use familiar phonograms or word parts, prefixes, and suffixes to both decode and spell words.

The easiest decoding assessment is to determine whether children can match pictures of words to alphabet letters corresponding to the beginning phoneme in the word. For the **letter–sound correspondence task** teachers gather pictures of objects that begin with ten or more consonant phonemes. The teacher pronounces the word in the picture and asks the child to say the letter associated with the sound they hear at the beginning of that word, or children can point to the letter on a card on which all the consonant letters have been printed.

A more sophisticated assessment is to ask children to read unfamiliar **decodable texts** while teachers record the words that are not correctly decoded and later analyze these miscues for which consonants and vowel letter–sound correspondences children use, use but confuse, or do not yet use. One set of decodable texts that teachers might use in a **decodable text reading task** is a series of books called *Dr. Maggie's Phonics Readers: A New View* (Allen, 1999a). This is a series of twenty-four books in which the text is carefully written to introduce children to a progression of phonics skills such as using just a few consonants with the short *a*, adding more consonants and gradually introducing short *o, i, u,* and *e*. Then children learn consonant digraphs and various spellings of long and other vowel sounds. The stories are interesting and well-illustrated and they include a few words that do not follow the phonics patterns being introduced but which add interest to the stories. High-frequency sight words are also included. We highly recommend assessing children's decoding using real words and texts rather than having children blend nonsense words.

To use decodable text to assess alphabetic decoding, teachers select a book not used in their instructional programs. They introduce the book by looking at its cover, reading its title, and talking with the child about what the book might be about. Then children read the book. As the child reads the teacher makes notes about miscues the child makes. For example, one teacher used *Top Job, Mom!* (Allen, 1999b) to assess an early reader's decoding. This text includes many three- and four-letter words with short *o* and *a* vowels. One child read, "It got hot, so Mom got a new" (p. 2), but got stuck on the next two words in the sentence (*tan fan*). The teacher waited to observe what the child would do. The child correctly pronounced the /t/ in the word *tan* but paused indicating her uncertainty about the rest of the word. The teacher then suggested she look all the way through the word, read the rest of the sentence, and then come back to work on this tricky word. The child read the word *fan* correctly. The teacher invited the child to reread the sentence and get her mouth ready to say the tricky word. Again the child pronounced the beginning letter's sound, but not the word. Now the teacher directed the child's attention to the letters *an* in *fan* and in *tan*. She asked, "Does that help you? If this word is *fan,* then this word could be" and she paused to let the child figure out the word. Now the child correctly said *tan fan*. From this the teacher noted that this child was not decoding unknown words by blending consonant, short vowel, consonant. Instead, she was using a strategy of relying on the first consonant and the context of the sentence. The teacher decided that this child needed more blending practice building new words from just a few letters and short vowels.

For children at a more advanced level, teachers can use *The Names Test of Decoding* (Cunningham, 2000, p. 137) to assess orthographic decoding. This assessment includes thirty-seven names carefully selected to include familiar word parts, prefixes, and suffixes including words with two or more syllables. Teachers present the list of names to children, and children read them aloud. Teachers record what children say (when they do not read the name correctly) and later analyze what this reveals about children's orthographic decoding. For example, one third grader read the name *Wendy Swain* as *Wendy Swan, Troy Whitlock* as *Troy Whitelock,* and *Vance Middleton* as *Vancee Midtown.* These miscues suggest that this child uses but confuses long and other vowels (sometimes he decodes words with these vowels successfully, but sometimes does not). In addition, he is not familiar with the *ton* suffix.

To assess alphabetic and orthographic strategies in spelling, teachers can examine children's spellings in first draft compositions looking for late emergent spellings, letter name-alphabetic spellings, within-a-word spellings, and syllable and affix spellings. A more systematic approach is to use a **developmental spelling inventory.** A developmental spelling inventory is a list of words children are asked to spell. The list is purposefully designed so that many different spelling patterns are included. For example, one list (Johnston, Invernizzi, & Juel, 1998) intended for first graders includes ten words (*van, pet, rug, sad, plum, chip, shine, skate, float,* and *treat*) that have initial and final consonants, short vowels, blends and digraphs, and long vowel markers (p. 49). We recommend using the *Elementary Spelling Inventory* (Bear et al., 2000) and its accompanying *Feature Guide.* The feature guide allows teachers to record which spelling patterns children use correctly or misspell. Teachers can determine whether children consistently use, use but sometimes confuse, or do not use particular spelling patterns including:

- Consonants
- Consonant clusters (*br, gl, st,* etc.)
- Consonant digraphs (*sh, ch, th, ph, wh,* and *ng*)
- Short vowels (m*a*d, etc.)
- Silent *e* long vowels (m*a*de, etc.)
- Long and other vowel combinations (m*ai*l, p*a*y, m*ea*t, t*oy*, etc.)
- Prefixes
- Suffixes
- Familiar word parts (*le* in *bottle,* etc.)

Assessing Comprehension and Vocabulary

Comprehension and vocabulary can be assessed in three ways: having children retell what they have read or heard their teacher read aloud, answer questions, or take part in a grand conversation. Teachers record what children say as they retell, answer questions, or make comments in the grand conversation. They use a retelling checklist to analyze children's comprehension as revealed in a retelling and a response to literature checklist to evaluate children's interpretation of literature as revealed in their participation in grand conversations or response journals. Using questions to determine comprehension is discussed later in the chapter when we describe how to take running records.

Using Retelling Checklists.   To assess retellings, teachers prepare a retelling checklist that includes all the important information from a story or informational text. As a child retells the story, the teacher checks off each event included in the child's retelling. After the child finishes retelling, the teacher may use several prompts to see whether the child has understood more about the story than he or she recalled at first. Depending on the parts of the story that were not recalled, teachers ask, "Do you remember any other characters?" "Where (when) did the story take place?" "What was (the main character's) problem?" "How did (the main character) solve the problem?" "Can you remember anything else that happened in the story?" "How did the story end?" Children's original retelling is called *unprompted recall,* and their responses to these questions is called *prompted recall.* The *retelling score* is the percentage of total ideas (prompted and unprompted) recalled.

To make retelling checklists, teachers select short stories of 100 to 300 words, read the stories carefully, and make a list of the important events. Retelling checklists can be constructed for informational texts as well. In this case, teachers make a list of all main ideas and supporting details or examples.

While a **retelling checklist** helps a teacher understand how much a child remembers after reading a storybook or informational book, it does not provide information about the quality of children's **retellings.** We recommend that teachers tape-record children's retellings so that they can better analyze their quality. Teachers can purchase a ninety minute audiocassette for each child in their class. They can use the tapes to record retellings at the beginning of the year, mid-year, and near the end of the year.

To analyze the quality of a retelling of a storybook, teachers consider whether children include none, some, or many details about the introduction, setting, main character, supporting characters, problem, events leading up to the solution of the problem, climax, and ending (Morrow, 1989). A high quality retelling includes many details about all of these components of a story presented in sequence. The highest quality narrative retelling would include a more abstract overall summary statement such as, "This story is about a homeless father and his son who try to make their lives better." This summary of *Fly Away Home* (Bunting, 1991) is nearly a theme statement. High quality retellings also include many of the vocabulary words used in the story. For example, *Fly Away Home* includes specialized vocabulary words and phrases such as *blue zippered bag, flight attendants, luggage, main terminal, hollow spaces, passengers,* and *noticeable.* These are more sophisticated words than *bag, people,* or *suitcase.* Teachers can make note when children include these more sophisticated words in their retellings.

To analyze the quality of an informational book, teachers consider whether children retell the topic, include the major information with supporting details, make explicit relationships between main ideas, and follow the organization of the text that was read (Cooper, 1993). High quality retellings of information books are not mere recitation of the facts; they reveal that children understand the purpose of the text and its underlying organization. High quality retellings of information books include many of the content-specific vocabulary found in the text.

Using Response-to-Literature Checklists. **Response-to-literature checklists** are used to analyze the nature of children's contributions to grand conversations or the content of their response journals. As children participate in grand conversations or write in response journals, they recall events, evaluate the text globally, make inferences or evaluations of characters and events, identify with a character, state themes, relate personal experiences, make connections to other literature, and comment on or evaluate literary structures or languages (McGee, 1992; Sipe, 2002). Children also make predictions, hypothesize about outcomes or reasons for actions, and ask questions or identify confusing parts of the text. These responses indicate children's personal involvement with the story or informational text and their ability to construct inferential, evaluative, and interpretive understandings. Figure 12.7 presents five first graders' grand conversation about *Hey, Al* (Yorinks, 1986), which illustrates the variety of different responses that teachers can expect in grand conversations (see also Figure 5.3 in Chapter 5).

Figure 12.8 on page 372 presents a response-to-literature checklist, which can be used to analyze children's responses in grand conversations and response journals. To use the response checklist, teachers audiotape or videotape grand conversations or collect entries from children's response journals. They review their recordings and focus on the contributions of one child at a time. They complete a checklist for each child participating in the grand conversation and note the levels of understanding reflected in children's responses.

FIGURE 12.7   Grand Conversation about *Hey, Al* (Yorinks, 1986)

Teacher (T): What did you think of the story?

Chris: I like the part when he turns into a bird. The dog and Eddie.

Ryan: Hey! Eddie's the dog. I like the part when he's laying down in the water, and the birds bring him food and stuff and he's wearing the old hat that he used to have and I like the dog, too.

Annie: I like the part when they were going back to their own house and Eddie fell into the ocean.

T: Why did you like that part?

Annie: Because it was gonna be okay.

T: Did you know that for sure?

John: No, no.

Chris: Yeah, because if they were on earth they wouldn't be birds.

Annie: I like the part when they got home and they painted everything yellow so everything would be okay. Al's dog came back so Al wouldn't be afraid that he didn't have a dog anymore.

Alice: I liked the part when he was a janitor but then he said, there's no— like when he was gonna go up there, and he was gonna change his mind, but he didn't.

Ryan: I like the part when the bird comes to say, "Hey, Al," and he jumps when he's shaving his face and the bird came and says, "Al, Al," and he jumped and said, "Who's that?" and the razor came out of his hand.

John: Yeah, it was funny.

Alice: I liked those birds with all those big, big legs.

FIGURE 12.7 Continued

Annie: I like the part when they were going up there and Al lost his luggage. Hey! Look at that! Look at that hand! (Annie points to illustration in which a bird has a human hand)

T: Oh, where?

Annie: He's turning back.

T: Look what Annie's found.

John: He was a person.

Annie: All of them were persons.

Ryan: They were all persons?

Annie: People! All of these were people! Look at his hands.

John: I know. That's what I said.

Chris: If they all stay there, they'll all be birds.

Annie: Oh, look. How can he be changed back?

Alice: I could tell he was an old man because look at his skin.

Annie: I think all the animals were humans before they came out there because one of these animals was the real one and they turn real people into

John: animals.

Ryan: Yeah, birds and they have to go back but they don't know how to get back because some of them don't have wings.

Eric: I like the bird there with the hand in the cage with the funny mouth.

John: I liked the part when he fell in that place up in the air.

Annie: In the water.

John: No. When he fell in the place in the sky. When the bird was dropping him down into the place.

T: Well, what do you think Al found out at the island?

Annie: I think he would be better as a janitor instead of up there. He learned never talk to strangers.

Ryan: If he stayed up there, he would really be a bird and we don't know if he could change back again and his whole body would be a bird.

John: He loves his home.

T: How do you know?

John: Because he was happy to be back and the dog came back and they painted it.

Annie: They painted it yellow like the place. He was happy at the end.

Chris: Yeah, and he got a new shirt like it wasn't the shirt from, like he was a janitor again, but he's got a nicer shirt and he looks happy.

Alice: Eddie is smiling. Yeah. The story has a happy ending.

FIGURE 12.8   Response-to-Literature Checklist

Name _____ Annie _____ Date _____ 4/16 _____

Title _____ Hey, Al _____

Other Children in Group _____ Chris, Ryan, John, _____

_____ Alice, Eric _____

Product (What child said or wrote)	**Comments**
Level 1: Recall and global evaluation	
✓ recalls story events and characters	Eddie fell ocean
makes global evaluations	
recalls text language	
✓ notes details in illustrations	notes hand
Level 2: Connections	
identifies with character	
relates personal stories	
relates personal feelings	
connects to other literature	
Level 3: Inferences and evaluations	
✓✓ makes inferences about characters' motivations,	birds are people
feelings, traits	Al doesn't have to be afraid
makes evaluations of characters' actions, traits,	doesn't have dog
motivations, feelings	
✓ makes inferences about events	gonna be ok
makes evaluations of events	
makes inferences about language meaning	
Level 4: Interpretation at the Story Level	
✓ states theme related to the story	better off janitor
✓ interprets literary elements (symbol, etc.)	yellow/happy
interprets author's use of literary structures	(symbol?)
Level 5: Interpretation at the Abstract and Personal Level	
✓ states theme at abstract level	don't talk to strangers
states theme at personal level	
interprets story as rejection of society	
Processes: Child's participation in group interactions	
✓ asks questions	how can be turned back?
✓ makes hypotheses	one person "real one"
acknowledges comments of others	
✓ contributes ideas to argument	
asks for clarifying or supporting evidence	
✓ uses appropriate turn-taking procedures	
	high level participation

Teaching Reading with Literature Case Studies by Tompkins/McGee, © 1993. Reprinted by permission of Pearson Education, Inc., Upper Saddle River, NJ.

The response-to-literature checklist in Figure 12.8 includes the teacher's analysis of Annie's participation in the grand conversation presented in Figure 12.7. The checklist shows that Annie recalled story events, responded to a symbol, made inferences, and used illustrations to support her responses.

Assessing Children's Ability to Read Texts of Increasing Difficulty

The most important assessment that teachers can make is to monitor children's progress in being able to read and write texts at increasingly more difficult levels with sufficient fluency and comprehension. This could be considered the *real* essential component of reading and writing. The first step in monitoring whether children are able to read text of increasing levels of difficulty is to determine children's **instructional and independent reading levels.** Instructional reading level is the level of text that children can read with support from their teacher. They can read most words (90% to 95%) correctly and, when asked questions, can answer most (70% to 90%) correctly. However, these texts are still challenging enough that teachers guide children as they read. Independent reading level is the level of text that children can read on their own. They read all or nearly all of the words (95% to 100%) correctly and, when asked questions, answer nearly all correctly (90% to 100%).

Over time, children's instructional and independent reading levels should increase. Traditionally, the progression of levels of difficulty at first grade included pre-primer, primer, and then first grade, second grade, and so on. More recent concepts of levels of text difficulty have arisen from levels used in Reading Recovery Instruction (Peterson, 1991). Reading Recovery includes more levels of difficulty; by the end of third grade proficient readers would have progressed from levels 1 to level 38 with levels 1 through 16 to 18 considered first grade level texts. Other leveling schemes use alphabet letters to indicate increasing difficulty (Fountas & Pinnell, 1996).

Using Running Records to Determine Reading Levels. A **running record** is used to analyze children's reading; it provides information about reading level and children's use of cueing systems during reading. A running record includes several steps. To begin, the teacher selects texts at several levels of difficulty. For example, the teacher can select books at each of the Reading Recovery levels. One commercial assessment, *Developmental Reading Assessment* (Beaver, 1997), provides books at levels 1, 2, 3, 4, 6, 8, 10, 12, 14, 16, 18, 20, 24, 28, 30, 34, and 38. Or, teachers may select texts from a basal reading series at several levels of difficulty. Another alternative is to use texts found in an **Individualized Reading Inventory,** a commercial collection of texts written at pre-primer to middle school or even high school levels of difficulty.

Next, children read texts that have been selected to reflect their level of reading. Teachers select a level of text that they believe the child can read with ease. The teacher records children's miscues as they read by either marking on a copy of the text or by using checks and other symbols on a separate sheet of paper.

Figure 12.9 presents a running record of Charlie's reading "The Three Little Pigs." This figure indicates words that Charlie omitted—crossed out in text; words

FIGURE 12.9   **Running Record for "The Three Little Pigs"**

TEXT: The Three Little Pigs

                        three sc
    Once upon a time there were three pigs. Mother pig|*said* sc sent the

                    the   T
three little pigs ~~out~~ to make their way in the world. The first

            sticks
pig made a house of straw. The second pig made a house of

sticks. The third pig made a house of bricks. A wolf came to

the first pig's house and said, "I'll huff and puff and blow your

house down." The wolf blew the house down and the little pig ran

                        little
away fast. The wolf came to the second∧pig's house and said,

"I'll huff and puff and blow your house down." The wolf blew the

            fast
house down but the little pig ran away faster. The wolf came to

the third pig's house and said, "I'll huff and puff and blow your

                        did   *down*
house down." He blew and blew but could not blow ~~down~~ the house∧

            s T
He tried to sneak down the chimney but the pig put a big pot of

water on the fire. The wolf came down the chimney and burned his

            fast sc
tail. He ran away the fastest of all.

EXAMPLES:	
child matches text	✓
child substitutes	*child* / text
child omits	• / text
child inserts	*child* / •
child repeats	└ text
child self-corrects	sc
teacher prompts	T

RUNNING RECORD

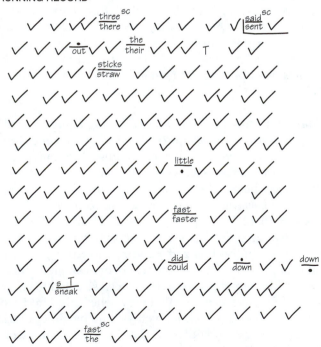

that he inserted—added above the text; words that he substituted—written over the text; and words that he self-corrected—marked with "SC." The figure also shows the teacher's running record, which captures Charlie's omissions, insertions, substitutions, and self-corrections (see the directions included in the figure).

Teachers then determine the child's **accuracy rate,** percentage of words read correctly, by counting the total number of miscues not including miscues that were self-corrected. The total number of miscues is subtracted from the total number of words in the passage to find the number of words read correctly. Finally, the number of words read correctly is divided by the total number of words in the passage. For example, Charlie read the "The Three Little Pigs" passage with 14 miscues including 3 self-corrected miscues for a total of 11 miscues. This number (11) is subtracted from the total number of words in the passage (181) to determine the number of words read correctly (170). The number of words read correctly is divided by the total number of words to reach the percentage of words read correctly—the accuracy rate. The accuracy rate for Charlie's reading of "The Three Little Pigs" is 93 percent. The accuracy rate is used to determine whether the text is on the independent, instructional, or frustrational reading level. Charlie's accuracy rate indicates that the passage "The Three Little Pigs" is at his instructional level.

The level of the text determines children's instructional reading level. For example, the *Three Little Pigs* text is approximately a first grade level text. Thus, Charlie's instructional reading level is first grade. The teacher would need to have Charlie read even easier text to determine his independent reading level.

Miscue Analysis.   A **miscue analysis** provides information about children's use of semantic (meaning), syntactic (language), and graphophonic cueing systems (Goodman & Burke, 1972). To assist in a miscue analysis, teachers construct a miscue analysis chart. Figure 12.10 displays the miscue analysis for Charlie's reading of "The Three Little Pigs." First, the teacher analyzes only substitutions to determine whether they are semantically acceptable (miscue has a similar meaning as the text word), syntactically acceptable (miscue is syntactically acceptable in the sentence), or graphophonically acceptable (miscue matches the text word at the beginning, middle, or end). The teacher also records whether the miscue was self-corrected.

According to the miscue analysis presented in Figure 12.10 none of Charlie's miscues were semantically acceptable, but Charlie self-corrected three miscues. Over half of his miscues were syntactically acceptable. All the miscues except two had the same beginning letters as the text word. According to this analysis, Charlie attends especially to beginning letters, but also to meaning. His miscues make sense and are often syntactically acceptable.

Using Running Records to Analyze Fluency and Decoding.   Running records and miscue analysis can also be used to assess children's strategy use (whether they are paying attention to meaning along with monitoring the letters in words, for example), their fluency, and use of alphabetic or orthographic decoding skills.

FIGURE 12.10   Miscue Analysis Chart for "The Three Little Pigs"

Child/Text	Semantically Acceptable	Syntactically Acceptable	Graphophonically same as			Self-Corrects	Comments
			B	M	E		
three/there			✓			✓	*
said/sent			✓			✓	*
the/their		✓	✓				
sticks/straw		✓	✓				
fast/faster	✓		✓	✓			
did/could	✓	✓			✓		
fast/the						✓	*
s/sneak			✓				
	2/8	3/8	6/8	1/8	1/8	3/8	

* sentence makes sense up to point of miscue

Fluency is the rate at which children read and their use of expression. That is, proficient readers beyond beginning early reading should read with fluency (a moderate pace) and with expression. Slow, word-by-word reading indicates children are paying too much attention to individual words rather than focusing on the meaning of what they are reading. Fluent reading emerges when children know most of the words they are reading by sight, when they can rapidly employ orthographic decoding strategies to identify unknown words quickly, and when their understanding is sufficient to allow them to read with intonation and phrasing that expresses the meaning of the text.

Children's miscues in running records provide excellent resources for determining their knowledge and use of alphabetic and orthographic principles (knowledge of sound–letter relationships, prefixes, suffixes, and familiar word parts). Teachers examine children's miscues to conduct a decoding analysis. A third grade teacher recorded the following miscues in Raymond's running record.

Text	Child
street	stairs
strutting	starting
mournful	m
deserted	distant
abruptly	ab
mysterious	mysteries

In a **decoding analysis** of Raymond's miscues, his teacher noted that Raymond consistently used beginning consonants but frequently omitted the *r* in the *str* consonant cluster and had difficulty decoding multisyllabic words (all the miscues were words of more than one syllable, except for *ceased*). However, Raymond is aware of some prefixes and familiar word parts (for example, he correctly read the *ab* prefix).

Using Questions to Analyze Comprehension and Vocabulary.   Teachers need to assess children's comprehension and their understanding of vocabulary as a part of their decision of determining a child's instructional or independent reading level. So far we have described how running records, miscue analyses, and decoding analyses provide evidence for determining children's word reading accuracy. However, teachers also need to consider comprehension when determining instructional level.

To assess a child's comprehension of a particular text a teacher could ask questions. The questions can probe children's literal, inferential, and evaluative understanding of the text as well as their understanding of vocabulary meanings within the context of the text. Teachers can construct their own questions being sure to include those that can be answered with information directly stated in the text (literal) or that require inferences (inferential).

When children can answer 70 percent or more of questions, the passage is at their instructional level. When they can answer 90 percent or more of the questions, the passage is at their independent level. When reading levels differ for children's accuracy rate and their comprehension, teachers usually use comprehension to establish instructional and especially independent reading levels. Children need to realize the importance of understanding what they read.

Analyzing Children's Ability to Write Texts of Increasing Complexity

Early childhood classrooms such as Ms. Orlando's provide children with many opportunities to try their hand at telling and retelling stories and writing at the writing center. Composing activities such as these provide opportunities for teachers to gather rich assessment information about their children's literacy development.

Teachers and older children select compositions to include in portfolios. These compositions may be written during writing workshop and may be highly polished stories that have gone through several drafts, or they may be informal compositions written at a writing center. Teachers analyze compositions for children's understanding of written forms and meanings.

Analysis of Form.   Young children's compositions can be examined for the following forms.

- Mock cursive (indicates awareness of linearity)
- Mock alphabet letters (indicates awareness of letter features)
- Conventional alphabet letters (indicates knowledge of alphabet formations)

- Copied words (indicates awareness of words in environment)
- Spelled words such as the child's name or other learned words such as *mom*, *dad*, and *love* (indicates learned spellings)
- Conventions (such as capitalization and punctuation)
- Invented spelling

In addition, teachers note whether children's writing shows awareness of linearity, for example, writing mock letters from left to right in lines, or spacing, for example, leaving spaces between strings of conventional letters as if writing words (Feldgus & Cardonick, 1999). Young children frequently circle words, place periods between words, or separate words with dashes. These unconventional strategies indicate that children are experimenting with word boundaries.

Older children's compositions can be analyzed for their knowledge of conventions, such as capital letters and punctuation. Teachers note all examples of children's use of these conventions and keep a list of all conventions the children use correctly. For example, a teacher may note that a child capitalizes the beginnings of sentences, the word *I*, the name of the local town, and the name of the school; consistently uses a period or question mark at the end of a sentence; uses apostrophes in the contractions *don't* and *I've;* and uses a comma after the greeting in a letter.

Story Form.   Teachers take special note of children's control over story form which include

- Setting, which identifies time, place, and weather
- Characters, who are revealed through their thoughts, actions, appearance, and dialogue
- Plot, which includes a problem, episodes, climax, and resolution—episodes consist of actions toward solving the problem and outcomes
- Point of view, which reveals who tells the story
- Mood
- Theme

Figure 12.11 presents a story composition dictated by five-year-old Kristen to her kindergarten teacher. The composition contains sixteen pages and a title page. As Kristen's kindergarten teacher analyzed the form of Kristen's story, she noted that Kristen had included three characters: a little girl, a cat, and baby cats. These characters were developed through the illustrations (which showed what the characters looked like), a few revelations of the cat's thoughts (she wanted to go home and she was happy), the girl's and cat's actions, and dialogue.

Kristen's story incorporates three plot episodes (rescuing the cat, the cat's birthday, and taking the baby cats to live in the woods). The first episode, about rescuing the cat, has a fully developed plot. It includes a problem (the cat was

FIGURE 12.11 **"The Girl with the Cat and the Babies"**

Title:	The Girl with the Cat and the Babies
page 1	The little girl took her cat for a walk.
page 2	She got caught in a trap.
page 3	The little girl came.
page 4	And she pulled, and she pulled, and she pushed, and she pushed on the trap.
page 5	She opened the cage and the cat was almost out.
page 6	The little cat was out. She was happy.
page 7	The cat was purring because the little girl was rubbing her.
page 8	The little girl was taking her home.
page 9	The sun was coming down.
page 10	Tomorrow was the cat's birthday. She was happy because she was going to have a party.
page 11	It was the cat's birthday and the people were fixing it up because they were awake.
page 12	One day the cat was knocking on the little girl's door because she had four babies on her birthday.
page 13	The cat asked, "Can I go out in the woods with my babies to live?"
page 14	Far, far away they went. She waved good-bye and so did the babies.
page 15	The cat built five houses.
page 16	They were all ready to go to sleep.

caught in a trap), actions toward solving the problem (the girl pulled and pulled, and pushed and pushed on the trap), a climax (the cat was almost out), and an outcome (the cat was out). The other episodes are descriptions of actions, and all the episodes are loosely connected through common characters.

Kristen relied on having the cats go to sleep to resolve the story. The story is told in the third person, with the cat's thoughts revealed. The mood of the story is pleasant except for when the cat is caught in the trap. Kristen's story shows her ability to manipulate all the literary elements of a story form except for theme.

Expository Text Form. Teachers also analyze the form of children's informational writing. At the simplest level, children's expositions consist of labels (see Chapter 5). They may be one-word, phrase, or sentence labels identifying objects, people, or events.

At the next level are couplets, two related sentences about the same topic. An attribute list includes a main idea and several supporting ideas, although the ideas are not ordered in any way. More complex expositions include complex couplets or ideas that are related to the main topic (they have consistency), but they also have ordered relationships (ideas that are presented in a sequence, explain cause and effects or problems and solutions, or compare and contrast). Usually children's first use of ordered relationships is embedded in an attribute list. Even more complex expositions include hierarchy, where a topic is introduced followed by subtopics. Teachers analyze children's expositions for their use of consistency, ordered relationships, and hierarchy. They also analyze expositions for topic presentation, description of attributes, characteristic events, category comparisons, and final summaries (Donovan, 2001).

Analyzing Meaning and Content. In analyzing the content in children's compositions, teachers consider the characters, events, settings, or information in relation to children's own experiences and to literature. They analyze the ideas included in compositions for consistency, believability, and unity. They examine children's use of dialogue, literary word order, or literary language such as alliteration, rhyme, repetition, simile, or imagery.

In the story presented in Figure 12.11, Kristen included a familiar character (she has a cat). Many of the actions of the story are from Kristen's own life—her cat often follows her on walks, she likes to rub her cat until he purrs, her birthday was less than a month away, she often explores the woods around her house, and she wishes that her cat could have babies.

Kristen also incorporated three examples of literary language in her composition. She used repetition of words and actions, including actions similar to those in the familiar folktale *The Enormous Turnip* (Parkinson, 1986) (And she pulled, and she pulled, and she pushed, and she pushed on the trap). She also used literary word order (Far, far away they went) and dialogue (Then the cat asked, "Can I go out in the woods with my babies to live?").

Chapter Summary

Teachers are responsible for supporting children's literacy learning, and assessing children's learning is an important part of that process. Classroom assessment relies on teachers' observations and analyses of children's work. Portfolio assessment is a systematic form of classroom assessment. Portfolios may include anecdotal notes, checklists, work samples, and performances from special literacy tasks, such as running records. Portfolios also include children's and teachers' reflections in the form of analyses, captions, and summaries.

Teachers analyze retellings, grand conversations, response journals, and compositions to reveal information about children's meaning making. They administer alphabet recognition tasks and concepts-about-print tasks and analyze children's compositions for understandings of written language forms. Phonemic awareness assessments, miscue analyses, decoding analyses, and analysis of spellings in compositions provide evidence of meaning-form link knowledge. Finally, observations of children's reading and writing document their under- standings of the functions of written language.

Portfolios are used to make instructional decisions, encourage children's reflections on their own learning, and share information about children's learning with parents. Assessments must be kept manageable by planning a reasonable time frame for collecting assessment information, selecting only a few most infor- mative assessments, and collecting information on a systematic basis.

Teachers are responsible for screening children's initial levels of achievement related to essential components of reading and writing. These components are sim- ilar for experimenting, early, and transitional readers and writers; however, as chil- dren progress through these phases of reading, they are expected to master more sophisticated and complex strategies and skills. Teachers monitor children's progress in these essential components. These assessments guide teachers as they make instructional decisions about individual children.

Applying the Information

We provide samples from Katie's third grade reading and writing portfolio. Katie selected a letter that she wrote to her grandmother and included the first two drafts as well as a copy of the final draft of the letter in her portfolio. Figure 12.12 presents Katie's drafts of her letter. Write a caption for the letter, analyzing Katie's knowl- edge of written language meanings, forms, meaning-form links, and functions.

Jonathan is a five-year-old beginning kindergarten. His teacher has observed him four times over the first two months of school. For three of the observations, she also collected work samples of his writing. Figure 12.13 presents Jonathan's work samples and his teacher's anecdotal notes about her observations. Write an analysis for the anecdotal note and captions for the compositions. Then write a portfolio summary that describes what Jonathan knows about written language meanings, forms, meaning-form links, and functions.

Going Beyond the Text

Interview a teacher who uses portfolio assessment about his or her classroom assessments. Find out what the teacher expects to collect in the portfolios, how he or she analyzes the information, and how he or she shares the information with parents. Examine the contents of several of the children's portfolios. Talk with chil- dren about the contents of their portfolios. Compare the results of your interview with Ms. Orlando's portfolio assessment plans and procedures.

Dear Grandma
~~wood~~ when I come to youor
hoose you ~~wod~~ ~~wde~~ ~~wood~~ ~~woud~~ Know Larven's triplets
she got this christmus? If its ok I'd like
them too! I can't vrat to see you! Bye Bye

first draft

Dear Grandma
when me and dad come for my present I wood like the triplets that
Lauren got for Chirstmas Dad wood like to golf if its
ok with you. Me and dad can't wait to see you.   Bye Bye

second draft

Dear Grandma
    when me and dad come
for my present I would like
the triplets that Lauren got
for Christmas. Dad would
like to golf if its ok with
Grandpa. Me and dad can't wait
to see you   Bye Bye

            Love
            Katie

P.S. the presents are
for our Birthday Party

final draft

FIGURE 12.12   Katie's Letter

9/20 Johnathan
at the computer
center
   Johnathan complains
his words are run
together. He is copying
words from around
the room. I show
him space bar. He
types discovery center
writing center /pet mouse
with spaces

a. Notes

9/24 Johnathan
at the library center
Johnathan is looking
at the tag on the stuffed
Snoopy dog and reads
"Snoop" "Snoopy". I ask
him which part spells
snoop - he spells snoop!
Earlier we were writing
notes to parents for open
house. He copied mom and
read mommy. I said no, it
only said mom. It would
have a y at the end to
say mommy.

b. Notes

10/7 Johnathan
at writing center
   Johnathan copies words
from letterhead of scrap
paper in the center. He
asks me to read what
he'd written. After he
reads he underlines
each word. He says I
can spell pub-pub. He
says I can spell comp-com!
I spell words and he writes.
I stress sounds but he wants
me to tell him letters. See sample

c. Notes

d. Sample

10/30 Johnathan
at writing center
   Johnathan wants to
write about Joker and
Batman. He says Joker and
I repeat segmenting /j/.
He writes 6 he says kills
I segment /k/ = K people
/p/ = p Batman /b/ = B bat =
/t/ = t helps /h/ = H people
/p/ = P I do all segmenting
* first invented
spelling I've observed
      see sample

e. Notes

f. Sample

FIGURE 12.13   Jonathan's Writing and His Teacher's Observations

REFERENCES

Adams, M. J., Foorman, B. R., Lundberg, I., & Beeler, T. (1998). *Phonemic awareness in young children: A classroom curriculum.* Baltimore: Paul H. Brookes.

Allen, M. (1999a). *Doctor Maggie's phonics reader: A new view.* Cypress, CA: Creative Teaching Press.

Allen, M. (1999b). *Top job, Mom!* Cypress, CA: Creative Teaching Press.

Ballenger, C. (1999). *Teaching other people's children: Literacy and learning in a bilingual classroom.* New York: Teachers College Press.

Barone, D. (1999). *Resilient children: Stories of poverty, drug exposure, and literacy development.* Newark, DE: International Reading Association.

Bauer, E., & Garcia, G. (1997). Blurring the lines between assessment and instruction: A case study of a low-income student in the lowest reading group. In C. Kinzer, K. Hinchman, & D. Leu (Eds.), *Inquiries in literacy theory and practice* (pp. 166–176). Chicago: National Reading Conference.

Bear, D. R., Invernizzi, M., Templeton, S., & Johnston, F. (2000). *Words their way: Word study for phonics, vocabulary, and spelling instruction* (2nd ed.). Columbus, OH: Merrill.

Beaver, J. (1997). *Developmental reading assessment.* Parsippany, NJ: Celebration Press.

Bergeron, B., Wermuth, S., & Hammar, R. (1997). Initiating portfolios through shared learning: Three perspectives. *The Reading Teacher, 50,* 552–561.

Bloodgood, J. (1999). What's in a name? Children's name writing and literacy acquisition. *Reading Research Quarterly, 34,* 342–367.

Brown, M. (1942). *The runaway bunny.* New York: Harper and Row.

Bunting, E. (1991). *Fly away home.* New York: Clarion.

Clay, M. (1993). *The early detection of reading difficulties* (4th ed.). Portsmouth, NH: Heinemann.

Clay, M. (1998). *By different paths to common outcomes.* York, ME: Stenhouse.

Cooper, J. (1993). *Literacy: Helping children construct meaning* (2nd ed.). Boston: Houghton Mifflin.

Cunningham, P. (2000). *Phonics they use: Words for reading and writing* (3rd ed.). New York: Longman.

Donovan, C. (2001). Children's development and control of written story and informational genres: Insights from one elementary school. *Research in the Teaching of English, 35,* 394–447.

Feldgus, E., & Cardonick, I. (1999). *Kid writing: A systematic approach to phonics, journals, and writing workshop.* Bothell, WA: The Wright Group.

Fountas, I., & Pinnell, G. (1996). *Guided reading: Good first teaching for all children.* Portsmouth, NH: Heinemann.

Goodman, Y., & Burke, C. (1972). *The reading miscue inventory.* New York: Macmillan.

Gronlund, G. (1998). Portfolios as an assessment tool: Is collecting of work enough? *Young Children, 53,* 4–10.

Hansen, J. (1996). Evaluation: The center of writing instruction. *The Reading Teacher, 50,* 188–195.

Hutchins, P. (1968). *Rosie's walk.* New York: Scholastic.

Johnston, F., Invernizzi, M., & Juel, C. (1998). *Book buddies: Guidelines for volunteer tutors of emergent and early readers.* New York: Guilford.

Kieffer, R. D., & Faust, M. A. (1994). Portfolio process and teacher change: Elementary, middle, and secondary teachers reflect on their initial experiences with portfolio evaluation. In C. K. Kinzer & D. J. Leu (Eds.), *Multidimensional aspects of literacy research, theory, and practice* (pp. 82–88). Chicago: National Reading Conference.

Kovalski, M. (1987). *The wheels on the bus.* Boston: Little, Brown.

Lonigan, C., Burgess, S., Anthony, J., & Baker, T. (1998). Development of phonological sensitivity in 2- to 5-year-old children. *Journal of Educational Psychology, 90,* 294–311.

McGee, L. (1992). An exploration of meaning construction in first graders' grand conversations. In C. Kinzer & D. Leu (Eds.), *Literacy research, theory, and practice: Views from many perspectives* (pp. 177–186). Chicago: National Reading Conference.

Morrow, L. (1989). Using story retelling to develop comprehension. In D. Muth (Ed.), *Children's comprehension of text: Research into practice* (pp. 37–58). Newark, DE: International Reading Association.

National Institute of Child Health and Development (2000). *Report of the national reading panel: Teaching children to read.* Available online at www.nichd.nih.gov/publications/nrp/pdf.

Parkinson, K. (1986). *The enormous turnip.* Niles, IL: Albert Whitman.

Peterson, B. (1991). Selecting books for beginning readers. In D. DeFord, C. Lyons, & G. Pinnell (Eds.), *Bridges to literacy: Learning from Reading Recovery* (pp. 119–147). Portsmouth, NH: Heinemann.

Porter, C., & Cleland, J. (1995). *The portfolio as a learning strategy.* Portsmouth, NH: Heinemann.

Rhodes, L., & Nathenson-Mejia, S. (1992). Anecdotal records: A powerful tool for ongoing literacy assessment. *The Reading Teacher, 45,* 502–509.

Roe, M., & Vukelich, C. (1998). Literacy portfolios: Challenges that affect change. *Childhood Education, 74,* 148–153.

Sarafini, F. (2001). Three paradigms of assessment: Measurement, procedure and inquiry. *The Reading Teacher, 54,* 384–393.

Seuss, Dr. (1963). *Hop on pop.* New York: Random House.

Sipe, L. (2000). The construction of literary understanding by first and second graders in oral response to picture storybook readalouds. *Reading Research Quarterly, 35,* 252–275.

Sipe, L. (2002). Talking back and taking over: Young children's expressive engagement during storybook read-alouds. *The Reading Teacher, 55,* 476–483.

Skillings, M., & Ferrell, R. (2000). Student-generated rubrics: Bringing students into the assessment process. *The Reading Teacher, 53,* 452–455.

Snow, C., Burns, M., & Griffin, P. (Eds.). (1998). *Preventing reading difficulties in young children.* Washington, DC: National Academy Press.

Stahl, S., & Murray, B. (1994). Defining phonological awareness and its relationship to early reading. *Journal of Educational Psychology, 86,* 221–234.

Tompkins, G., & McGee, L. (1993). *Teaching reading with literature: Case studies to action plans.* New York: Merrill/Macmillan.

Valencia, S. (1990). A portfolio approach to classroom reading assessment: The whys, whats and hows. *The Reading Teacher, 43,* 338–440.

Yopp, H. (1988). The validity and reliability to phonemic awareness tests. *Reading Research Quarterly, 23,* 159–177.

Yopp, H. (1995). Read-aloud books for developing phonemic awareness: An annotated bibliography. *The Reading Teacher, 48,* 538–542.

Yorinks, A. (1986). *Hey, Al.* New York: Farrar, Straus and Giroux.

APPENDIX

Children's Literature

Alphabet Books

Anno, M. (1976). *Anno's alphabet*. New York: Crowell.

Archambault, J., & Martin, B. (1989). *Chicka chicka boom boom*. New York: Scholastic.

Baskin, L. (1972). *Hosie's alphabet*. New York: Viking Press.

Bruna, D. (1967). *B is for bear*. New York: Macmillan.

Burningham, J. (1964). *John Burningham's ABC*. London: Johnathan Cape.

Ehlert, L. (1989). *Eating the alphabet*. New York: Harcourt Brace Jovanovich.

Eichenberg, F. (1952). *Ape in cape*. San Diego, CA: Harcourt Brace Jovanovich.

Elting, M., & Folsom, M. (1980). *Q is for duck*. New York: Clarion.

Hoban, T. (1987). *26 letters and 99 cents*. New York: Greenwillow.

Holtz, L. T. (1997). *Alphabet book*. New York: DK Publishing.

Ipcar, D. (1964). *I love an anteater with an A*. New York: Knopf.

Isadora, R. (1983). *City seen from A to Z*. New York: Greenwillow.

Johnson, S. T. (1995). *Alphabet city*. New York: Penguin.

Kellogg, S. (1987). *Aster Aardvark's alphabet adventures*. New York: Morrow.

Lionni, L. (1985). *Letters to talk about*. New York: Pantheon.

Lobel, A. (1981). *On Market Street*. New York: Greenwillow.

McCurdy, M. (1998). *The sailor's alphabet*. Boston: Houghton Mifflin.

McMillan, B. (1986). *Counting wildflowers*. New York: Lothrop.

Schnur, S. (1997). *Autumn: An alphabet acrostic*. New York: Houghton Mifflin.

Seuss, Dr. (Theodore Geisel). (1963). *Dr. Seuss's ABC*. New York: Random House.

Shannon, G. (1996). *Tomorrow's alphabet*. New York: Greenwillow.

Tudor, T. (1954). *A is for Annabelle*. New York: Walck.

Wildsmith, B. (1963). *Brian Wildsmith's ABC*. Danbury, CT: Franklin Watts.

Books for Very Young Children

Baker, K. (1994). *Big fat hen*. New York: Harcourt Brace.

Berenstain, J., & Berenstain, S. (1971). *Bears in the night*. New York: Random House.

Brown, M. (1942). *The runaway bunny*. New York: Harper.

Brown, M. (1947). *Goodnight moon*. New York: Harper.

Burningham, J. (1971). *Mr. Grumpy's outing*. New York: Holt.

*Carroll, R. (1932). *What Whiskers did*. New York: Walck.

*Carroll, R. (1970). *The Christmas kitten*. New York: Walck.

Cauley, L. (1982). *The three little kittens*. New York: Putnam.

Chorao, K. (1977). *The baby's lap book*. New York: Dutton.

Clifton, L. (1977). *Amifika*. New York: E. P. Dutton.

Crews, D. (1978). *Freight train*. New York: Greenwillow.

de Paola, T. (1985). *Tomie de Paola's Mother Goose*. New York: Putnam.

Eastman, P. D. (1960). *Are you my mother?* New York: Random House.

Freeman, D. (1968). *Corduroy*. New York: Viking.

Galdone, P. (1973). *The little red hen*. New York: Scholastic.

Galdone, P. (1973). *The three bears*. New York: Scholastic.

Galdone, P. (1985). *Cat goes fiddle-i-fee*. New York: Clarion.

Galdone, P. (1986). *Three little kittens*. New York: Clarion.

Havill, J. (1986). *Jamaica's find.* Boston: Houghton Mifflin.

Hill, E. (1982). *The nursery rhyme peek-a-book.* New York: Price/Stern/Sloan.

Hill, E. (1989). *Where's Spot?* New York: Putnam.

Hort, L. (2000). *The seals on the bus.* New York: Henry Holt and Company.

Hughes, S. (1985). *Bathwater's hot.* New York: Lothrop, Lee and Shepard.

Hutchins, P. (1971). *Rosie's walk.* New York: Macmillan.

*Keats, E. (1974). *Kitten for a day.* Danbury, CT: Franklin Watts.

Kuskin, K. (1959). *Which horse is William?* New York: Harper and Row.

Lewis, K. (1991). *Emma's lamb.* Cambridge: Candlewick.

Lewis, K. (1996). *One summer day.* Cambridge: Candlewick.

Lewis, K. (1997). *Friends.* Cambridge: Candlewick.

Marshall, J. (1979). *James Marshall's Mother Goose.* New York: Farrar.

*Ormerod, J. (1981). *Sunshine.* New York: Puffin.

*Oxenbury, H. (1982). *Good night, good morning.* New York: Dial.

Rice, E. (1981). *Benny bakes a cake.* New York: Greenwillow.

Shannon, D. (1998). *No, David!* New York: Scholastic.

Slobodkina, E. (1947). *Caps for sale.* New York: Addison.

Steen, S., & Steen, S. (2001). *Car wash.* New York: G. P. Putnam's Sons.

Tolstoy, A. (1968). *The great big enormous turnip.* Danbury, CT: Franklin Watts.

Wright, B. F. (Illustrator). (1916). *The real Mother Goose.* New York: Rand McNally.

Wordless Picture Books

Baker, J. (1991). *Window.* New York: Greenwillow.

Day, A. (1985). *Good dog, Carl.* New York: Scholastic.

de Paola, T. (1978). *Pancakes for breakfast.* San Diego: Harcourt Brace Jovanovich.

Goodall, J. (1988). *Little red riding hood.* New York: McElderry Books.

Hoban, T. (1972). *Push-pull, empty-full.* New York: Macmillan.

Hoban, T. (1980). *Take another look.* New York: Greenwillow.

Hoban, T. (1988). *Look! Look! Look!* New York: Greenwillow.

Mayer, M. (1974). *Frog goes to dinner.* New York: Dial.

Mayer, M. (1977). *Oops.* New York: Dial.

McCully, E. (1984). *Picnic.* New York: Harper and Row.

McCully, E. (1985). *First snow.* New York: Harper and Row.

McCully, E. (1987). *School.* New York: Harper and Row.

McCully, E. (1988). *New baby.* New York: Harper and Row.

Rohmann, E. (1994). *Time flies.* New York: Crown.

Spier, P. (1982). *Peter Spier's rain.* New York: Doubleday.

Turkle, B. (1976). *Deep in the forest.* New York: Dutton.

Weisner, D. (1991). *Tuesday.* New York: Clarion.

Winter, P. (1976). *The bear and the fly.* New York: Crown.

Predictable Books

Burningham, J. (1978). *Would you rather . . . ?* New York: Crowell.

Carle, E. (1977). *The grouchy ladybug.* New York: Crowell.

Fleming, D. (1993). *In the small, small pond.* New York: Scholastic.

Fox, M. (1987). *Hattie and the fox.* New York: Bradbury.

Galdone, P. (1968). *Henny Penny.* New York: Scholastic.

Ho, M. (1996). *Hush! A Thai lullaby.* New York: Orchard.

Hutchins, P. (1982). *Goodnight, owl!* New York: Macmillan.

Jackson, A. (1997). *I know an old lady who swallowed a pie.* New York: Dutton.

Kavalski, M. (1987). *The wheels on the bus.* Boston: Little, Brown.

Kent, J. (1971). *The fat cat.* New York: Scholastic.

Kraus, R. (1970). *Whose mouse are you?* New York: Collier.

Lexau, J. (1969). *Crocodile and hen.* New York: Harper and Row.

Martin, B., Jr. (1983). *Brown bear, brown bear.* New York: Henry Holt.

*Wordless books

Martin, B. (1991). *Polar bear, polar bear, what do you hear?* New York: Scholastic.

Root, P. (1998). *One duck stuck.* Cambridge: Candlewick.

Schneider, R. M. (1995). *Add it, dip it, fix it.* Boston: Houghton Mifflin.

Sendak, M. (1962). *Chicken soup with rice.* New York: Harper and Row.

Smith, M., & Ziefert, H. (1989). *In a scary old house.* New York: Penguin.

Sweet, M. (1992). *Fiddle-i-fee.* Boston: Little, Brown.

Tabak, S. (1997). *There was an old lady who swallowed a fly.* New York: Scholastic.

Tafuri, N. (1984). *Have you seen my duckling?* New York: Greenwillow.

Tresselt, A. (1964). *The mitten.* New York: Lothrop, Lee and Shepard.

Weiss, N. (1989). *Where does the brown bear go?* New York: Trumpet Club.

Westcott, N. B. (1987). *Peanut butter and jelly.* New York: Trumpet Club.

Williams, L. (1986). *The little old lady who wasn't afraid of anything.* New York: Harper and Row.

Wood, A. (1982). *Quick as a cricket.* Singapore: Child's Play (International).

Zemach, M. (1965). *The teeny tiny woman.* New York: Scholastic.

Language Play Books

Ahlberg, J., & Ahlberg, A. (1978). *Each peach pear plum.* New York: Scholastic.

Benjamin, A. (1987). *Rat-a-tat, pitter pat.* New York: Harper.

Brown, M. (1994). *Four fur feet.* New York: Hyperion.

Carlstrom, N. W. (1987). *Wild wild sunflower child Anna.* New York: Macmillan.

Demming, A. G. (1994). *Who is tapping at my window?* Puffin.

Edwards, P. M. (1996). *Some smug slug.* New York: Harper-Collins.

Koch, M. (1991). *Hoot howl hiss.* New York: Greenwillow.

Komaiko, L. (1987). *Annie Bananie.* New York: Harper and Row.

LeCourt, N. (1991). *Abracadabra to zigzag.* New York: Lothrop, Lee and Shepard.

Melser, J. (1998). *One, one, is the sun.* Bothell, WA: Wright.

Most, B. (1996). *Cock a doodle moo.* New York: Harcourt Brace.

Noll, S. (1987). *Jiggle wiggle prance.* New York: Greenwillow.

Paparone, P. (1995). *Five little ducks.* New York: Scholastic.

Plourde, L. (1997). *Pigs in the mud in the middle of the rud.* New York: Blue Sky.

Raschka, C. (1992). *Charlie Parker played be bop.* New York: Orchard.

Reddix, V. (1992). *Millie and the mud hole.* New York: Lothrop, Lee and Shepard.

Root, P. (1998). *One duck stuck.* Cambridge: Candlewick.

Seuss, Dr. (Theodore Geisel) (1957). *The cat in the hat.* New York: Random House.

Seuss, Dr. (Theodore Geisel) (1963). *Hop on pop.* New York: Random House.

Silverstien, S. (1964). *A giraffe and a half.* New York: Harper and Row.

Sonneborn, R. A. (1974). *Someone is eating the sun.* New York: Random House.

Thomas, P. (1990). *The one and only, super-duper, golly-whopper, Jim-dandy, really-handy, clock-tock-stopper.* New York: Lothrop, Lee and Shepard.

Watson, C. (1971). *Father Fox's penny-rhymes.* New York: Scholastic.

Wells, R. (1973). *Noisy Nora.* New York: Dial.

Wildsmith, B. (1986). *Goat's trail.* New York: Knopf.

Wood, A. (1987). *Heckedy Peg.* New York: Harcourt Brace Jovanovich.

Ziefert, H. (2002). *Who said moo?* New York: Handprint Books.

Multicultural Books

Barnwell, Y. (1998). *No mirrors in my nana's house.* New York: Harcourt Brace.

Baylor, B. (1986). *Hawk, I'm your brother.* New York: Scribner's.

Bruchac, J. (1985). *Iroquois stories: Heroes and heroines, monsters and magic.* Freedom, CA: The Crossing Press.

Bruchac, J., & Longdon, J. (1992). *Thirteen moons on turtle's back: A Native American year of moons.* New York: Philomel.

Bryan, A. (1977). *The dancing granny.* New York: Atheneum.

Bryan, A. (1986). *Lion and the ostrich chick and other African folk tales.* New York: Atheneum.

Bunting, E. (1998). *So far from the sea.* New York: Clarion.

Caines, J. (1982). *Just us women.* New York: Harper and Row.

Choi, S. (1993). *Hal Moni and the picnic.* Boston: Houghton Mifflin.

Clifton, L. (1970). *Some of the days of Everett Anderson.* New York: Holt, Rinehart and Winston.

Connolly, J. (1985). *Why the possum's tail is bare and other North American Indian nature tales.* Owings Mills, MD: Stemmer House.

Coutant, H., & Vo-Dinh. (1974). *First snow.* New York: Knopf.

Crews, D. (1991). *Big Mama's.* New York: Greenwillow.

Cruz Martinez, A. (1991). *The woman who out-shone the sun/La mujer que brillaba aun mas que el sol.* San Francisco: Children's Book Press.

Delacre, L. (1989). *Arroz con leche: Popular songs and rhymes from Latin America.* New York: Scholastic.

Delacre, L. (1990). *Las Navidades: Popular Christmas songs from Latin America.* New York: Scholastic.

Dorros, A. (1991). *Abuela.* New York: Dutton.

Garcia, R. (1987). *My Aunt Otilia's spirits.* San Francisco: Children's Book Press.

Garza, C. (1990). *Family pictures.* San Francisco: Children's Book Press.

Giovanni, N. (1985). *Spin a soft black song.* New York: HarperCollins.

Goble, P. (1989). *Iktomi and the berries.* New York: Orchard.

Goble, P. (1992). *Crow chief: A Plains Indian story.* New York: Orchard.

Greene, B. (1974). *Philip Hall likes me. I reckon maybe.* New York: Dial.

Greenfield, E. (1975). *Me and Nessie.* New York: Crowell.

Greenfield, E. (1978). *Honey, I love.* New York: Harper and Row.

Greenfield, E. (1988). *Grandpa's face.* New York: Philomel.

Greenfield, E. (1988). *Nathaniel talking.* New York: Black Butterfly Children's Books.

Hamilton, V. (1985). *The people could fly.* New York: Knopf.

Hamilton, V. (1992). *Drylongso.* New York: Harcourt Brace Jovanovich.

Havill, J. (1989). *Jamaica tag-along.* Boston: Houghton Mifflin.

Howard, E. (1991). *Aunt Flossie's hats (and crab cakes later).* Boston: Houghton Mifflin.

Johnson, A. (1989). *Tell me a story, Mama.* New York: Orchard.

Johnson, A. (1990). *Do like Kyla.* New York: Orchard.

Martin, F. (2000). *Clever tortoise: A traditional African tale.* Cambridge: Candlewick.

Martinez, E., & Soto, G. (1993). *Too many tamales.* New York: Putnam.

Mathis, S. (1975). *The hundred penny box.* New York: Viking.

McKissack, P. (1986). *Flossie and the fox.* New York: Dial.

McKissack, P. (1989). *Nettie Jo's friends.* New York: Knopf.

Mollel, T. (1993). *The king and the tortoise.* New York: Houghton Mifflin.

Mollel, T. M. (1995). *Big boy.* New York: Clarion.

Ortiz, S. (1988). *The people shall continue.* San Francisco: Children's Book Press.

Pena, S. (1987). *Kikiriki: Stories and poems in English and Spanish for children.* Houston: Arte Publico Press.

Price, L. (1990). *Aida.* New York: Harcourt Brace Jovanovich.

Rohmer, H., & Anchondo, M. (1988). *How we came to the fifth world: Como vinimos al quinto mundo.* San Francisco: Children's Book Press.

Say, A. (1982). *The bicycle man.* Boston: Houghton Mifflin.

Say, A. (1988). *The lost lake.* Boston: Houghton Mifflin.

Say, A. (1990). *El Chino.* Boston: Houghton Mifflin.

Say, A. (1991). *Tree of cranes.* Boston: Houghton Mifflin.

Say, A. (1993). *Grandfather's journey.* Boston: Houghton Mifflin.

Say, A. (1997). *Allison.* Boston: Houghton Mifflin.

Sneeve, V. (1989). *Dancing teepees: Poems of American Indian youth.* New York: Holiday House.

Soto, G. (1993). *Too many tamales.* New York: Putnam.

Steptoe, J. (1969). *Stevie.* New York: Harper and Row.

Steptoe, J. (1987). *Mufaro's beautiful daughters.* New York: Lothrop, Lee and Shepard.

Strete, C. (1990). *Big thunder magic.* New York: Greenwillow.

Tafolla, C. (1987). *Patchwork colcha: A children's collection.* Flagstaff, AZ: Creative Educational Enterprises.

Takeshita, F. (1988). *The park bench.* New York: Kane/Miller.

Wright, C. (1994). *Jumping the broom.* New York: Holiday House.

Xiong, B. (1989). *Nine-in-one grr! grr! A folktale from the Hmong people of Laos.* San Francisco: Children's Book Press.

Yashima, R. (1958). *Umbrella.* New York: Viking.

Young, E. (1989). *Lon po po.* New York: Putnam.

Zhensun, A., & Low, A. (1991). *A young painter.* New York: Scholastic.

Informational Books

Burton, J. (1989). *Animals keeping safe.* New York: Random House.

Canizares, S., & Chanko, P. (1998). *Water.* New York: Scholastic.

Copeland, C., & Lewis, A. (2002). *Funny faces, wacky wings, and other silly big bird things.* Brookfield, CT: Millbrook Press.

Editions, G. (1994). *A first discovery book: The rain forest.* New York: Scholastic.

Fletcher, N. (1993). *See how they grow: Penguin.* London: Dorling Kindersley.

Fowler, A. (1992). *Rookie read-about science: It could still be water.* Chicago: Children's Press.

George, J. (1999). *Morning, noon, and night.* New York: HarperCollins.

Gibbons, G. (1997). *The honey makers.* New York: Scholastic.

Intrater, R. (1995). *Two eyes, a nose, and a mouth.* New York: Scholastic.

Kottke, J. (2000). *How things grow: From seed to pumpkin.* New York: Scholastic.

Llewellyn, D. (1995). *Mighty machines: Tractor.* London: Dorling Kindersley.

Morris, A. (1989). *Bread, bread, bread.* New York: Scholastic.

Parsons, A. (1990). *Eyewitness juniors: Amazing spiders.* New York: Alfred A. Knopf.

Rehm, K., & Loike, K. (1991). *Left or right?* New York: Scholastic.

Walker-Hodge, J. (1998). *Eyewitness readers: Surprise puppy!* London: Dorling Kindersley.

AUTHOR INDEX

SUBJECT INDEX